Coming
Up
Short

Coming
Up
Short

A Memoir of My America

Robert B. Reich

ALFRED A. KNOPF · NEW YORK · 2025

A BORZOI BOOK
FIRST HARDCOVER EDITION
PUBLISHED BY ALFRED A. KNOPF 2025

Published in the United States by Alfred A. Knopf, a division of Penguin Random House LLC, 1745 Broadway, New York, NY 10019.

Knopf, Borzoi Books, and the colophon are registered trademarks of Penguin Random House LLC.

Portions of this book appeared previously in my books *Locked in the Cabinet* (1997) and *The Common Good* (2018), in *The Guardian,* and on my Substack.

penguinrandomhouse.com | aaknopf.com

Library of Congress Cataloging-in-Publication Data
Names: Reich, Robert B. author
Title: Coming up short : a memoir of my America / Robert B. Reich.
Description: First edition. | New York : Alfred A. Knopf, 2025. |
Includes bibliographical references and index.
Identifiers: LCCN 2025001241 (print) | LCCN 2025001242 (ebook) |
ISBN 9780593803288 hardcover | ISBN 9780593803295 ebook
Subjects: LCSH: Reich, Robert B. | Cabinet officers—United States—
Biography | United States. Department of Labor—Biography |
College teachers—United States—Biography | United States—
Politics and government—1945–1989 | United States—Politics and government—1989– |
LCGFT: Autobiographies
Classification: LCC E840.8.R445 A3 2025 (print) |
LCC E840.8.R445 (ebook) | DDC 352.2/93092 $a B—dc23/eng/20250527
LC record available at https://lccn.loc.gov/2025001241
LC ebook record available at https://lccn.loc.gov/2025001242

Manufactured in the United States of America
5th Printing

The authorized representative in the EU for product safety and compliance is Penguin Random House Ireland, Morrison Chambers, 32 Nassau Street, Dublin D02 YH68, Ireland, https://eu-contact.penguin.ie.

For Edwin Reich
(1914–2016)

For no part of life, neither public affairs nor private, neither in the forum nor at home, neither when acting on our own nor in dealings with another, can be free from duty. Everything that is honorable in a life depends on its cultivation, and everything dishonorable upon its neglect.

—Cicero (44 BC)

•

Potter: Have you put any real pressure on those people of yours to pay those mortgages?
Bailey: Times are bad, Mr. Potter. A lot of these people are out of work.
Potter: Then foreclose! . . . Are you running a business or a charity ward?

—*It's a Wonderful Life* (1946)

•

I give to everybody. When they call, I give. And you know what? When I need something from them two years later, three years later, I call them. They are there for me.

—Donald J. Trump (2016)

Contents

Coming
Up
Short

Introduction

I was born on June 24, 1946, ten days after the birth of Donald John Trump, twelve days before the birth of George Walker Bush, and fifty-six days before the birth of William Jefferson Blythe III, whose name was later changed to Bill Clinton. I did not become president but among my earliest memories is my grandmother Minnie Reich telling me that I *would* become president. I think she was trying to reassure herself that despite my being a runt, fully a head shorter than other little boys, I'd make her proud.

When Trump first ran as a candidate for president in 2015, I viewed him as an anomaly, a cartoon caricature of a con man trying to gain political power. He spent most of his life bullying others—employees, contractors, vendors, women, tenants, lawyers, bankers, politicians, producers. He was and is a bully's bully—vulgar, chaotic, angry, uninformed, impulsive, vindictive.

I have seen the harm bullies cause, and I have spent much of my life trying to stop them. I fought schoolyard toughs who teased and harassed me for being short. I was protected by a teenager who subsequently was murdered by the Ku Klux Klan for trying to register Black voters in Mississippi. I marched for civil rights, protested the Vietnam War, and worked to elect Minnesota senator Eugene McCarthy, the antiwar candidate for president in 1968. I interned for Bobby Kennedy, argued two Supreme Court cases, and advised at the Federal Trade Commission. As labor secretary to Bill Clinton, I tried to protect workers who were bullied by employers. When I ran for governor of Massachusetts, I became the first candidate for major office in America to endorse gay marriage. I taught several generations of students at Harvard, Brandeis, and Berkeley, and wrote a bunch of books.

I always believed America was not a nation of bullies. We protected the vulnerable, comforted the afflicted, gave refuge to those fleeing violence and persecution, and gave voice to those who otherwise would not be heard. I found these ideals in the Declaration of Independence, the Constitution and the Bill of Rights, Lincoln's Gettysburg Address, Emma Lazarus's poem affixed to the Statue of Liberty, FDR's second inaugural address, and Martin Luther King, Jr.'s "free at last" sermon at the 1963 March on Washington. My parents and grandparents espoused these ideals and my teachers expounded them, connecting me with previous generations of Americans and the sacrifices they endured to preserve our democracy and achieve a greater good. We did not always live up to these ideals, of course, but through most of my life they continued to guide the nation. I cherished these ideals and hoped to pass them on.

When I was secretary of labor, I had an office near the U.S. Capitol from which I had a close-up view of the Capitol building's large, majestic dome. When I worked late, which was most nights, I'd look up from my desk and see its hulking beauty lit up like a great monument to the idea of American democracy. I was often exhausted, sometimes discouraged, but the sight of that great dome filled me with the sense that I was taking part in something hugely important. It seemed to illuminate everything I was trying to do and vindicate the frustrations I felt, trying but often failing to keep the economic bullies at bay.

Yet Trump was elected president in 2016 and then—after losing reelection in 2020 and instigating a coup and an attack on the U.S. Capitol, on American democracy itself—he was reelected in 2024. And on January 20, 2025, he took the oath of office for a second time, right under the great dome of the Capitol.

I asked myself how a plurality (albeit a razor-thin one) of American voters could possibly choose to put him in the Oval Office again and trust that he would abide by his oath when he betrayed it the first time. There are many explanations, but for me the most convincing one began to unfold more than four decades ago when I noticed that most Americans' incomes were flattening even though the economy continued to grow. Since then, the lion's share of economic gains have gone to the top. Most Americans, especially those without college degrees, have felt very little improvement in their lives and their jobs have grown less secure. Vast swaths of the country have been abandoned by industry. The basic bargain used to be that if you worked hard and played by the rules, you'd do better than your parents, and your children would do even better than you. But since the late 1970s, that bargain has become a sham. The middle class has shrunk. Some $50 trillion has been siphoned from the bottom 90 percent of Americans to the richest 1 percent.

Many Americans feel frustrated and angry. Trump gave voice to that anger, although he directed it at scapegoats who did nothing to cause it—undocumented workers, the "deep state," transgender people, "communists," and Democrats. And he did nothing whatsoever to address the underlying cause—the corruption of American democracy by big money intent on rigging the system to its advantage, and against average working people. In fact, the major legislative achievement of Trump's first term was a big tax cut to the wealthy, and, as I write this, he is planning another.

Through these years, I watched as other Republican presidents also cut taxes on the wealthy, arguing that the government should allow the so-called free market to operate without constraint— perpetuating the "trickle-down" myth that great wealth in the hands of a few will benefit the many as the rich make the nation more productive. But as I came to understand, the "free market" is a misnomer and little or nothing has trickled down.

Meanwhile, I watched Democrats abandon the working class. John F. Kennedy was the last Democratic president to depend on the votes of working-class Americans while losing the votes of white, college-educated Americans by two to one. Sixty years later, Joe Biden depended on the votes of college-educated Americans while losing the votes of the white working class by two to one. Kamala Harris lost the working class by an even larger margin.

I saw Democratic leaders embrace free trade and lower tariffs on Chinese goods. I witnessed them deregulate finance and allow Wall Street to become a high-stakes gambling casino. I was there when they let big corporations gain enough market power to keep prices and profit margins high. I saw them look away when corporations busted unions and slashed payrolls. I had a front-row seat when they bailed out Wall Street because its gambling addiction threatened to blow up the entire economy but never bailed out homeowners who lost everything. I saw them welcome big money into their campaigns and deliver quid pro quos that rigged the market in favor of big corporations and the wealthy.

To his credit, Joe Biden redirected the Democratic Party back toward its working-class roots, but many of the changes Biden catalyzed wouldn't be evident for years and could easily be reversed. And he had great difficulty communicating effectively about them. In her brief, bright campaign, Kamala Harris rarely mentioned inequality. (She said she'd end corporate price gouging but never explained what it was or how she'd stop it.) Her campaign had enormous energy but was on a perilously short runway, and she was not able to address why so many Americans were working harder than ever yet still struggling economically.

Over the decades, I have participated in some of the nation's failed responses to widening inequality. I have also spoken up against policies I feared would widen it further—into presidents' ears, to any member of Congress who'd listen, and, whenever I had the chance, to the American public. I urged Democratic candidates and lawmakers to tell Americans why their pay continued to be lousy and their jobs less secure: certainly not because of immigrants, the "deep state," transgender people, "communists," or any other bogeyman, but because of the power of large corporations and the rich to rig the market and siphon off most of the economy's gains.

I asked Democrats to stop doing the bidding of big corporations and the wealthy and instead champion the working class: demand paid family leave, Medicare for all, free public higher education, stronger unions, and higher taxes on great wealth, and create the biggest boom in residential home construction since World War II. I argued that corporations must share their profits with their workers and limit CEO pay, that stock buybacks should be illegal, that corporate welfare (subsidies and tax credits unrelated to the common good) be stopped and giant corporations busted up.

I warned that widening inequality and the corruption that accompanied it would eventually invite a demagogue who'd exploit the powerlessness and rage of Americans who felt economically bullied.

It's possible that the arguments I've made over the decades have been wrong and my warnings alarmist. But they have been based on what I have seen and experienced. And now that the nation has reelected exactly the kind of demagogue I portended, I feel added urgency in explaining why it is so important to reverse the staggering inequalities and legalized bribery that characterize today's America.

That is the lesson of this book. It is, in many respects, the lesson of my life.

I love America and am proud of much that this nation has accomplished over my lifetime. I remain doggedly hopeful about the long-term future. But, undeniably, we and much of the world now face a brutal set of crises, headed by the decline of democracy and the deterioration of the rule of law. My father and his Greatest Generation won the Second World War and created the most powerful economy and strongest democracy the world had ever seen, populated by the largest and most prosperous middle class in history. My "boomer" generation and I then failed to create the decent, sustainable, and just society that was within our grasp. In this regard, I'm sorry to say, we all came up short.

PART I

The Bullies

Starters

My father, Ed Reich, was a medic during the Second World War. Fred Trump, Donald's father, built barracks for Navy personnel. George W.'s father, George H.W., was a Navy pilot. Bill Blythe, who fathered Bill Clinton, repaired ships and tanks. At the end of the war, Ed, Fred, George, and Bill returned to Mildred Reich, Mary Anne Trump, Barbara Bush, and Virginia Blythe, respectively, to stoke what would be known as the postwar baby boom. More babies were born in 1946 than in any other year in American history to that time—3.4 million of us little darlings, 20 percent more than the year before. We were born into an America that felt proud of its war victory but also exhausted by the experience.

Surprising almost everyone, the nation emerged economically stronger. Almost all Americans had been put to work during the war and almost every factory was run at full capacity, ending the Great Depression more effectively than any of the many programs that President Franklin D. Roosevelt launched.

We were born to men and women whose futures were now filled with more possibility than they had ever known. They had survived the economic cataclysm of the Great Depression. They had been part of a nation that confronted and ended fascism. They had witnessed (and were soon to learn more about) the horrific results of genocide. Because they faced this together, it's likely they felt more connected to other Americans of their generation than has any generation before or since. The GI Bill offered many a means to a college degree. The soaring postwar economy offered bountiful opportunity.

Black Americans and women, though, were still second-class citizens. Black men had served in segregated units during the war. Millions of women, like my mother, had taken factory jobs, but with the end of the war many of their jobs were filled by blue-collar men. The rights of Black Americans and women, in the economy and our political system, would make for a central struggle in postwar America.

The war and the Depression decade before it had obliterated the fortunes of the Gilded Age. Industrial robber barons, monopolists, titans of Wall Street, and heirs to vast wealth lost almost everything they had accumulated or had it taxed away. The vast playing field of the American economy was greatly leveled, opening the way to the largest middle class the world had ever seen.

When I was a toddler, Ed had saved just enough money to rent a store on Lackawanna Avenue in Scranton and buy the only things he had learned to sell before the war—women's dresses, blouses, and stockings. The shop was called Beverly's, named after his sister. His customers were the wives of factory workers. Most were now homemakers who helped save what they could of their husband's paychecks and spent the rest.

When Donald was a toddler, Fred was a real estate developer in the Bronx who acquired a mortgage-servicing company with access to the titles of many properties nearing foreclosure, which he bought cheaply and sold at a profit.

When little George W. was a toddler, George H.W. was in the oil business in Texas.

Bill's father had been a traveling salesman who died in an automobile accident three months before Bill was born. Four years after Bill's birth, Virginia married Roger Clinton, co-owner of an automobile dealership.

What did Donald, George, Bill, I, and millions of other boomers do for the next seventy-nine years? Did we make America better, more inclusive, more tolerant? Did we strengthen American democracy?

The beginning of an answer might be found in *It's a Wonderful Life,* Frank Capra's ode to America, released to the public on December 21, 1946, the same year little Donald, George, Bill, and I were released on America.

It's a Wonderful Life

If you don't already know it, the movie's central conflict is between Mr. Potter (played by Lionel Barrymore) and George Bailey (Jimmy Stewart). Potter is a greedy, cruel banker, in whose Social Darwinist view of America people compete with one another for scarce resources. Those who succeed deserve to win because they've outrun everyone else in that competitive race.

George is the generous, honorable head of Bedford Falls' building-and-loan company, the one entity standing in the way of Potter's total domination of the town.

After the death of George's father, who founded the building-and-loan company, Potter—who sits on the bank's board—seeks to dissolve it. Potter claims George's father "was not a businessman. He was a man of high ideals, so-called, but ideals without common sense can ruin a town." For Potter, common sense is not coddling the "discontented rabble."

To George, though, Bedford Falls is a community whose members help each other. He tells Potter that the so-called "rabble . . . do most of the working and paying and living and dying in this community." His father helped them build homes on credit so they could have a decent life. "People were human beings to him," George tells Potter, "but to you, they're cattle."

When George accidentally loses some bank deposits that fall into Potter's hands, the banker sees an opportunity to ruin George. This brings George to a bridge where he contemplates suicide, thinking his life has been worthless, before a guardian angel counsels him to think about what Bedford Falls would be like if George hadn't been born—poor, fearful, and completely dependent on Potter. The movie ends when everyone George has helped—virtually the entire town—pitches in to bail out George and his building-and-loan.

It's a cartoon, of course—both a utopian and a dystopian version of America—but the cartoon poses a choice that's become all too relevant. Do we join together or do we let the Potters of America own and run everything?

The movie, in that sense, was a prelude to modern Republican ideology. Since the political rise of Ronald Reagan, his party and the moneyed interests have used Potter-like Social Darwinism to justify tax cuts for the wealthy, union-busting, and cutbacks in social safety nets.

Above all, they have developed and executed a philosophy that has divided Americans (a kind of *political* Social Darwinism). That way, many Americans stay angry and suspicious of one another and don't look upward to see where all the money and power have gone. And we don't join together to claim it back.

What would Republicans and America's moneyed interests say about *It's a Wonderful Life* if it were released today? They'd probably call it socialist, maybe even communist, and it would make them squirm—especially given the eerie similarity between Lionel Barrymore's Mr. Potter and you-know-who. As America has moved closer to being an oligarchy, with staggering inequalities of income, wealth, and power not seen in over a century, and closer to Trumpian neofascism (the two moves are connected, as I'll make clear), *It's a Wonderful Life* speaks to what's gone wrong and what must be done to make it right.

When *It's a Wonderful Life* was released, the FBI considered it evidence of Communist Party infiltration of the film industry. Either a movie was subversive or it wasn't, and in the Bureau's broad framing, this one certainly was. The organization handed over the results of its investigation to the House Un-American Activities Committee (HUAC).

The FBI's Los Angeles field office, using a report by an ad-hoc group that included *Fountainhead* author and future Trump pinup girl Ayn Rand, warned that the movie represented "rather obvious attempts to discredit bankers by casting Lionel Barrymore as a 'scrooge-type' so that he would be the most hated man in the picture." The movie "deliberately maligned the upper class, attempting to show the people who had money were mean and despicable characters. This . . . is a common trick used by Communists." The Bureau's report compared *It's a Wonderful Life* to a Soviet film and alleged that Frank Capra, its director, was "associated with left-wing groups" and that the film's screenwriters, Frances Goodrich and Albert Hackett, were "very close to known Communists."

This was all rubbish, of course, and a prelude to the witch hunt led by Republican senator Joseph McCarthy of Wisconsin, who launched a series of highly publicized probes into alleged Communist penetration of Hollywood, the State Department, and even the U.S. Army.

Few people got my father as riled up as Joe McCarthy.

My Father and the SOBs

My father called himself a liberal Republican in the days when such creatures still roamed the earth. He voted for Thomas Dewey in the 1948 presidential election (canceling my mother's vote for Harry Truman) and then for Dwight Eisenhower for president in 1952 and 1956 (canceling my mother's votes for Adlai Stevenson), and he thought highly of New York State's Republican governor, Nelson Rockefeller, and one of its Republican senators, Jacob Javits, neither of whom would last a nanosecond in today's GOP.

But Ed Reich could not abide political bullies. He gave up on the Republican Party when Richard Nixon became president. He would have detested Trump. (My father died nine months before Trump was elected to his first term of office.) He thought anyone who had to bully someone else to feel good about himself was despicable. If they did their bullying through politics, they were doubly despicable. In my father's mind, political bullying had led to the Holocaust.

At the start of September 1947, my father moved us from Scranton to a small town some sixty miles north of New York City, South Salem, to be within driving distance of the two stores he then owned, in Norwalk, Connecticut, and Peekskill, New York. On Labor Day, just after we moved in, a delegation of older men came by our house. When they knocked on the door, my mother thought they were a welcoming committee and opened the door with a big "Hello!" But when she saw the expressions on their faces, she became alarmed.

She invited them into the living room and asked if they'd like coffee. They declined.

My father greeted them stiffly, suggesting they sit down. They did not.

"What's this about?" he asked. "What's happened? Is there a problem?"

"Mr. and Mrs. Reich," one of them spoke gravely, "we've come to inform you that South Salem is a Christian community."

There was a long pause. My father reddened.

"So, we're not welcome here?" His voice was tight.

"Legally, you have a right to be here, of course," the speaker said. (New York State had just enacted a law prohibiting homeowners from including "restrictive covenants" in their deeds that barred sales to "Negroes or Hebrews.") "But we don't think you and your family will be happy here."

"Thank you for coming by," my father said flatly, opening the front door for them. Then he exploded: "Now get the hell out of my house!"

That was the day my father decided we'd stay put in South Salem forever. "I showed those sons of *bitches*," he said some years later.

"Son-of-a-*bitch*!" was the worst epithet my father could hurl at someone. It burst out of him like a volcanic eruption. For many years I didn't know it contained separate English words, including a term many would find offensive. To my young ears it might have been Russian or Yiddish, but it was frightening.

Joe McCarthy held a special place in Ed Reich's pantheon of horrible people not only because he bullied those he claimed were members of the Communist Party, but because he did so with malice. McCarthy ridiculed the "pitiful squealing" of "those egg-sucking phony liberals" who "would hold sacrosanct those Communists and queers." Every time McCarthy's image came across the six-inch screen of the Magnavox television in our living room, my father would shout "Son-of-a-*bitch*" so loudly it made me shudder.

McCarthyism was the by-product of the Republican Party's postwar effort to eradicate the New Deal. The GOP had portrayed the midterm election of 1946 as a "battle between Republicanism and communism," and the Republican National Committee chairman claimed that the federal bureaucracy was filled with "pink puppets."

Southern segregationist Democrats joined in the red-baiting. Mississippi senator Theodore Bilbo, a Klansman who had filibustered to block anti-lynching legislation, described multiracial labor unions' advocacy for civil rights as the work of "northern communists." Representative John Elliott Rankin, a racist and antisemitic Mississippi Democrat who helped establish the House Committee on Un-American Activities (HUAC), called the Congress of Industrial Organizations' Southern organizing campaign "a communist plot" and feared it would give more voting rights to Black people. "We're asleep at the switch," he warned. "They're taking over this country; we've got to stop them if we want this country."

The tactic was temporarily successful. In the 1946 midterms, Democrats lost control of both the Senate and the House. Wisconsin ended its era of progressive Republicanism and sent McCarthy to the Senate. California replaced New Dealer Jerry Voorhis in the House with a young Republican lawyer who had already figured out how to use red-baiting as a political tool, Richard Nixon.

In December 1946, at the founding convention of the Progressive Citizens of America, Henry Wallace called the red scare a tool used by the most powerful economic forces in our country and warned us not to give in to it. "We shall . . . repel all the attacks of the plutocrats and monopolists who will brand us as Reds," he said, adding: "If it is traitorous to believe in peace—we are traitors. If it is communistic to believe in prosperity for all—we are communists. If it is un-American to believe in freedom from monopolistic dictation—we are un-American. We are more American than the neo-fascists who attack us. The more we are attacked the more likely we are to succeed, provided we are ready and willing to counterattack."

But, for years, there was no pushback. The red-baiting escalated, encouraged by J. Edgar Hoover, the first director of the FBI, and President Truman succumbed to the mounting hysteria. On March 21, 1947, he signed Executive Order 9835, which ushered in loyalty oaths and background checks and created the attorney general's List of Subversive Organizations.

As the 1950 election approached, a *New York Times* headline announced that the "Left Is Silent in Campaign." Even the American Civil Liberties Union, whose roots lay in the red scare of the World War I era, was reluctant to take the lead in opposing the threat to civil liberties in the second red scare. California representative Helen

Gahagan Douglas, dubbed the "Pink Lady" for her supposed communist sympathies, ran for the Senate in 1950. She survived a bitter primary battle only to be beaten in November by Nixon.

On June 9, 1954, I sat at my father's side on our living room couch watching the Army-McCarthy hearings. The senator had accused the U.S. Army of having poor security at a top-secret facility. He charged that one of the young attorneys on the staff of Joseph Welch, who was representing the Army, was a communist. The charge could destroy the young man's career.

"Son-of-a-*bitch*!" my father shouted. I hid my head.

As McCarthy continued his attack on the young attorney, Welch broke in: "Until this moment, Senator, I think I never really gauged your cruelty or your recklessness."

I was only eight years old, but I was spellbound.

McCarthy didn't stop. "Son-of-a-*bitch*!" my father shouted even more loudly.

At this point, Welch demanded that McCarthy listen to him. "Let us not assassinate this lad further, Senator," he said. "You have done enough. Have you no sense of decency?"

Almost overnight, McCarthy imploded. His national popularity evaporated. Three years later, censured by his Senate colleagues, ostracized by his party, and ignored by the press, McCarthy drank himself to death, a broken man at the age of forty-eight.

During those hearings, McCarthy's chief counsel was Roy Cohn, who became one of America's most notorious bullies. Cohn had gained prominence as the Department of Justice attorney who successfully prosecuted Julius and Ethel Rosenberg for espionage, leading to their execution in 1953. (Evidence made public afterward confirmed that Julius was a spy but that Ethel, while aware of her husband's activities, was not.)

In public, Cohn was homophobic. Privately, he was gay at a time when being gay was a crime. A character in Tony Kushner's play *Angels in America* describes him as "the polestar of human evil. The worst human being who ever lived . . . the most evil, twisted, vicious bastard ever to snort coke at Studio 54."

The Rosenberg trial brought the twenty-four-year-old firebrand to the attention of Hoover, who convinced McCarthy, chairman of the Senate Permanent Subcommittee on Investigations, to hire Cohn as its chief counsel. He soon became known for his aggressive questioning of suspected communists.

My father, who thought Roy Cohn almost as despicable as Joe McCarthy, shouted "Son-of-a-*bitch*!" whenever Cohn's name was in the news. After the senator's downfall, it was assumed that Cohn's career was also over, yet he reinvented himself as a power broker in New York and survived scandals, indictments, and accusations of tax evasion, bribery, and theft.

Cohn proved himself useful to a young real estate developer named Donald Trump, whose father had started his son's career by bringing him into the family business of renting apartments in Brooklyn and Queens. Cohn introduced Donald to New York's social and political elite. By then, Donald was undertaking several large construction projects in Manhattan and needed both a fixer and a mentor. Cohn filled both roles. Along the way he bequeathed to Trump a penchant for ruthless bullying, profane braggadocio, opportunistic bigotry, lying, and more lying. Like Trump, Cohn was utterly without principle and prioritized personal power that could be leveraged for wealth, influence, and celebrity.

In 1973, the Justice Department alleged that Trump Management, Inc., its twenty-seven-year-old president, Donald, and chairman, Fred, violated the Fair Housing Act of 1968 in thirty-nine of its properties. The company was said to have quoted different rental terms and conditions to prospective tenants based on their race and made false "no vacancy" statements to Black people seeking to rent. Trump employees had secretly marked the applications of Black people with codes, such as "C" for "colored," according to documents filed in federal court. The employees allegedly directed Black people away from buildings with mostly white tenants, steering them toward properties that had many Black tenants.

Representing the Trumps, Cohn filed a countersuit against the government for $100 million, asserting that the charges were "irresponsible and baseless." Trump settled the charges out of court in

1975, asserting he was satisfied that the agreement did not "compel the Trump organization to accept persons on welfare as tenants unless as qualified as any other tenant." Three years later, when the Trump Organization was in court for violating terms of the 1975 settlement, Cohn called the charges "nothing more than a rehash of complaints by a couple of planted malcontents." Donald Trump denied the charges.

Cohn was also involved in the construction of Trump Tower, helping to secure concrete during a citywide Teamster strike via a union leader linked to a mob boss. At about this time, Cohn introduced Trump to another of Cohn's clients, Rupert Murdoch.

During Ronald Reagan's 1980 presidential campaign, Cohn helped another young man named Roger Stone. As Stone later recounted, Cohn gave him a suitcase filled with money that Stone dropped off at the office of a lawyer influential in Liberal Party circles: "Legal fees. I don't know what he did for the money." In fact, the money was given to New York's Liberal Party to support Illinois congressman John Anderson's campaign, with the intention of splitting New York's opposition to Reagan. It worked. Reagan carried the state with 46 percent of the vote. (My Republican father voted for Jimmy Carter.)

In 1986, Cohn was disbarred by the New York State Bar for unethical conduct after attempting to defraud a dying client by forcing him to sign a will amendment leaving Cohn his fortune. (Cohn died five weeks later from AIDS-related complications.)

In his first and best-known book, *The Art of the Deal,* Trump drew a distinction between integrity and loyalty. He preferred the latter, and for him, Roy Cohn exemplified it. Trump contrasted Cohn with "all the hundreds of 'respectable' guys who make careers out of boasting about their uncompromising integrity but have absolutely no loyalty. . . . What I liked most about Roy Cohn was that he would do just the opposite."

My father would vehemently disagree.

McCarthy, Cohn, and the old men who came to our door and told my parents that Jews weren't welcome in South Salem typified for me Mr. Potter—people who abused their power to make life harder for the weaker and more vulnerable. It was a child's notion (apparently shared by Frank Capra) that the world could neatly be divided between the bullies and the bullied, and that the most courageous act was to stand up to the bullies. Much of my early education centered on that. Arrayed against such people in my young mind were the George Baileys of the world, such as my father.

My Expulsion

My formal education did not get off to an auspicious start: I was expelled from Miss Bouton's nursery school because of excessive sarcasm. I was four years old.

The Bouton family had lived in South Salem since the Revolutionary War. One of Miss Bouton's ancestors had served under George Washington and received a large parcel of land on which a farmhouse still stood. The main road was Bouton Road.

I remember Miss Bouton as a character in a child's cartoon—tall and angular, with a thin nose, sharp chin, and arms and shoulders like the sawed-off limbs of a tree. In my four-year-old eyes, she seemed very old. She spoke in a high, raspy voice, and rarely smiled. Miss Bouton ran the only nursery school in South Salem, in the main room of the farmhouse, where she lived with her brother, Billy. It smelled of antiseptic. A potbellied stove kept part of it warm but the rest of it—where I often sat alone on the floor playing with wooden blocks, fearing that the other children would tease or taunt me because of my height, or lack thereof—was cold. The hook rug covering most of the floor chafed my arms and legs. Next to the farmhouse was a barn where Billy fed the cows and slopped the pigs.

A photo shows sixteen of us—seven three-year-olds and nine four-year-olds—standing in front of a scraggly Christmas tree. I'm a head shorter than the others, mouth agape.

My mother was an artist who loved beautiful objects and conversations with interesting people. Yet she was trapped in a little house in South Salem with a demanding little boy who wouldn't leave her alone. In the afternoons she'd sometimes lock herself in her bedroom to get some time for herself, leaving me alone in a hallway outside the bedroom. Miss Bouton's nursery school must have been a godsend to her.

I didn't understand this at the time, of course. All I knew was that my mother dropped me off at the farmhouse at 9 a.m. in an old Nash Rambler whose brakes didn't work well, and I had to endure school until 3 p.m., when my mother rescued me. It felt like punishment, but I had no idea what I did wrong. I always tried to please my mother and father and every other adult, to do and say exactly what I thought they wanted. If I didn't, I feared they'd abandon me—as my mother did when she dropped me off at Miss Bouton's every weekday. My life was conditional.

Looking back, I'm grateful to Miss Bouton for opening her farmhouse to toddlers and preschoolers, for giving my mother some freedom, and for coping day after day with sixteen screeching, yelling, often wild little people, along with one who played alone and felt kind of sorry for himself. (Seventy-five years later, most mothers in America are working and most parents are feeling the stress of rising costs and shrinking availability of childcare. On average, according to a 2024 survey, parents spend one quarter of their income on childcare.)

At the time, though, I disliked Miss Bouton intensely. Her lunches consisted of lukewarm beef stew and a vegetable, usually lima beans. The food was spiky and hard, like my image of her. She prepared lunch during morning nap time, and when she served it to us on a little table in the center of the main room, she smelled of it. In my mind, she and her meals blended into a sharp, fearsome, indigestible problem.

Day after day, I could barely eat her lunch but managed it because I didn't want to offend her. One day, though, I simply couldn't. She asked me why. I didn't say anything. She fumed, telling me that it was good food and she had spent time preparing it so the children would have a nourishing meal. I remained silent and wouldn't touch it.

"Eat some," she said.

I stabbed at a tiny bit of stew with my fork and put an even smaller amount into my mouth.

"What do you think?" She bent down so her face was close to mine. I said nothing.

"What do you think of my lunch, Bobby?" she asked again.

It was at this moment that, according to my mother's account, I spit out the small amount in my mouth and said, "It's *delicious*!" Then I refused to take another bite. Miss Bouton phoned my mother and told her that she was expelling me because I was sarcastic.

My mother was devastated. I was happy to be free of Miss Bouton, but I hated to disappoint my mother. I took my expulsion as further evidence that if I weren't perfect, I would be abandoned.

On the other hand, if I hadn't been expelled from nursery school, I wouldn't have met Vice President Henry Wallace.

Sitting on the Vice President's Lap

Henry Wallace, who was Franklin D. Roosevelt's vice president from March 1941 to January 1945, was not just a champion of democracy and fierce opponent of American fascism. He was also one of America's most outspoken environmentalists, writing presciently in 1936 that "the most damaging indictment that can be made of the capitalistic system is the way in which its emphasis on unfettered individualism results in exploitation of natural resources in a manner to destroy the physical foundations of national longevity."

Wallace saw what Hitler did in Nazi Germany and feared the same could happen in America. He worried that an unprincipled sociopath with a gift for marketing and self-promotion could turn some Americans into violent bullies if they felt abandoned and angry enough.

With Roosevelt's encouragement, Wallace spoke out against American fascism. "The dangerous American fascist is the man who wants to do in the United States in an American way what Hitler did in Germany in a Prussian way," Wallace wrote in his essay "The Danger of American Fascism," published in *The New York Times Sunday Magazine* on April 9, 1944.

A fascist is one whose lust for money or power is combined with such an intensity of intolerance toward those of other races, parties, classes, religions, cultures, regions, or nations as to make him ruthless in his use of deceit or violence to attain his ends. . . .

The American fascist would prefer not to use violence. His method is to poison the channels of public information. With a fascist the problem is never how best to present the truth to the public but how best to use the news to deceive the public into giving the fascist and his group more money or more power. . . .

It has been claimed at times that our modern age of technology facilitates dictatorship. What we must understand is that the industries, processes, and inventions created by modern science can be used either to subjugate or liberate. The choice is up to us. . . .

The American fascists are most easily recognized by their deliberate perversion of truth and fact. Their newspapers and propaganda carefully cultivate every fissure of disunity, every crack in the common front against fascism. They use every opportunity to impugn democracy. They use isolationism as a slogan to conceal their own selfish imperialism. . . . They claim to be superpatriots, but they would destroy every liberty guaranteed by the Constitution. They demand free enterprise but are the spokesmen for monopoly and vested interests. . . .

Still another danger is represented by those who, paying lip service to democracy and the common welfare, in their insatiable greed for money and the power which money gives, do not hesitate surreptitiously to evade the laws designed to safeguard the public from monopolistic extortion. . . .

Monopolists who fear competition and who distrust democracy because it stands for equal opportunity would like to secure their position against small and energetic enterprise. In an effort to eliminate the possibility of any rival growing up, some monopolists would sacrifice democracy itself. . . .

Their final objective toward which all their deceit is directed is to capture political power so that, using the power of the state and the power of the market simultaneously, they may keep the common man in eternal subjection.

Wallace saw the connection between Hitler's preachments about racial "purity" and the language of Southern segregationists who spoke of a master race. "Those who fan the fires of racial clashes for the purpose of making political capital here at home are taking the first step toward Nazism," he warned. And "the second step toward fascism is the destruction of labor unions."

To avert the rise of American fascism, Wallace argued that his party and country must champion "the democracy of the common man," embracing "not just the Bill of Rights but also economic democracy, ethnic democracy, educational democracy, and democracy in the treatment of the sexes."

Wallace scorned the America First rhetoric that was being mouthed by prominent Democrats as well as Republicans. "We must remember that down through the ages one of the most popular political devices has been to blame economic and other troubles on some minority group," he said. "The survival and strength of American democracy are proof that it has succeeded by its deeds thus far," he continued:

> But we all know that it contains the seeds of failure. I for one will not be confident of the continued survival of American democracy if millions of unskilled workers are condemned to [near poverty] all their lives, with no place in our industrial system. I will not be confident of the survival of our democracy if half our people must be below the line of a decent nutrition [and] if most of our children continue to be reared in surroundings where poverty is highest, and education is lowest.

Wallace called for massive investment in job creation, education, social services, and peacemaking. Because Wallace was increasingly seen as too sympathetic to Soviet Russia and the Democratic Party bosses couldn't control him, FDR was forced to drop him from the ticket in the 1944 election in favor of a little-known Missouri senator and former haberdasher named Harry Truman, whom they assumed they could control. FDR died in 1945, and Truman became president.

As the midterm elections of 1946 loomed, Wallace feared that without a strong progressive message and platform, Democrats would not be able to mobilize their base to beat the Republicans. He warned that "if the Democrats fail to control the Eightieth Congress there is only one way in which we get control again and that is by becoming more progressive."

He was correct. In the first midterm election of Truman's presidency, the Democrats lost control of both the House and the Senate for the first time since Herbert Hoover occupied the Oval Office in 1932. The Democrats' abandonment of progressive populism and the redistributionist policies FDR championed did much to destroy the New Deal coalition that spawned leaders like Wallace. Years later, Ronald Reagan would exploit that void in American politics by drawing so-called Reagan Democrats to the extreme right. Thirty-five years later, as Democrats continued to divorce themselves from the working class, an even larger void would be exploited by the bully in chief, Donald Trump.

Wallace came close to defeating Truman for the presidential nomination at the Democratic convention of 1948. When that bid failed, Wallace launched a third-party presidential campaign under the banner of the Progressive Party, calling for the desegregation of public schools, racial and gender equality, national health insurance, and sharp cuts in military spending.

The Cold War threatened Wallace's dream of achieving global peace. In Wallace's mind, Washington, D.C., was responsible for the growing hostility between the United States and the Soviet Union. On May 11, 1948, before a full crowd at Madison Square Garden, he called for a new dialogue with Russia. Reading aloud an open letter to Josef Stalin, he offered a six-point plan, including arms reductions and a ban on weapons of mass destruction, and a proposal that neither the United States nor the USSR maintain military bases in other countries.

Stalin was one of the worst bullies of the twentieth century. Wallace was blind to the atrocities he was committing within Russia. Wallace's seeming embrace of him was too much even for Wallace's admirers. After losing the 1948 election, Wallace retired from politics to the largest farm in South Salem.

My mother recognized Wallace in the South Salem post office one day and summoned the courage to introduce herself and her little boy, who had just been expelled from nursery school. Wallace invited us to tea on his large porch. I remember him as a kindly old man with a bright shock of white hair who pulled me up onto his lap while spending what seemed interminable hours talking to my mother. She was thrilled. I was bored.

After we left, she told me Henry Wallace was a great man, and that someday most Americans would agree. But when my mother mentioned to a neighbor that we had tea on Wallace's porch and I had sat on his lap, the neighbor was horrified. She called him a communist.

Sitting on Wallace's lap, I of course knew nothing about his warnings about American fascism. But I did know about bullying. And I was about to learn even more.

The Dangers Lurking in
Lewisboro School

In kindergarten, I was the shortest kid in South Salem's Lewisboro Elementary School. The other children called me names ("midget," "mouse," and "runt" were among the kindest) and hurled insulting jokes at me. (What's the difference between a dwarf and a midget? Very little! Why are midgets constantly thirsty? They can't reach the drinking fountains!) When they spotted me walking down the corridor, they sang "Shrimp Boats Is a Comin'." I didn't yet know the word "humiliated," but that's how I felt.

On the school playground, I tried to stay within eyesight of a teacher so the bullies wouldn't dare harass me. It didn't always work. Once, when the teacher had gone inside, I was dragged off to a mock court behind a large tree where the child bullies charged me with being too short to be in school and threatened to punish me by whacking me over the head with a baseball bat. A kind third-grade boy came over to defend me, saying, "This is unfair!" and commanding them to release me in so loud a voice that they did. I ran. A narrow escape.

When some second graders found me alone in the boys' room, they threatened to hold me upside down and dunk my head in the toilet. I escaped by screaming as loud as I could, which stopped them long enough for me to escape to the safety of the kindergarten room.

For the next six months I refused to reenter the boys' room, which led to some embarrassingly close calls. My tactic was not to drink or eat anything after breakfast. But on one occasion I needed to empty my bowels so badly that I had to hop around the kindergarten room to avoid letting go. I was too embarrassed to explain that to my teacher, so she sent me to the principal's office. The principal, a kind man named Charles Helmes, looked directly into my eyes and asked if I was all right. Continuing to hop, I told him I was fine. But when he put his hands on my shoulders, I couldn't control myself and let loose. I felt ashamed, my life a disaster.

When my mother arrived, I tearily explained to her and Mr. Helmes why I didn't want to use the boys' room. They came up with a solution. From then on, when I wanted to go to the bathroom, I would knock on the classroom door of a third grader named Jimmy Hoffman, who would accompany me and protect me from the bullies. Jimmy, the son of a friend of my mother's, was judged by her to be sufficiently mature to take on this responsibility.

Summoning Jimmy became an excruciating but necessary ritual. Whenever I did so, other third graders snickered. I was embarrassed but I knew the alternative was worse. After several months, Jimmy tired of being my protector, so I found another third grader who'd take on the role. And then another. I became adept at finding older boys who'd protect me from bullies.

When it came time for the school Christmas pageant, the music teacher who directed the show naturally cast me, the shortest boy in the school, as Baby Jesus. The role didn't require much preparation or talent. I just had to lie on some straw strewn on the stage and look at children playing Mary and Joseph, the three Wise Men, and assorted angels, and then sit up and join the rest of the school in prayer and Christmas carols.

The problem was that even at the tender age of five, I felt I was doing something profoundly wrong. I knew Jesus was Jewish, but my family did not celebrate Christmas and did not believe Jesus was the Messiah. Yet here I was playing him onstage and praying and singing songs praising him. As I lay on the straw, I apologized to God under my breath, so no one else would hear, and then again during the prayers and carols. I whispered, "God, I didn't have a choice, I was cast as Baby Jesus. Please forgive me. Thank you."

Soon afterward, the U.S. Supreme Court fortified the wall separating church and state, and public schools no longer had Christmas pageants. But seventy years later, the Supreme Court made a U-turn, ruling in favor of a former high school football coach who repeatedly led his players in prayers in the locker room and on the field after games. At the homecoming game, the coach was joined in the postgame prayer by members of the public, a state legislator, and the media. Justice Neil M. Gorsuch, writing for his fellow Republican appointees in the 6-to-3 decision, ruled that the coach's prayers were protected by the Constitution's guarantees of free speech and the free exercise of religion. Writing in dissent, Justice Sonia Sotomayor said: "Official-led prayer strikes at the core of our constitutional protections for the religious liberty of students and their parents. . . . The Court now charts a different path."

As I write this, the MAGA governor of Louisiana has signed into law a bill passed by the state's MAGA legislature requiring all public schools (including public colleges and universities) to post the Ten Commandments in every classroom.

I remember how unprotected I felt as a five-year-old. Those feelings of vulnerability—to the bullies in the boys' room and on the playground, to the snickering third graders in Jimmy Hoffman's classroom, and to God, whom I let down by playing Baby Jesus—continued to haunt me until I reached Mrs. Camp's third-grade classroom.

How Alice Camp Saved Me

I arrived in that classroom a shy, insecure eight-year-old who felt like a loser and had no particular interest in school. But Mrs. Camp saw something in me. She fed me books, projects, ideas. She challenged me and praised me. She made me feel special.

Her slightly wacky sense of humor connected with mine. Her curiosity fueled mine. She didn't mind if I stayed in at recess and barraged her with questions. Her enjoyment of literature fueled my love of books. She made me understand that I wasn't a freak, that I might even be talented, that the drawings and writing I did were pretty good. She made clear there was no reason for me to feel so sad and ashamed, so fearful, so alone in the world.

One day toward the end of the school year she announced to the class that she was about to write a very important word on the blackboard—a word, she said, that described one student in the class. In huge letters that spanned most of the blackboard she wrote out A-M-B-I-T-I-O-U-S, and then asked if we knew what it meant and to whom she was referring. The class was silent. She said it meant being strongly motivated to succeed. Then she pointed to me and said, "This describes Bobby Reich." Smiling at me, Mrs. Camp walked up to my desk and said to me, out loud, "It's been a pleasure having you in my class, Bobby."

I began to tremble. I wanted to cry. I was embarrassed and elated. I had never felt successful at anything.

I think of Mrs. Camp now when I hear America's teachers blamed for almost everything imaginable—yelled at by parents over the insistence that their children wear masks during the pandemic, reprimanded by school boards about books they assign or let their students read, vilified by politicians for teaching about America's history of racism, even told to arm themselves on the chance that their classrooms will be invaded by murderous young men with semi-automatics.

Instead of berating them, we should be honoring them. Rather than impose ludicrous demands on them, we should free them to teach and inspire. Instead of demeaning them, we should express our gratitude to them—every day—and pay them twice as much as they're earning. Why should investment bankers get paid fortunes for moving money from one set of pockets to another when our teachers can barely afford to live on what they make? Bankers watch over our financial capital. Teachers watch over our *human* capital, and therefore our future.

Mrs. Camp saved me, or, more accurately, she discovered me. And her discovery of me allowed me to discover myself.

I never saw Mrs. Camp again after third grade ended for me in June 1954. I never thanked her, although I do remember sitting cross-legged on the floor at the end-of-year school assembly, choking up about leaving her. She passed long ago.

I had the great fortune to have other wonderful teachers over the rest of my years of public elementary and high school, and then in

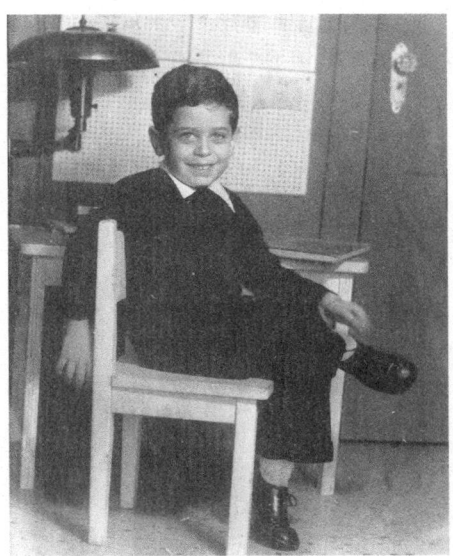

college and graduate school. I don't recall thanking any of them, either. But I think of them often, and I know I am forever in their debt. I suppose I managed to pay back a small portion of that debt by teaching, which I did for more than four decades. I loved teaching. I loved my students. I can't imagine a more rewarding or noble profession.

My father, on the other hand, never enjoyed his work.

My Father's Recitations

My father, as I said, owned a series of women's clothing shops over the course of his working life. His goal was to have a chain of them, but he kept having to close ones that lost money and open new ones with the hope they'd do better, so he never had more than two at a time, and was just getting by. Often, he'd arrive home late, having driven forty miles or more from one of his stores. My mother would be waiting for him with dinner on the stove. She'd open the front door cautiously and ask, "How did it go?" I'd be right behind her. Sometimes he looked happy to be home, but I mostly remember his long, tired face. "My stomach is on the blink," he'd say, kissing her and giving me a hug and then disappearing into the bathroom. He'd emerge later, trying his best to look cheerful, but I knew it had been another disappointing day at the store.

In the summer of 1954, Hurricane Carol swept through Torrington, Connecticut, where he had opened his most recent store. The hill behind turned into a mudslide that washed through the store, taking everything with it. He was almost washed up. My grandmother offered to pay for a two-week vacation in Florida to get my father "back on his feet," as she put it.

My father, mother, sister Ellen, and I, along with my grandmother and her brother Morris, crowded into Morris's 1944 Cadillac for the trip south. I don't think it got my father back on his feet because Morris's radiator kept overheating, which caused several stops along the way at garages that charged so much as to provoke several "son-of-a-*bitch*" explosions. But the vacation did give my mother's creative mind time to ponder.

When we returned, she proposed that he open a new store in Ridgefield, Connecticut, several miles east of South Salem. Instead of selling cheap cotton dresses, blouses, and undergarments to working-class women, she suggested he try appealing to the wives of wealthy business executives who were starting to move into the area, as corporate headquarters moved out of New York City and into southern Connecticut. She offered to run the day-to-day operation of the store. My father agreed to give it a try. They got a small loan from the local bank, found a tiny space on a side street, filled it with what my mother called "country casual" attire—cardigans, skirts, quilted jackets, fitted coats, polo shirts, and knitted jumpers—and named it "Ellen Roberts," after my sister and me.

Ed Reich was a practical man, not prone to personal reflection or philosophy. The closest he came to introspection was to recite a portion of Thomas Gray's "Elegy Written in a Country Churchyard."

> *The boast of heraldry, the pomp of pow'r,*
> *And all that beauty, all that wealth e'er gave,*
> *Awaits alike th' inevitable hour.*
> *The paths of glory lead but to the grave.*

And he had a favorite recitation from *Macbeth*.

> *Tomorrow, and tomorrow, and tomorrow,*
> *Creeps in this petty pace from day to day,*
> *To the last syllable of recorded time;*
> *And all our yesterdays have lighted fools*
> *The way to dusty death. Out, out, brief candle!*
> *Life's but a walking shadow, a poor player,*
> *That struts and frets his hour upon the stage,*
> *And then is heard no more. It is a tale*
> *Told by an idiot, full of sound and fury,*
> *Signifying nothing.*

He recited these two excerpts frequently. They seemed to give him comfort. He often smiled while reciting them, occasionally laughing as he concluded. When his store was washed away in Hurricane Carol, he recited them repeatedly.

"Ellen Roberts" kept the family going. My mother loved her new-found role, which enabled her to use her artistic talents in selecting merchandise for the store and helping women choose their ensembles. She proved a remarkable salesperson. My father was appreciative of her. The next year he closed the remaining Beverly's and opened another Ellen Roberts in the upscale town of Bedford Village, which did even better and took even fuller advantage of my mother's artistry and taste. Years later I began to see the larger pattern enveloping my parents' change of fortune: an American economy tilting ever more toward business executives and college-educated professionals, such as those whose wives bought country casuals at Ellen Roberts, and away from the working-class women who no longer sustained stores such as Beverly's.

The year my father turned forty—the same year as the flood—I became desperately afraid he would die. His health was good, but I worried about his age. His repeated recitations from these two literary works about the temporariness of life made me particularly sensitive to the passage of time. I had heard that forty marked the start of something called "middle age." To my eight-year-old self, that seemed to border on being old, as if my father had reached the top of a mountain and was now about to fall down the other side in a mudslide, toward the "inevitable hour."

I began to record our lives in my head as if I were making a scrapbook that I'd return to in the future, a kind of internal home movie that I'd be able to watch whenever I wanted to recall these years.

My father did not die soon after he turned forty. In fact, he lived until two weeks before his 102nd birthday. He was lucid right up to the end.

A week before he died, I lay next to him on his bed with my arms around him. He was staring at the ceiling.

"I love you, Dad," I said.

He looked puzzled.

"Does that surprise you?" I asked.

"No," he said softly. "It's just that we were never a very demonstrative family."

That made no sense. My life had been filled with his affection.

Then I remembered something he had told me years before. He said that when he was a boy, *his* father—my grandfather, Alexander Reich—was not demonstrative with his love for Ed. Quite the opposite. Alexander had told little Ed he'd never amount to anything. It seemed such a cruel thing to say to a little boy. The grandfather I knew was sweet and gentle, and laughed easily. When I came to visit him, he hugged me close. But apparently he hadn't always been that way. He had come from a family of strict and formal Austrian Jews, influenced more by the norms of the Victorian era than by Jewish tradition. Whatever love they felt for each other they kept buried.

I came to understand that my father's recitations from Gray's "Elegy" and *Macbeth* were ways of dealing with his sense of failure. It was okay that he never amounted to much, that he became little more than a storekeeper whose stores often failed, because even people who obtain glory, wealth, and power inevitably end up the same way everyone else ends up. Life is nothing more than a shadow play where actors briefly strut and fret but then disappear regardless of their achievements.

Although he never said it, I suspected that his runt of a son confirmed his sense of failure. Little Bobby, the shortest kid in Lewisboro Elementary School, was probably an embarrassment to a man whose father told him he'd never amount to anything. I suppose that's one reason I worked so hard to achieve something in my own life—why I was "ambitious," as Mrs. Camp put it—not just to compensate for my shortness but to give my father a vicarious sense of success.

To me, Ed Reich was hardly a failure. He was a wonderful man, full of integrity and deeply held views about decency and fairness—and passionately opposed to bullies. When I felt small and vulnerable, which was most of the time, he was a mountain of strength. He kicked out of our house the men who wanted us to leave town because we were Jewish. He worked very hard, six days a week.

Ed Reich's strength gave me strength. Alice Camp's encouragement gave me courage. But I still needed older boys to protect me.

What Happened to My
Protector, Mickey

My grandparents on both sides spent summers in tiny cabins in Sacandaga Park, New York, a small vacation community nestled in the foothills of the Adirondack Mountains.

Its heyday had been at the turn of the previous century when the Fonda, Johnstown, and Gloversville Railway built a resort on the Sacandaga River, replete with a hotel, outdoor dance pavilion, and small cabins with wraparound porches. The railroad made big profits bringing thousands of tourists there until the early 1920s, when the river was dammed and turned into a reservoir, flooding most of the resort. By the time my grandparents got there in the late 1930s, Sacandaga Park was already in decline. But some cabins survived, surrounded by tall pines. The air was cool. The Adirondack Inn still stood, although its paint was peeling and its broad lawns were less manicured than in its prime. It hosted live bands on the weekends.

That's where my parents met, on the dance floor, in 1941. Ed was a great dancer—fox trot, rumba, swing. He swung Mildred off her feet. Ed and Mildred announced their engagement on December 7, 1941—hardly a propitious day. Shaken by the Japanese invasion of Pearl Harbor, they decided to marry as soon as they could find a ballroom in which to do so, which turned out to be Christmas Day, just over two weeks later. A few weeks after that, Ed went into the Army. Five years later, when the war was over, I was born.

My earliest and happiest memories are of our Adirondack summers—the sweet aroma of pine needles; my parents relaxed and happy; my grandparents doting on their first grandchild; a cascade of relatives and friends visiting on weekends, eager to have me come by and sit on their porches, offering hugs and noshes; everyone crowding into bedrooms with two or more double beds: Morris playing the upright piano; my father and mother dancing and laughing. I had

free rein in Sacandaga, but I stayed clear of older kids who might bully or tease me.

The summer after third grade, I met Mickey, whose family had rented one of the cabins. I was eight and he was a teenager. We were not friends, yet I came to love him.

Mickey was kind and gentle, with a ready smile. I don't recall asking him to protect me. He wasn't the kind of hulking kid I usually chose as protector; he was on the short side and thin. He wore a sailor's cap and seemed forever cheerful. I don't remember him fighting to defend me or even quieting the kids who made fun of me, but I do remember his warmth and reassuring presence. His calm good nature seemed to cast a positive spell over kids who might otherwise turn to teasing or bullying.

Years went by and I grew into a teenager who no longer needed older boys to protect me from bullies, and I lost track of Mickey. It wasn't until September 1964, the start of my freshman year at Dartmouth College, that I heard what had happened to him. Early that summer, Mickey—whose full name was Michael Schwerner—

had traveled to Mississippi. The civil rights movement was gaining strength. Martin Luther King, Jr., had given his famous "I have a dream" speech at the August 1963 March on Washington, where 250,000 people had gathered at the Lincoln Memorial to hear him. "Freedom Summer" of 1964 brought college students, both Black and white, Mickey among them, from northern schools together with Black people from Mississippi, to educate and register Black voters, under the aegis of the Student Nonviolent Coordinating Committee (SNCC). Mississippi was chosen because only 7 percent of the state's eligible Black voters were registered, in a state that was about 40 percent Black. Most had been frozen out of the polls with poll taxes, subjective literacy tests, and brutality. It had been that way since 1877. The system was enforced by white supremacists who could commit crimes with impunity because the entire region had become a one-party state run by white supremacists.

Mickey was among the first wave of volunteers to arrive in Mississippi for Freedom Summer. On the afternoon of June 21, he and two other student volunteers—Andrew Goodman, also white, and James Chaney, a young Black man—were driving near the town of Philadelphia, when Neshoba County deputy sheriff Cecil Ray Price stopped them for allegedly speeding. Price locked them up in the local jail. That night, after they paid their speeding ticket and left the jail, Price followed them in his police car, stopped them again, ordered them into his car, and took them down a deserted road, where he turned them over to a group of his fellow Ku Klux Klan members. They beat Mickey, Andrew, and James with chains. Then they killed them and buried their bodies in an earthen dam under construction.

For weeks, no one knew what had happened to the three volunteers. Lyndon Johnson used concern over their disappearance to pressure the House to pass the Civil Rights Act of 1964 on July 2. Just before he signed the bill, Johnson addressed the American people on television "to talk to you about what that law means to every American." He said:

One hundred and eighty-eight years ago this week, a small band of valiant men began a long struggle for freedom. They pledged their lives, their fortunes, and their sacred honor not only to founding a nation, but to forge an ideal of freedom—not only for political independence, but for personal liberty; not only to eliminate foreign rule, but to establish the rule of justice in the affairs of men. . . . That was a triumph, but those who founded our country knew that freedom would be secure only if each generation fought to renew and enlarge its meaning. . . . Americans of every race and color have died in battle to protect our freedom. Americans of every race and color have worked to build a nation of widening opportunities. Now our generation of Americans has been called on to continue the unending search for justice within our own borders.

Johnson was proud that his bill had the bipartisan support of more than two-thirds of the lawmakers in Congress, along with "the great majority of the American people." He said:

The purpose of the law is simple. It does not restrict the freedom of any American, so long as he respects the rights of others. It does not give special treatment to any citizen. . . . It does say that . . . those who are equal before God shall now also be equal in the polling booths, in the classrooms, in the factories, and in hotels, restaurants, movie theaters, and other places that provide service to the public. . . . Its purpose is not to punish. Its purpose is not to divide, but to end divisions—divisions which have lasted all too long. Its purpose is national, not regional. Its purpose is to promote a more abiding commitment to freedom, a more constant pursuit of justice, and a deeper respect for human dignity. . . . We will achieve these goals because most Americans are law-abiding citizens who want to do what is right. My fellow citizens, we have come now to a time of testing. We must not fail.

On July 16, two weeks after Johnson signed the Civil Rights Act and a little more than three weeks after James Chaney, Andrew Goodman, and Mickey Schwerner disappeared, Senator Barry Goldwater accepted the Republican nomination for president at the Cow Palace in Daly City, California. Goldwater told Republican delegates that "extremism in the defense of liberty is no vice. And . . . moderation in the pursuit of justice is no virtue."

Meanwhile, Alabama's segregationist governor, George Wallace, running in Democratic primaries against incumbent Lyndon Johnson, won 34 percent of the vote in Wisconsin and 30 percent in Indiana. A significant share of those votes came from working-class Democrats. In the presidential election that fall, voters backed Johnson's vision of America and rejected Goldwater by a landslide, the loser prevailing only in his own state of Arizona and five states of the Deep South—Mississippi, Alabama, Louisiana, Georgia, and South Carolina.

Mickey's body and those of Chaney and Goodman were found on August 4. Their murders were illustrations of extremism in the defense of what white supremacists defined as liberty. The state of Mississippi refused to bring murder charges against any of the killers, but eventually Price and Neshoba County sheriff Lawrence Rainey, also a Klan member, and sixteen others, including Samuel Bowers, the Imperial Wizard of Mississippi's White Knights of the Ku Klux Klan, were arraigned for the federal crime of conspiracy to violate the civil rights of the murdered young men. An all-white jury found seven of them guilty, including Price and Bowers. After several unsuccessful appeals, each received a sentence of between three and ten years. None would spend more than six years behind bars.

When the news reached me that Mickey had been beaten and murdered by white supremacists, by adult bullies who would stop at nothing to prevent Black people from exercising their right to vote, something snapped inside me. It was as if I had gotten a new pair of eyes and began to see everything differently. Before then, I understood bullying as a few kids picking on me for being short, making me feel bad about myself. After I learned what happened to Mickey, I began to see bullying on a larger scale, all around me: Black people bullied by whites; workers bullied by employers; girls and women bullied by men; the disabled or gay or poor or sick or immigrant bullied by politicians, insurance companies, landlords, and bigots. I saw the powerful and the powerless, the exploiters and the exploited.

It seemed as if the world had changed, when in fact it was me who had changed. I had a different understanding of the meaning of injustice. It became as personal to me as were the bullies who called me names and threatened me in the boys' room and on the playground—but larger, more encompassing, more urgent.

After the murders, Freedom Summer continued. Civil rights activists were stirred to greater action rather than intimidated. Almost a thousand volunteers bolstered SNCC's voter registration drives, Freedom Schools, and literacy and civics classes.

That fall, some University of California, Berkeley, students who had participated in Freedom Summer tried to set up tables to recruit students to register Black voters the next summer and raise money for SNCC. But the university had banned all political activity and fundraising on campus—a legacy of Joe McCarthy's communist witch hunt, which by then had morphed into HUAC's ongoing search for communists. Four years before, the committee's hearing at the Civic Center in San Francisco had been stormed by Berkeley students and other protesters. After police attacked them with fire hoses, sixty-four were arrested, twelve hospitalized.

In the fall of 1964, Berkeley's university police arrested a student who was staffing the table in the middle of Sproul Plaza and put him in a police car. Someone in the surrounding crowd of students yelled, "We can see better if we sit down," and hundreds of students sat, trapping the police car for the next thirty-three hours. Berkeley administrators negotiated an end to the siege but refused to end the ban on political activity.

The student protests grew. At an even larger rally, a graduate student named Mario Savio, who had been in Mississippi for Freedom Summer, addressed the crowd. He soon emerged as the leader of what came to be known across America as the Free Speech Movement. His words criticized not only Berkeley but America itself.

There is a time when the operation of the machine becomes so odious, makes you so sick at heart, that you can't take part, you can't even tacitly take part, and you've got to put your bodies upon the gears and upon the wheels, upon the levers, upon all the apparatus, and you've got to make it stop. And you've got to indicate to the people who run it, to the people who own it, that unless you're free, the machine will be prevented from working at all.

Hundreds of Berkeley students occupied its administration building, leading police to make the largest mass arrest of students in American history and shocking a public accustomed to campus conformity. As Savio later told *The Washington Post,* the Free Speech Movement was an outgrowth of the civil rights movement. "Are we on the side of the civil rights movement? Or have we gotten back to the comfort and security of Berkeley, California, and can we forget the [Black] sharecroppers whom we worked with [to register to vote] just a few weeks back? Well, we couldn't forget."

A few days after Savio's speech, FBI director J. Edgar Hoover told aides that he feared that Savio and other protesters would inspire student rebellion "at other colleges across the land. We need to and will give continuous attention to this matter." Hoover turned his secret surveillance machine on Savio, including covert action to "disrupt" and "neutralize" him, for more than a decade. In 1976, a U.S. Senate subcommittee exposed these activities and forced the Bureau to restrict those it investigated and what measures it could take. The guidelines remained in effect until September 11, 2001, after which time George W. Bush's attorney general, John Ashcroft, loosened them to "fight terrorism," and the Patriot Act gave the FBI more power to pry.

The Free Speech Movement and Hoover's secret surveillance were not the only consequences of the Berkeley demonstrations that fall. A Hollywood actor named Ronald Reagan successfully campaigned for governor of California by connecting the student protesters at Berkeley to the need for "law and order."

The following summer, 1965, I volunteered to be a counselor at Dartmouth for Project ABC—"A Better Chance"—which selected mostly poor Black and Latino teenagers from disadvantaged communities for an intensive two months of summer "enrichment" education, the kind kids from advantaged families routinely got to boost their chances of getting into prestigious colleges. We spent seven days a week together.

The kids were smart and tough. They also loomed over me, taller and heavier than I was. The one time I had to break up a knife fight, the participants could easily have resisted my intervention. But they were also generous and kind.

Years later, when I was about to give a speech at a conference of state officials, a man approached me with a wide grin. "Remember me?" he asked. I searched my memory and came up empty.

"I'm Frank!" he said.

Still blank.

"Francisco! Francisco Borges!" he said with a laugh.

"Francisco!" I finally remembered the tall, thin, awkward teenager from New Haven whom I'd tutored that summer. We embraced. "What are you doing here?" I asked.

His laugh turned into a sly grin. "I was elected treasurer of Connecticut," he said modestly.

My eyes welled up.

In 1965, with the leadership of Martin Luther King, Jr., and others in the civil rights movement, Congress passed the Voting Rights Act, protecting the right of Black people to vote. After that, the stranglehold of the white supremacists on the one-party South began to loosen. At the center of the law's success was Section 5, commonly referred to as the "coverage formula," which determined which states had to receive clearance from the Justice Department before changing their election rules, based on their histories of race-based voter discrimination. In the twenty years following the law's passage, the disparity in registration rates between whites and Blacks dropped from nearly 30 percent in the early 1960s to 8 percent. Based on its continuing success, the Voting Rights Act was repeatedly reauthorized by Congress. But the forces of racism and violence did not disappear.

On August 3, 1980, Reagan launched his presidential campaign with a rally at the Neshoba County Fair, only a few miles from where Cecil Ray Price had stopped Schwerner, Chaney, and Goodman on that fateful night sixteen years earlier. In defending "states' rights" that day, Reagan, the cheerful "morning in America" candidate, was sending a dark dog-whistle to racist bullies, telling them he was on their side.

Twenty-three years later, on June 25, 2013, the Supreme Court struck down the coverage formula in the Voting Rights Act, in *Shelby County v. Holder*. The Court's five conservatives decided that the formula was out of date, despite Congress's repeated reauthorizations, effectively ending preclearance. The court's opinion was written by Chief Justice John Roberts and joined by Antonin Scalia, Anthony Kennedy, Samuel Alito, and Clarence Thomas. Reagan had put Scalia and Kennedy on the court.

The decision opened the floodgates to state laws restricting voting throughout the United States. Within twenty-four hours of the ruling, Texas announced that it would implement a strict photo ID law. Mississippi and Alabama began to enforce the same photo ID laws that federal preclearance had previously barred. Other states began to purge voters from their rolls, curtail early voting, eliminate same-day registration, and prevent county boards of elections from opening polls for an additional hour.

In 2021 and 2022, in response to record voter turnout in the 2020 election, nineteen states passed more than thirty laws making it harder to vote. The United States Senate, although nominally under Democratic control, did not have the votes needed to overcome a Republican filibuster and restore Section 5.

Stopping Bullies

I began to view the central struggle of civilization as fighting bullies—standing up against brutality. Absent laws and norms, we'd be in a continuous war in which only the fittest survive, where lives are "nasty, brutish, and short," in the words of English philosopher Thomas Hobbes. Unless we prevented the stronger from attacking or exploiting the weaker, none of us would be safe. Even the most powerful would live in fear of being attacked or deposed.

I saw civilization as the opposite of this Darwinian competition to survive. A civil society doesn't allow the strong to brutalize the weak. A decent society is one that has moved as far as possible from a brutal state of nature. Of course, certain inequalities of power are expected, even in a civil society. Some people are bigger and stronger than others. Some are quicker of mind and body. Some have more forceful personalities. Some have fewer scruples. Some inequalities of income and wealth may be necessary to encourage hard work and inventiveness, from which everyone benefits. But when inequalities become too wide, they invite abuses. Without laws and norms that protect the weaker, the stronger will abuse their positions of power. Such abuses invite further abuses, until society degenerates into a Hobbesian survival of the most powerful.

I came to understand that every time the stronger bully the weaker, the social fabric is tested. If bullying is not contained, the fabric unwinds. The stronger may be white supremacists who make it harder for Black and Latino people to vote; giant corporations that drive small mom-and-pops out of business; people with great wealth who use their money to lobby for tax cuts and government subsidies that impose costs on the rest of us; powerful men who harass and debase women; members of a dominant religion who scapegoat religious minorities; native-born people who demean immigrants; or politicians who use hatefulness and bigotry to build their political base. Unless the bullies are stopped, an entire society—even the world—can descend into chaos.

Some posit a moral equivalence between those who seek social justice and those who want to protect individual liberties, between so-called left and right. But I have come to believe that there is no moral equivalence between bullies and the bullied, between tyranny and democracy, between brutality and decency. No individual can be free in a society devoid of justice. There can be no liberty where brutality reigns. The struggle for social justice is the most basic struggle of all because it defines how far a civilization has developed.

We inhabit a society and a world growing more unequal, in which political and economic power are becoming ever more concentrated. Trump and the multi-billionaire entrepreneur Elon Musk epitomize this trend in America. To claim that "both sides"—the more powerful who seek individual liberty and the weaker who seek social justice—have equal moral claims is to avert one's eyes from this reality. Lobbyists for large corporations, publicists for the wealthy, lawmakers for the privileged, pundits for the powerful, celebrity peddlers of racism and xenophobia—none of them deserve equal space in the public square with those fighting against abuses of power. The powerful *already* have the largest megaphones and the deepest pockets. They grow even more powerful when they're allowed to own Internet platforms, television and radio stations, newspapers, and satellites—as do the three richest people in America (as I write this). Centralized power over how the truth is communicated endangers self-government and must not be carelessly allocated to the highest bidders.

We must also be vigilant against those who use their wealth and power to deceive us with big lies. To allow the worst demagogues free rein is to open wide the gates to tyranny.

Our duty, as I've come to understand it, is to stop brutality. Our responsibility is to hold the powerful accountable. Our challenge is to stand up to abuses of power. Our moral obligation is to protect the vulnerable.

As I write this, it seems to me imperative that voting rights be restored, that Vladimir Putin's aggression be stopped, that Donald Trump eventually be held accountable for seeking to overturn the results of the 2020 election. Pundits who fuel racism and xenophobia must be denounced. Social media platforms that amplify hate must be boycotted. Police who kill innocent Black people must be brought to justice. Powerful men who sexually harass or abuse women must be prosecuted. CEOs who treat their employees badly must be exposed and censured. Billionaires who bribe lawmakers with campaign donations to cut their taxes or exempt them from regulations must be penalized, and lawmakers who accept such bribes must be sanctioned.

There will always be bullies. But in a civil society those bullies can be constrained with powerful social norms, ideals, and laws. At least, that's been my faith. I would not survive a minute in a society based on brute force.

Why I'm So Short

Starting when I was around six years old, my mother and grandmother Minnie told me not to worry that I was at least a head shorter than other kids my age because I'd "shoot up" when I got to be thirteen or fourteen years old. I pictured a magic beanstalk; one morning, I'd wake up and be six-foot-ten. But by the time I was fifteen, I remained an inch under five feet, and never got any taller.

Soon after John F. Kennedy's inauguration in 1961, when the whole country seemed to be bubbling with optimism, my optimistic mother took me to see a doctor in New York who specialized in bone growth. He took a bunch of measurements, asked questions about the heights of my grandparents and great-grandparents (they were all normal), made some X-rays, drew some blood samples, and three weeks later phoned to say he had no idea why I was so short.

Reluctantly, I gave up waiting to shoot up. By that time, I wasn't particularly worried about being bullied or ridiculed. But being a very short young man was not especially helpful when it came to dating. A few years later, the college I chose, Dartmouth, which was then all-male, seemed composed almost entirely of big young men able to swoop the inhabitants of women's colleges literally off their feet. When I swooped in, they seemed to flee.

That's where things stood, as it were, until some twenty years later, when my then wife (about five inches taller than me) and I contemplated having children. Medical science had advanced considerably over the two decades, because there *was* an answer to why I was so short.

I had inherited a mutation called Fairbank's disease, or multiple epiphyseal dysplasia, a rare genetic disorder that slows bone growth. (The actor Danny DeVito also has this condition.) Normal bones grow when cartilage is deposited at their ends. The cartilage then hardens to become additional bone. But my cartilage didn't work that way.

Not only were my bones short, but the experts predicted I'd also have pain in my joints. I'd often tire, they said, and have problems with my spine. I'd have arthritis all over and I'd waddle when I walked. Other things would go wrong as well. Their predictions were fairly accurate. I have had problems with my hips, and in my late thirties had to replace both. I had a bout of grand mal seizures in my late thirties, which neurologists couldn't explain. There's no need to bore you with my aches and pains. But the geneticist I consulted explained that the odds of passing this mutation to my children were very small. Even if they had it, the odds that it would slow their bone growth or cause any other irregularities, or be passed on to their own children, were minuscule.

We decided to have kids. And our sons turned out perfectly normal. But what's "normal" anyway? And why is normal so important? Apart from being bullied when I was a kid, I've had a wonderful life. I have a loving family. I've had good friends, work that I consider satisfying and important, reasonably good health except for the above-mentioned problems. So what if I'm very short?

From time to time, worried parents of abnormally short children phone or email me seeking reassurance. I tell them what I've told you just now. I also tell them that if they or their children are desperate, they can resort to limb-lengthening surgeries; growth hormone treatments—Humatrope—with unknown and potentially dangerous side effects; or a wide variety of homeopathic and crank remedies. But I gently urge them not to do any of these things. I tell them to love their short kids, to inundate them with affection, and they'll be okay.

I'm not sure why so many parents seem to be worried about their child's height these days. Dr. Adda Grimberg, a pediatric endocrinologist at Children's Hospital of Philadelphia, told Jane Brody of *The New York Times* that "twenty years ago, families were focused on health. They came in with a child who was not growing right and wanted to know if there was an underlying disease. Now, more and more, they're focused on height. They want growth hormone, looking for a specific height. But this is not like Amazon; you can't just place an order and make a child the height you want."

David Sandberg, a psychologist at the University of Michigan, studied hundreds of children in the Buffalo area and found no real problem with being short and little benefit to being tall. In fact, height didn't affect the number of friends those kids had, or how well they were liked by others, what others thought of them, or even their own perception of their reputation. Yet when psychologists Leslie Martel and Henry Biller asked several hundred university students to rate the qualities of men of varying heights on seventeen criteria, short men were assumed to be less mature, less positive, less secure, less masculine, less successful, less capable, less confident, less outgoing, more inhibited, more timid, and more passive. In another study, only two of seventy-nine women said they'd go on a date with a man shorter than themselves (the rest, on average, wanted to date a man at least 1.7 inches taller).

Heightism has even infected our language. Respected people have "stature" and are "looked up to." People are more likely to make disparaging cracks about short people because nobody gets pulled up short for doing it—except for Randy Newman, who went too far with his song "Short People (Got No Reason to Live)," which he has apparently regretted ever since.

When it comes to choosing leaders, our society is exceptionally heightist and seems to be getting more so. My dear friend and mentor, the late economist John Kenneth Galbraith, was six foot eight. He once said that favoring the tall was "one of the most blatant and forgiven prejudices in our society." (When we walked around together, chatting away, people stared at us as if we were a carnival act. We laughed it off.)

When I ran for the Democratic nomination for governor of Massachusetts in 2002, it seemed that the only attribute reporters wanted to cover was my height. Regardless of what I said in my speeches, the *Boston Globe* ran photos of me standing on boxes so I could see over the podium. The right-wing *Boston Herald* ran a headline on its front page charging "Short People Are Furious with Reich" because I had joked about my height on the campaign trail. None of it helped me with that election. But I didn't lose because of my height. I lost because I was a lousy campaigner.

Research shows that voters *do* prefer taller candidates. A paper published in 2013 by psychologists at the University of Groningen in the Netherlands analyzed the results of American presidential elections dating back to 1789. They found that taller candidates received more votes than shorter ones in roughly two-thirds of those elections. And the taller the candidates were relative to their opponents, the greater the average margin of their victory. Among presidents who have sought a second term, winners have been two inches taller, on average, than losers. The authors conclude that height may explain as much as 15 percent of the variation in election outcomes. Presidents are becoming taller relative to average Americans (as measured by Army records of recruits of the same age cohort). The last president shorter than this average was William McKinley, elected in 1896.

A survey of the heights of CEOs of Fortune 500 companies showed they were on average six feet tall, about 2.5 inches taller than the average American man.

Why are we so heightist? Probably because of some genetic trigger in our brain that told early humans they needed the protection of very big men. Other things being equal, large males are more to be feared and they live longer. An impulse to defer to them, or prefer them as mates, makes evolutionary sense in a survival-of-the-fittest world. In *Size Matters,* Stephen S. Hall writes that in the eighteenth century, Frederick William of Prussia paid huge sums to recruit giant soldiers from around the world, thereby giving tangible value to matters of inches, and revealing "the desirability of height for the first time in a large, post-medieval society." Maybe parents these days are more desperate for their children to be tall because, in an era of record-breaking inequality, they believe greater height will give their kid a leg up. But hey, I'm okay with being protected by giant soldiers, big security guards, and massive first responders. I don't want to do these sorts of jobs anyway. I'm fortunate to have grown up (or at least grown upward) in a society that values brains at least as much as brawn.

PART II

Coming Up

The Old Left, the New Left, and the Left Out

By the time I was a teenager in the early 1960s, the labor union movement, the heart of the Old Left of the 1930s and 1940s, was considered ancient history. Although my mother's stepfather (who died before I was born) had been a union lawyer and my mother's mother, my grandma Frances, was an activist firebrand, no one in my family spoke of the labor movement as a contemporary phenomenon.

The Old Left had faded because of Joe McCarthy's red scare, labor leaders' concerns about being seen as "soft" on communism, and the effects of the Taft-Hartley Act of 1947, which limited the power of labor unions. It also faded because of soaring prosperity and the extraordinary growth of the American middle class in the post-war years. The Old Left had focused on material concerns such as employment, wages, pensions, and job security, seeking to give the working class a larger slice of the economic pie. Now, all that seemed irrelevant. The working class—at least the white working class—was doing wonderfully well.

The *New* Left that I discovered in the 1960s focused on the needs of a burgeoning middle class that took material comfort for granted. It centered on college students and people who had graduated from college, and sought to protect consumers from unsafe products, limit pollution, win new rights for women and people of color, reduce dire poverty, and spread participatory democracy.

My introduction to the New Left was the Port Huron Statement, issued in June 1962 by a group of mostly white, middle-class college students from the University of Michigan. It was written largely by a twenty-one-year-old activist there named Tom Hayden, a recent graduate of the university who had been editor of the *Michigan Daily*. A friend lent me a copy, and I read it in the summer of 1963. From its very first line, I was transfixed. "We are people of this generation," it read, "bred in at least modest comfort, housed now in universities, looking uncomfortably to the world we inherit."

It seemed to be talking directly to me. I wasn't yet in college but was planning to attend one that fall. And although reared in modest comfort, I felt increasingly uncomfortable with the direction America was taking. Segregationists and white supremacists seemed on the rise in reaction to the civil rights movement and Martin Luther King, Jr., who was about to lead a March on Washington for social and economic justice. The previous fall's Cuban missile crisis had brought the world perilously close to a nuclear holocaust. The war in Vietnam was already becoming a quagmire. Rachel Carson's book *Silent Spring* warned that pesticides and other toxins put into the environment were having devastating effects. My mother saw herself in Betty Friedan's book *The Feminine Mystique,* which described suburban housewives trapped in "dependent, passive, childlike" roles.

The Port Huron Statement claimed America's arms race heightened the risk of nuclear war. It challenged the nation's faith in technology, affluence, and materialism, which encouraged consumerism and conformity. "The goal of man and society should be human independence: a concern not with . . . popularity but with finding a meaning in life that is personally authentic . . . This kind of independence does not mean egotistic individualism—the object is not to have one's way so much as it is to have a way that is one's own." It took on university education, asserting:

> Our experience in the universities [has not] brought us moral enlightenment. Our professors and administrators sacrifice controversy to public relations; their curriculums change more slowly than the living events of the world; their skills and silence are purchased by investors in the arms race; passion is called unscholastic. . . . The questions we might want raised— what is really important? can we live in a different and better way? if we wanted to change society, how would we do it?—are not thought to be questions of a "fruitful, empirical nature," and thus are brushed aside.

In response to these failings, the statement called for participatory democracy—across college campuses, in the South, and in inner cities. Seeing the effectiveness of the young civil rights protesters in SNCC, the authors believed that ordinary citizens, particularly students, could create change through nonviolent means.

It was the most ambitious manifesto I had come across (apart from Karl Marx and Friedrich Engels's communist one), proposing nothing less than an "agenda for a generation." At just over 25,000 words, it was also the longest and the most eloquent, combining existential longings inspired by Albert Camus, a quote from an encyclical by Pope John XXIII, urgent descriptions of the most serious issues facing humankind (then known as "mankind"), and far-reaching, detailed proposals for how to go about the task of democratizing the nation and the world.

In many ways, it became *my* manifesto.

Once in college, I came to see university students and intellectuals as the vanguard of progressive change in America and the world. And I assumed that college students such as those who drafted the Port Huron Statement and founded SNCC would lead the charge. I saw in Mickey Schwerner, Andrew Goodman, and James Chaney martyrs who inspired the civil rights movement. I thought students like Mario Savio and Berkeley's Free Speech Movement would lead the way to a new form of democratized education. I started an alternative university at Dartmouth called the "Dartmouth Experimental College" in which anyone—students, townies, spouses of faculty members—could teach anything they were enthusiastic about. I believed that the students I eventually would recruit for Eugene McCarthy's presidential campaign in 1968 would end the Vietnam War.

In hindsight, this was a mistake. I overlooked the non-college working class. I didn't recognize how tiny my cohort of college students was. By the mid-1960s, fewer than 10 percent of Americans had graduated from a four-year university. Even now, more than a half century later, fewer than 40 percent of adult Americans have a four-year college degree.

The New Left had relegated the depredations and indignities of *class*—and the need for strong labor unions to lift workers' wages, protect jobs, provide pensions, and give workers more job security—to the backwater of activism. By the late 1960s, it felt as if all Americans, apart from the very poor and the very rich, were on the way to enjoying middle-class life. To me, the central problem wasn't inequality but drab conformity, crass materialism, and the hypocrisy of American ideals—as illustrated in the classic 1967 film *The Graduate,* in which Dustin Hoffman, playing Benjamin Braddock, a newly minted college graduate, is told that the future is in "plastics" and is seduced by the mother of the girl he loves.

The trail-blazing progressive authors of the late 1950s and 1960s whose books I devoured barely mentioned the working class. As John Kenneth Galbraith wrote in *The Affluent Society,* published in 1958, America had become a society of abundance. *The Feminine Mystique* grew out of a fifteenth anniversary reunion survey at Smith College; its message that women should join the workforce was of little relevance to the working-class women already in it. *Silent Spring* spurred the environmental movement. Ralph Nader's 1965 bestseller, *Unsafe at Any Speed,* gave birth to the consumer movement. Michael Harrington's 1962 eye-opener, *The Other America,* exposed American poverty and inspired Lyndon Johnson's War on Poverty. But the working class and the labor movement were all but forgotten.

Not even President Johnson's Great Society aimed to strengthen and expand the rights of workers. Initially, he intended to repeal the part of the Taft-Hartley Act that allowed so-called open shops, but he backed off when corporate lobbyists attacked. America had a civil rights movement, a women's rights movement, a gay rights movement, a consumer movement, an environmental movement, a poor people's campaign, and an anti–Vietnam War movement, but no movement to lift the living standards of the working class.

That neglect became a giant political void that lasted for decades and would eventually be filled by Donald Trump's angry, bigoted cultural populism. Bernie Sanders sought to become the Democratic presidential candidate in 2016 and 2020 on a platform based on *economic* populism—focusing on America's soaring inequalities of income, wealth, and political power. But the Democratic Party never embraced Sanders or his platform. As early as 1993, when I became secretary of labor, the Democratic Party focused instead on what were called "suburban swing" voters, mostly college-educated professionals who tended to be liberal on social issues and more conservative on economic ones. Labor unions were still part of the party but of diminishing importance; the percentage of unionized workers in the private sector had fallen precipitously from over a third in the 1950s to around 10 percent in the 1990s. Most union presidents were more interested in protecting the jobs of existing members than expanding their membership.

Democratic presidents took organized labor for granted if they thought about unions at all. When Jimmy Carter as president had to choose between spending his political capital on a bill to strengthen labor unions or a treaty to hand over control of the Panama Canal to Panama, he chose the treaty and the labor bill died. Bill Clinton didn't push for labor law reform in his first two years as president when Democrats held a majority in both houses of Congress, nor did Barack Obama in his first two years, when Democrats also had a congressional majority. In 2021 and 2022, when Democrats again narrowly controlled Congress, President Joe Biden did not fight to make it easier for workers to form unions, although, to his credit, he did appoint a pro-union National Labor Relations Board and he walked a union picket line.

In the twenty-first century, millions of American workers—most of them with no college education and no union to support them—lacked a political home. Without the alternative of economic populism, Americans were more susceptible to right-wing cultural populism. Eventually, this political void was filled by someone only pretending to be on their side: Donald Trump.

The Absurdity of Ayn Rand

As a teenager, I also read the novel *Atlas Shrugged,* by Ayn Rand. One of my uncles had left the voluminous paperback on a shelf in my grandma Frances's cabin. I knew it was controversial—I had heard him arguing about it with my mother—and was intrigued.

Published in 1957, the novel centers on Dagny Taggart, operating vice president of a railroad that's struggling to stay in business during an economic downturn; her brother, Jim, the railroad's president; Hank Rearden, a self-made steel magnate; and an engineer named John Galt, who hacks into a national radio broadcast to give a three-hour speech about freedom. I had no idea at the time that I was reading a political tract extolling laissez-faire capitalism—a tract that a generation of economic bullies would use to justify their bullying. Galt's long speech encapsulated Rand's philosophy: that the only moral purpose of life is the pursuit of one's own happiness and that the only system consistent with this central goal respects individuals' rights to do whatever they wish to increase their own happiness.

Rand was a Russian émigré to the United States whose father's business had been confiscated during the Russian Revolution. Her most influential writing occurred in the 1940s and 1950s in the shadow of European fascism and Soviet communism. In addition to *Atlas Shrugged,* it included a 1943 opus, *The Fountainhead,* along with other writings and interviews in which Rand expounded her views about what she called the "virtue of selfishness."

Rand saw government actions that require people to give their money and resources to other people under the pretext of a "common good" as steps toward tyranny. It was far better, in her view, to base society on autonomous, self-seeking, and self-absorbed individuals. She believed the only community that any of us has in common are family and friends, maintained voluntarily. If we want to be generous, she thought, that's fine, but no one should coerce us into generosity and nothing beyond our circle of voluntary associations merits our trust. No institutions or organizations should be able to demand commitments from us. All that can be expected or justified from anyone is selfish behavior, she thought. That behavior is expressed most clearly through the acts of selling what we want to sell and buying what we want to buy in a free market. For her, the common good did not exist.

Rand's philosophy was updated and formalized in 1974 by Harvard philosopher Robert Nozick in his bestselling book *Anarchy, State, and Utopia.* Nozick argued that individual rights are the only justifiable foundation for a society. Instead of a common good, he wrote, "there are only individual people, different individual people, with their own individual lives."

When Rand and Nozick propounded these ideas, they seemed quaint if not far-fetched. Anyone who lived through the prior half century had witnessed our interdependence during the Great Depression and World War II. In the 1950s and early 1960s, Americans had pooled our resources to finance all sorts of public goods— schools and universities, a national highway system, and healthcare for the aged and poor (Medicare and Medicaid). We rebuilt war-torn Europe. We sought to guarantee the civil rights and voting rights of African Americans. We opened doors of opportunity to women.

Even as an adolescent, I understood there was a common good that transcended the selfish needs of individuals. After all, the U.S. Constitution was designed for "We the people" seeking to "promote the general welfare," not for *me the selfish jerk seeking as much wealth and power as possible.* Yet Rand saw the common good as "an undefined and undefinable concept," a "moral blank check for those who attempt to embody it." When the common good of a society is regarded as something apart from and superior to the individual desires of its members, she argued, "it means that the good of some men takes precedence over the good of others, with those others consigned to the status of sacrificial animals."

Starting in the late 1970s, Rand became the intellectual godmother of modern-day American conservatism, especially its libertarian strand. Ronald Reagan professed to being a follower of hers. His policies—and those of his contemporary conservative leader, Margaret Thatcher of Great Britain—appeared to draw inspiration from her thoughts and writing. Years later, Donald Trump called Rand his favorite writer and said he identified with Howard Roark, the protagonist of *The Fountainhead,* an architect who dynamites a housing project he designed because the builders did not precisely follow his blueprints. (I doubt Trump ever read Rand, but for the sake of this discussion, let's assume he has.)

Rex Tillerson, secretary of state in the first Trump administration, called Rand's *Atlas Shrugged* his favorite book. Trump's first CIA chief Mike Pompeo cited Rand as a major inspiration. Before Andrew Puzder withdrew his nomination to be Trump's first secretary of labor, he said he devoted much of his free time to reading Rand. Paul Ryan, former Republican speaker of the House of Representatives, required his staff to read her books. Rand fans were also found at some of the high reaches of American business: Uber's co-founder and former CEO, Travis Kalanick, described himself as a Rand follower, even using *The Fountainhead*'s original cover art as his Twitter avatar.

I think Rand, Nozick, and their more modern incarnations are dangerously wrong. Not only does the common good exist, but it is essential for a society to function. Without voluntary adherence to a set of common notions about right and wrong, we would be living in a jungle where only the strongest, cleverest, and most wary could hope to survive. This would not be a civilization because there would be no civility at its core.

Americans sharply disagree about what we want for our country or for the world, but we must agree on basic principles—such as how we deal with our disagreements. Our obligations to a democratic form of government, toward the law, and to the Constitution are essential if we're to participate in the same society. These obligations connect us.

Consider what would happen if no one voluntarily obeyed the law without first calculating what they could gain by violating it, as compared with the odds of the violation being discovered multiplied by the size of the likely penalty. We'd be living in bedlam.

If everyone behaved like Donald Trump, both as a businessman and then as president, much of our time and attention would have to be devoted to outwitting or protecting ourselves from other Trumps. We would have to assume everyone else was out to exploit us if they could. Every interaction would need to be carefully hedged. Penalties would need to rise and police enforcement to increase, to prevent the Trumps among us from calculating they might have more to gain by violating the law and risking the penalty than by abiding by it. And because laws can't possibly predict and prevent every potential wrong, laws would have to become ever more detailed and exacting to prevent the Trumps from circumventing them.

Even then we'd be in trouble. We couldn't rely on legislators to block or close legal loopholes, because Trump lobbyists would bribe legislators to keep them open, and Trump legislators would be open to taking such bribes. (Many Americans understandably view politics this way even now.) If we managed to close the loopholes, we couldn't rely on police to enforce the laws, because Trump supporters would bribe the police not to, and Trump police would accept bribes.

Without a shared sense of responsibility to the common good, we would have to assume that everybody—including legislators, judges, regulators, and police—was acting selfishly, making and enforcing laws for their own benefit.

The followers of Ayn Rand who glorified the "free market" and denigrated "government" fooled themselves if they thought the "free market" got them off this Trumpian hook. As I came to understand, the market is itself a human creation—a set of laws and rules that define what can be owned and traded and how. Government doesn't "intrude" on the "free market"; it *creates* the market. Government officials—legislators, administrators, regulators, judges, and heads of state—must decide on and enforce such laws and rules for a market to exist. Without norms for the common good, officials have no way to make these decisions other than their own selfish interests.

Hopefully, government officials base these sorts of decisions on their notions about the common good. But if Trump and people like him were making and enforcing such rules, the rules would be based on whatever it took for these officials to gain personal wealth and power. The "free market" would be a sham, and most people would lose out in it. (As we will see in the pages to come, something close to this has in fact occurred.)

Truth itself is a common good. Throughout history, one of the first things tyrants have done is to attack independent truth-tellers—philosophers such as Plato, scientists including Galileo, and the free and independent press—thereby confusing the public and substituting their own "facts." Without a shared truth, democratic deliberation is hobbled. As poet and philosopher Václav Havel put it, "If the main pillar of the system is living a lie, then it is not surprising that the fundamental threat to it is living in truth."

Yet in a world populated by people like Trump, we could not trust anyone to be truthful if they could do better for themselves by lying. (Here again, much of the public believes America is already at this point.) We couldn't count on any claim by sellers of any product or service. Internet-based "reputational ratings" would be of little value because Trump raters would be easily bribed. Journalists would shade their reports for their own selfish advantage, taking bribes from advertisers or currying favor with politicians. Teachers would offer lessons to satisfy wealthy or powerful patrons. Historians would alter history if by doing so they gained wealth or power. Scientists would doctor evidence for similar selfish motives. The truth would degenerate into a cacophony of competing factual claims, as, in part, it has.

We couldn't trust doctors or pharmacists to give us the right medications. We couldn't trust bankers and accountants not to fleece us, restaurants not feed us tainted food, lawyers not to hoodwink us. Professional ethics would be meaningless.

The common good is especially imperiled when a president of the United States claims that an election was stolen from him, with no evidence that it was. Such baseless assertions erode trust, fuel conspiracy theories, and can lead to violence.

Most basically, the common good depends on people trusting that most others in society will also adhere to the common good, rather than lie or otherwise take advantage of them. In this way, civic trust is self-enforcing and self-perpetuating, while civic distrust can corrode the very foundations of a society.

Polls tell us that many of today's Americans worry that the nation is losing its national identity. The core of that self-definition has never been *We're better than anyone else* nationalism. Nor has it been the whiteness of our skin or the uniformity of our ethnicity. Our core identity—the most precious legacy we have been given by the generations who came before us—consists of the ideals we share and the obligations we hold in common, especially political equality. If we are losing our national identity, it is not because we are becoming blacker or browner or speak in more languages than we once did. It is because we are losing our sense of the common good.

The genius of a system based on political equality is that it doesn't require us to agree on every issue, but only to agree to be bound by decisions that emerge from the system. Some of us want to prohibit abortions because we believe life begins at conception; others believe people should have the right to determine what happens to their bodies. Some of us want stricter environmental protections, others, more lenient ones. We are free to take any position on these and any other issues, but as political equals, we are bound to accept the outcomes even if we dislike them. This requires enough social trust for us to regard the views and interests of those with whom we disagree as equally worthy of consideration to our own. And it requires that we trust the system to be fair.

Ayn Rand had it completely wrong. Moral choices logically involve duties to others, not just calculations about what's best for our selfish selves. When members of a society ask, What is the right or decent thing to do? they necessarily draw upon an understanding of these mutual obligations. America's culture of self-promotion, iPhones, selfies, and personal branding churns out cynics and narcissists like Trump, to be sure. But our larger loyalties and attachments define who we are.

In the fall of 1964, I headed off to college and learned this lesson repeatedly.

My Unforgivable Hypocrisy

Dartmouth College in Hanover, New Hampshire, in the early 1960s consisted of 3,400 young male undergraduates and no young women. Unlike Columbia, Harvard, and Brown, which were also "all-male" but had managed to create women's colleges under their misogynistic male banners, the closest women's college to Dartmouth was several hours away. To make matters worse, the interstate highway system had not yet paved the way from Dartmouth to Smith, Mount Holyoke, or numerous female two-year "junior colleges." In the winter, which in the Upper Valley of the Connecticut River ran from mid-November to mid-March and reached such low temperatures that one's nostril hairs froze and broke off on the way to morning classes, ice and snow often blocked the roads. In other words, Dartmouth in the early 1960s was a monastery in Siberia.

The College Handbook, distributed the very first day of matriculation, warned that students would unceremoniously be expelled for, among other things, engaging in "lewdness or fornication." It did not spell out in detail what behavior qualified as "lewdness," but there was no question about fornication. It's what almost all 3,400 of us hoped for.

In 1960, the Food and Drug Administration had approved the nearly foolproof contraceptive that came to be known as "the Pill." Now, it was gaining wide circulation among college-aged women. It ushered in what came to be known as the sexual revolution. As the poet Philip Larkin wrote,

Sexual intercourse began
In nineteen sixty-three
(which was rather late for me)—
Between the end of the Chatterley ban
And the Beatles' first LP.

During the first weeks of my freshman year, I decided to run for class president. I had a vague sense I could make the place more livable, more enjoyable, and more, well, grown-up. Dartmouth was a picture-postcard-gorgeous campus, and the professors were superb. But the lack of coeds made dorm life raunchy and adolescent, centered on *Playboy* centerfolds and boasts of sexual exploits. I thought I could improve the quality of dorm life by, say, encouraging student-led seminars. I also sensed that being class president would somehow compensate for my being by far the shortest person in the class. I relished the thought of phoning my father and telling him I had been elected, and knowing how proud it would make him that his half-pint son had been chosen to lead.

I visited every freshman dormitory room and introduced myself to almost all of my eight hundred classmates, most of whom had no idea why anyone in their right mind would barge in on them and ask for their vote. I won handily.

My classmates had only one thing they wanted me to do as class president: invite busloads of young women students to Dartmouth for the weekends. I didn't give up on the student-led dorm seminars, but I also had to respond to my constituents. So on a Friday night several weeks after I was elected, dozens of buses arrived in Hanover containing over four hundred young women invited from every women's college in New England. Dartmouth had never seen anything like it. To avoid having the young women snaked by upper-classmen, I allowed only freshmen through a makeshift fence sur-rounding the paved area where the buses unloaded their passengers and had klieg lights directed at the bus doors from which the young women disembarked. Unfortunately, this had the effect of forcing each young woman to make a rather theatrical entrance onto the campus from her bus, prompting my freshmen constituents to holler numbers from one to ten, reflecting their judgments about her looks. The spectacle made me cringe. It was worse for the young women, many of whom were humiliated. Some even refused to get off the bus. A few convinced the bus drivers to take them home immedi-ately. I felt awful—complicit in the bullying of these young women.

The larger problem was perhaps more predictable—the College Handbook. As class president, I was automatically a member of the student court, which heard complaints from the dean's office about alleged violations of it. The student court interviewed alleged offend-ers and dispensed appropriate punishment. It was an inquisitorial form of justice. By tradition, as the youngest member of the court, I was responsible for asking what was known as "the penetrating ques-tion." As the accused young man sat before us trying to explain how it came to be that the dorm janitor found him in bed with a young woman at seven o'clock in the morning, it was my duty to ask, "Did you penetrate?" If he answered in the affirmative, the student court was obliged to send him packing.

You see my dilemma. As class president, I was procuring hundreds of young women for my classmates, who seemed to have little else on their minds other than fornication. As a member of the student court with the job of asking the penetrating question, I was obliged to vote to expel any young man honest enough to admit to it. The hypocrisy was overwhelming. I did attempt to improve the intellectual life of the college, and spearheaded efforts to make everyone more attentive to civil rights. But what of the civil rights of the young fornicators?

In 1968, I warned the college president, a giant of a man named John Sloan Dickey, who talked so ponderously we called him John Slow Diction, that if he did not put an end to the obnoxious and demeaning in loco parentis rules, he'd have a revolt on his hands—and that is what transpired. The year after I graduated, some under-graduates even lifted Slow Diction out of his chair in his second-floor office in the administration building and deposited him on the sidewalk before taking over the building.

My dilemma came to a head during my sophomore year. I had been reelected class president and by then had figured out how to lure even more young women to Hanover, weekend after weekend, without subjecting them to ritual humiliation. But the Vietnam War was coming into view, and the moral universe was shifting. A case came to the student court from the dean, who had been contacted by the dean of a woman's college. A Dartmouth student had been caught in bed with a student from the woman's college, *but* the nefarious coupling had occurred during spring break when both were vacationing in Mexico. My peers on the court were unsure how to proceed. Did the College Handbook's prohibition of fornication apply when neither perpetrator was on campus? And even if it did, did the long arm of the college's law extend outside the United States?

I said no to both questions, but my judicial brethren decided otherwise, and when the young accused offender—let's call him Tom—appeared before the court, and answered the penetrating question in the affirmative, the court voted to expel him. (A similar fate apparently befell his love interest.) Tom was promptly drafted and sent to Vietnam.

My conscious mind repressed all of this until one day, roughly twenty years later, my then wife and I were sitting at the counter in Lou's Restaurant on Main Street in Hanover and Tom walked in, now twenty years older. Everything came rushing back with frightening clarity. The question of whether he had been killed in Vietnam must have been reverberating in the recesses of my brain because the moment I saw him I felt an overwhelming sense of relief that caused tears to well up.

My wife had no idea what was going on. I asked her to ignore me and hoped that Tom would ignore me as well. I tried to hide behind a menu, but he saw me and strode toward where I was sitting.

"Bob!" he said, putting a large arm around my shoulders. "Good to see you!"

"Tom!" I said. "I'm so delighted to see you, too." And I was, giddy with relief. Tears streamed down my face.

My Date with Hillary

I did find a few young women willing to go out with me but rarely on formal "dates." Instead, I came up with subterfuges for getting together with them that didn't require me to issue a formal invitation and suffer almost certain rejection.

Being reelected president of my class in my sophomore year (credit the busloads of young women) gave me carte blanche to arrange conferences and events on serious topics, like educational reform. While I was sincerely interested, there was an ulterior motive: the conferences attracted sincerely interested young women from other colleges.

In the fall of 1965, I met a sophomore from Wellesley College named Hillary Rodham. She was president of her freshman class and interested in ideas for reforming college education. (Six years later I introduced her to Bill Clinton, but that's a later story.) Hillary had long blond hair and thick glasses, and an infectious laugh. She was whip smart. I was smitten. I invited her to Hanover for a kind of "presidential summit" where we could talk about educational reform. Not a date, you see, but a conference. She accepted.

I recall nothing about that get-together except that we talked about Bob Dylan ditching his acoustic guitar for a Stratocaster at the Newport Folk Festival and we went to the Nugget Theater in Hanover to watch Michelangelo Antonioni's film *Blow-Up*. (I cannot recall how either of these cultural phenomena connected with educational reform.)

Fifty years later, when she ran for president of the United States, a reporter from *The New York Times* phoned me. She had come across some of Hillary's letters from college. In one of them Hillary mentioned our "date." The reporter's voice grew serious. "Is there anything you can remember from your date with her that might shed light on how she would perform as president?"

I didn't know how to respond. This was *The New York Times,* for crying out loud.

I told the reporter we had gone to see *Blow-Up.*

"Anything else?" she asked.

I paused. I couldn't resist. "I probably shouldn't be saying this," I said mischievously.

"What's that?" I could hear the eagerness in her voice.

"She wanted an inordinate amount of butter on her popcorn."

There was a long silence.

"Hello?" I asked, fearing my lame attempt at humor had put her off.

"Still here," the reporter said. "Just writing all this down." And she did; and the *Times* actually reported on my "date" with Hillary and her supposed penchant for butter on her popcorn.

Educational reform remained a live issue. The Free Speech Movement spread rapidly from Berkeley to other college campuses, along with demands for more input from students on what was taught and how universities were administered. Civil rights and the Vietnam War added to student demands to be heard. The tumult was beginning to penetrate even relatively staid and conservative Dartmouth. Students lined up on the college green to protest the Vietnam War. When segregationist Alabama governor George Wallace visited campus in May 1967, students charged the stage where he spoke and surrounded the car he tried to escape in. As class president, I felt torn between egging on my fellow students and making sure their protests didn't turn violent.

"Help me!" the dean of students yelled across the green when students were rolling Wallace's car. The dean was well over six feet tall. He was running around the mob, ineffectually telling them to stop.

"What do you want me to do?" I yelled back.

"You're the president of the class! Tell them to stop!" As if I could possibly influence hundreds of young men determined to block Wallace's departure. I ran to the college radio station, where I told the students who were broadcasting about the tumult that the dean was taking down names, and anyone causing violence would be held accountable. It appeared to work. Wallace got away.

But what could I possibly do about the larger issues roiling college campuses and the country? I was president of my class, but I was nobody. Ever since Michael Schwerner had been murdered, I felt a vague sense of uselessness. Dartmouth was a privileged white male bastion, a beautiful New England college campus that had almost nothing to do with the larger struggles America was then engaged in—to guarantee equal rights to Black people and women, and to get out of Vietnam.

I applied to be a summer intern in Bobby Kennedy's Senate office. He was crusading for economic and political justice, and I wanted to be part of that. I got the job.

Getting Chewed Out by Bobby Kennedy

The job had nothing to do with civil rights or social justice, though, and it required only half a brain. I ran the signature machine in a tiny office next to where Kennedy's secretaries typed out responses to a torrent of mail that streamed into Kennedy's Senate office daily.

My machine mechanically scrawled "Robert F. Kennedy" on thousands of photographs and constituent letters; my responsibility was to ensure the photos and letters were lined up properly so the signature would appear at the right place. Halfway through the summer I was so bored that I started composing mock letters to friends. ("Congratulations, Mr. Dworkin, on possessing the largest nose in the entire Hudson Valley. Yours sincerely, Robert F. Kennedy.")

One day, I was standing in front of an elevator in the Senate office building when it opened to reveal Bobby himself, surrounded by supercharged aides, all of whom were talking to him simultaneously. As Kennedy moved into the corridor, he saw me and took half a step in my direction. "How are ya, Bob? How's the summer going?" he asked and gave me a toothy grin. He was whisked away before I had a chance to respond. No matter. That he *knew my name* was more than enough to keep me going through the rest of the summer.

It doesn't take much to inspire; sometimes a smile and a hello can do it. Alan Simpson, a former Republican senator and dear friend, once told me that remembering someone's name is often the highest compliment you can pay them. I was so inspired by Bobby Kennedy's hello that I got all the young people who were interning that summer for Democratic senators to sign a petition calling for Lyndon Johnson to end the Vietnam War.

A few days later, one of Kennedy's political assistants popped his head into the signature machine room. "The senator would like to see you," he said.

"Really?" I beamed, putting down my stack of unsigned letters and almost running through the rabbit warren of offices to the desk just outside the senator's own office, where his scheduler sat. As I stood there, I told myself he was so impressed with my organizing skills that he wanted to thank me directly, maybe even offer me a permanent job on his staff when I finish college.

"You may go in," his scheduler said.

And there he was, sitting behind his desk. I felt humbled but excited.

"Sit down," he said without looking up. I took the chair next to his desk. "So," he continued, reading pieces of paper as he talked. "You organized that antiwar petition?"

"I did, Senator," I said, proudly.

"Well, here's what I want you to do," he said, finally raising his head and looking at me, expressionless. "Get your name off it, *now*."

"Sorry?" I said, confused and shaken.

"And for the rest of the summer, don't identify yourself publicly as working in my office."

"I, er, of course, Senator, if that's . . . but . . ."

I felt as if I'd been punched in the gut. What had I done?

"Look," he said with a raised voice. "I'm having enough fucking trouble with Johnson as it is. The last thing I need is a goddamn anti-war petition from my summer *intern*."

I didn't know what to say. I was stunned.

"That's it," he said, waving me off and turning back to his work.

I walked out of his office crushed like a pesky insect.

He was right, of course. It had never occurred to me that as one of his interns my actions would reflect on him. I didn't think about his delicate political relationship with Johnson. I assumed without asking that Kennedy was against the Vietnam War, even though he hadn't yet come out publicly against it. That was one of many mistakes I've made.

I took my name off the petition.

Sometimes I wonder where America would be today had Bobby not been murdered the following June. I believe he would have been nominated for president that summer and elected in November 1968, instead of Richard Nixon. Had that happened, I tell myself, we would have gotten out of Vietnam far sooner and tens of thousands of lives would have been saved on both sides. If he had been elected, America would have had a different trajectory. It would be in a far better place now.

But am I fooling myself? And what possible purpose is served by an "if only" dream, anyway?

Getting Clean for Gene

I was in my senior year and the Vietnam War was escalating. Nearly half a million American combat troops were already there and nine thousand Americans had died in the war the year before. Hundreds of thousands of Vietnamese had been killed. It was a catastrophe.

Citing the importance of ending the war, Senator Eugene McCarthy from Minnesota entered the Democratic presidential race against President Johnson. McCarthy was a tall, thin, mild-mannered politician whom some found remote and professorial. He wrote poetry and spoke eloquently about the ideals of America. He claimed that America was suffering from a "deepening moral crisis" and a helplessness that he hoped to alleviate. McCarthy rejected the long-accepted wisdom that stopping communism required resisting it actively everywhere, including in Vietnam, and the supposed necessity of sending half a million troops to fight in jungles half a world away. He especially rejected the practice of propping up unpopular dictators.

McCarthy had encouraged Bobby Kennedy to enter the race, but Kennedy said he didn't want to challenge Johnson and publicly announced he'd support Johnson as the nominee. Kennedy predicted that McCarthy's campaign would have a "healthy influence" on Johnson, whom he assumed would win the nomination.

On January 30, 1968, North Vietnam launched the Tet Offensive, a ferocious attack on the cities of South Vietnam, including the U.S. embassy in Saigon. The assault's perceived success belied Johnson's claim that the Americans and the South Vietnamese were winning the war. After three years of escalation, bombing, and mounting casualties, America seemed further from victory than ever.

I felt I had to do something. Soon after the Tet Offensive, I got a call from a friend who had left college to work on the McCarthy campaign. Students were needed to go door-to-door for the candidate in every state with Democratic primaries or caucuses. My friend suggested I help recruit them.

Within hours I was in my green VW Beetle, heading west. My first stop was Antioch College in Yellow Springs, Ohio, where Sarah, whom I had met at an educational reform workshop at Dartmouth, was a senior. (To protect her privacy, I won't use her real name.) I thought she might lend a hand to the McCarthy campaign. Indeed, within hours she had packed her things and was sitting next to me in my Beetle, heading toward other college campuses. Over the next few months, we visited more than forty universities across Indiana, Pennsylvania, Minnesota, Wisconsin, New Hampshire, and California.

Sarah wasn't much taller than me. She had bright blue eyes and an impish grin. Her voice was low and melodic, her laugh infectious. She could also be deadly serious when talking politics or about the future of the world.

At whatever school we visited, we hauled out an old 35-millimeter projector, set it on a table in whatever room we could find, and looped through its sprockets a ten-minute film of McCarthy talking directly to the camera about the importance of his campaign and why he needed students to join him. After every session, hundreds of students signed up. We collected their names and passed them on to the campaign staff. Like us, most of these students left their campuses and courses behind to join the McCarthy campaign.

Sarah and I also gave short lectures on how to go door-to-door, what to ask for, how to ask, what to wear, and the importance of looking respectable—keeping "clean for Gene." We were part of what the press dubbed "McCarthy's children's crusade."

McCarthy seemed to be gaining ground. We were on a roll. Three precincts in Minnesota supported McCarthy delegates, a blow to Johnson, whose vice president, Hubert Humphrey, was a Minnesotan. Sarah and I felt like revolutionaries in a peaceful revolution that was succeeding beyond anyone's expectations. The number of students showing up at our recruitment sessions grew larger at every stop.

But we didn't think much about the thousands of young men *not* attending college who were being drafted into the war, nor about their families and communities for whom patriotism took precedence over qualms about the war. Nor did we focus our efforts on members of labor unions, Black Americans, or Latinos. Our world was the growing antiwar movement on mostly white college campuses. That was a profound error. The coalition that had propelled the New Deal and had been temporarily revived by John F. Kennedy connected unionized workers, the poor, Catholics, Black and Latino Americans, students, and intellectuals. But the antiwar movement we participated in was mostly white students and intellectuals. Martin Luther King, Jr., was attempting to broaden it.

Sarah and I reached New Hampshire at the beginning of March. Opinion polls prior to that first-in-the-nation primary showed McCarthy's support at only 10 to 20 percent of likely Democratic voters. Johnson's campaign circulated pamphlets saying that "the communists in Vietnam are watching the New Hampshire primary . . . don't vote for fuzzy thinking and surrender." But the polls didn't show the depth of disaffection among independents and others who could vote in the Democratic primary, and the polls missed a late surge in voter interest spurred in part by hundreds of young college volunteers who streamed into the state to campaign for McCarthy—some of them, courtesy of Sarah and me.

On March 12, McCarthy stunned the political establishment by winning 42.2 percent of the vote in the New Hampshire primary. Johnson got 49.4 percent. The result was seen as an upset and a huge blow to the incumbent president. On primary night, McCarthy was jubilant: "People have remarked that this campaign has brought young people back into the system," he said, "but it's the other way around. The young people have brought the country back into the system."

McCarthy's surprise showing in New Hampshire contributed to Johnson's announcing on March 31 that he would not run for reelection.

The New York Times ran a three-tiered headline:

JOHNSON SAYS HE WON'T RUN;
HALTS NORTH VIETNAM RAIDS;
BIDS HANOI JOIN PEACE MOVES.

It is hard to convey to you now, more than a half century later, the sense of triumph we experienced. Johnson would be gone! The dreadful Vietnam War would end! The "children's crusade" had slain the dragon!

And I had fallen for Sarah. She was my first unbridled romance. Like Philip Larkin, it was rather late, but the delight made up for my tardiness.

The victory would have felt clearer to me had Bobby Kennedy not suddenly entered the race on March 16. In announcing his candidacy, Kennedy said, "I do not run for the presidency merely to oppose any man, but to propose new policies. I run because I am convinced that this country is on a perilous course and because I have such strong feelings about what must be done, and I feel that I'm obliged to do all I can." Almost immediately, Kennedy soared to first place in polls of Democratic voters.

What was I to do? I'd worked for Kennedy the preceding summer. I knew many of his key staffers and political advisers. Yet I had been pouring my heart into McCarthy's campaign. I believed in McCarthy, admired his courage and his integrity. I had convinced thousands of students to join his children's crusade. How could I possibly switch to Kennedy? And, of course, there was Sarah. What would she think of me if I abandoned McCarthy? Moreover, Kennedy's decision to run struck me as patently opportunistic. Only months before, he said he wasn't going to. Only after McCarthy demonstrated the public's antipathy to the war and the popularity of an antiwar candidate did Kennedy jump in. I recalled how angry Kennedy had been with me for getting interns on Capitol Hill to sign my little antiwar petition, worried about his relationship with Johnson.

I would stay with McCarthy.

On March 27, Kennedy announced his intention to run against McCarthy in the Indiana primary. It would be the first head-to-head race between them. At Indiana University in Indianapolis, Sarah and I collected names of hundreds of student volunteers for McCarthy. That same afternoon, I ran into Kennedy's chief of staff, Joe Dolan.

"Well, look who's here!" Joe said with a slight grin. "Didn't know you were on the campaign."

"Joe," I said haltingly, "I'm here for McCarthy."

Without a word, Dolan spun around and walked in the opposite direction.

—

On Thursday, April 4, Martin Luther King, Jr., was assassinated by a white ex-convict while standing on a balcony outside his second-floor room at the Lorraine Motel in Memphis, Tennessee. King had come to the city to lead a march by striking sanitation workers, and to criticize the Vietnam War. King's condemnation of racial inequalities had grown to embrace economic inequalities, including those faced by the sanitation workers. King's views about the Vietnam War had likewise grown to include a more radical critique of what he saw as U.S. militarism and imperialism.

As news of King's murder spread, riots broke out in 130 cities, resulting in more than forty deaths nationwide. It felt to me as if America was coming apart. Without skipping a beat, California's then governor, Ronald Reagan, called King's assassination part of the "great tragedy that began when we began compromising with law and order, and people started choosing which laws they'd break."

Stokely Carmichael, who headed SNCC, told a crowd in Washington, D.C., that "white America killed Dr. King" and had "declared war on black America," and that they should "go home and get your guns."

McCarthy tried to calm the crowds, but he had a hard time connecting with Black Americans. Kennedy, speaking from the back of a flatbed truck in Indianapolis, delivered the news of King's assassination to people in a Black neighborhood, without a script. "What we need in the United States is not division, not hatred, not violence and lawlessness," he said, "but love and wisdom and compassion toward one another, and a feeling of justice toward those who still suffer within our country, whether they be white or they be black." I was moved by Kennedy's eloquence. I was impressed by the way he connected both with Black people and working-class whites.

Kennedy won the Indiana primary with 42 percent of the vote. A native son came in second. McCarthy was third, with 27 percent. But among white-collar professionals and college-educated voters, Kennedy finished last and McCarthy first. McCarthy's constituents—including those who embraced the New Left and the Port Huron Statement, who were against the Vietnam War, who were suspicious

of any politician who promoted "law and order" (as Kennedy did)—
were a minority of Americans.

Sarah's and my attention shifted to the upcoming primary in California. We assumed it would be decisive. Kennedy said he'd exit the
race if he lost. We drove up and down the huge state, recruiting hundreds of students for McCarthy at every stop. McCarthy visited many
of the same California colleges and universities. He was treated as
a hero for being the first presidential candidate to oppose the war.
Meanwhile, Kennedy campaigned in the ghettos and barrios of the
state's larger cities, and connected with Cesar Chavez and Dolores
Huerta, who were organizing farmworkers.

On the night of June 4, just after winning the California primary,
Kennedy was shot while leaving the ballroom of the Ambassador
Hotel in Los Angeles, where his supporters had gathered to cheer
his victory. McCarthy immediately canceled his campaign plans and
was placed under heavy guard in his hotel. Kennedy died the next
day. McCarthy was grief-stricken and considered dropping out of
the race. I was devastated. All my ambivalence about Kennedy disappeared. I thought about his powerful words, his commitment to
social justice. I even questioned why I had campaigned for McCarthy.

The assassinations of Kennedy and Martin Luther King, Jr.,
seemed to transform America from hope to despair. Both men had
appealed to the best in us, to the ideals we held in common, and told
us we could achieve those ideals. Both had inspired millions—Black
people and white, poor, working class and middle class, students and
non-students—to strive for those ideals. Both had moved us with
their eloquence, their courage and commitment. Now that both were
gone, the nation felt barren, the ideals hollow.

Hope needs leaders to provide a moral compass. Those leaders
don't need to be vested with official authority—King held no national
office, but he spoke as the conscience of the nation; Kennedy was but
one of a hundred senators, but he carried the ideals and hopes first
kindled by John F. Kennedy. Millions of Americans wanted to believe
that these men would lead us to a moral high ground, a common
good that would transcend the crass, selfish brutality of America.
That belief had its own moral momentum, captivating so many of
us. And now that both had been gunned down, there didn't seem to

be anywhere else for that momentum to go. We were thrown into a moral abyss.

I wanted nothing more to do with American politics. Sarah couldn't stop crying. She was overcome by darkness. She wanted to go back to Ohio. We packed up my Beetle, I dropped her off in Antioch, and barely made it back to Dartmouth in time to graduate.

For some, the moral void was filled by violence. When the Democratic National Convention opened in Chicago, delegates were greeted with demonstrations against the war. During the following days, young people who had been lured into politics by the idealism of McCarthy's antiwar campaign or Robert Kennedy's calls for social justice were beaten by the Chicago police.

The delegates chose as their presidential nominee vice president Hubert Humphrey, whose name hadn't appeared on any primary ballot. His campaign had concentrated on winning delegates from non-primary states where party leaders controlled the votes. Humphrey was reluctant to come out against the war, waiting until the final weeks of the presidential campaign to break with Johnson over Vietnam. My friends and I had numerous debates about whether we could support Humphrey. But if we didn't, wouldn't that help the right-winger, Richard Nixon? It would not be the last time that the idealists of my generation, and of generations to come, had to choose between the lesser of two perceived evils.

After ending his campaign, McCarthy said he had "set out to prove . . . that the people of this country could be educated and make a decent judgment . . . but evidently this is something the politicians were afraid to face up to."

Humphrey's loss to Nixon represented the end of the Democrats' New Deal coalition, and it seemed to be the end of idealism. I was disgusted by American politics and told myself I was through with it. This was also the end of my romance with Sarah. It broke my young heart.

When Bill Clinton and I
Didn't Inhale Together

I met Bill Clinton a few months later on the SS *United States,* sailing from New York City to Southampton, England. We were twenty-two years old. He and I, along with thirty other young American men, had won Rhodes Scholarships to study at Oxford. (Women were not allowed to compete then.) We were heading to England by ship because that had been the tradition for newly selected Scholars. Five days at sea were supposed to give us time to get to know one another, but on this voyage the crossing was so stormy that most of us spent a good part of the time alone in our cabins, seasick. I was one of them. By our second day at sea, I disappeared below deck.

I didn't mind being alone in my cabin. Despite the rough seas, the journey felt restorative—an escape from a nation that seemed to be losing its mind and moral purpose.

That evening, there was a loud knock on my cabin door. I staggered over to open it. In front of me was a tall, curly-haired fellow with a big grin, holding a bowl of chicken soup.

"Hi, my name is Bill," he said in a syrupy Southern accent as the ship rolled and the soup sloshed. "I hear you weren't feeling well. Thought this might help."

He handed me the bowl. (He didn't say "I feel your pain." That came years later in his presidential campaign.)

"Well, that's awfully kind of you," I said, taking the bowl in both my hands while trying to steady myself and not barf on him.

"I'm Bob," I stammered. "I'd invite you in, Bill, but . . ."

"Oh, that's okay. We'll have time later. . . . I'm from Arkansas."

"Well, that's really great. I'm from a little town in New York State."

"It's amazing, isn't it?" He grinned. The soup was sloshing over the sides of the bowl, and I desperately needed to use the john.

"Er, what's amazing?"

"Small-town boys. Did you ever think you and I would be *here*?"

"No. But sorry, I've got to . . ." I didn't want to vomit all over the kind young man from Arkansas.

"Don't worry, I'll be gettin' on." He turned and walked off, his hand on the wall of the corridor as the ship rolled.

"Thanks, again," I called after him. "Very nice of you." I was genuinely touched. He waved as he walked away.

My other recollection from that voyage occurred in the ship's stateroom, on one of my few outings from my cabin. The stateroom was almost empty except for a pale, gray-haired man sitting at a far table, smoking a cigarette. I sat down and introduced myself. He told me his name was Bobby Baker. Of all the people to be on this ship, he was the last I expected—or wanted to talk with.

If you don't remember or weren't around at the time, Baker had been a crony of Lyndon Johnson's. He was secretary to the Democratic Party when LBJ was Senate majority leader—until Robert Kennedy, as attorney general, exposed Baker's alleged deals with organized crime and he was forced to resign. Kennedy's investigation led to allegations that Johnson himself had received kickbacks from military contractors. It was rotten stuff, even worse when several newspapers found evidence that Baker had also been involved in procuring women for JFK.

Baker and I exchanged a few polite words and then I excused myself, pointing to my stomach. He said he understood. I headed back to my cabin. That Baker had chosen to travel to England at this particular time, on this particular ship, seemed a cruel joke—as if to tell me there was no real escape from the vileness of America.

Days later, after landing in Southampton and taking a bus to Oxford, Bill and I were assigned "digs" at University College. Legend had it that the college was founded around 866 by King Alfred. I recall hearing of a disagreement among the faculty over whether it should celebrate its 1,100th anniversary in 1966, detractors grousing that once they began celebrating every hundred years there'd be no end to it.

Bill and I spent much of the next two years talking about Vietnam, American politics (he already had his eye on becoming governor of Arkansas), food (he liked British hamburgers, which I found revolting), and British girls. He had an endless stream of stories about people he knew from Arkansas, including politicians, and odd and funny bits of American history he'd picked up along the way.

Oh, and we did not inhale together.

To say that Bill Clinton at the age of twenty-two enjoyed people and conversation is to understate the voraciousness of his appetite. I was struck by his affability, his desire to connect, his empathy. I mean, when I was seasick, why should he come down to give me chicken soup? I was also struck by his delight in telling stories. He loved an audience, even if it was an audience of one. I was also impressed by his ambition. He knew where he was going.

We were so young then, and we were out of America for the first time in our lives. It was glorious, except for the sword of Damocles hanging over all of us—the draft.

The Biggest Moral Quandary
of Our Young Lives

In 1968, tens of thousands of us graduating from college were subject to being drafted and very possibly going to Vietnam. Many of us opposed the war, and not only because we were afraid of being wounded or killed in it. We believed the war was insane and unjust.

It was a time of wrenching decisions. Some of us got deferments from obliging draft boards. Others with trick knees, bad eyesight, allergies, and even self-induced maladies were classified as not fit for duty. A few became conscientious objectors. Draft resistance meant going to prison, or Canada, or elsewhere.

Our small band of Rhodes Scholars was in continuous tumult. The war created a tight bond among us. For me and many of the others, it was our first personal moral struggle, and the stakes could not have been higher.

One of us, Frank Aller, was determined to resist the draft. We urged him to apply for conscientious objector status, but Frank felt he could not honestly claim to oppose all wars. On the day Frank was supposed to report for induction, I held a party for him in my digs at University College; it was both a festive and a grim occasion. Frank had decided to remain in England, a fugitive. "I hoped that the spectacle of young men refusing to fight would somehow move the conscience of America" is how he explained his decision in a letter to a friend two years later. "The problem is that, while the exile goes on and on and on, the effect does not."

Frank never told any of us how much his decision to resist was torturing him, nor did he show how much he was hurting. We were unaware of the psychological toll. In the end, it was part of his undoing. Frank died by suicide, in despair over a decision that he felt had ruined his life.

Bill and I didn't consider becoming conscientious objectors because, like Frank, we weren't opposed to all wars. The larger reason was Bill had a political future to think about. I didn't want to close off possibilities, either. Bill got his extended deferment by signing a letter of intent to join the Reserve Officers Training Corps (ROTC) after Oxford. During our first year at Oxford, he said he was haunted by his decision, that it didn't feel right to him. In December of our second year there, after Bill drew a draft-lottery number that ensured he wouldn't be drafted, he wrote a letter to Colonel Eugene Holmes, the head of ROTC at the University of Arkansas, essentially withdrawing from the program.

Bill's decision and letter would become controversial twenty-three years later when he ran for president. Reading it now, decades after that, I'm struck by its thoughtfulness.

Dear Colonel Holmes,

First, I want to thank you, not just for saving me from the draft, but for being so kind and decent to me. . . .

For years I have worked to prepare myself for a political life characterized by both practical political ability and concern for rapid social progress. It is a life I still feel compelled to try to lead. I do not think our system of government is by definition corrupt, however dangerous and inadequate it has been in recent years (the society may be corrupt, but that is not the same thing, and if that is true we are all finished anyway).

When the draft came, despite political convictions, I was having a hard time facing the prospect of fighting a war I had been fighting against, and that is why I contacted you. ROTC was the one way left in which I could possibly, but not positively, avoid both Vietnam and resistance. . . .

After I signed the ROTC letter of intent I began to wonder whether the compromise I had made with myself was not more objectionable than the draft would have been, because I had no interest in the ROTC program in itself and all I seemed to have done was to protect myself from physical harm. Also, I began to think I had deceived you, not by lies—there were none—but by failing to tell you all the things I'm writing now. I doubt that I had the mental coherence to articulate them then. At that time, after we had made our agreement and you had sent my 1-D deferment to my draft board, the anguish and loss of self-regard and self-confidence really set in. I hardly slept for weeks and kept going by eating compulsively and reading until exhaustion brought sleep. Finally on September 12th, I stayed up all night writing a letter to the chairman of my draft board . . . stating that I couldn't do the ROTC after all and would he please draft me as soon as possible.

I never mailed the letter, but I did carry it on me every day until I got on the plane to return to England. I didn't mail the letter because I didn't see, in the end, how my going in the Army and maybe going to Vietnam would achieve anything except a feeling that I had punished myself and gotten what I deserved. So I came back to England to try to make something of this second year of my Rhodes scholarship.

And that is where I am now, writing to you because you have been good to me and have a right to know what I think and feel. I am writing too in the hope that my telling this one story will help you to understand more clearly how so many fine people have come to find themselves still loving their country but loathing the military, to which you and other good men have devoted years, lifetimes, of the best service you could give. To many of us, it is no longer clear what is service and what is disservice, or if it is clear, the conclusion is likely to be illegal. Forgive the length of this letter. There was much to say. There is still a lot to be said, but it can wait. Please say hello to Colonel Jones for me. Merry Christmas.

    Sincerely,

    Bill Clinton

As for me, I had read the Selective Service's physical requirements for being drafted, which set the minimum height at five feet. So, at four feet, eleven inches, I assumed I wouldn't make the grade. Before heading back to England for my second year at Oxford, I decided to get the matter officially out of the way. At the time, I had a summer job with a professor of architecture in Berkeley who was working on designing sustainable buildings in poor communities. I liked him and was learning a great deal from the work he was doing, but I wasn't very good at taking direction. I had a problem with authority, perhaps another vestige of my early experiences with bullying.

I went over to the Oakland Induction Center, which had been the scene of some violent antiwar protests, to receive my 4-F classification—"unfit for military service." The center was almost empty when I arrived. An examining sergeant sitting at a desk at the end of the corridor caught sight of me. "Hey!" he shouted, beckoning me. "Just what we've been waiting for!"

"Sorry, sir?" I asked as I reached his desk, hoping I'd misheard. My heart raced. Was he joking?

"You're perfect!" he said, smiling and standing up as if to give me a bear hug. "A tunnel rat!"

"A . . . what?"

"We need shorties like you to go into tunnels under the rice paddies! Smoke out the Cong with grenades!"

Fear rose in me like an explosion. My stomach knotted. My knees felt weak.

"Let's just measure you." He asked me to strip down to my underwear and socks, and then ushered me to the measuring stand about ten feet away. He turned me so I was looking outward, away from the vertical measure.

"Just stand up v-e-r-y straight," he said in a somber tone as he slid the horizontal metal strip down to the top of my head.

I couldn't see the measurement, but I could hear my heart pounding. In his enthusiasm for tunnel rats, would he declare I was five feet tall regardless of my one-inch deficiency?

There was a long pause that seemed to go on and on. Then his large hand came down on my shoulder as he ushered me off the platform.

"I'm sorry, son," he said solemnly.

Sorry? Was he sorry I was heading under the rice paddies with hand grenades, or sorry I wasn't? I suddenly remembered that the Army height regulation allowed examining sergeants to round up or down: (1) If the height fraction is less than half an inch, round down to the nearest whole number in inches. (2) If the height fraction is half an inch or greater, round up to the next highest whole number in inches. If this sergeant rounded up, I'd be down under the rice paddies with grenades. Forget Oxford. Hell, forget life.

"So," I said, trying to hide the tremor in my voice, "wha . . . what's the measure show?"

He frowned. "You're just a bit too short."

I was tempted to let out a yell but stopped myself for fear he'd take offense and draft me out of spite. I simply nodded and said, "Okay," trying my best to act disappointed.

"But, son . . ."

Shit. Was I *too* disappointed? Was he going to round up out of sympathy?

". . . Don't give up hope." He smiled. "Maybe you'll grow!"

I grinned.

A second later he let out a loud guffaw, probably relieved I wasn't upset by his lame attempt at humor. Then I felt my own relief overwhelm me—the unmitigated joy of having my life back—and I laughed too. Yet at the same time, I felt sick to my stomach—not just with relief but also with the ache of knowing I had just slipped by the whole catastrophe of the Vietnam War without any personal sacrifice at all.

That's the image I'm left with now, fifty-seven years later: the two of us, the examining sergeant and me, doubled up there in the Oakland Induction Center, while tens of thousands of young Americans, most of them without college degrees, and hundreds of thousands of Vietnamese, were being slaughtered for no good reason.

The sharp class division—between those of us who served, and those of us who found ways to avoid military service—would form one of the central elements of the coming culture wars. The late 1960s was a time of experimentation—"sex, drugs, and rock-and-roll" and a lot more. The giant baby-boom generation was heading out into the world that seemed to many of us to be nuts. Some of us joined cults; others, urban communes; others, utopian communities in the countryside. I wasn't courageous (or foolhardy) enough to do any of these. The closest I came was participating in a T-group (sometimes referred to as a "training" or "sensitivity training" group) later that same summer of 1969.

My T-Group in Big Sur

T-groups were big in the late 1960s. The idea was to help people learn more about themselves through their interactions with others in groups of complete strangers.

One weekend, soon after I was told I was too short for the military, I headed down the California coast to a magical stretch called Big Sur. Its rugged beauty captivated me—the mountains rising straight up from the Pacific, the pungent eucalyptus, the roar of the ocean. I had admired Jack Kerouac's 1962 novel *Big Sur* (which he typed over a ten-day period onto a teletype roll) and had loved the works of Lawrence Ferlinghetti, Allen Ginsberg, and William Burroughs, who appear in the novel pseudonymously but clearly recognizable. That they inhabited this same stretch of extraordinary coastland made it feel even more enchanted. I was feeling in a celebratory mood, free of worry about being drafted and enjoying the bright sunshine and extraordinary coastline. So, when I read a notice at the Big Sur post office of a T-group to be held that very evening in the local school, it caught my attention. I had only the vaguest idea of what a T-group was but felt so intoxicated by the place and the associations it spurred that I figured why not.

I arrived just as about twenty-five adults ranging in age from the early twenties to early seventies were assembling. All seemed to be feeling as tentative as I was, but excited. We gathered in a large empty room, in the center of which was a square athletic mat. There were chairs along all four walls.

Already seated along the far wall was a large balding man with dark hair extending from the sides of his head to below his shoulders, and a big belly. Without standing, but in a firm voice, he asked us to choose a chair and sit down as soon as possible so we could begin. When we had settled in, he looked slowly around the room, making eye contact with each of us. His face was stern. He said he was the "facilitator" of the group, then asked us to state our names and what we hoped to achieve in the group.

When it was my turn, I gave my name and said I was curious about T-groups and eager to see how he would be facilitating it.

After everyone had spoken, there was silence. Then the large balding man looked directly at me. "You and I are gonna wrestle," he said.

Several people in the group laughed. A few gasped.

"Sorry?" I said, pretending I hadn't heard him, buying some time to decide what to do or say.

He stood up. He was immense. He pointed to the mat. "You ever wrestle?"

"Well . . ." I stammered. "A bit." In fact, I had wrestled in high school. It was the one sport I was fairly good at, although I didn't stick with it for long.

"Get into the starting position," he said. "Hands and knees down." More laughter from the group.

Despite my problem with authority, I did as he ordered. I walked to the center of the mat and fell to my hands and knees. Then he got down on his knees next to me. He put one of his big arms and hands around my waist, and with his other hand he held one of my arms—the standard referee's position for beginning a match. But this was absurd. Wrestlers are matched according to weight. His was at least three times mine.

"Ready?" he asked without waiting for my answer. "Go!"

In a split second, he was on top of me. I felt as if I was caught in a landslide and had been buried. I knew from my high school days that if I could just squeeze myself out from under him, I might be able to use his body mass against him. Most of wrestling is about leverage. If I could flip him on his back, he would have a hard time moving. So the moment I escaped from under him, I angled my body on top of and across his back, grabbed one of his arms and legs, and pulled with all my might, forcing him onto his back. Then I pivoted myself crossways over his shoulders and chest and held him down for several seconds.

It was over. Several members of the group applauded. I stood up, panting heavily, and unsteadily began to walk back to my chair. Suddenly he grabbed my ankle from behind. I lost my balance and fell onto the mat, on my back. I was too startled to yell. His entire body was on my chest. I could barely breathe. I was shocked and panicked. What's happening? Who is this man?

With the little remaining air in my lungs, I called out to the group. "Help! Please! Pull him off me!" They were just as shocked as I was. Several rose from their chairs and grabbed him. He resisted for a moment, then rolled over. I got up and collapsed in a chair. He quickly walked out of the room.

I was dazed, out of breath, confused, and upset. "Thank you," I whispered to my rescuers, who had returned to their chairs. They seemed equally perplexed and alarmed. I expected the group to grab their things and leave, but they remained in their chairs.

"What the hell was that all about?" I asked no one in particular.

"I think he's nuts," said one of my rescuers.

"He didn't expect you to pin him, and when you did he went crazy," said another.

"I thought it was just play-acting until he grabbed your ankle," said a third.

"He looked angry when he stormed out," said another.

"I doubt he's coming back."

"Anyone know anything about him?" No one did.

I asked the group whether they wanted to leave. They all chose to stay and talk. Some spoke of their personal experiences with violent parents or partners. They were asked how they had coped. A few broke down in tears.

I talked about being bullied as a kid because of my height. I told them about the second graders who held me upside down over the toilet in the boys' room and threatened to plunge my head in, and that after that I didn't want to use that bathroom. I talked about feeling humiliated that I had to find protectors, about Mickey and the Klan who murdered him. Others told equally harrowing personal stories.

I don't remember how long this went on. At one point, the large balding man came back into the room and quietly sat down. Our conversation stopped. All of us looked at him. He smiled rather sheepishly.

"Can you tell us what that was about?" I asked him.

"What?" he asked, as if he hadn't almost killed me.

"The wrestling. Grabbing me by the ankle as I was heading back to the chair. Putting all your weight on my chest. My having to call out for help. Then you stormed out of the room. What were you doing? And why *me*?"

He looked around at the group, then at me. After a long pause, he answered, "I didn't think you'd pin me."

A few people laughed. I was angry. "So, it was revenge? You were upset that I pinned you and your pride was hurt, and you had to take it out on me?"

"No, no," he said.

"Then why the hell did you do that?"

"Because I knew you and I had to fight it out."

"What are you talking about?"

"From the moment we went around the room introducing ourselves, I figured you were gonna challenge me. You were gonna try to run this group."

"That's absurd," I said.

"Not at all," he said. "Look at you, right now. You're running the group. You've taken over my role."

"You're wrong. I just stepped in. You'd left. We didn't know what to do. I just asked people if . . ."

"Exactly," he said. "And look where you're sitting."

Suddenly I realized that I had taken the seat he occupied when the group began.

"We would have had to fight it out, sooner or later," he said. "Much better to get it over with right away. And how wonderfully it's worked out!" He looked around the room and smiled. "Some of you came to his rescue. You worked together. And since then, I expect you've been having a fine discussion. You've learned a lot."

At that, he rose from his chair—the chair I had been sitting in at the start—and said, "My work here is done. Thanks for coming." Then he walked out of the room, for the second and last time.

It was about then, after my T-group experience in Big Sur in the summer of 1969, that I began to understand I could no longer separate my earlier feelings of being bullied when I was a kid from the issues I was repeatedly confronting as a young man: When to respect authority. How to exercise authority wisely and avoid hypocrisy. How to escape the violence and upheaval gripping America but do what I could to constrain the bullies in America. How to prevent *myself* from eventually becoming a bully.

The Riot That Started
the Culture Wars

May 8, 1970, marked the twenty-fifth anniversary of the Allied victory over Germany in World War II. It was also just weeks after Richard Nixon expanded the Vietnam War into Cambodia. And four days after Ohio National Guardsmen shot dead four students during antiwar protests at Kent State University. It was also the day several of my friends had come to New York City to demonstrate against the war and a riot broke out. I was there because I was on my way home from Oxford.

Around noon, near the intersection of Wall and Broad Streets in Lower Manhattan, more than four hundred construction workers—steamfitters, ironworkers, plumbers, and other laborers from nearby construction sites like the emerging World Trade Center—attacked around one thousand student demonstrators (including two of my friends) protesting the war and the Kent State shootings. The workers were armed with lengths of steel rebar, their tools, and steel-toe boots. They carried U.S. flags and chanted "U.S.A., all the way" and "America, love it or leave it" as they chased the students through the streets, attacking those who looked like hippies.

The police did little to stop the mayhem. Some even egged it on. When a group of hardhats moved menacingly toward Wall Street Plaza, a patrolman shouted: "Give 'em hell, boys. Give 'em one for me!" The workers then stormed a barely protected City Hall, where the mayor's staff, to the hardhats' rage, had lowered the flag in honor of the Kent State dead. They pushed their way to the top of the steps and attempted to gain entrance, chanting "Hey, hey, whatcha say, we support the U.S.A.!" Fearing the mob would break in, a person from the mayor's staff raised the flag. The workers then stormed the newly built main Pace University building, smashing lobby windows and beating students and professors with their tools.

More than one hundred people were wounded. The typical victim was a twenty-two-year-old white male college student, though one in four was female. Seven police officers were also hurt. Most of the injured required hospital treatment. Six people were arrested, but only one construction worker. My friends who had been demonstrating against the war phoned me later that day. They had escaped injury, but they were traumatized. I remember them describing the rioting construction workers as a "pack of animals."

The hardhat riot was the first major salvo in America's culture wars, and it had been planned in the Oval Office. Nixon hatchet man Chuck Colson can be heard on a White House tape recording made May 5, three days before the riot, urging several New York union leaders to organize an attack against student protesters in New York.

Nixon then exploited the riot for political advantage. His chief of staff, H. R. Haldeman, wrote in his diary: "The college demonstrators have overplayed their hands, evidence is the blue-collar group rising up against them, and [the] president can mobilize them." Patrick Buchanan, then a Nixon aide, wrote in a memo to his boss that "blue-collar Americans" are "our people now." (Colson's dirty work didn't end with the riot. He subsequently hired E. Howard Hunt, a former CIA agent, to spy on Nixon's political opponents. Hunt then led a break-in of the Democratic National Committee headquarters at the Watergate building in June 1972.)

Peter J. Brennan, president of the Building and Construction Trades Council of Greater New York, claimed "the unions had nothing to do with" the riot, even though it occurred just after Brennan held a rally of construction workers to show support for Nixon's Vietnam policies. Brennan explained that workers were "fed up" with violence and flag desecration by antiwar demonstrators. In the wake of the riot, Nixon invited Brennan and a delegation of twenty-two union leaders, representing more than 300,000 tradesmen, to the White House. They presented Nixon with several hard hats and a flag pin, after which Nixon praised the "labor leaders and people from Middle America who still have character and guts and a bit of patriotism."

After the 1972 election, Nixon appointed Brennan labor secretary. Brennan did not distinguish himself in that position. He strongly opposed affirmative action. He also prevented Labor Department officials from investigating allegations of corruption in the Teamsters Union and of its president, Frank Fitzsimmons, who had helped secure labor support for Nixon's election.

The hardhat riot revealed a deep split in America's left that had begun to show itself during the 1968 Democratic convention—dividing the coalition of workers and progressives that Franklin D. Roosevelt had knitted together in the 1930s. It showed that working-class whites could be peeled away from middle-class liberals and college-educated professionals on cultural issues involving nationalism and class as well as race and gender.

The riot's class-based and race-based tensions would worsen over the next half century, as America's college-educated middle class and wealthy began seceding from the white non-college working class. The construction men who attacked the demonstrators on May 8, 1970, and the police who egged them on were more likely to have family and friends in Vietnam than the college students who demonstrated. Many were veterans of World War II and Korea. They also lived in the same working-class neighborhoods. They despised the protesters as a bunch of pampered, long-haired, draft-dodging, flag-desecrating snots.

They felt abandoned by the middle class and the college-educated who deserted their communities, stiffed by the clever kids with draft deferments, forced to bus their kids to Black neighborhoods and accept Black kids into their schools, and burdened by an economy no longer delivering upward mobility. As the journalist Pete Hamill observed at the time, the workingman "feels trapped and, even worse, in a society that purports to be democratic, ignored."

Pat Buchanan, writing in 1988 about the future of the GOP, argued that the Republican Party should take more advantage of these growing working-class resentments. "The Republican moment slipped by, I believe, when the GOP refused to take up the challenge from the left on its chosen battleground: the politics of class, culture, religion, and race." Three years later, Buchanan openly questioned whether democracy was the best form of government. "The American press is infatuated to the point of intoxication with democracy," he wrote, comparing the Marine Corps and corporations like IBM to the federal government. "Only the last is run on democratic, not autocratic principles. Yet who would choose the last as the superior institution?"

Buchanan sought the Republican presidential nomination in 1992, 1996, and 2000. He lost, but his culture war claimed increasing ground in the GOP. His rallies prefigured Trump rallies two decades later. The crowds he drew included many men wearing military fatigues. The press corps traveling with Buchanan were reviled and subjected to verbal threats that have become commonplace today. In 1992, Buchanan argued that Republicans should oppose the North American Free Trade Agreement (NAFTA). Years later, Buchanan argued that Republicans should support Russian president Vladimir Putin because he was anti-gay. Buchanan lost the Republican nomination in 1996 to Bob Dole. But Buchanan won about a third of the Republican primary vote, chiefly from the party's blue-collar members.

Buchanan's presidential bids epitomized Republican cultural populism before Trump—exploiting the nationalist, anti-gay, racist anger of the white working class. Buchanan faded, but cultural warfare claimed ever more Republican ground. Yet the Democratic Party did not re-embrace the *economic* populism that had been central to Franklin D. Roosevelt's coalition, although it would have offered a powerful counterpoint. For many years I was frustrated and mystified by this.

At Yale Law with Bill, Hillary, and Clarence

Soon after the hardhat riot, in September 1970, I packed up my VW and drove to New Haven, Connecticut, and Yale Law School. Oxford had given me a respite from the chaos and moral rot of America and a chance to better understand myself. Now I had to get on with whatever it was I was going to do. In those days, Yale Law School was where you went if you wanted to "do good" in the world but were uncertain of how to do it.

Bill was there, too, as was Hillary (she had matriculated the year before). In the law school cafeteria, on the very first day, I was having lunch with Bill when Hillary came up behind me.

"Bob! Good to see you!"

"Hillary! I didn't even know you were here."

"Already finished the first year. Two to go."

"Let me introduce you. This is Bill Clinton."

"Hi, Bill," Hillary said, extending her hand.

"Bill, this is Hillary Rodham."

"Hi, Hillary," he said, shaking hands.

My introduction obviously didn't take, because they claim to have met days later in the law library.

Also in my class was Clarence Thomas.

All of us were there when the Supreme Court decided *Roe v. Wade,* protecting women's rights to do what they want with their bodies, under the Fourteenth Amendment to the Constitution.

The professors used what you may know as the "Socratic method," asking hard questions about the cases they were discussing and waiting for students to raise their hands in response, and then criticizing the responses. It was a hair-raising but effective way to learn the law.

One of the principles guiding those discussions is called *stare decisis,* Latin for "to stand by things decided." It's the doctrine of judicial precedent. If a court has already ruled on an issue (say, on reproductive rights), future courts should decide similar cases the same way. Supreme Courts can change their minds and rule differently than they did before, but they need good reasons to do so, and it helps if their opinion is unanimous or nearly so. Otherwise their rulings appear (and are) arbitrary—even, shall we say, partisan?

In those classroom discussions a half century ago, Hillary's hand was always the first in the air. When she was called upon, she gave perfect answers—whole paragraphs, precisely phrased. She distinguished one case from another, using precedents and *stare decisis* to guide her thinking. I was awed.

My hand was in the air about half the time, and when called on, my answers were *meh.*

Clarence's hand was never in the air. I don't recall him saying anything, ever.

Bill was never in class.

As I write this, only one of us sits on the Supreme Court. In 2023, he and four of his colleagues—all appointed by Republican presidents, three by a president who instigated a coup against the United States—decided to repeal *Roe* and violate *stare decisis.* Neither he nor they gave a coherent argument for why.

In October 1991, during what became known as the Clarence Thomas–Anita Hill hearings, Hill, who had worked for Thomas at the Equal Employment Opportunity Commission, testified before the Senate Judiciary Committee—then headed by Delaware senator Joe Biden—about the sexual harassment she endured under Thomas. Thomas had been nominated by George H. W. Bush to fill the Supreme Court seat vacated by Justice Thurgood Marshall, who announced his retirement the previous June due to ill health. Facing a committee comprised entirely of white men, Hill, a Black woman, recounted many raunchy sexist remarks made by Thomas. Her claims were often dismissed. "You testified this morning, in response to

Senator Biden, that the most embarrassing question involved—and this is not too bad—women's large breasts," then–Pennsylvania senator Arlen Specter said to Hill at one point. "That is a word we use all the time." Other Republicans called her "a little nutty, a little slutty." But she did not back down. In the end, though, Thomas's nomination was confirmed.

I got to know Hill in the late 1990s when we were both professors at Brandeis University and her office was next to mine. I've met few people over the course of my life with more humility, intelligence, and integrity than her. I don't have a scintilla of doubt that what she told the committee about Thomas's harassment of her was true.

Hill has devoted her scholarship and activism to the cause of stopping sexual harassment. The data she has gathered—on children in elementary schools who are bullied and sexually harassed, university students who are sexually assaulted, sexual harassment in the workplace, sexual assault by athletic coaches and doctors, and harassment and assault inside people's homes—is chilling. The #MeToo movement exposed some of this—rapes, assaults, and sexual extortion in the entertainment industry and elsewhere. But our society is still averting its eyes. Ten million people are victimized by an intimate partner every year in this country. Many become homeless as a result.

In 1994, Congress enacted, and Bill Clinton signed into law, the Violence Against Women Act, which provided victims of gender-motivated violence the right to sue their attackers in federal court. But in 2000, in a case entitled *United States v. Morrison,* the Supreme Court, in a six-to-three decision, including Thomas's concurring opinion, held that key parts of the act were unconstitutional because they exceeded the powers granted to Congress under the commerce clause, which gives the federal government authority to regulate commerce among the states. Violence against women, the court assumed, was a "domestic" problem whose reach did not extend beyond state lines. Therefore, it could not be a *federal* crime. The court did not explain why.

In 2018, Christine Blasey Ford appeared before the Senate Judiciary Committee with detailed allegations of sexual assault by Supreme Court nominee Brett Kavanaugh. The outcome was the same as the Senate's response to the allegations of sexual harassment by Clarence Thomas: Kavanaugh was confirmed.

To Be Borked

I met Robert Bork when I took his class on antitrust law at Yale Law School. I recall him as a large, imposing man in his midforties, with a red beard and a perpetual scowl, seemingly impatient and bored with us (Hillary and Bill were also in that class). We kept challenging his view that the only legitimate purpose of antitrust law was to lower consumer prices.

"What about the political power of giant corporations?" we asked.

His retort: "How do you expect courts to measure political power?"

"But what about the power of big corporations to suppress wages?"

Bork: "Employees are always free to find better jobs."

"What about their power to undercut potential rivals with lower prices?"

Bork: "Lower prices are good for consumers."

"What about the sheer power that comes from their gigantic size?"

Bork: "Also good for consumers. Large size means lower costs through efficiencies of scale."

His answers never satisfied us. He spouted economic theory based on the dubious assumptions that all economic players have perfect information and can immediately enter or leave any market they wish, without cost. Bork had attended the University of Chicago and its law school and was influenced by economist Milton Friedman's and his disciples' belief in laissez-faire economics. The same year Bork joined the Yale faculty, Friedman published *Capitalism and Freedom,* an ode to the free market (Rose Friedman, Milton's wife, had written much of it, editing Milton's academic language for a general audience).

Even in our early and mid twenties, we knew Bork's faith in the free market was nonsense. Bork refused to recognize the centrality of *power* in our political-economic system, even though antitrust laws emerged from the Gilded Age of the late nineteenth century when a central concern was the untrammeled power of giant corporations. A few years after I finished law school, Bork wrote a book called *The Antitrust Paradox* that summarized his ideas. The staff of a conservative California governor bound for the White House read it and passed it along to their boss, and Bork's book formed a basic tenet of Reaganomics.

Federal judges read it, too. Most judges didn't (and still don't) know much economics and hated getting bogged down in interminable and almost incomprehensible antitrust trials that could last for years. They found Bork's simplicity and cogency helpful in limiting such lawsuits. As a result, antitrust cases nearly became a dead letter, until Joe Biden revived them.

I didn't hold Bork's narrow approach to antitrust against him. I enjoyed sparring with him, appreciated his wry sense of humor, and respected his intellect. Hell, I even came to like him.

Soon after, Richard Nixon appointed Bork solicitor general, the third-ranking official in the Justice Department, representing the United States before the Supreme Court. Bork was known as a conservative, but as solicitor general he filed liberal friend-of-the-court briefs on the side of litigants seeking expansive rights as often as Thurgood Marshall had when he served as solicitor general in the Johnson administration, and even more often than Wade McCree would do during the Carter administration.

In 1970, Nixon authorized break-ins or "black bag jobs" of people considered domestic threats to him. As I've noted, Nixon's bagman Chuck Colson, who instigated the hardhat riot, was the ringleader. One early goal was to destroy the reputation of Daniel Ellsberg, who, while working for the RAND Corporation, a defense contractor, had leaked to the news media the Pentagon Papers, showing that the Johnson administration had lied to the American people about the Vietnam War. Nixon's burglars broke into the office of Ellsberg's psychiatrist, seeking information that might smear Ellsberg and undermine his credibility in the antiwar movement. "You can't drop it, Bob," Nixon told his assistant H. R. Haldeman in June 1971, referring to Ellsberg. "You can't let the Jew steal that stuff and get away with it. You understand?"

Early in 1972, Nixon launched a plan for spying on and sabotaging Democrats in the upcoming presidential campaign, including wiretaps and burglaries. His henchmen paid the chauffeur of Senator Ed Muskie, whom Nixon considered his most likely Democratic opponent, to photograph Muskie's internal memos and strategy documents, and paid others to dig up dirt on the sex life of Senator Ted Kennedy, a potential opponent in 1976. "I'd really like to get Kennedy taped," Nixon told Haldeman.

They inserted a retired Secret Service agent into the team protecting Kennedy who, Haldeman assured Nixon, would "do anything that I tell him." Nixon replied, "We just might get lucky and catch this son of a bitch and ruin him for '76," adding, "That's going to be fun." Nixon ordered another assistant, John Ehrlichman, to direct the Internal Revenue Service to investigate the tax returns of all likely Democratic presidential candidates, including Kennedy. "Are we going after their tax returns?" Nixon asked. "You know what I mean? There's a lot of gold in them thar hills."

In the early morning of June 17, 1972, a team of burglars wearing business suits and rubber gloves broke into the headquarters of the Democratic National Committee in the Watergate complex in Washington. The burglars were discovered and arrested, and the FBI immediately began an investigation. Six days later, Attorney General John Mitchell proposed to Nixon that he order the CIA to claim national security secrets would be compromised if the FBI didn't halt its investigation. Nixon agreed. "Play it tough," he directed. "That's the way they play it, and that's the way we are going to play it." Six weeks after the burglars' arrest, Nixon and Haldeman discussed paying them off to keep them from talking to federal investigators. "They have to be paid," Nixon said. "That's all there is to that."

On March 21, 1973, Nixon counsel John W. Dean reported that the burglars were still demanding money. Nixon asked, "How much money do you need?" Dean estimated a million dollars over the following two years. Nixon responded, "You could get it in cash, and I know where it could be gotten." They discussed using a secret stash hidden in the White House, laundering the money through bookmakers, and empaneling a grand jury so the burglars could plead the Fifth Amendment or claim memory loss. Nixon praised Dean's efforts. "You handled it just right. You contained it. Now after the election, we've got to have another plan." On August 9, 1974, four days after the tapes revealing much of this malfeasance were released, and facing the almost certain prospect of being impeached and convicted by Congress, Nixon resigned.

I relate these details to remind you just how far Nixon went in violating the norms of the modern presidency to retain power. Even though his actions led to many reforms, Americans' trust in politics was deeply shaken. Public outrage continued when Nixon's successor, Gerald Ford, granted him a full pardon. Ford believed the nation had to be shielded from the pain and disruption of a president put on criminal trial and possibly imprisoned. Yet to many Americans, the fact that Nixon would not be held fully accountable felt like another assault on the common good.

To make matters worse, Nixon continued to insist he had not participated in any crimes. In his 1977 television interviews with British journalist David Frost, he conceded he had "let the American people down" but refused to admit to any illegality. "I didn't think of it as a coverup. I didn't intend a coverup. Let me say, if I intended the coverup, believe me, I would have done it." Nixon added, "When the president does it, that means it is not illegal." Those words would continue to haunt America.

Notwithstanding all of this, Nixon pulled off an extraordinary political heist. He persuaded millions of working-class Americans that the Republican Party was their home. Beginning in 1968, Republicans won five of the next six presidential elections. All used Nixon's playbook, relying on a coalition of corporate America and the white working class, and using racial dog-whistles like "law and order" and "welfare queens."

In what came to be known as the "Saturday Night Massacre" of October 20, 1973, several high-ranking members of the Justice Department chose to resign rather than follow Nixon's order to fire special prosecutor Archibald Cox, who was investigating the Watergate scandal. Bork's superiors, attorney general Elliot Richardson and deputy attorney general William Ruckelshaus, had promised the senators who confirmed them that they would allow the investigation to move forward. Bork, who had never made that promise, felt bound to follow Nixon's order to fire Cox, which he did. Bork served as acting attorney general until January 4, 1974, and then resumed his duties as solicitor general. Gerald Ford kept Bork in that job.

I went from Yale Law to clerk for Judge Frank M. Coffin, who sat on the court of appeals for the First Circuit, which included most of New England. His office was in the federal courthouse in Portland, Maine. A law clerk is like an apprentice who learns a craft by working closely with a master craftsman. Judge Coffin blended sharp intelligence and wit with compassion for the underdog. I learned a lot about the law that year but even more about how one person could make America better and kinder.

Ten months later, Bork offered me a job as one of his assistants. Maybe he remembered me from his Yale Law classes and my pugilistic responses to his arguments, or maybe, after firing Archibald Cox, he couldn't find anyone else. I took the job because I was still in my twenties and thrilled at the prospect of briefing and arguing cases before the Supreme Court. I was sure I wouldn't have to compromise my beliefs because, given my lack of experience, I wouldn't be assigned an important case. Still, I was conscious that my first full-time job in the executive branch of government was in a Republican administration that was headed by the president who pardoned Richard Nixon. I could live with that, I told myself, as long as I didn't help any awful bullies.

In any event, I did not distinguish myself in the job. In one of my two arguments before the Court, I mistakenly referred to Justice Potter Stewart as Justice William Brennan, an error that the two justices found amusing but made me want to disappear under the podium where I was standing. Bork was forgiving.

The solicitor general's office was not only responsible for representing the United States in all cases that went to the Supreme Court but also had to approve all briefs that went to the courts of appeal. We were just five deputies and fifteen assistants, so it was a huge workload. All of us put in long hours trying to get the briefs exactly right, including every footnote. When we argued a Supreme Court case, we spent days preparing for it.

A photo of the group shows Bork, bearded and wearing glasses, sitting in the middle of the front row, surrounded by a mostly dour group of white males and one white woman. Some would go on to become judges, such as Paul Friedman, whom Bill Clinton nominated to the District Court of the District of Columbia; Frank Easterbrook (standing next to me on the far right), whom Ronald Reagan nominated to the Court of Appeals for the Seventh Circuit; and Danny Boggs, nominated by Reagan to the Court of Appeals for the Sixth Circuit.

I was too junior to participate in *Buckley v. Valeo,* the first of a series of cases in which the Supreme Court began expanding the right of corporations to influence politics. In the wake of Watergate, Congress had passed the Federal Election Campaign Act of 1974, limiting the amount of money that could be contributed to political campaigns. In January 1975, a coalition of plaintiffs, including New York senator James L. Buckley, filed a lawsuit claiming that the contribution limits violated the First Amendment's guarantee of freedom of speech. The solicitor general's office filed a friend-of-the-court brief on the side of preserving the act and its spending limits.

The Supreme Court, on which by then Lewis Powell sat, upheld the act's limits on individual contributions to political campaigns and candidates, which, it said, enhanced the "integrity of our system of representative democracy" by guarding against corruption. But the Court found that the act's limits on spending for "issue advocacy" violated the First Amendment because, in the Court's view, such spending by independent committees didn't increase the risk of corruption. The ruling led to a flood of so-called soft money for TV advertising that indirectly advocated the election or defeat of candidates without explicitly doing so. By the 1996 elections, both major parties were spending more soft money than hard money. *Buckley v. Valeo* offered the first hint that the Court would henceforth equate spending money on politics with the exercise of free speech.

The cases I argued were insignificant. I was a rookie in the Justice Department who was given either sure winners or sure losers to argue because the department didn't want to take a risk on a rookie. It was a wise move. But I was in awe of the Supreme Court, which at the time understood its responsibility to balance the scales of justice in favor of the powerless—something Congress and the executive branch could not be relied on to do. Even Nixon's appointees—Harry Blackmun, Lewis Powell, and Warren Burger—seemed to understand this important role. Blackmun wrote the Court's decision in *Roe v. Wade,* and Powell and Burger joined him, as did four Democratic appointees to the Court—William O. Douglas, Thurgood Marshall, William Brennan, and Potter Stewart.

I recall Douglas, who had recently suffered a stroke and was in obvious discomfort, looking sharply at me as I made my arguments. From where I stood, I could see only his light blue eyes and bright white hair. Here was the justice who wrote the 1965 decision in *Griswold v. Connecticut,* finding that a constitutional right to privacy forbids states from banning contraception—a right that would become endangered years later by Justice Samuel Alito, who doesn't recognize a privacy right in the Constitution. Douglas was also the man who decided that the Vietnam War was illegal and issued an order that temporarily blocked the sending of Army reservists to Vietnam. He was the justice who wrote in the 1972 case *Sierra Club v. Morton* that any part of nature feeling the destructive pressure of modern technology should have standing to sue in court—including rivers, lakes, trees, and even the air—because, he reasoned, if corporations, which are legal fictions, have standing, why shouldn't the natural world?

Sitting not far from Douglas on the bench was Thurgood Marshall, who two decades before had succeeded in having the Supreme Court declare segregated public schools unconstitutional, in the landmark 1954 decision, *Brown v. Board of Education*. Marshall did more than any person then alive to break down the shameful legal edifice of Jim Crow.

Douglas, Marshall, and Blackmun were the intellectual leaders of that Supreme Court. Their opinions gave the Court its moral heft. They drew not only from the Constitution as written but also from their understanding of how the nation had evolved. They understood the moral leadership America needed in the Supreme Court to protect the rights of the voiceless and the powerless, the bullied from the bullies.

Today's Supreme Court majority doesn't have a clue about the court's moral authority and apparently couldn't care less. The Republican appointees to the court are mostly political hacks, rigid ideologues, and small minds intent on entrenching the power of the already powerful, comforting the already comfortable, and inflicting pain on the already afflicted. Five were nominated by presidents who lost the popular vote; three were nominated by a president who instigated a coup against the United States and were confirmed because a rogue Republican Party mounted scorched-earth campaigns to put them on the Court.

In 2005, I testified before the Senate Judiciary Committee against the confirmation of John Roberts as chief justice. I had reviewed his legal work and found that as an assistant to the attorney general in the Reagan administration he wrote a memorandum arguing that Section 5 of the Voting Rights Act of 1965 unnecessarily intruded on the states; as deputy solicitor general in the George H. W. Bush administration, he argued against abortion rights and against affirmative action; and as a judge on the Court of Appeals for the District of Columbia, he issued a series of opinions that expanded the power of the presidency but limited civil rights. (In the 2004 case of *Hedgepeth ex rel Hedgepeth v. Washington Metropolitan Area Transit Authority*, he even ruled that Washington police had properly detained a twelve-year-old girl who ate a snack in violation of a "zero tolerance" policy against eating in a Metro station.) I concluded that although Roberts was "a very bright, if not brilliant jurist and an extremely thoughtful lawyer," his "values are way to the right of mainstream America" and it was up to the Judiciary Committee "to decide whether you want to put somebody in as Chief Justice who's that far to the right."

The intellectual leader of today's majority (if "intellectual" is the appropriate adjective) is Samuel Alito, perhaps the most conceptually rigid and cognitively dishonest justice since Chief Justice Roger Taney, who found in the infamous *Dred Scott v. Sandford* case in 1857 that Congress had no power to exclude slavery from the territories and that Black people could not become citizens.

The extremism of today's six Republican appointees to the Supreme Court was on full display in their 2022 opinion in *Dobbs v. Jackson Women's Health Organization,* overruling *Roe v. Wade. Roe* had been the law of the land for almost fifty years. Even more ominous was Clarence Thomas's concurring opinion, which pointed the way for the radicals on the Court. If the due process clause of the Fourteenth Amendment to the Constitution doesn't protect abortion, said Thomas, the court "should reconsider" other cases that rely on the same clause: *Griswold v. Connecticut*; *Lawrence v. Texas,* a 2003 case invalidating sodomy laws and making same-sex sexual activity legal across the country; and *Obergefell v. Hodges,* the 2015 case establishing the right of gay couples to marry. Thomas said the court had a duty to "correct the error" established in those precedents. After "overruling these demonstrably erroneous decisions, the question would remain whether other constitutional provisions" protected the rights they established, Thomas wrote, demonstrating once again that he learned nothing decades before about *stare decisis.* The Supreme Court, in fact, is now firmly in the hands of radical justices who are eager to throw it out the window. They are part of the anti-democracy movement now threatening America.

The authority of the Supreme Court derives entirely from Americans' confidence and trust in it. As Alexander Hamilton wrote in *Federalist* No. 78, the judiciary has no influence over "the sword" (the executive branch's power to compel action) or "the purse" (Congress's power to appropriate funds); it has only the trust of the people, which is derived from its moral authority. The Supreme Court I was privileged to argue before a half century ago protected the less powerful with arguments that resonated with the core values of the nation. Americans didn't always agree with its conclusions, but they respected them. Tragically, today's cruel and partisan Supreme Court majority is squandering what remains of the Court's moral authority.

I saw Bork just once after he left the Justice Department, at the start of the 1980s at a dinner party at his house in Washington. He was in a festive mood. He had remarried (his first wife had died of cancer a few years before) and seemed happy. His sharp wit was much on display. In 1982, Reagan appointed him to the Court of Appeals for the District of Columbia, a hugely influential position, and in 1987, after Powell announced his retirement, Reagan nominated Bork to the Supreme Court.

Bork's nomination was controversial from the start, not just because of his role in the Saturday Night Massacre but also because of his increasingly pugnacious conservative views. The then chairman of the Senate Judiciary Committee, Joe Biden, warned Reagan, "If you nominate him, you'll have trouble on your hands."

Bork's nomination precipitated the first scorched-earth, no-holds-barred combat I had witnessed in Washington. Someone went through his home trash cans looking for anything that might incriminate him (and found nothing of the kind). Someone else went to his local video rental store seeking records of what films he'd checked out (again, nothing out of the ordinary). TV ads produced by People for the American Way and narrated by Gregory Peck attacked him as an extremist.

Senator Ted Kennedy (who later became a good friend) gave a speech on the floor of the Senate in opposition to Bork's nomination.

Robert Bork's America is a land in which women would be forced into back-alley abortions, blacks would sit at segregated lunch counters, rogue police could break down citizens' doors in midnight raids, schoolchildren could not be taught about evolution, writers and artists could be censored at the whim of the government, and the doors of the federal courts would be shut on the fingers of millions of citizens for whom the judiciary is, and is often the only, protector of the individual rights that are the heart of our democracy.

This struck me as unfair. I had worked closely with Bork. Yes, his views had become more conservative over time, but he was not the extremist Kennedy described. Bork did not help himself in his confirmation hearing. When asked why he wanted to be a Supreme Court justice, he said the job "would be intellectually stimulating." His nomination was ultimately rejected by the Senate, 58 to 42.

We will never know whether Bork would have followed the somewhat progressive trail blazed by Nixon's nominees—Blackmun, Powell, and Burger—or the cruel and pinched trail of Thomas, Alito, and Trump's three nominees. But from what I knew of Bork before the hearing on his nomination, I would have given fair odds that he'd have taken the more progressive path.

The campaign against Bork added a new verb to the American lexicon: to be "Borked," defined by the *Oxford English Dictionary* as "to defame or vilify someone systematically, especially in the mass media, usually to prevent his or her appointment to public office." In the years since that nomination fight, many people have been Borked—notably, Bill and Hillary, and John Kerry when he ran for president. After his own Senate confirmation fight, Brett Kavanaugh claimed that his opponents had engaged in "a good old-fashioned attempt at Borking," but the analogy doesn't hold. Serious accusations had been leveled against Kavanaugh touching directly on his moral character and capacity to be a Supreme Court justice, charges that continue to color the public's view of him. Bork's moral character was never questioned.

The fight over Bork's nomination marked the beginning of the end of civil discourse in American politics. Bork was treated horribly, which shocked me. The boundary separating George Bailey from Mr. Potter—the bullies from the bullied—wasn't nearly as clear-cut as I had thought. In the fight over Bork, Kennedy and the other Democrats on the Judiciary Committee acted like bullies. Angry and bitter, Bork resigned his judgeship the following year, and subsequently became one of the nation's most inveterate cultural warriors.

I find the following excerpt from his 1996 book, *Slouching Towards Gomorrah: Modern Liberalism and America's Decline*, especially poignant because it shows how the fight over his nomination affected how he came to view his students from decades before. We had morphed into leftist extremists.

One morning on my way to teach a class at the Yale law school, I found on the sidewalk outside the building heaps of smoldering books that had been burned in the law library. They were a small symbol of what was happening on campuses across the nation: violence, destruction of property, mindless hatred of law, authority, and tradition. I stood there, uncomprehending, as a photograph in the next day's *New York Times* clearly showed. What did they want, these students? What conceivable goals led them to this and to the general havoc they were wreaking on the university? Living in the Sixties, my faculty colleagues and I had no understanding of what it was all about, where it came from, or how long the misery would last. It was only much later that a degree of understanding came.

Bork viewed the 1950s and 1960s as sources of everything that he reviled—including Bill and Hillary.

We noticed (who could help but notice?) Elvis Presley, rock music, James Dean, the radical sociologist C. Wright Mills, Jack Kerouac and the Beats. We did not understand, however, that far from being isolated curiosities, these were harbingers of a new culture that would shortly burst upon us and sweep us into a different country. The Fifties were the years of Eisenhower's presidency. Our domestic world seemed normal and, for the most part, almost placid. The signs were misleading. Politics is a lagging indicator. Culture eventually makes politics. The cultural seepages of the Fifties strengthened and became a torrent that swept through the nation in the Sixties. . . . The spirit of the Sixties revived in the Eighties and brought us at last to Bill and Hillary Clinton, the very personifications of the Sixties generation arrived at early middle age with its ideological baggage intact.

What Bork described as "ideological baggage" emerged from our generation's experience with the civil rights movement, the Vietnam War, and Richard Nixon. We were weaned on the moral necessity of remedying abuses of power. The antitrust movement that began more than a century ago had similar roots. Bork was unable to understand that.

He died in December 2012.

PART III

The Giant U-Turn

The Worst Memo in
American History

In 1971, unbeknownst to me at the time, the U.S. Chamber of Commerce asked Lewis Powell, then an attorney in Richmond, Virginia (and future Supreme Court justice), to report on the political activities of the left. Richard Nixon was still president, but the Chamber (along with some prominent Republicans like Powell) worried about the left's effects on "free enterprise."

Powell's memo, distributed widely to Chamber members, argued that the American economic system was "under broad attack" from consumer, labor, and environmental groups. These groups were doing nothing more than enforcing the implicit social contract that had emerged at the end of World War II, ensuring that corporations were responsive to *all* their stakeholders, not just their shareholders but also their workers, their consumers, and the environment on which everyone depends. But Powell and the Chamber saw it differently.

Powell urged businesses to mobilize for political combat: "Business must learn the lesson . . . that political power is necessary; that such power must be assiduously cultivated; and that when necessary, it must be used aggressively and with determination—without embarrassment and without the reluctance which has been so characteristic of American business." He stressed that the critical ingredients for success were organization and funding: "Strength lies in . . . the scale of financing available only through joint effort, and in the political power available only through united action and national organizations."

On August 23, 1971, the Chamber distributed Powell's memo to leading CEOs, large businesses, and trade associations. It had exactly the impact the Chamber sought, galvanizing corporate America into action and releasing a tidal wave of corporate money into American politics. The memo caused CEOs and Wall Street bankers to cough up huge amounts of money to finance the campaigns of members of Congress who would do their bidding. All the moneyed entities had to follow suit lest they find themselves at a disadvantage politically and, assuming the money would change the rules of the game, economically.

An entire corporate-political complex was born, including tens of thousands of lobbyists, lawyers, political operatives, and public relations flacks. Within a few decades, big corporations would become the largest political force in Washington and most state capitals. The number of corporate political action committees (PACs) mushroomed from under 300 in 1976 to over 1,200 by 1980. Between 1974 and 1980, the Chamber of Commerce doubled its membership. (This was thirty years before the Supreme Court, in its infamous *Citizens United* decision, decided that corporations are people under the First Amendment, thereby opening the floodgates even further to big money in politics.) It didn't matter whether a Democrat or Republican occupied the White House. The corporate-political complex continued to expand.

By the 1990s, when I became secretary of labor, corporations employed some 61,000 people to lobby for them, including registered lobbyists and lawyers. That came to more than a hundred lobbyists for each member of Congress. Corporate money also supported platoons of lawyers who represented corporations and the very rich in court, often outgunning the Justice Department and state attorneys general, and small armies of public relations flacks who sought to turn public opinion against corporate critics and regulators. Trade associations, law firms, lobbying firms, political operatives, and public relations specialists swarmed Washington, offering their partners and executives so much money that, by 2024, half of all retiring members of Congress were joining the corporate-political complex.

Between the late 1970s and the late 1980s, corporate PACs increased their expenditures on congressional races nearly *fivefold*. Labor union PAC spending rose only about half as fast. By the 2016 campaign cycle, corporations and Wall Street contributed $34 for every $1 donated by labor unions and all public interest organizations combined.

I saw Washington change. When I arrived there in 1974 to work with Robert Bork, Washington was a rather seedy town. One of my favorite haunts was a dilapidated used furniture store just off Pennsylvania Avenue owned by a Fred Litwin, who had taken it over from his father. Fred sold me tables and lamps at bargain-basement prices and was a reliable source of hilarious gossip about the Washington bigwigs to whom he delivered furniture. A thin wisp of a balding man, Fred had a big heart and a keen sense of humor.

By the time I returned as secretary of labor in 1993, Washington had been transformed into a glittering center of corporate America— replete with elegant office buildings, fancy restaurants, pricey bistros, five-star hotels, major conference centers, beautiful town houses, and a booming real estate market that pushed Washington's poor, most of whom were Black, out of the increasingly upscale Northwest portion of the city and made two of Washington's adjoining counties among the wealthiest in the nation. There was no trace of Fred and his secondhand furniture store.

Big money in politics corrupted many lawmakers, who changed the rules of the economic game to favor the moneyed interests that financed their campaigns. In the following decades, laws attacking monopolies were defanged. Laws protecting workers' rights to unionize were diluted. Laws discouraging hostile takeovers were neutered. Laws allowing average people to reorganize their debts under bankruptcy were replaced by laws making it harder for average people to use bankruptcy to prevent banks foreclosing on their homes or garnishing their wages if they couldn't pay their student debts. (Those student debts had soared due in part to laws that dramatically cut state funding for higher education.)

Trade agreements were enacted that protected corporations' intellectual property and financial assets but not the jobs and wages of the people who had worked for those firms. Patents, trademarks, and copyrights were enlarged and extended—allowing pharmaceutical, high-tech, biotechnology, and entertainment corporations to preserve their monopolies longer, which meant higher prices for consumers (including the highest pharmaceutical costs of any advanced nation).

Corporate raiders (today dubbed "shareholder activists" and "private equity managers") were allowed to mount hostile takeovers of large corporations, forcing CEOs to abandon all *other* stakeholders. Hence, corporations busted unions. (The unionized portion of the American workforce dropped from 35 percent of all private-sector workers in the 1950s to 6 percent today.) They cut jobs and wages. They moved production abroad. They even eliminated pensions. (The portion of workers with pensions fell from just over half in 1979 to under 35 percent by 2024.)

Laws preventing Wall Street from gambling with other people's money were repealed, allowing high-paid bankers to expose Americans to extraordinary economic risks—which came to a head in the financial crisis of 2008 and the taxpayer-funded bailout of large Wall Street firms. Securities laws were relaxed to allow more insider trading of confidential information, and permit corporations to manipulate stock prices through stock buybacks. CEOs were allowed to use buybacks to boost share prices and cash in their stock options. Contract laws were altered to require mandatory arbitration before private judges selected by big corporations.

Taxes on corporations and wealthy individuals were slashed, while additional tax loopholes were enacted for partners of hedge funds and private equity funds, for the oil and gas industry, Big Pharma, Wall Street, Big Agriculture, and Big Tech. When I was in high school, the top income tax rate had been over 90 percent. Today, it's less than 40 percent. Meanwhile, a growing portion of government revenue came from Social Security taxes, sales taxes, property taxes, and user fees (such as tolls), all of which took larger portions out of the pay of working-class and poor people than of the wealthy.

These and thousands of other policy decisions were pushed by wealthy elites on Wall Street and in corporate C-suites, who made mammoth donations to politicians on both sides of the aisle—mostly but not exclusively Republican—to ensure that their wishes would be honored. As these changes, and thousands like them, went into effect, wealth and power shifted upward.

I saw the consequences, but it was many years before I understood why it had happened. Powell's memorandum to the Chamber of Commerce unleashed a form of economic bullying less visible than the bullying I was subjected to as a boy but no less brutal in its ultimate result. I've shared with you my abiding faith that a civil society uses laws to constrain bullies. When economic bullies set the laws, civility is undermined.

Ironically, Powell wrote his memo the same year that Harvard philosopher John Rawls wrote *A Theory of Justice,* in which he argued that a fair allocation of wealth and power in a democratic capitalist society would be one to which we would agree if we thought about the characteristics of a fair system under a "veil of ignorance" as to what our own position would be in it. We'd never approve of slavery since *we* might be enslaved. We'd want to lift more children out of poverty because *our* children might be impoverished. By the same logic, and in direct contradiction to Lewis Powell's recommendations to the Chamber of Commerce, we would not give CEOs and Wall Street investment bankers more political power since this might disempower *us.* We wouldn't allow unbridled election spending by corporations and wealthy individuals—in effect, legalized bribery—because this would make democracy less responsive to *our* needs and wants.

Under a veil of ignorance, argued Rawls, we'd choose two basic principles. First, we'd decide to protect our most important personal and political liberties. After all, if we didn't know who we'd end up being in a society, we wouldn't want to risk being persecuted for our religious beliefs or sexual preferences or denied the right to vote because of the color of our skin or our gender. Second, we'd want to live in a society where everyone has an equal chance to succeed regardless of their race, class, or gender. We'd accept inequalities only if they benefited everyone, and we'd try to organize society to maximize the life chances of the least well-off among us.

Rawls's argument struck me as so reasonable and persuasive that I bought his book for many friends and arranged dinners where we could discuss it while at law school. One recurring question among us was, Who is included in the "we" who contemplate a fair system under Rawls's veil of ignorance? Is the "we" limited to full citizens, or does it include undocumented people? Inhabitants of the nation or everyone in the world? Another question was where this thought experiment was supposed to occur. Was it intuitive and subconscious in all of us, or more likely found in the musings of people specifically vested with responsibility for determining fairness, such as judges and justices?

Rawls's book was influential in colleges and universities, but Powell's memo was influential in Washington, the center of power in America, where the moneyed interests and the lawmakers they courted did not operate under a "veil of ignorance" about where they'd come out if the outcomes they sought were put into effect. They knew exactly how they'd fare. Rawls's theory of fairness proved no match for Powell's invitation to engage in legalized bribery and mass corruption. Rarely before in American history has one document— the Powell memorandum—had such nefarious consequences. By unleashing big money into American politics, it distorted American democracy and shifted power upward in a way that would have appalled John Rawls.

The Truth About Jimmy Carter

After two years at the Justice Department, I took a job at the Federal Trade Commission as one of Jimmy Carter's political appointees. I met him only twice, once at a Rose Garden ceremony and years later at a dinner party at the home of Senator Dianne Feinstein. On the latter occasion, Carter was uncharacteristically late for dinner because he had taken a nap in an upstairs bedroom. He apologized profusely. "I'm getting old and need my nap, but I should have told someone," he said with a self-effacing grin.

For years, it's been said that Carter's presidency failed but his *post-*presidency was the best in modern history. That's too simplistic. Carter's life after his presidency was exemplary for the same reason that he was elected president: his modesty, decency, and humanity. Not only were these traits the opposite of Richard Nixon's but they would shine even brighter forty years later in contrast to the loathsome Donald Trump.

One-term presidents are always presumed failures because voters chose not to reelect them. But Carter lost his reelection bid (as would George H. W. Bush twelve years later) not because his presidency failed but because the Federal Reserve Board—mandated by Congress to keep prices as stable as possible, normally by controlling short-term interest rates—raised interest rates so high as to bring on a recession. During Carter's term of office, the OPEC oil cartel increased oil prices from $13 a barrel to over $34, resulting in double-digit price increases across the economy. Paul Volcker, Carter's appointee as Fed chair, determined to "break the back of inflation," hiked interest rates to nearly 20 percent by 1981, bringing on a deep recession and causing millions of people to lose their jobs—including Carter.

Many of Carter's initiatives—ending funding for the B-1 bomber; seeking a comprehensive consumer-protection bill; proposing broad-based tax reform; opposing traditional "pork barrel" spending; establishing a "superfund" to clean up toxic waste sites; and deregulating the airline, trucking, and railroad industries (resulting in lower transportation costs for industry and consumers)—were commendable. At the same time, he appointed consumer, labor, and environmental advocates to his administration, which seemed to confirm Lewis Powell's warning to corporate America in 1971 that corporations must bulk up their lobbying muscle in Washington or suffer political defeat.

My boss at the FTC was Michael Pertschuk, an energetic and charismatic chairman. Consumer advocate Joan Claybrook chaired the National Highway Traffic Safety Commission. Other friends and followers of Ralph Nader were spread throughout the administration. All were ready to battle big corporations that for years had been deceiving or injuring consumers.

Yet almost everything we initiated at the FTC, and just about everything undertaken by these activists elsewhere in the administration, was met by unexpectedly fierce political resistance from Congress. At one point, when the FTC began examining advertising directed at children, Congress stopped funding the agency altogether, scuttling it for weeks. Washington lobbyists for advertisers, broadcast television, cereal and candy manufacturers, and the sugar industry had organized seemingly overnight to stop the FTC's efforts.

It was the first of many Republican-initiated government shutdowns. I was dumbfounded. I still didn't understand the power shift that was occurring. The untold story of the Carter years is the vast increase in corporate political firepower in the wake of the Powell memo.

With the defeat of Carter's consumer protection legislation in 1978 at the hands of corporate lobbyists, Richard Lesher, then president of the U.S. Chamber of Commerce, presciently boasted: "Thirty to forty years from now people will look back and say 'These were the years when the transition took place.' . . . We're waking up. And big business is going to be in the forefront of this drive." He was right. Big business was behind America's giant U-turn. Perhaps Carter could have prevented all this had he been more politically cunning, but I doubt it. Despite Carter's best efforts, big business paved the way for Ronald Reagan and America's return to the corporate capitalism that had dominated the nation before the Great Depression and Franklin D. Roosevelt. Jimmy Carter died December 29, 2024, at the age of one hundred.

Reagan fired me, and every other Carter appointee. That was to be expected. Political appointees are different from permanent civil servants—more power, less job security. Yet Reagan was far from a traditional Republican in the mold of Dwight Eisenhower or Thomas Dewey. He told Americans that government was the problem. It was one of the most damaging things Reagan did because only government can fix certain public problems. He thereby eroded public confidence in the whole project of self-government. He also brought show business to the office of the presidency. His simplistic, distorted patriotism—seeing America as the rider on a white horse at the top of the hill—appealed to many Americans (and still does).

Before I left the FTC, two young professors from Harvard's Kennedy School came to visit me, asking if I might be interested in joining the faculty. A life of teaching and researching hadn't previously occurred to me. But when Harvard Law School offered my then wife a position at the same time, the decision became easy. We'd head for Cambridge, Massachusetts.

Looking back, I'm grateful. Harvard gave me a chance to think through what I had learned about the structure of the economy and its relationship to the rising tide of corporate money. I could synthesize law, economics, and politics to understand the system, including what I witnessed as a massive shift in power toward the top. I had seen how corporate money was affecting decisions about how the market was organized, creating winners and losers.

But, I wondered, how could American workers adapt to the changing economy? The growing tide of big money in Washington increased the profits of large corporations but did nothing to help workers adapt to the inevitable shift from an industrial to a knowledge-based system. Surely, the American economy was more than the sum of the profits of American corporations. While at Harvard, I began interviewing CEOs, visiting worksites, talking with various groups of workers, and investigating the emergence of a high-tech corridor around Boston. I started writing articles about what I was seeing and learning, how the economy was changing and why we needed an industrial policy that included workers and aimed at the common good.

Harvard also gave me the chance to know Ken Galbraith.

My Six-Foot, Eight-Inch
Mentor and Friend

No one has influenced my thinking and my sense of what a public life could be more than John Kenneth (he preferred to be called Ken) Galbraith. Ken had run the Office of Price Administration in World War II. John F. Kennedy appointed him ambassador to India. He was often consulted by national leaders, especially Democrats, and he gave his advice freely, though it may have been ignored as often as it was taken.

He was the most widely read economist of the twentieth century—forty-six books that together sold more than seven million cop-

ies, not one of them a textbook—as well as one of America's most engaged and celebrated public intellectuals. Many of his compelling phrases—among them "the affluent society," "conventional wisdom," and "countervailing power"—became part of our language. I had read his books in high school and college, and they formed the basis of my understanding of how the world worked. I gulped down *American Capitalism: The Concept of Countervailing Power* (1952), *The Affluent Society* (1958), and *The New Industrial State* (1968). His writing was urbane and witty, fluid, even on complex subjects, and his arguments were richly provocative, especially to a young person curious about the system.

Ken didn't regard economics as a form of applied mathematics. He understood it as embedded in politics, sociology, history, and moral philosophy. He was fascinated by power—who had it, how they used it, how it was countered by others. In this, he drew from earlier traditions: In the eighteenth century, thinkers like Adam Smith called themselves "moral philosophers"; in the nineteenth century, the study of economics was called "political economy."

I had never aspired to a career like Ken's, but here I was on the Harvard faculty after years of public service, advising Democrats on what they should do. I responded to Ronald Reagan's brainless and ineffective trickle-down economics with articles advancing the idea that public investments in the American workforce—in their education, training, and health, and in the infrastructure linking them together—were critical to the future competitiveness of the nation. I argued for an industrial policy that would shift the American economy to the technologies of the future rather than simply maintain the status quo, and bring most Americans along with it. Ken was eager to discuss all of this, and more. We began meeting regularly for lunch. He was then seventy-six, with more energy and intellect than people half his age.

Larry Summers represented the other extreme on the Harvard economics faculty. Squat and rotund with a round face and sharp nose, and definitive views that he communicated by waving his arms and nearly shouting, Larry stood out almost as much as I did. He was not exactly conservative, but he espoused all the conventional wisdom of modern economics. We often met for lunch at the Wurst Haus on Harvard Square, and I looked forward to our discussions. He could almost always tear apart with vivid metaphors and rapier logic the weakest parts of my arguments. Our lunches were great fun.

Although Larry had never served in government, he was dismissive of my ideas about industrial policy. He said government couldn't possibly push the economy toward emerging industries such as semiconductors or help workers adapt to the new economy and shouldn't even try to "pick winners." When I asked him how he developed his understanding of what government could and couldn't do, he answered that such things should be obvious to anyone. Ken, on the other hand, understood that with the amounts of money corporations were starting to pour into politics, absent an explicit industrial policy government would be at the mercy of the largest and most powerful corporate interests, which would get government subsidies, loan guarantees, trade protection, and lax antitrust enforcement— everything that was necessary to increase their wealth and power. Most workers, indeed, most of the public, would be left out.

Ken was an imposing presence, lanky and angular at six feet, eight inches tall. I was four feet, eleven inches (now even shorter). The gap didn't much matter when we were dining together, but *vertical* conversations—say, walking along the streets of Cambridge, or in his backyard at his annual commencement party—were always challenging (and becoming more so as he became hard of hearing). Our *average* height was five foot nine, but that was irrelevant. When the distribution of anything becomes widely disparate, talk of "averages" can mislead.

So it was with American incomes. Although the *average* American's income was much higher by 2000 than it had been nearly a half century before when Ken wrote *The Affluent Society,* the *typical* American couldn't afford to pay higher taxes because his own income had barely increased for decades. Most gains had gone to the top. By then, America had the most unequal distribution of income among all advanced countries, and inequality was increasing further and faster than in any comparable nation.

Ken didn't want to focus on income inequalities among individuals, lest we lose sight of the more crucial battle to improve the "social balance" between the production of private goods and the supply of public amenities. I disagreed. I thought it was impossible to achieve a better social balance without addressing income inequality. When he wrote *The Affluent Society,* in 1958, Ken had assumed that income inequality would continue to decline as the rising economic tide lifted all boats. The book appeared in the middle of a historic, some might say unique, shift: between 1950 and 1978, families in the top fifth of income doubled their intake, adjusted for inflation, but families in the bottom fifth did even *better.* As Ken wrote then:

> The first reason inequality has faded as an issue is that it has not been showing the expected tendency to get worse. And thus the Marxian prediction, which earlier in this century seemed so amply confirmed by observation, no longer inspires the same depth of fear. It no longer seems likely that the ownership of the tangible assets of the republic and the disposal of its income will pass into a negligible number of hands despite the approving sentiment of those who would abandon the progressive income tax or widen its present loopholes. Meanwhile there has been a modest reduction in the proportion of disposable income going to those in the very highest income brackets and a larger increase in the proportion accruing to people in the middle and lower brackets. Full employment and upward pressure on wages have increased well-being at the bottom.

But, starting in the late 1970s, the trend reversed. The economic tide continued to rise, but it lifted only the pleasure craft; the row-boats were barely staying afloat. The median income, which had risen steadily along with productivity gains during the three decades after the Second World War, stopped rising. More of the nation's income was becoming concentrated in the hands of a few at the top, and wealth was becoming even more concentrated than income. Upward mobility could no longer be taken for granted. The American middle class started to shrink.

Cumulative percent change in real annual wages, by wage group, 1979–2022

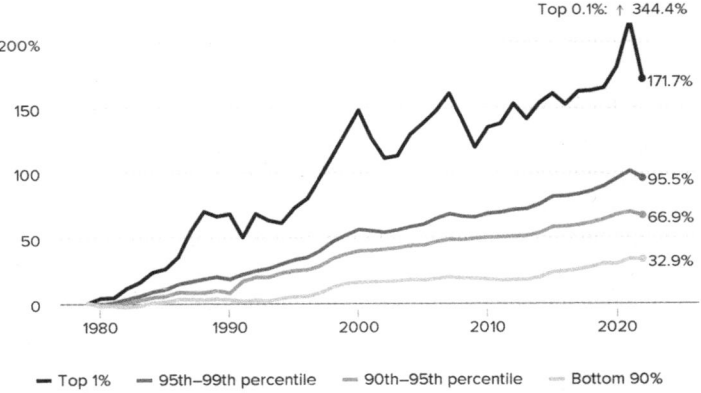

Source: EPI analysis of Kopczuk, Saez, and Song, "Uncovering the American Dream: Inequality and Mobility in Social Security Earnings Data Since 1937" (2007) and Social Security Administration wage statistics.

Economic Policy Institute

This didn't have to be the case. Steps could have been taken so the economy continued to work for everyone. The nation could have invested substantially more in the education and healthcare of average workers. It could have attracted new industries to communities in danger of being abandoned. It could have prevented corporations from busting unions and outsourcing large numbers of jobs abroad. It could have fortified safety nets and stopped Wall Street from gambling with millions of people's savings, homes, and jobs. But many of the laws that were subsequently enacted, starting with Ronald Reagan's giant tax cuts that disproportionately benefited the rich, did the opposite, causing inequality to widen further—eventually fanning anger and resentment at a system deemed increasingly unfair. Ken's social balance was becoming ever more elusive.

Yet Ken and I knew that the fundamental question wasn't the size of government. It was whose side it was on. We agreed that Reagan's so-called supply-side tax cut was wrongheaded. The highest marginal income tax rate had been 70 percent when Reagan took office. He dropped it to 50 percent in 1982 and then to 28 percent in 1989. Since then, it has never risen above 39.6 percent. Reagan also cut taxes on inheritances, corporate profits, and capital gains. The net result was a dramatic decline in total tax payments by the wealthy and the start of an explosion in the federal deficit and debt. In effect, America's wealthy went from supporting government through their tax payments to supporting it through lending it money.

Meanwhile, in firing the air traffic controllers for going on strike (to be sure, they had no legal right to strike), Reagan legitimized the practice of fighting labor unions—in effect pushing America back to before the enactment of the National Labor Relations Act in 1935.

Overall, Reagan's economic record was lousy. Under the broadest measure of economic success—the growth of total output divided by the size of the population—the economy did better under the Kennedy and Johnson administrations than under Reagan. It also did better under Franklin D. Roosevelt. Under Reagan, inequality surged.

Ken had undaunted optimism about American capitalism. Always lurking within it, he argued, were corrective forces that would put back into balance whatever may temporarily have gone awry. He conceded that large corporations were coming to dominate every industry, but he believed that over the long term, the system would achieve a balance between the private interests of those corporations and the public's interest in the common good.

I was skeptical. It seemed to me that America had already entered a vicious cycle in which the power of giant corporations, as well as Wall Street and wealthy individuals, was increasing, their growing influence over the rules of the game siphoning ever more wealth and power to the top. He countered that as the nation became wealthier, it had more capacity to achieve social balance. When the Cold War ended, which both of us assumed would happen soon, America would have even more capacity for social balance as it shifted from military to civilian needs.

When Bill Clinton was elected president, Ken and I expected him to lead the charge toward a better social balance. During his campaign Clinton had promised major spending on education, job training, "lifelong learning," and social insurance that would help American workers adapt to the new economy—the agenda I had been urging. When Clinton asked me to run his economic transition team, Ken was delighted. When Clinton asked me to join his cabinet as labor secretary, Ken was exuberant. "Now you'll have a chance to put in place everything you've been advocating," he told me over coffee in the oval dining room of his house. "We shall have social balance! How wonderful!" But Clinton's Wall Street advisers—chiefly Robert Rubin, who had been co-chairman of Goldman Sachs before joining the administration as director of the National Economic Council—were adamant that before Clinton could do anything else, he had to reduce the budget deficit, which Clinton did over the next four years. The bar was lifted again in 1995 when Newt Gingrich, then the Republican Speaker of the House, along with several Democrats, threatened to seek a constitutional amendment to balance the budget. To forestall it, Clinton postponed his agenda once again, until the budget was, in fact, balanced. Far from the social balance that Ken had advocated, the balanced federal budget would exclude all sorts of things Americans needed.

A few years later, when the federal budget showed a surplus, Ken was certain the time had come. "Splendid! Clinton can now do what he promised for social balance!" I wasn't sure there was political will for it. By then I was out of the administration, and Rubin and his protégé at the Treasury Department, Larry Summers, were the loudest economic voices inside. Ever optimistic, Ken prophesied that to win the 2000 election, Democrats would have no choice but to propose a bold social agenda. Instead, the bar was lifted once again. Afraid that the Republicans would use the surplus to reduce the national debt, Bill, at the urging of Rubin and Summers, urged that the surplus be used to "rescue" Social Security (which was facing insolvency because of anticipated spending on the retirements of baby boomers). Yet Social Security could be made fully solvent forever if the cap was removed on incomes subject to Social Security taxes. Al Gore, running for president, agreed with Rubin and Summers. So much for social balance.

Ken and I discussed the possibilities for a progressive wealth tax, which he thought Gore and the Democrats should push for. I agreed, but I feared they were so dependent on campaign funding from the wealthy (including large corporations and Wall Street) that they would not. The public, meanwhile, was becoming ever more convinced of the Reagan Republican view that government was the problem, mainly because Democrats—dependent as they were on campaign funding from big corporations and the rich—weren't telling the public the truth: the *real* problem was an ever more lopsided distribution of income and wealth, driven largely by the moneyed interests. The public's growing cynicism about government was in stark contrast to the public's attitude when *The Affluent Society* was published. As Ken wrote then, "in the last half century, the power and prestige of the US government have increased. If only by the process of division, this has diminished the prestige of the power accruing to private wealth."

In *The New Industrial State,* Ken even envisioned government as part of an industrial "planning system," sharing responsibility with large corporations for determining the direction of the economy. To make sure the common good was fully considered, he urged that "the educational and scientific estate" take more political leadership. But Ken's hope for such leadership had not borne much fruit. Over the years, the professoriate had become more specialized and technical. Economists, most of whose theories were expressed in mathematical formulae and grounded in "rational self-interest," tended to overlook the values of community, mutual obligation, and compassion, or the centrality of political power in determining how the market functioned.

Rational self-interest might explain much that people do, but it offers only limited guidance for determining what society should try to accomplish. In one of our last conversations, Ken and I talked about America's lack of social cohesion. Americans no longer faced the common perils of Depression, hot war, or cold war, which almost all citizens had experienced directly or indirectly in the middle years of the twentieth century when Ken had written his most influential books. These common perils created a palpable sense of mutual dependence and shared responsibility, which exacted sacrifices for the common good. But in the emerging global economy, those who were better educated or wealthier were not nearly as dependent on their compatriots. They were linked by modem and fax to the great financial or commercial centers of the world. Social cohesion also depends on "it could happen to me" thinking—as in John Rawls's theory of fairness. Support for social insurance, education, and infrastructure depends on widely shared risks. But America's wealthy knew they would be fine, regardless. They also knew that achieving any social balance for the rest of society would require large tax increases on them.

After the 2000 election, when I again met with Ken in his oval dining room, I detected for the first time a slight gloom in him. "What happened to your Democrats?" he asked, emphasizing the "your" as if he no longer had any stake in the party. "The nation is richer than ever! Surely . . ." His voice trailed off. He was by then ninety-two years old—still formidable, still writing, still sending letters off to politicians telling them what they should do. I explained that although America could easily afford and profit from a better social balance, balancing the federal budget had taken precedence.

The last time I saw Ken, he was bedridden. His voice had become a high chirp. I had to yell for him to hear me. But his mind was as sharp and subtle as ever, his activism as undeterred. When I entered his bedroom, he was writing a letter to George W. Bush, explaining why the president's idea for turning Social Security payments into personal investments on Wall Street—creating what Bush called the "ownership society"—would fail.

"Do you think Bush or even one of Bush's underlings will be persuaded?" I said loudly so Ken could hear me.

"Not at all," he said.

"Then why write the letter?" I asked, genuinely curious.

"It's therapeutic for me!" he said and then grinned.

Ken died on April 29, 2006, at the age of ninety-seven.

Two years later, Wall Street imploded, nearly taking the world economy with it.

When I Became a Feminist

Harvard was becoming more difficult to endure. It wasn't just that my writings were provoking envy at the higher reaches of the faculty (my skin was thick enough to survive that), but some of them seemed so insecure about their own standing that they looked for ways to lower mine. One even berated my assistant for answering my phone "Professor Reich's office" because I was not a full professor.

My then wife was experiencing much the same at Harvard Law School, where the arrogance came mixed with sexism. I knew misogyny existed—I had witnessed Anita Hill's excruciating treatment by the Senate Judiciary Committee—but I assumed sexism was the product of backward and parochial cultures. It might show up in an entrenched Senate committee dominated by an old-boy network or in working-class neighborhoods where Rambo still reigned, but I didn't expect to encounter such noxious bias in the overwhelmingly liberal, intellectual, worldly, and high-minded university community we inhabited. Surely, such bullying would not be tolerated here.

Yet a string of males had been voted tenure at the law school and my wife hadn't. Most had not written as much as she had, nor had their writings engendered as much praise from specialists around the nation as hers had. In addition, none of their writings had been subject to the same detailed scrutiny, footnote by footnote, to which the senior faculty—all men—had subjected her latest manuscript. Not one of the male candidates had aroused the degree of anger and bitterness that characterized the fight over her tenure.

I was bewildered. I knew most of the men who voted against her, a few of whom were narrow-minded. One or two I suspected of misogyny. But most were thoughtful and intelligent, read widely, traveled widely, had held positions of responsibility and trust. I was sure that they felt they had been fair and impartial in judging her work. They would be appalled at any suggestion of gender bias.

Gradually, I came to understand. They would be aghast to think they were sexist bullies. They were applying their standard of scholarship as impartially as they knew how. But they assumed that the person to whom they applied their standard had gone through the same training with the same formative intellectual experiences, and the same understanding of society, as they had. Yet my wife had been shaped in part by the irrefutable reality of gender. The perspectives she brought to bear on the world of ideas were different from theirs because she had experienced the world differently. It was the very uniqueness of her female perspective that animated her scholarship and gave it its intellectual bite.

Had they been able and willing to expand their standard, not to compromise it but to broaden it to include a woman's way of knowing, they might have recognized what she accomplished. But they didn't try. Moreover, she had not laughed at the jokes of the older men on the faculty, massaged their egos, or pretended to be one of them, speaking loudly and talking tough. To the contrary, she made them uncomfortable.

This was 1987. There are now far more tenured women on law school faculties. Women are university presidents. Sixty percent of American undergraduates are now women. But sexism, on university faculties and everywhere else, is still very much with us.

After the vote, my wife remained as confident of the worth of her scholarship and of herself as before. Many women colleagues, and many men, rallied to her cause. There were student demonstrations. The Equal Employment Opportunity Commission brought a lawsuit against Harvard, and she won a generous settlement, which she invested in an institute to combat domestic violence. She was offered a faculty position elsewhere, accepted it, and found a professional home.

The experience shook me. I began to notice things that I'd ignored previously. A recruiter for a large company called to ask about a student of mine who was being considered for a job. "Does she plan to have a family?" he asked. "Is she, er, serious about a career?" A male colleague was critical of a young woman assistant professor when we met to consider offering her tenure: "She's not assertive enough in the classroom." Then another male colleague said about the same young woman, "I find her very abrasive." I couldn't help wondering whether these characterizations reflected how my two male colleagues felt about women in general—their wives, mothers, or girlfriends— rather than about this young woman. At a board meeting of a small nonprofit foundation, a female director tried to express doubts about a pending decision, but several loquacious men repeatedly interrupted her. Even after she finally stated her objection, her concerns were ignored, as if she had never raised them.

If being a "feminist" means seeing these sorts of things, I became a feminist the day my wife was denied tenure. But my responsibility beyond merely noticing was, at the very least, to remind recruiters that they shouldn't be asking about whether prospective female employees want to have a family, to warn male colleagues against sexual biases in their evaluations of female colleagues, and to make sure that women who voice concerns and comments in meetings are listened to. In other words, just as I had to educate myself, I had to help educate other men.

This was no small task. The day after the Harvard Law faculty voted against offering my wife tenure, I phoned one of the curmudgeons who had voted against her and without the slightest sense of irony called him—in the tradition of Ed Reich—a son of a bitch.

The Raiders of the Lost Economy

My skepticism about American capitalism—in contrast to Ken's confidence in its "corrective forces"—was compounded by so-called corporate raiders who were mounting hostile takeovers of corporations, financed by risky bonds. The raiders were making fortunes, Wall Street was becoming the most powerful force in the economy, and CEOs had begun to devote themselves entirely and obsessively to maximizing the short-term value of their shares of stock. The new rule was: Do whatever it takes to make huge profits and maximize shareholder returns.

Before then it was assumed that large corporations had responsibilities to all their "stakeholders," including their workers and communities, not just their shareholders. "The job of management," proclaimed Frank Abrams, chairman of Standard Oil of New Jersey, in a 1951 address, "is to maintain an equitable and working balance among the claims of the various directly affected interest groups . . . stockholders, employees, customers, and the public at large." In November 1956, *Time* magazine noted that business leaders were willing to "judge their actions, not only from the standpoint of profit and loss but of profit and loss to the community." (I'm sure Abrams would have agreed.) CEOs had become "corporate statesmen," responsible for the common good of the nation. General Electric, the magazine noted, sought to serve the "balanced best interests" of all its stakeholders. As J. D. Zellerbach, chair of Crown Zellerbach, one of America's largest producers of paper, told *Time*, Americans "regard business management as a stewardship, and they expect it to operate the economy as a public trust for the benefit of all the people."

These sentiments may seem quaint today, but in the three decades after World War II they laid the basis for rapid economic growth and, with strong unions, an equally rapid expansion of the American middle class. They reflected the views of many corporate executives who had endured the Great Depression and the war along with the rest of the nation and felt some responsibility for America's future well-being. These views were in sharp contrast with the dominant views of corporate executives before World War II and the views of executives today. But in the early postwar decades they helped legitimize the role of the large corporation in the public's mind.

Ken shared these views about the large corporation and its leadership. But the corporate raiders—Michael Milken, Ivan Boesky, Carl Icahn, and others—believed that the only legitimate goal of the corporation was to maximize share prices. They targeted companies that could deliver higher returns to shareholders if the companies abandoned their *other* stakeholders—by fighting unions, cutting workers' pay or firing them, automating as many jobs as possible, and abandoning their original communities by shuttering factories and moving jobs to states with lower labor costs, or moving them abroad. The raiders pushed shareholders to vote out directors who wouldn't make these sorts of changes and vote in directors who would (or else sell their shares to the raiders, who'd do the dirty work).

The raiders did not happen by accident. They were the result of changes in laws promoted by corporate and Wall Street executives who saw a chance to make a lot more money, and who armed themselves with platoons of lobbyists and corporate campaign donations—another legacy of Lewis Powell's 1971 memo to the U.S. Chamber of Commerce.

In 1974, at the urging of pension funds, insurance companies, and Wall Street, Congress enacted the Employee Retirement Income Security Act. Before then, pension funds and insurance companies could only invest in high-grade corporate and government bonds. Now they could invest in the less reliable but often more profitable stock market, thereby making a huge pool of capital available to Wall Street financiers.

In 1982, more capital became available when Congress gave savings-and-loan banks, the bedrocks of local home mortgage markets, permission to invest their deposits in a wide range of financial products, including "junk" bonds that promised investors high returns for lending to enterprises that posed a higher than normal risk of not being able to pay back the loans. Government insurance of savings-and-loan banks against losses made these investments hugely tempting, and ultimately cost taxpayers some $124 billion when many of those banks went bust. Meanwhile, the Reagan administration loosened other banking and financial regulations. All this allowed corporate raiders to get the capital and the regulatory approvals necessary to mount unfriendly takeovers of companies whose management didn't want to be taken over.

In 1985, after winning control of the now-defunct Trans World Airlines, Carl Icahn stripped its assets, pocketed nearly $500 million in profits, and left the airline more than $500 million in debt. Former TWA chair C. E. Meyer, Jr., called Icahn "one of the greediest men on earth." Another of Icahn's raids involved RJR Nabisco, the food and tobacco giant, which he pushed to spin off its food business, leading Icahn to make a cool $884 million when he sold his stock in late 2000. Toward the end of his career, Icahn estimated that his activist campaigns at a dozen companies, including Apple, eBay, PayPal, Forest Labs, Xerox, Herbalife, and Netflix, had helped generate $300 billion in additional value for the shareholders of those companies. But the social costs of Icahn's deals fell on hundreds of thousands of people who lost their jobs, and hundreds of communities that lost their major employers. Few individuals have done more to harm America's working class than Icahn.

Not surprisingly, Icahn was a Trump backer from the start, and benefited immensely from his first presidency. Trump made Icahn his special regulatory adviser, until lawmakers raised concerns about potential conflicts of interest. Days before Trump announced hefty tariffs on foreign-made steel, Icahn sold off $31.3 million in stock he owned in the Manitowoc Company, an American manufacturer of steel cranes. Manitowoc and other American-based construction equipment manufacturers relied heavily on foreign steel in their manufacturing work, making Icahn's sale just before the tariff announcement look mighty suspicious. After the announcement, the company's shares tumbled. Icahn said he had no inside knowledge of Trump's move, but it was hard to believe him. Trump's first presidency was awash in conflicts of interest, lies, payoffs to friends, insider deals, and utter disdain for the public. (His second would be even worse.)

Icahn's steel deal was chickenfeed relative to the billions Icahn pocketed courtesy of Trump's tax cut during his first administration. Icahn is said to have spent $150 million lobbying for it, which made it one of his best investments. In 2023, Forbes estimated Icahn's fortune at $18 billion.

During the 1970s there were only thirteen hostile takeovers of big companies valued at $1 billion or more. During the 1980s, there were one hundred fifty. Between 1979 and 1989, financial entrepreneurs mounted more than two thousand leveraged buyouts, in which they bought out shareholders with borrowed money, each transaction exceeding $250 million. The shareholders who sold out did well; the raiders did even better. The losers were workers who lost their jobs, communities that lost their core businesses, and a nation that had to cope with ever angrier politics.

CEOs across America who had managed their corporations for the benefit of all stakeholders now faced the possibility of being replaced by CEOs who would maximize shareholder value. Few events change minds more profoundly than the imminent possibility of being sacked. CEOs became so obsessed by shareholder value that Roberto Goizueta, CEO of Coca-Cola, proclaimed in 1988 that he "wrestle[d] with how to build shareholder value from the time I get up in the morning to the time I go to bed. I even think about it when I am shaving." Goizueta's obsession was quite different from the views of his predecessor, Coca-Cola's president William Robinson, who in 1959 told an audience at Fordham Law School that executives should *not* put stockholders first. They should "balance the interests of the stockholder, the community, the customer, and the employee."

The easiest and most direct way for CEOs to increase profits and share prices is to cut costs—especially payrolls, which are the largest single expense for most firms. The nearly exclusive focus of the corporate butchers of the 1980s and 1990s was, in the meat-ax parlance that became fashionable then, to "cut out the fat," "cut to the bone," and make their companies "lean and mean." I began writing articles, op-eds, and books pointing out that the raiders were forcing a profound change in the purpose of the corporation that would generate huge social costs. Workers who lost good, unionized jobs would have to settle for lower-paying and less stable jobs in the service sector. Communities that had grown up around major corporations would be abandoned. Large swaths of the Midwest would be emptied.

Ken and I spent long hours discussing all this. He continued to believe that large corporations would over the long term reflect the interests and needs of all stakeholders. I disagreed. I pointed to Jack Welch, who took the helm of GE in 1981, when the company was valued by the stock market at less than $14 billion and retired in 2001 when GE was worth about $400 billion. Welch had increased the value of GE shares largely by cutting payrolls. Before his tenure, most GE employees had spent their entire careers with the company; between 1981 and 1985, a quarter of them—one hundred thousand people—lost their jobs, earning Welch the moniker "neutron Jack." Even when times were good, Welch encouraged his senior managers to replace 10 percent of their subordinates every year to keep GE competitive.

Other CEOs tried to outdo Welch. In the early 1990s, by the time I was labor secretary, Scott Paper hired Al Dunlap as CEO. Within Dunlap's first two years at the helm, the company's stock price rose some 200 percent and the value of the company (measured by the total value of outstanding shares) grew from $2.5 billion in 1993 to $9 billion in 1995. Dunlap accomplished this by firing over 70 percent of upper management employees and trimming more than 11,200 jobs from the payroll for a total reduction of 35 percent. Another 6,000 jobs were transferred to the payrolls of other companies when Dunlap sold non-core businesses. After this he was called, admiringly, "Chainsaw Al."

Dunlap rejected the idea that executives should manage companies for their "stakeholders." Not only did he fire a large portion of his workforce, but he also moved corporate headquarters from Philadelphia to Boca Raton, Florida, where Scott saved another $6 million each year in maintenance and climate-control costs. He authored a memoir outlining his strategy, entitled *Mean Business,* in which he stressed that "the most important person in any company is the shareholder," and the only legitimate goal was to "make money for the owners."

Dunlap then sold Scott Paper to Kimberly-Clark, creating the second largest consumer products company in the United States, and leaving Dunlap with $100 million after just twenty months in the job. I publicly criticized both Dunlap and Welch for treating American workers as costs to be cut rather than as assets to be developed. Dunlap countered that "the $100 million I got from Scott Paper was less than two percent of the wealth I created for all Scott shareholders. Did I earn that? Damn right I did."

I duked it out with Dunlap on Ted Koppel's ABC-TV show *Nightline.*

KOPPEL: . . . If the current trends continue, we can expect
to see the biggest businesses laying more people off at the
same time that government is less able to provide additional
support. . . . Mr. Dunlap, do you think that benign
leadership is workable at a large company?
DUNLAP: Here, the reason to be in business is to make
money for your *shareholders.* The shareholders *own* the

company. They take all the *risk*. No company ever gives the shareholders their money back when they go bust, and you have an awesome responsibility to see that they get the proper return for their risk.

KOPPEL: Mr. Secretary, isn't what's good for business in the long run good for the American people?

ME: Not necessarily, Ted. The stock market is soaring, but wages are stuck because people are scared to ask for a raise. They're afraid they may lose their job, and they don't have any bargaining leverage. . . . There are social consequences to all of this. It's not just a matter of maximizing shareholder returns.

KOPPEL: Mr. Dunlap?

DUNLAP: Business is not a social experiment. . . . And you know, socialism has failed the world over, yet we in America want to reinstitute socialism into our economic situations, and I think that's dead wrong.

KOPPEL: Are you proposing some form of socialism here, Mr. Secretary?

ME: I'm talking about *corporate responsibility*. Millions of Americans are trapped in the old economy. If the *public* sector can't help them because it has to balance the budget, then the private sector is going to have to do more. Corporate responsibility extends beyond maximizing shareholder returns. There's also a responsibility to employees and to communities.

DUNLAP: Number one, that is *not* the role of business. . . . And the *last* person that should arbitrate that is the *government*, the largest business in America with the worst balance sheet, the poorest management, services people don't want, and a bloated cost structure.

ME: We've got to think of society as a whole. America isn't simply a bunch of businesses. It's a group of people. If businesses are highly profitable, they *at least* owe it to their employees to upgrade their skills. And if they're downsizing, they have a responsibility to find their employees new jobs that pay as well. . . .

The cameras stopped, the klieg lights went off, and I rose out of my chair. A studio technician unfastened my microphone and earpiece. "I heard you just now," he said. "Right on."

"Thanks," I said, pulling up the cord from inside my shirt.

"This used to be a full-time job for me," he continued, "but the network laid me off six months ago. Now they call me back when they need me. I work three jobs with no benefits. All the networks are the same."

"That true for most employees?"

"Yup," he said, beginning to wind the cord. "Almost no one is on full-time payroll anymore. Camera crew, control room, makeup. We're all freelance. Even a lot of the producers are freelance. Giant corporations are buying and selling networks like playing cards. A few people at the top, making hundreds of millions. But the little guys like me don't count."

Chainsaw Al appeared from around the corner. I hadn't met him in person; during the program, he and I had talked into separate cameras from adjoining studios. Dunlap was built like a tank. He had been a boxer in college, and he still swaggered. He walked directly to me. He was flushed.

"Who the hell are *you* to talk about working people?" he barked, pointing his finger in my face. I half expected him to land me one on the jaw. "I was brought up in a working-class family. *You* had a silver spoon in your mouth!"

I wasn't ready for his assault. The unwritten rule of TV debates is that it's over when the lights and cameras are off. "You don't . . . know a thing . . . about me," I stammered. "Both my parents worked six days a week."

"That's not what my researchers say," he hissed.

"Then your researchers are incompetent. Fire them. You've fired everybody else."

He burst past me and out of the studio.

A few months later, in July 1996, Sunbeam's board hired Dunlap to revive the struggling home appliance maker. By then his reputation for delivering high share prices was well established. "I'm a superstar in my field, much like Michael Jordan in basketball and Bruce Springsteen in rock 'n' roll," Dunlap bragged in his memoir. Wall

Street seemed to agree. On the day his appointment was announced, Sunbeam's stock jumped 60 percent. After less than four months, Dunlap announced plans to eliminate half of Sunbeam's 12,000 employees worldwide.

Again, I criticized Dunlap publicly, arguing that there was no excuse for treating employees like disposable pieces of equipment. Dunlap shot back that Sunbeam was a "dismally sick" company, and drastic measures were necessary. With the payroll cuts, Sunbeam could bring out the new products "and the kind of advertising and marketing that will make Sunbeam a global leader." He projected sales growth of 20 percent a year. Sunbeam's stock reached a high of $53 a share in March 1998.

Dunlap's undoing was accounting fraud. He used a bill-and-hold strategy—selling Sunbeam products at large discounts to retailers and holding them in third-party warehouses to be delivered later. By booking sales months ahead of actual shipments, Sunbeam could report higher revenues in the form of accounts receivable, which inflated its quarterly earnings. Sunbeam was borrowing against the future, and its balance sheet was beginning to suffer. In June 1998, twenty-three months after his arrival, Sunbeam's board fired Dunlap for withholding information about the company's deteriorating condition. On February 6, 2001, Sunbeam filed for bankruptcy. In August 2002, Dunlap paid $15 million to settle a class-action lawsuit brought by shareholders against him. In September 2002, the Securities and Exchange Commission charged him with devising illegal accounting maneuvers to mask Sunbeam's financial troubles. Dunlap agreed to be banned permanently from serving as a public company official and to pay a $500,000 penalty to settle the SEC charges. *The New York Times* discovered that Dunlap had engaged in similar accounting fraud twenty years earlier in a position that he never included in his résumé.

In 2009, *Condé Nast Portfolio* named Dunlap the sixth-worst CEO of all time. He died on January 25, 2019, at the age of eighty-one.

In recent years, corporate raiders have morphed into "private equity managers" and "activist investors," but they're no different from the raiders of the 1980s. They buy struggling companies with borrowed money, often using the companies' assets as collateral for the loans. They then make the purchased company profitable by cutting payrolls, outsourcing jobs, and selling off some of its assets. Then they resell what's left of the company and pocket the returns.

Hostile takeovers have become rare because it is now *assumed* that corporations exist only to maximize shareholder returns. Businesses have used their profits to give shareholders dividends and buy back their shares of stock, reducing the number of shares outstanding and thereby giving stock prices short-term boosts. More money is now paid to the top executives, whose pay began to be linked to share prices due to the change in tax law that came out of a meeting I had with Bob Rubin and Lloyd Bentsen in 1993 (which I'll be getting to).

Some say shareholder capitalism has proven to be more "efficient" than stakeholder capitalism, moving economic resources to where they're most productive, enabling the economy to grow faster. In stakeholder capitalism, they say, CEOs employed workers they didn't need, paid them too much, and were too tied to their communities. The free-market theorist Milton Friedman, in a 1970 essay in *The New York Times Magazine* entitled "A Friedman Doctrine—the Social Responsibility of Business Is to Increase Its Profits," argued that a business that "takes seriously its responsibilities for providing employment, eliminating discrimination, and avoiding pollution is preaching pure and unadulterated socialism."

But shareholders are not the only ones who invest in corporations and bear some of the risk. Workers who have been with a company for years often develop skills and knowledge unique to it. Others may have moved their families to take a job with the company. The community itself has invested in roads and other infrastructure to accommodate the corporation and its employees. When a firm decamps, these investments lose their value. In standard microeconomics, the costs to workers and communities abandoned by profit-maximizing corporations are deemed "externalities," social costs lying outside the deals struck between managers and investors. But why should these costs not be included in deciding whether the deals are good? Over the last four decades, such "externalities" have grown so large as to swamp so-called efficiencies. Entire regions of America have been denuded of good jobs, leaving stranded legions of (mostly) men without college degrees. The bottom half of the American workforce, those who still have jobs, have been left with stagnant pay and decreasing job security. The results: rising rates of drug addiction, family violence, child abuse, deaths of despair, and an increasingly angry working class susceptible to demagogues like Trump.

Executives claim they have a "fiduciary obligation" to maximize investors' returns, which assumes that investors are the only people worthy of consideration. What about the common good?

Jared Kushner's real estate company used arrest warrants to collect debts owed by low-income tenants, often tacking on thousands of dollars in legal fees, because of its perceived need to satisfy investors—the largest of whom were Jared Kushner and his family. After the company sued one of its tenants for moving out of her apartment without giving the company two months' notice, the company won an almost $5,000 judgment against her, and then garnished her wages—as a home healthcare worker—and her bank account. When asked to justify such tactics, the Kushner Companies' chief financial officer told *The New York Times* that the company had a "fiduciary obligation" to collect as much revenue as possible.

The goal of maximizing profits has leached into sectors of the economy that had once been responsible to the common good. The original purpose of health insurance plans, for example, devised in the 1920s at the Baylor University Medical Center in Dallas, was not to generate profits but to cover as many people as possible. The non-profits Blue Cross and Blue Shield accepted everyone who wanted to become members, and all members paid the same rate regardless of age or health. By the 1960s, Blue Cross provided hospital coverage to more than fifty million Americans.

Now, it's all about profits. Between 2014 and 2024, private equity in healthcare exploded from $5 billion to over $100 billion a year, from buying hospitals, staffing emergency rooms, taking over nursing homes, and other moneymaking steps. TeamHealth, a staffing agency owned by Blackstone, one of the largest private equity firms in the world, charges about six times what Medicare charges in emergency rooms. TeamHealth and Envision, another such firm, are notorious for surprise medical bills. Patients can also expect lower-quality care. A sweeping study examined private-equity-owned nursing homes and found staff hours were slashed, jobs disappeared, and the use of anti-psychotic medications to make patients more tractable—but which have a host of dangerous side effects—skyrocketed. All this contributed to a 10 percent increase in patient mortality. That's more than one thousand lives lost every year on average.

Private-equity-backed real estate corporations have bought up both single-family homes and apartment buildings at record rates, contributing to soaring housing costs. In 2021, those corporations bought nearly one in seven homes in the country's top metro areas, and by 2023 private equity owned at least 260,000 homes across the country. Blackstone made $7 billion when it sold off its shares of the rental company it created, Invitation Homes—more than double what it initially invested.

When a landlord is a private equity firm, rents go up, evictions come faster, and there are punitive fees and shoddier repairs and services (if someone even shows up). Such firms drive rents up in general. When corporate landlords turn already scarce homes into rental properties, they shut out millions of people from being able to buy their own homes, preventing them from building financial stability and generational wealth. In essence, it's a direct siphoning of wealth from the middle and working classes into the pockets of private equity managers.

The damage being done by private equity is not front-page news in part because, by 2024, hedge funds and such firms owned half the nation's daily papers. Over the past decade and a half, they've stripped thousands of publications of their assets (such as real estate) and sold their equipment for scrap, fired their reporters and staff, and then taken huge tax write-offs. Readers lose while private equity managers get even richer. A 2022 study found that after newspapers are bought out by private equity, the number of reporters and editors declines by nearly 10 percent. The *East Bay Times* in Oakland, California, owned by Alden Global Capital, laid off twenty employees just one week after the paper won a Pulitzer Prize. Declines in local news coverage are associated with lower voter turnout, less competitive local elections, and more government corruption. Subscription prices are jacked up, sticking readers with a lower-quality product for a much higher cost.

To remedy this, first and foremost, private equity managers' favorite tax loophole must be closed, the one that allows them to keep their taxes low: carried interest, which treats their income as capital gains, taxed at a top rate of just 20 percent, instead of the ordinary income it really is, subject to a top tax rate of 37 percent.

When the only purpose of business is to make as much money as possible in the shortest time, regardless of how it's done, the common good is sacrificed. There can be no social balance. In pursuit of high profits, CEOs have ignored, circumvented, or worked to change laws intended to protect workers, communities, the environment, and consumers. They have abandoned the principle of equal economic opportunity that underlay their obligations to all stakeholders and have too often put themselves first. Like Chainsaw Al Dunlap, they have also lied about financial results.

The "efficiency" benefits have not been widely shared. As I've noted, the average worker today is barely better off than his or her equivalent forty years ago, adjusted for inflation. Most are less economically secure. Not incidentally, few own any shares of stock. By 2024, the richest one percent of Americans owned more than half of the shares of stock owned by Americans. The richest 10 percent owned more than 90 percent. The nation's economic gains, once distributed broadly to the working and middle classes, have been siphoned to the top.

America's giant U-turn—from a growing to a shrinking middle class, from upward mobility for most to soaring wealth for a few, from stakeholder capitalism to shareholder capitalism—was occurring with little public awareness. Power quietly shifted to the moneyed interests. They invested in politicians who changed laws and regulations to make them even more money, and in the prestigious institutions that enhanced and perpetuated their status and wealth. Harvard, for example, was growing extraordinarily wealthy as rich alumni donated large sums toward its endowment and buildings with their names etched on pediments (deducting all such contributions from their income taxes). It was becoming a stepping stone for many of its graduates on the way to Wall Street and the riches of shareholder capitalism, and a vehicle for their children to receive preferential admissions—thereby perpetuating such dynasties.

The obvious remedy was to change the laws, enabling working

people to enjoy more of the fruits of their labors and to achieve a better social balance. But how to do this when so much wealth and power were becoming concentrated at the top? I would get a chance to try. I became the Democrat's "new guru" and then, after Bill became president, secretary of labor.

PART IV

Failure

The New Democrats

When my book *The Next American Frontier* came out in 1983, the publisher went into overdrive to market it. *Newsweek* even did a feature on me headlined "The Democrats' New Guru." It was heady stuff, although the hype did not endear me to my Harvard faculty colleagues. With the notable exception of Ken Galbraith, they assumed that public popularity was inversely related to academic rigor. My writings were also beginning to arouse opposition on Wall Street and in corporate C-suites. But it was easy to be the Democrats' new "guru" because the Democrats were on the defensive and desperate for new ideas. I had a lot of them and wasn't shy about sharing.

GEORGE HERMAN (host of CBS's *Face the Nation,* April 1983): Mr. Reich, in addition to advocating a whole series of what some people would call revolutionary economic and business ideas and proposals, you've also been advising some Democratic presidential aspirants. As you look at the economy about which you have some serious questions, what do you tell Democratic candidates and aspirants?

Twenty minutes of blather followed.

HERMAN: Who has the moxie . . . to make the changes you're suggesting?
ME: The first step is to acknowledge that the real choice is not between the free market and centralized economic planning. It's between government intervention to maintain the status quo through tariffs, subsidies, and bailouts, as demanded by business, or government intervention to push businesses into higher value-added production and help workers adjust to the new economy.

The first to seek me out was Gary Hart, the young and telegenic senator from Colorado who was eyeing the 1984 presidential race. He described himself as an "Atari Democrat," evoking the transition of the economy from industrialized manufacturing to the information age. He was part of a cohort of "New Democrat" politicians—including California governor Jerry Brown, Senator Tim Wirth of Colorado, Congressman Paul Tsongas of Massachusetts, Massachusetts governor Michael Dukakis, and an obscure Arkansas governor named Bill Clinton—who attracted the support of suburban professionals by promoting liberal stances on foreign policy, civil rights, feminism, and the environment, while also celebrating entrepreneurship and private-sector growth. But in their eagerness to distance themselves from the "old Democratic politics" of the New Deal, Hart and other New Democrats left out one important challenge: how to bring the working class into the new economy. As I've emphasized, the wages of blue-collar workers had stagnated.

I urged Hart to include workers as part of a new industrial policy and help them get additional skills through "lifelong learning," such as community colleges offering technical skills that were needed by emerging industries. But Hart wanted America to move to the new economy as quickly as possible, not to spend money on workers in the old one.

Some months later, former vice president Walter Mondale, also running for president, reportedly exclaimed that my book "will do it for the Democrats!" He phoned to ask if I would visit him in Minneapolis. I was flattered, of course, and hopped on the next available flight.

Mondale met me at his home with a warm handshake and a big smile. We sat in his study. He was filled with energy and enthusiasm. He wanted to know everything—how best to rebut Reaganomics, what a new industrial policy might look like, which public investments had the biggest payoff, what I meant by "lifelong learning," and on and on. His questions continued at a fast pace.

I told him that a deepening rift in American politics had begun, related to a change in the structure of the economy from industrialized manufacturing to the information age, from standardized high-volume production to high-value production, from routine assembly-line jobs to knowledge-intensive jobs. American workers needed help making this shift. He wrote everything down. Two of his campaign advisers joined us. After several hours I was exhausted, but he was just starting.

I went further than I went with Hart, urging Mondale to advocate more generous safety nets to protect workers when they lost their jobs, such as turning the unemployment compensation system into a *re-employment* system that would help workers who had lost their jobs to find new ones. I suggested incentives for profit-sharing with employees. I added that big corporations should be required to devote at least 2 percent of their net profits to giving their workers more valuable skills. Corporations that were scaling back production or abandoning their communities should give notice of their plans at least six months beforehand so their workers and communities had more time to adjust, and they should help attract new industries to those communities. Otherwise, I warned, the working class would be abandoned.

Mondale wasn't particularly interested in smoothing the way to a new economy; he wanted to preserve the old one. The irony wasn't lost on me: Here we were in the Orwellian year of 1984, and one leading Democratic presidential candidate wanted to rush into the new economy at the cost of abandoning most workers trapped in the old one, while the other leading hopeful wanted to preserve the old economy at the cost of slowing America's move into the new one.

In the all-important New Hampshire primary, Mondale lost to Hart, but he went on to win the Democratic nomination. Mondale then lost to Reagan in a landslide.

Four years later, Michael Dukakis was running for president. He was a policy wonk, which the media never quite understood. He was also short, serious, kind, and high-minded. He spoke in quick bullet-like bursts. I got to know Mike (he insisted on being called Mike) when he invited me to talk about policy in his governor's office on Beacon Hill and at Harvard's Kennedy School, where he occasionally lectured.

As governor, he had presided over what many called the "Massachusetts miracle," an economic renaissance in what had been a rather backwater state. By 1985, Massachusetts had the highest average per capita income of any state in the nation. The engines of that miracle were Harvard, MIT, and the Department of Defense, which financed much of the two schools' high-tech research. The added ingredients were entrepreneurs who applied the research to a slew of innovations, forming a ring of high-tech companies around metropolitan Boston in an efflorescence of office parks and labs. Much the same was unfolding in the Bay Area, in North Carolina's "research triangle," and in Atlanta—wherever there were research universities, financial hubs, and international airports.

Suburban knowledge workers—engineers, tech executives, academics, lawyers, and financiers—were replacing manufacturing workers as the fastest-growing occupational sector in "post-industrial society," as Harvard sociologist Daniel Bell famously labeled the emerging system. And because many of them contributed bundles of money to Democratic campaigns and engaged in issue-based advocacy that received outsized media attention, those knowledge workers—like me—began to exert disproportionate influence over the Democratic Party, eclipsing labor unions and workers from the party's old industrial base.

As governor, Mike brokered deals between high-tech companies and Boston-based venture capital firms, leading to a surge of new software, data processing, and computer manufacturing. In 1988, he rode the high-tech wave into the Democratic presidential primaries, making the "Massachusetts miracle" the centerpiece of his campaign.

Mike sought my policy advice, as well as that of Larry Summers. Again, I pushed for an industrial policy to ease the adjustment of workers into the new economy. Larry wanted to reduce the federal budget deficit and promote savings and investment. The *Washington Post*'s Hobart Rowen wrote that Dukakis's "two key economic advisers are engaged in a bitter battle" for the candidate's heart and mind. "It would be disturbing," Rowan continued, "if the public saw confusion and disarray on what the basic economic policy of a Dukakis administration would be." It was hardly a bitter battle. Moreover, Larry and I disagreed in private but didn't air our disagreements publicly. I told Rowen that some 60 percent of the nation's problems could be solved by traditional macroeconomic remedies. "That leaves 40 percent," I said, "an awful lot, for micro approaches—on investment, training, trade policy" and industrial policy. Larry also played down our differences, saying "the direction of Reich's thinking" was the same as "the direction the policies of the state of Massachusetts has taken, and so far as I know, that's the orientation of the governor."

One of Mike's rivals in the crowded Democratic field, Senator Al Gore from Tennessee, mentioned in a primary debate that Mike had supported furloughs for prisoners, including murderers. This led Mike to publicly urge his rivals to wage positive campaigns rather than throw dirt at each other. Then Mike's key campaign aide, a brilliant young political operative named John Sasso, gave reporters a video showing that another of Mike's primary opponents, Delaware senator Joe Biden, had quoted liberally without attribution from a British politician's speech. This and other disclosures forced Biden out of the race. High-minded Mike promptly fired Sasso, thereby losing his most important adviser.

Mike won the Democratic nomination but lost the presidential election after a brutally negative campaign waged by George H. W. Bush. A video of Mike driving an Army tank in a helmet that seemed three times too large for his head was used by Bush to ridicule him and describe Mike as soft on defense. Then there was the infamous Willie Horton ad, featuring a photo of a disheveled Black man accompanied by a voice stating that Dukakis "allowed first-degree murderers to have weekend passes from prison. One was Willie Horton, who murdered a boy in a robbery, stabbing him nineteen times. Despite a life sentence, Horton received ten weekend passes from prison. Horton fled, kidnapped a young couple, stabbing the man and repeatedly raping his girlfriend. Weekend prison passes—Dukakis on crime." The ad was the brainchild of Republican political strategist Lee Atwater, who bragged that "by the end of the campaign, you're going to think that Willie Horton is Michael Dukakis' running mate." At the time, all fifty states had furlough programs for prisoners, including for murderers in many states. Even Ronald Reagan, when governor of California, had such a program. But the charge stuck. What also stuck were the scurrilous tactics Atwater brought into Republican politics.

Atwater's ad stifled criminal justice reform for a generation. In response, Democrats thought they needed to be tough on crime. This eventually led to Bill Clinton's 1994 crime act, which included nearly $10 billion for building more prisons, adding 100,000 more cops on the streets, and revoking Pell education grants for prison inmates. (The law was drafted by Biden.)

My candidates all struck out. I assumed my days as a policy adviser to aspiring presidents were over. But then the Democratic Leadership Council—which claimed to represent America's future of high-tech and suburban professionalism, in contrast to what it described as America's past of blue-collar workers and labor unions—proclaimed Bill Clinton its leader.

Watch Bill Run!

Ever since I met Bill on the ship heading for England in September 1968, he had talked about running for office. As I said, he was then eyeing the governorship of Arkansas, but I assumed his eventual aim was the presidency. It wasn't until the spring of 1991 that I knew for sure.

I'd arranged for Bill to give a talk at Harvard about his economic thinking, and he had done a splendid job. Modesty aside, he had taken themes from my articles and books and explained them with such clarity and compassion that it made me proud. It was a warm evening, and Strobe Talbott, a journalist and Russian scholar who had translated Khrushchev's memoir into English, had joined Bill and me on my porch. Strobe was tall and balding, and he wore thick glasses. He had been a Rhodes Scholar in Oxford at the same time Bill and I were and was a close and trusted friend to both of us.

"Are you serious about running for president?" I asked Bill, in my typical jump-in-with-both-feet way.

Bill smiled. "Maybe," he said.

"You think you really have a chance?" Strobe asked.

"I wouldn't do it if I didn't think I had a chance."

"But Bill, you're a governor of a small Southern state," I said.

"You're not well known. George H. W. Bush is an incumbent president. I don't want to discourage you, but this is a leap."

Bill's smile broadened. "Which is why this might be a good time. Even if I don't get the nomination, I can establish myself as a credible candidate for 1996."

"What exactly do you run on?" Strobe asked, purposeful and precise as always.

"There's a lot wrong with the country," Bill said softly.

"The economy is already starting to bounce back," I offered.

"Most people don't feel it," he said.

Strobe and I were playing naysayers, but for every question, Bill had a good response. We knew each other well enough to feel comfortable being candid, but neither Strobe nor I wanted to broach the question of Bill's notorious extracurricular activities. I opted for indirection. "Any skeletons in the closet? Anything the press or your opponents could slam you with?"

Bill's expression changed. I couldn't tell whether he was turning angry or inward. "No," he said flatly.

Strobe and I knew he was running.

On October 3, I flew to Little Rock, Arkansas, to watch Bill announce his bid. I didn't tell him I was coming. I stood quietly behind a Doric column on the porch of the Old State House as he and Hillary, and little Chelsea, strode out onto the marble steps. He waved at the crowd. They roared back. They held signs reading "Clinton for President." A remarkable number of TV cameras and reporters were bunched up in front of him. I asked myself if Bill and Hillary knew what they were getting into.

As he began his announcement, I feared he'd go on too long, as he had when he introduced Dukakis for the Democratic nomination in Atlanta in 1988. But he kept it within half an hour. His words, mostly platitudes with occasional points of sharp clarity, flew by, but what struck me most was his energy, intelligence, and youthfulness. He said, in part:

> I refuse to be part of a generation that commits hardworking Americans to a lifetime of struggle without reward or security . . . refuse to stand by and let our children become the first

generation of Americans to do worse than their parents . . . [I] don't want our children to grow up in a country that's coming apart instead of coming together. . . .

Middle class people spending more time on the job, less time with their children, bringing home less money to pay more for healthcare and housing and education. . . . While the incomes of our wealthiest citizens went up, their taxes went down. That's wrong. . . . The country is headed in the wrong direction fast, slipping behind, losing our way. . . . All we have out of Washington is status quo paralysis. . . . No vision, no action. Just neglect, selfishness, and division. . . .

A Clinton administration will put government back on the side of the working class . . . together we can make America great again. . . . We need a new leadership. . . . That is why I proudly announce my candidacy for presidency of the United States.

The crowd exploded. Fleetwood Mac's "Don't Stop Thinking About Tomorrow" blared.

Bill and Hillary were inundated by admirers. I scooted out unnoticed from behind the Doric column and headed back to the airport and the comparative calm of Cambridge. The Associated Press's story about Clinton's announcement noted simply that he was "the second governor and fifth major Democratic candidate to join the 1992 Democratic field" and that "all are newcomers to national politics, positioning themselves as outsiders ready to seize a government they portray as short-sighted and gridlocked." I wondered how Bill would break out of the pack. Strobe and I traded frequent phone calls. We tried not to get our hopes up.

The Iowa caucuses were held on February 10. Not surprisingly, Iowa's Democratic U.S. senator, Tom Harkin, came in first. The media treated it as a non-event. All eyes shifted to the New Hampshire primary on February 18. Bill seemed to be doing well, with a bottomless storehouse of energy, campaigning from early morning to late at night, shaking hands with everyone within reach, talking endlessly, earnestly, intently.

But then, suddenly, Bill's campaign was threatened by allegations of an extramarital affair with an Arkansas state employee and cabaret singer named Gennifer Flowers. The *Star,* a trashy supermarket tabloid, "broke" the Flowers story on January 23. Armed with damning taped phone conversations, she claimed a twelve-year affair with Clinton and said he had assisted her in securing a job as an administrative assistant with the state appeals board.

To counter the allegations, Clinton appeared on CBS's *60 Minutes* immediately following the Super Bowl on Sunday, January 26. Hillary would be part of the interview. Strobe and I met them beforehand to lend moral support. They seemed nervous but very much in command. Minutes before the interview was to begin, a part of the scaffolding holding a large klieg light toppled down, nearly hitting Hillary. Her anger flared, but in a few seconds she seemed to regain her cool.

Fifty million Americans tuned in to what was really Hillary's show. As she defended her husband, she spoke somewhat sympathetically of Flowers. "When this woman first got caught up in these charges, I felt as I felt about all of these women [who had been rumored to be involved with Bill] . . . that they had just been minding their own business and they got hit by a meteor," adding: "I felt terrible about what was happening to them." Hillary said that Flowers had called her husband frequently and he had attempted to calm her nerves: "Bill talked to this woman every time she called, distraught, saying her life was going to be ruined, and . . . he'd get off the phone and tell me that she said sort of wacky things, which we thought were attributable to the fact that she was terrified."

Bill did not explicitly deny the affair. Instead, he deflected. "No matter what I say, to pretend that the press will then let this die, we're kidding ourselves." I told myself his deflection didn't matter. By then, the public knew about JFK's love life and LBJ's dalliances.

The interviewer, Steve Kroft, then lobbed a softball: "Most Americans would agree that it's very admirable that you've stayed together, that you've worked your problems out, that you seem to have reached some sort of an understanding and an arrangement." Bill interjected, "Now wait a minute, wait a minute. Wait a minute. You're looking at two people who love each other. This is not an 'arrangement' or an 'understanding.' This is a marriage. That's a very different thing." In the green room, Strobe and I gave each other a thumbs-up.

Then it was Hillary's turn: "You know I'm not sittin' here as some little woman, standing by my man like Tammy Wynette. I'm sittin' here because I love him, and I respect him, and I honor what he's been through and what we've been through together." It would become the most famous soundbite of the interview, one of the most famous of her career. Hillary continued: "You know, if that's not enough for people, then heck, don't vote for him."

The interview saved the Clinton campaign. It also introduced the world to Hillary. The couple walked back into the green room. Strobe and I congratulated them. They seemed pleased but dazed.

It would not be the last time Bill would be called to account for his dalliances. Six years later, in his deposition to lawyers representing former Arkansas state employee Paula Jones in her sexual harassment lawsuit against him, Bill acknowledged that he did have sexual relations with Flowers, saying it occurred just once in 1977.

Clinton's popularity rebounded after the *60 Minutes* interview. Although Massachusetts senator Paul Tsongas won the New Hampshire primary, Bill scored a strong second-place showing—a performance for which he labeled himself the "Comeback Kid." As his campaign turned southward, he found more and more success, not losing a state after April 2.

I did what I could to help, sending a slew of memos into the great maw of the campaign, replete with policy ideas and suggestions for speeches. The overall theme was that in a global economy a nation's people are its only unique resource. Capital can go everywhere; investors put their money all over the world seeking the highest return. Consumers buy products and services from everywhere. Technology is developed in one country and assembled in another. In the new global economy, everyone and everything is footloose except for a nation's *people*. Their level of education, skills, capacity to work together, and the infrastructure linking them determine the current and future standard of living of people in that country, so a nation should invest in its people and what they need to be more productive. If these investments are done on a large scale and done wisely, I argued, private investment will follow.

Bill and I talked over this theme by phone whenever he could break away from the campaign. It seemed to make intuitive sense to him. It justified government spending in a way that would appeal to Democrats but also be understandable to corporate Republicans. It became the essence of Bill's agenda, "putting people first," which became the title of Bill's campaign book and the campaign's basic promise. It's what Bill would go to Washington to accomplish, or so I hoped.

For the most part, Strobe and I remained in the bleachers, cheering Bill and Hillary on, amazed at their tenacity, fascinated by the tortuous path they had chosen. We didn't believe Bill would win the nomination and were amazed when he did. We were even more amazed that he was elected president. That wouldn't have happened but for the third-party candidacy of Ross Perot, the maverick Texas multimillionaire industrialist. At one of the presidential debates, Perot was asked about the North American Free Trade Agreement (NAFTA) that George H. W. Bush had negotiated with Mexico and Canada. Perot was strongly against it: "If you're paying $13 or $14 an hour for factory workers and you can move your factory south of the border, pay $1 an hour for labor, have no health care . . . have no environment and no pollution controls and no retirement, and you don't care about anything but making money, there will be a giant sucking sound going south."

I worried that Perot might be right. NAFTA would reduce the bargaining power of American workers to get better wages because companies could so easily threaten to move to Mexico. So the only justifiable way for Bill to endorse it would be to condition the endorsement on a slew of things to improve the lives of American workers, such as national health insurance. Bill's economic team was divided. Ultimately, Bill endorsed NAFTA while saying that as president he would not sign it in its current form. An acceptable trade agreement, he said, should include provisions that would toughen environmental and worker-safety standards in Mexico and allow the president to establish a commission to monitor NAFTA's impact. "I believe we can address these concerns without renegotiating the basic agreement," which, he said, should be part of a "larger economic strategy" designed to raise the incomes of American workers, a strategy that would include major investments in healthcare, lifelong education, job training, and assistance in finding new jobs that paid as well as the old. "If it is not done right, however, the benefits of the agreement are far less clear," he said. "And the burdens will be significant. I'm convinced that I will do it right. I am equally convinced that Mr. Bush won't."

I was teaching a class at the Kennedy School when a staff member poked her head in. "Sorry to interrupt, Professor Reich, but the president-elect is on the phone. He says it's important that he speak with you."

My class hooted. I excused myself and ran down a corridor to take the call.

"Bob?"

"Bill! Congratulations! I never thought, er, never expected . . . er, what I mean to say is . . ."

"How soon can you get down here to Little Rock?"

"Well, I'm teaching now, and I have to check in with . . ."

"Tomorrow would be great. I'd like you to head up my economic team. Get everyone together. Help organize the economic transition. Okay?"

"Sure, but . . ."

He was gone. I was shocked. I had just spoken with the next president of the United States. He wanted me to run his economic transition team but I had no idea what an economic transition involved. I headed back to my class.

"That was the president-elect," I told them. They hooted again. "He wants me to join him in Little Rock tomorrow," I said. They applauded and cheered. "But my first responsibility is to you. I'll do this only if you say it's okay."

More applause. More hoots. Several students stood up and continued applauding. "Okay. I take that as a yes."

"Yes!" they shouted amid laughter.

The next month was a blur of flights, meetings, phone calls, reports, conversations with Bill and Hillary in their kitchen in Little Rock, and press briefings in preparation for the transition. Even if I'd been normal height, I'd have been over my head, trying to get it right and afraid of making a mistake. I would be consulting with the economic team; gathering economic data; aware of the importance of what I was doing; worried about letting Bill down; missing my wife and two young boys; excited; frightened; exhausted.

At one point, in the middle of the tumult, Bill smiled at me and asked, "Did you ever think you and I would be *here*?" It was the same question he had asked twenty-four years before when we were steaming across the Atlantic on the SS *United States*.

The Deficit Obsession

On December 7, 1992, Pearl Harbor Day, the economic team met with Bill at Blair House, across the street from the White House. As head of the team, I had to deliver the bad news that the federal budget deficit was much bigger than we anticipated. "We certainly have our work cut out for us!" Bill said enthusiastically. (At the end of the meeting, he almost leaped out of his chair.) I was glad he was not depressed by the news, but I was worried that the deficit was already framing our discussions; getting it "under control," reducing it, was becoming the most important measure of success.

The deficit had ballooned largely because Reagan had radically lowered taxes, especially on the rich. He had inherited a manageable debt and a modest deficit, but he began running deficits of $200 billion a year. Now, the debt was more than $4 trillion and the yearly deficit more than $300 billion, projected to be $350 billion by 1997, as I pointed out to Bill. He didn't want to raise taxes, so the only realistic option appeared to be cutting spending. We had to clean up the mess Reagan and Bush left behind.

Interest on the national debt was mainly owed to wealthy Americans who had previously financed the government through their taxes. Because of Reagan's tax cuts, they were now financing the government by lending it money, and the rest of America had to pay them interest on those bonds, a double irony. The huge federal deficit made it harder for the government to do anything to help the rest of America, most of whose earnings had been stagnant for more than a dozen years. The deficit had become a symbol of a failure of government when large numbers of people were feeling they had less and less control over their lives and needed help. The ambition of "putting people first" would have to give way to deficit reduction.

The reporters who wouldn't stop asking me about the federal deficit had been indifferent to it during the dozen years when Reagan and Bush caused the deficit to balloon. That was because the mainstream media had succumbed to conservative economists' concerns about the deficit, and stereotypes of Democrats as spenders and Republicans as skinflints.

Reagan and David Stockman, his budget chief, wanted to make it hard for any potential Democratic administration to execute its spending agenda. Bill feared that if we didn't get the deficit under control, Alan Greenspan—the chairman of the Federal Reserve, the nation's central bank, who had been appointed by Reagan and reappointed by George H. W. Bush—would raise interest rates. That would cause the economy to slow and push millions of people out of work. It might even cost Bill reelection in 1996, just as Greenspan's hiking interest rates two years earlier had brought on a recession and caused Americans to boot Bush out of office.

We shouldn't have focused on the deficit at our meeting. We should have discussed how to increase public investments in education, job training, healthcare, and everything else Americans needed, and how to encourage corporations to share more of their profits with their workers. I had succumbed to the deficit obsession. That required us to go through the federal budget line by line and cut whatever could be sacrificed. I asked two members of the economic transition team representing opposite views to come up with ideas that would test their own assumptions. I tasked Larry Summers, a deficit hawk, with identifying priorities for public investment, and Ira Magaziner, a management consultant who wanted more public investment, to guide the discussion for budget cuts.

Al Gore was upset that Larry was on the team. The vice president–elect had come across a memo Larry wrote when chief economist of the World Bank suggesting that the world's toxic wastes should be stored in poor countries where lifespans were already short, thereby minimizing the social costs of the storage. "I've always thought that under-populated countries in Africa are vastly UNDER-polluted," Larry's memo said. "I think the economic logic behind dumping a load of toxic waste in the lowest wage country is impeccable and we should face up to that." After all, he reasoned, the rest of the world would not lose out on much money or value if poor people with shorter lifespans sickened and died. It would be more efficient to keep healthier populations with higher incomes alive. It was a ludicrous and insensitive position, a parody of what an economist might suggest. José Lutzenberger, Brazil's environment minister, called the memo "perfectly logical but totally insane."

At our meeting, I told Gore that Larry assured me he hadn't read the memo although it had gone out under his name (an excuse almost as damning as its content). Larry later told a Senate committee that the memo was satirical and "never intended in any way as a serious policy recommendation."

Larry would go on to become deputy treasury secretary when Bob Rubin became treasury secretary, and treasury secretary when Rubin returned to Wall Street, then briefly president of Harvard University, where his suggestion that women were innately disinclined toward science got him fired. Then he became a top economic adviser to Barack Obama, to whom he argued that the economic stimulus necessary to rescue the economy from the financial crisis should be no greater than $700 billion, an amount that proved far too little, thereby prolonging a perilously slow recovery. Subsequently, he became a critic of Joe Biden's stimulus package, which he claimed was responsible for the surge of inflation that would not abate unless or until unemployment skyrocketed. He was proven wrong again. I liked Larry personally but came to believe his judgment was terrible. Would America have been better off had I not convinced Al Gore that Larry should be on Clinton's economic team in the first place?

I still didn't know if Bill wanted me to be part of his administration. Half of me hoped he didn't. The other half thought it an opportunity of a lifetime to do some of the things I'd been writing and speaking about for years.

Becoming Secretary

In early December, a lawyer who'd been retained by the Clinton campaign phoned to say he'd been asked to investigate me in case the new president wanted to appoint me to high office. He was a bit vague about who made the request, but said the matter was urgent. When I arrived at his law office, he and two colleagues (all in starched-white shirts and dark suits) invited me to sit on a large couch. His two colleagues settled in armchairs on either side. He sat behind a large mahogany desk. He was friendly but firm. "Our purpose is to discover any embarrassing item that might turn up in a confirmation hearing," he said.

I thought to myself: Confirmation? So Bill is considering me for a cabinet job that needs Senate confirmation? Wow!

"Anything I can do to help," I chirped, trying not to reveal my sudden excitement. "Nothing to hide *here*."

My mind flashed back to third grade. Ronny Elliott and I sawed almost clear through the large maple that held Richard Merrick's tree house. I was grounded for a week.

"I expect this will be pretty routine," he said. "We've already done a preliminary check and you're fine."

My mind flashed on kindergarten, when I paid Holly Knox a nickel to do a somersault on the jungle gym so I could get a good peek at her underwear. She promised not to tell a soul, but she ratted. Miss Welch sent a note home, suggesting counseling.

"You're pretty boring, as these things go," said another member of the trio. They chuckled.

My host looked at me intently. "We're on your side," he said. "We're on your team. If you can think of anything that, if revealed, might taint your confirmation, you probably should share it with us now."

There was Miss Bouton's Nursery School when she expelled me for being sarcastic. There was the time I dumped a load on the carpet of Charles Helmes, the principal of Lewisboro Elementary School.

"Can't think of anything," I said.

"The late nineteen sixties? That's a tricky period for some people. Anything you might be, er, ashamed of?"

I remembered my time as president of my class at Dartmouth, and some of my regrettable decisions.

"Ashamed?" I asked with sudden nervousness. "Nothing immediately comes to mind."

"If it does, give a call," said my host, with a smile. "In the meantime, we need to discuss *this*." He reached under his desk and handed me a large black three-ring binder. "We did a search of all the negative things critics have written about your books over the years." The binder contained at least two hundred pages, single-spaced, indexed by year, cross-indexed by topic. I hadn't intended my books to be particularly provocative, but they turned out that way. Orthodox economists, committed to their beliefs, had been upset by them. Conservative theorists were even less enthusiastic. Republican political hacks hated them. Fortunately, Bill Clinton was a fan. Yet because many of the ideas in my most recent book had found their way into his campaign book, I had become an even bigger target.

My host gently took the binder out of my hands and placed it on the desk. "Quite a collection," he said, still smiling. "If you're nominated, you'll need to be ready to respond." His two colleagues looked at the volume, then up at me again, smiling politely and nodding in agreement.

"No problem," I said, as gloom descended on me.

My host leaned toward me. "You'll have your work cut out for you." He pointed to the label on the side of the black binder: "Critics of Reich, Volume I."

Some days later, Bill and I were going over some budget numbers in his temporary office when he told me he wanted me to be in his administration. It was an offhand comment, as if he were telling me he wanted me over for lunch. I didn't have a chance to respond before he stood up and started for the door. "Have to run," he said. Just

before leaving, he looked back and asked me what position I'd like. I said I'd been fantasizing about secretary of labor, which seemed the right place for acting on my concerns about American workers. His eyes lit up. "Perfect!" he said and was out the door.

My coaches helped me cram for my Senate confirmation hearing. It was intense. I felt like a prizefighter getting ready for the big one. We did a mock run. My coaches played the parts of senators on the committee. I sat facing them. They tried to be as difficult and nasty as possible.

"Mr. Reich, you've had absolutely no experience managing a big organization, have you?"

"Mr. Reich, do you believe employers should have the right to permanently replace striking workers?"

"Mr. Reich, are you a socialist?"

"Mr. Reich, you have argued that government has the competence to pick industrial winners. Why do you assume this?"

"Mr. Reich, have you ever met a payroll?"

"Mr. Reich, do you believe that defined-benefit pension plans are underfunded, and if so, what should be done about the problem?"

I groped for words. I babbled. I got angry. On the rare occasions when I had something intelligent to say, I gave long and complicated answers.

"Time *out*," said my chief interrogator, a rotund, middle-aged Hill staffer with graying red hair and a decade of experience at this sort of thing. "Let's stop here and critique your performance so far. You gotta understand . . ." he said, stepping out from behind the table that served as a mock committee rostrum. "This hearing isn't designed to test your *knowledge*. It's designed to test your *respect*. For *them*. You don't have to come up with the *right answer*," he continued, pacing around the room. "I hope you don't take offense, but you've got a big handicap, *professor*. Your whole life you've shown people how smart you are. That's not what you should do before the committee. You try to show them how smart you are, you're in big trouble."

"But I have to answer their questions, don't I?"

"Yes and no. You have to *respond* to their questions. But you don't have to *answer* them. You *shouldn't* answer them. You're not *expected* to answer them."

The others laughed. I was bewildered. "What's the difference between answering and responding?"

"Respect! *Respect!*" my chief interrogator nearly shouted.

My interrogator walked over to me and leaned down so his face was close to mine. "This is all about respect. *Your* respect for *them*. The *president's* respect for them. The *executive branch of government's* respect for the legislative branch. Look: The president has nominated you to be a cabinet secretary. The senators must *consent* to the nomination. The Democrats are in control of the Senate, so barring an unforeseen scandal, they will. But first you have to *genuflect*." He got down on his knees, grabbed my hand, and kissed it. The others roared. "You have to let them know you respect their power, and you'll continue to do so for as long as you hold office."

I joined in the laugh but was still confused. "What does this have to do with the difference between answering their questions and responding to their questions?"

He sat down on the chair again. He lowered his voice. The others in the room enjoyed the spectacle. "If you *lecture* them, they won't feel you respect them. But if you respond to their questions with utter humility, they will feel you do."

"Utter humility?"

"Have you ever in your life admitted you don't know something?" He grinned, relishing the moment.

"Sure."

"But have you ever admitted you didn't know when you knew just enough to bullshit your way through?"

I paused. "Not often."

My trainer was up again, pacing. "So when you're sitting there in front of the committee and one of the senators asks you a question that you're not absolutely sure of the answer to, I want you to say simply 'I don't know, Senator.'"

"Okay."

He stopped and pointed his finger at me. "*Practice* saying it. *I . . . don't . . . know . . . , Senator.*"

"I don't know, Senator."

"Good! Again!"

"I don't know, Senator."

"Again!"

"*I don't know, Senator.*" The others applauded.

"Fine." He looked toward the group. "I think he's catching on."

Laughter. Then back to me again. "And even when you're absolutely *sure,* and you have it all worked out in your head, I want you to give a *simple* answer. One sentence. Two at most. Simple and general. No specifics."

This was going to be hard.

"*And*"—he brought his face closer and looked me dead in the eye—"as often as you can say it without it sounding contrived, I want you to tell them how much you look forward to working with them. *I look forward to working with you on that, Senator.*"

"I look forward to working with you on that, Senator."

"*I don't know, Senator. But I look forward to working with you on it.*"

"I don't know, Senator, but I look forward to working with you on it," I repeated.

"G-o-o-o-o-d." My trainer smiled and was up and pacing again. "And whenever you can do so without sounding like your nose is completely up their assholes, I want you to *compliment* them. Praise their leadership on this issue. Tell them you'll need their help and guidance. Mention their years of diligence and hard work."

I rehearsed. "Senator, you know far more about that issue than I do, and I look forward to hearing your views in the months and years to come."

"Wonderful!" My trainer beamed and pointed at me. "And remember, if they ask anything personal—about your writings, your political views, even your friendship with the president, whatever—*don't* take it personally. They are not interested in an answer. They're interested in *how* you respond."

"*How* I respond?"

"Deferentially. Good-naturedly. If they are nasty, don't be nasty back. If they're sarcastic, refrain from sarcasm. *Never* get angry. *Never* lose your balance. *Never* take the bait."

My interrogator put an arm around my shoulder and addressed the others. "He'll do just fine, won't he?"

His colleagues said encouraging things, but they weren't convinced.

The session ended. We'd try again tomorrow. I wished the hearing were two weeks away instead of two days.

When the big day arrived, I walked as confidently as I could into the large room in the Senate office building where my confirmation hearing was to be held. I hadn't counted on all the cameras and journalists in front of the witness table: C-SPAN, CNN, reporters on their knees taking notes. It would be hard enough to fight the impulse to show the senators how smart I was. Could I resist the temptation to show all of America?

After introductions, Ted Kennedy, the committee chairman, lobbed me some softballs about school-to-work apprenticeships and worker training. Then Kansas senator Nancy Kassebaum, the ranking Republican on the committee, wanted to draw me into a discussion of government waste and inefficiency. I respectfully resisted. Rhode Island Democratic senator Claiborne Pell digressed on the subject of worker membership on corporate boards. Minnesota Republican senator David Durenberger wanted me to talk about changes in the workplace. Ohio Democratic senator Howard Metzenbaum tweaked me about the North American Free Trade Agreement. Connecticut Democratic senator Chris Dodd wanted my views on the pending Family and Medical Leave Act. South Carolina Republican senator Strom Thurmond asked me about unions.

I fought off all temptation. I remembered the rules: It wasn't about my answers. It was about demonstrating respect.

"I agree, Senator."

"I don't know, Senator."

"I look forward to working with you on that, Senator."

"I look forward to reading that report, Senator."

"No decision has been made about that, Senator, and I'm eager to have your views."

"I will look into that, Senator."

"Thank you for your leadership on the issue, Senator."

It was like a game of tennis. I was swatting the balls back as gently and respectfully as I could, no matter how hard they came at me.

Then an unexpected question came from Indiana Republican senator Dan Coats: "Mr. Reich, I enjoyed reading your recent book, *The Work of Nations*," he said, smiling slyly and holding up a copy. "I was interested in some of your proposed recommendations and solutions to the challenge which you outlined in Chapter 20. . . . I figured if I read that, I could skip the first nineteen chapters." (This prompted laughter in the room.) "The first response you suggest is to make the income tax much more progressive and closing what you call some gaping tax loopholes, and in doing so, you reference Woodrow Wilson's proposal to Congress to enact a steeply progressive tax code with the top rate on an individual of 83 percent. Is *this* the kind of proposal you're going to be advocating to the Clinton economic team relative to how to deal with this basic challenge that we face?"

Don't defend yourself. Don't lecture. Don't take the bait.

"No," I said, without elaboration.

His smile broadened. "I'm happy to hear that."

But further words welled up inside my throat and then out of my mouth. "The president-elect's economic proposals include an increase in the marginal tax rate on families with an adjusted gross income in excess of $200,000, to 36 percent."

Coats said 36 percent sounded good compared to 83 percent, snarking, "It's a tried and tested political technique to offer a high number and have everybody say, 'Wow, it's only going to be 36 percent.'" He continued, a snake slowly coiling around its victim, referring to another chapter of my book where I argued against making sharp cuts in the federal budget deficit. "Why is that so wrong," he asked, "when the president-elect has made it one of his top priorities?"

C-SPAN and CNN were broadcasting this. The world was watching.

Now was my chance to give the lecture of my life. What I wanted to say was: *If it weren't for twelve years of Republican supply-side, trickle-down bullshit, no one would be worrying about the budget deficit to begin with. Besides, if public investments like education and job training and infrastructure are deducted from government spending, and if the remaining amount is expressed as a percentage of the whole economy, it's not nearly as large a problem as it might seem. And if we cut defense spending as we should—now that the Cold War has ended—and taxed the very wealthy at the rate they were taxed as recently as the 1970s, we could both lower the deficit and have a large pot of money to help all Americans get the skills they need for higher wages.*

Instead, I took a deep breath and told myself not to say any of this. *Remember the rules!* "President-elect Clinton is committed to reducing the budget deficit." I paused, amazed and relieved at my self-control. Yet I couldn't resist making a tiny provocative point: "The objective . . . is to move from too much public *and* private consumption to a greater degree of public *and* private investment. That's what will get our country back on the right economic track."

Oops. I've invited a debate. Coats saw his opening and rushed in. "Would entitlement spending on Medicare and Medicaid be investment or consumption?" Coats and I both knew that Medicare and Medicaid costs were soaring and that no one had any idea how to slow them. Clinton still hadn't figured out an approach. I had to be *very careful.*

"Well, again, that's an issue that I want to leave for—for the—for the president-elect." Stop here, I told myself. But my mouth kept going. "At this very moment, he and some of his advisers are working, developing the package which members here will be—have an opportunity to examine and be involved with, so I don't want to— I don't want to spill the beans, I don't want to get out ahead of him." The voice in my head told me to cease, but I couldn't. "The criterion for separating consumption and investment is to determine what spending is merely enhancing the well-being of people here today and what is building the future productivity of the nation." *Don't say another word!*

Coats lunged at the opportunity to expose the contradiction at the heart of Clinton's economic policy: "It seems to me just on the face of it that we have some incompatible goals here: A pledge by the president-elect to halve the budget deficit while indicating substantially more investment. . . . I can't see how you can accomplish that without a very substantial reduction in entitlement spending."

Ted Kennedy interjected, as is the chairman's prerogative. "As you know, 85 percent of the increase in entitlement spending is on health care, and that's only a quarter of the federal budget. You could cap it today and all you'll do is shift the costs onto the private sector. . . . We all understand these issues are complex." Kennedy signaled Coats's turn was over. He wasn't getting another try.

I could have drowned. Kennedy saved my life.

The hearing ended a half hour later. Flashbulbs exploded all around. I saw my burly chief interrogator across the hearing room. He was beaming. I couldn't reach him in the crowd, but our eyes met. He pointed his thumb straight upward.

I was confirmed by the Senate unanimously and went to work. But the budget deficit got in the way. Bill couldn't get anything done with the deficit hawks breathing down his neck. Alan Greenspan, the Fed chair, held all the cards. I needed to meet with Greenspan, but how? The secretary of labor couldn't just call up the chairman of the Federal Reserve Board and ask for a meeting. The Fed is supposed to be politically independent. Fortunately, Greenspan invited me to breakfast.

Breakfast with Greenspan

Bill would reappoint Greenspan again, although Greenspan didn't know it at the time—which, I suspected, was why he invited me. He probably assumed I had the president's ear on economic policy, and because he was a deficit hawk and I was the opposite, it couldn't hurt his chances to try to charm me.

We'd never met before but as soon as he greeted me, I instinctively knew him. I knew where he grew up (New York), and where he got his drive and his sense of humor (he's Jewish). I felt like we'd been together at countless weddings, bar mitzvahs, and funerals. Our breakfast was pleasant, our conversation easy. He deftly avoided talking about the deficit, jobs, and inflation. In fact, he avoided talking about anything that mattered. I left feeling pampered and charmed. Greenspan got out of the breakfast exactly what he wanted. Yet I never asked him the questions I intended to ask and never got the answers I imagined he'd give.

Here's a version of the conversation I had anticipated:

ME: *Mr. Chairman, how did a shy little Jewish guy like you get to be the most powerful man in the American economy?*
HE: *I'm cunning and ambitious and very, very smart.*
ME: *You're a Republican and follower of Ayn Rand?*
HE: *And proud of it. Nixon, Ford, Reagan, and Bush all appointed me to powerful positions.*
ME: *What's your purpose in life?*
HE: *To stamp out inflation.*
ME: *Even if that means high unemployment?*
HE: *You bet.*
ME: *Even if it requires slow growth and stagnant wages?*
HE: *Right you are.*
ME: *Even if it means drastic cuts in federal programs that help working people and the poor?*
HE: *Absolutely, if that's what it takes to balance the budget and remove all temptation to inflate away the government's debt.*
ME: *But why? A little inflation never hurt anybody.*
HE: *You're wrong. It hurts bond traders and lenders.*
ME: *But why place their interests over everybody else's interest in good jobs?*
HE: *Because I'm a capitalist and capitalism is driven by the filthy rich. They make their money off bonds. Your constituents are just plain filthy. They have to work for a living.*
ME: *You're the nation's central banker. You should be accountable to all Americans.*
HE: *But I'm not, and neither is the Fed.*
ME: *That's not fair, it's not right.*
HE: *Nah-na-na-nah-na. You can't stop me.*

ME: *Can too.*

HE: *Can not.*

ME: *Can too. The president's my friend.*

HE: *So what?*

ME: *He won't reappoint you.*

HE: *Oh, no?*

ME: *No.*

HE: *Well, we'll see about that.*

ME: *You think he'll reappoint you?*

HE: *No doubt about it.*

ME: *Why are you so sure?*

HE: *Because he needs me.*

ME: *Oh, yeah?*

HE: *Yeah.*

ME: *What does he need you for?*

HE: *He needs me because he needs to have the confidence of Wall Street, and only I can deliver that to him.*

ME: *Oh, yeah?*

HE: *Yeah. That's why Bush reappointed me in 1992, even though he hated me for keeping interest rates high as the economy slipped into recession in 1990. That's why he lost the presidency to your man. I could do it to your man too. I could do worse. He'll reappoint me. He'll do whatever I want him to do.*

ME: *Well, you can take your crummy lunch and cram it, you robber-baron pimp.*

HE: *Go suck on a pickle, you Bolshevik dwarf.*

The Real Reason CEO Pay Exploded

Cutting the deficit meant cutting back on the public investments Bill had promised—education, job training, healthcare, and many other things middle-class families needed. That worried me. A priority of the Clinton administration was to be reviving wages and reducing inequality.

Bill had also promised in his campaign to stop allowing corporations to deduct from their taxable earnings executive pay exceeding a million dollars. But now CEOs' pay was exploding as they received mountains of shares of stock. In 1980, when Reagan was elected president, CEOs of major companies made, on average, 35 times the pay of the typical worker. In the 1992 election, when Bill promised to limit executive pay, CEOs made 109 times as much as a typical worker. By 2000, Bill's last year in office, the pay ratio had more than tripled. CEOs made as much in a day as the average worker made in a year.

The bulk of these lavish compensation packages came in the form of shares of stock. The Clinton administration had exempted shares of stock from the million-dollar cap because of a decision made in a meeting soon after we took office—Bill didn't attend—that would have enormous repercussions. It was one of many in which yours truly was railroaded.

> BOB RUBIN: During the campaign the president said he didn't want companies to be able to deduct executive pay exceeding $1 million from their taxable earnings. We need to pin this down for the budget and get him a recommendation.
> LLOYD BENTSEN (secretary of the treasury, former senator from Texas, sitting to Clinton's right in the photo): He proposed a lot of things during the campaign. Circumstances change.

ME: It got a lot of press. A lot of people out there think corporate executives are overpaid. He can't reverse himself without being accused of waffling.

BENTSEN: Well, they're wrong. It takes a lot more than a million dollars to attract a talented CEO these days, and he's worth every penny if he can make the company more competitive and raise the value of its shares.

LEON PANETTA (chief of staff, former member of Congress from California): Maybe there's some way we can do this without actually limiting executive pay.

ME: Look, we're *not* limiting executive pay. Companies could still pay their executives whatever they wanted to pay them. We're just saying that society shouldn't subsidize through the tax laws any pay over a million bucks.

LAURA TYSON (chair of the Council of Economic Advisers, former University of California–Berkeley professor): What are we really trying to accomplish with the proposal? Discourage companies from paying their executives more than a million dollars, or making sure that when they do, they're really acting in the best interest of their shareholders?

BENTSEN: We have no business doing either, but the second is more valid.

RUBIN: I agree with Lloyd. Why not require that pay over
a million dollars be linked to company performance?
Executives have to receive it in shares of stock or
stock options, that sort of thing. If no linkage, no tax
deduction.

PANETTA: Good idea. It's consistent with what the president
promised, and it won't create flak in the business
community.

ME: But we're not just talking about *shareholders*. The wage
gap is widening in this country, and it affects everybody.

BENTSEN: Look, Bob, we shouldn't be social engineering
through the tax code. And there's no reason to declare class
warfare. I think we've arrived at a good compromise.
I propose that we recommend it to the president.

RUBIN: Fine. Now to a few other items on the agenda. . . .

The Battle of the Bobs

It is difficult to describe conflicting points of view among a president's top advisers without assuming personal animus. But I held no personal grudge against Bob Rubin, and I don't believe he did against me. He was giving Bill the best advice he could, just as I was. Yet as time went on, it became clear that Bob and I had fundamentally different views, not only about what Bill should do but more generally about the role of government as the United States shifted from an old manufacturing economy to a new digital one.

I liked Bob. We often had dinner together at the Jefferson Hotel, where he had a suite. I found him charming, thoughtful, and curious. He had a good sense of humor and laughed easily. His graying hair was always carefully combed, with a straight part to the side, and he dressed impeccably—the tells of a Wall Street investment banker. But unlike most Wall Street bankers, Bob felt strongly that America's poor needed better healthcare, education, and more routes to the middle class.

Our differences came from very different understandings of the working and middle classes, which the media sensationalized. To my surprise and irritation, that battle would define the poles of Democratic Party economics for years. As *The New York Times*'s usually thoughtful David Leonhardt summarized it more than a decade later:

> For 15 years, Democratic Party economics have been defined by a struggle that took place during the start of the Clinton administration. It was the battle of the Bobs. On one side was Clinton's labor secretary and longtime friend, Bob Reich, who argued that the government should invest in roads, bridges, worker training and the like to stimulate the economy and help the middle class. On the other side was Bob Rubin, a former Goldman Sachs executive turned White House aide, who favored reducing the deficit to soothe the bond market, bring down interest rates and get the economy moving again. Clinton cast his lot with Rubin, and to this day the first question about any Democrat's economic outlook is often where his heart lies, with Reich or Rubin, the left or the center, the government or the market.

I didn't see it that way. "Government or the market" *wasn't* the fundamental choice. As I've stressed, it is impossible to have a market without government. Government defines and enforces it, determining how much monopoly power big corporations can assert; whether and how workers can form unions; the duration of patents, copyrights, and other intellectual property; what happens when debtors can't pay what they owe; how to control inflation and avoid recession; the rules of international trade; how much money government can borrow, and much more.

The real choice is *who benefits* by the decisions government makes about the rules of the game—people who are wealthy and privileged or those who are not, and *who pays the costs*—those who can most easily afford to or those who are barely getting by. Viewing it as a debate between those who want more government and less—the mythic "battle of the Bobs"—disguises this more basic choice. My real concern was I didn't want the rules to favor those at the top at the expense of average working Americans. That had been going on ever since the Powell memo, followed by the Supreme Court opening the floodgates to big money in politics. The resulting rules were already making the wealthy even wealthier and keeping most people down.

Bob had a different perspective. From his standpoint, it was critical that Clinton gain the confidence of the borrowers and lenders on Wall Street. Bob had spent his life on Wall Street—twenty-five years at Goldman Sachs, one of the nation's most profitable investment banks. It was a place of giant egos, sharp elbows, and smart dealmakers. Through a combination of intelligence and diplomacy, Bob gradually worked his way up to co-chairman of the firm, becoming fabulously wealthy. During our years in the Clinton administration, he commuted from and to his home in New York by private jet. It was natural that he saw things differently from how I did. By reducing the deficit, he argued, we'd win the confidence of Wall Street. This would lead to lower interest rates, which would prompt businesses to invest in new plants, equipment, and technologies. The result would boost the economy more effectively than all the public investments Clinton had promised during the campaign.

I disagreed. It seemed to me that businesses would be more likely to invest when average working people had more money to spend on all the things that were being produced. And average people would have more money to spend on goods and services if they didn't have to spend so much on things like healthcare, education, and childcare. These *public* investments would do more to boost business investment than private investments fueled by lower interest rates.

Bob and I had ongoing discussions about this. He assumed that if the economy grew, everyone would gain, and inequalities of income and wealth would take care of themselves. I pointed out that the economy had been growing for years and such inequalities were widening; most of the gains had gone to the top. He responded that it would be unwise to trade off some economic growth for a more equal distribution of income and wealth; better to seek maximum growth and *then* figure out how to get a more equal distribution. I thought this naïve. If the gains from growth continued to go disproportionately to those at the top, I argued, there'd be no way to redistribute it because those at the top would have that much more political power to resist any redistribution, and they'd fight tax increases to pay for better education, healthcare, childcare, and everything else most people needed if they were to do better. In fact, I thought it a false tradeoff. I was sure a more equal distribution would generate even greater growth because more people would feel a stake in the system.

Often, Bill went along with Rubin, but not because Bob had the better arguments. Bill was intimidated by Wall Street and feared that bond traders would punish him by raising interest rates on long-term bonds, thereby slowing the economy and potentially putting millions of people out of work, if he didn't cut the deficit. (This prompted James Carville, one of Bill's political advisers, to quip that "I used to think if there was reincarnation, I wanted to come back as the president or the pope or a .400 baseball hitter. But now I want to come back as the bond market. You can intimidate everybody.") I think Bill was haunted by his desertion of the activist ideas that had attracted so many voters to his campaign. At one point he snapped: "Where are all the Democrats? I hope you're all aware we're all Eisenhower Republicans. We're Eisenhower Republicans here, and we are fighting the Reagan Republicans. We stand for lower deficits and free trade and the bond market. Isn't that great?" Nevertheless, he didn't dare raise hackles on Wall Street.

Bob Rubin also believed in free trade. He was eager for Bill to push Congress to ratify the North American Free Trade Agreement, which would make the continent a free-trade zone. Bob argued that by increasing trade, NAFTA would create hundreds of thousands of new American jobs. Bill was inclined to go along on this, too. Bill bought into the textbook view that trade benefits all parties. He didn't see globalization as something that could be turned off. "It is the economic equivalent of a force of nature, like wind or water," he said.

I thought this view as nonsensical as the idea of a "natural" free market. How globalization works and whom it benefits or hurts depend on specific, negotiated rules determining which assets will be protected from global competition and which will not. In most trade deals, the assets of American corporations—their factories, equipment, financial assets, and intellectual property—are well protected. But the jobs and wages of American workers are *not*. Why shouldn't American corporations that profit from trade be required to compensate American workers for losses of jobs or wages due to trade?

Other questions gnawed at me. The age-old economic doctrine of "comparative advantage" assumes that more trade is good for all nations because each trading partner specializes in what it does best. But what if a country's comparative advantage comes from allowing its workers to labor under dangerous or exploitative conditions? Why shouldn't America's trading partners be required to have the same level of worker safety as in the United States and give their workers the same right to organize unions?

The proposed North American Free Trade Agreement didn't address these sorts of questions. Instead, NAFTA reflected domestic politics. As such, I worried that American workers would get shafted by NAFTA. I feared there would be no bold plan to get them new jobs if they lost their old ones, no system to get new businesses into communities and regions abandoned by corporations heading to Mexico. Organized labor was against NAFTA from the start, but the unions had become politically weak relative to big corporations and Wall Street, and Bill didn't want to listen to the unions anyway, thinking them "old Democrat." I wasn't allowed to speak out publicly against NAFTA, of course, but I dreaded media interviews where I had to defend it.

The Clinton administration lobbied hard for NAFTA. In the end, Congress ratified it, with more Republican than Democratic votes. Additional trade agreements followed, along with the creation of the World Trade Organization (WTO) and the opening of trade relations with China, which joined the WTO in 2001. Proponents of trade with China assumed it would speed China toward democracy. That assumption proved to be wrong.

All told, trade increased from 19 percent of the U.S. economy in 1989 to 31 percent in 2011, according to the World Bank. (By 2021, following Trump's economic battles with China and the pandemic, trade's share of the U.S. economy drifted down to 25 percent.) These deals benefited corporations, big investors, executives, Wall Street traders, and other professionals. The pharmaceutical industry won extended drug patents in Mexico, China, and elsewhere. Wall Street banks and investment firms made sure they could move capital into and out of these countries regardless of local banking laws. American oil companies won the ability to seek compensation if a country adopted environmental standards that hurt their bottom lines. The stock market responded favorably. In 1993, when Clinton took office, the Dow-Jones Industrial Average peaked at 3,799. By the time he left office in 2001, it had topped 11,000.

Middle- and working-class Americans benefited from these deals as *consumers,* gaining access to lower-priced goods from China, Mexico, and other countries where wages were lower than in the United States. But the trade deals also caused millions of Americans to lose their jobs or settle for stagnant or declining wages. Between 2000 and 2017, some 5.5 million American manufacturing jobs vanished. Automation accounted for about half of the loss; imports, mostly from China, for the other half. Whole regions became economic wastelands.

Milwaukee, for example, had been known as the "machine shop of the world" in the 1950s and 1960s when most of the city's adult population had well-paying union jobs in manufacturing. As late as 1969, the city's inhabitants enjoyed the second-highest median income of any large American city. But many of those jobs went abroad; others were replaced by automated equipment and software. Since then, Milwaukee lost more than 80 percent of its manufacturing jobs and now has the second-highest poverty rate of any large American city.

You can trace a direct line from these trade deals and the subsequent job or wage losses to the rise of Donald Trump in 2016. A 2021 study documented steep job losses starting in the mid-1990s in counties tied to industries exposed to competition from Mexico. Most of these counties had long voted Democratic. By the year 2000, they tilted toward Republicans in House elections.

More manufacturing jobs were lost after China joined the World Trade Organization and began assembling and exporting products to the United States (many of them under the brands of U.S. corporations). The college educated were better suited to a tech-heavy globalized economy that rewarded their insights and skills. But blue-collar workers without college degrees gave every indication of wanting to keep their old jobs, even if that meant somewhat higher prices. Democrats responded to the preference of the college-educated, and blue-collar workers moved toward the GOP. Economists have estimated that if America had imported only *half* of what China exported to us during these years, Michigan, Wisconsin, Pennsylvania, and North

Carolina would have swung Democratic in 2016, delivering their electoral votes and the presidency to Hillary Clinton.

Theoretically, the winners from trade could compensate the losers and still come out ahead. As a practical matter, the winners did not do this, and we failed to devise a way to make them. Too many American workers got shafted.

Bob and I also had different views about the role of finance in the economy. In the 1950s and 1960s, banking was a dull, quiet profession. The financial sector accounted for 10 to 15 percent of U.S. corporate profits; by the mid-1980s, 30 percent. By the time Bob and I were working for Bill Clinton, it accounted for nearly 40 percent. That was more than four times the profits in all U.S. manufacturing.

For years, I'd been concerned about the growing dominance of finance. In early 1980, I wrote an essay for *The New York Times,* which eventually became a book, warning that the economy was shifting from making real products to making financial products and that financial entrepreneurs were winning out over product entrepreneurs. The latter innovate by creating better products at less cost, I wrote. They enlarge the economic pie. But financial entrepreneurs do not enlarge the economic pie; their efforts only redivide the slices. For an economy to maintain its health, entrepreneurial rewards should flow primarily to producers rather than to financiers.

Financial entrepreneurialism has prevailed over product entrepreneurialism because our economic system has become so complex and interdependent that capital is allocated according to *symbols* of productivity rather than to productivity itself. The symbols lend themselves to profitable manipulation more readily than do the underlying processes of production. It takes time and effort to train workers, improve product quality, develop manufacturing efficiencies, build reliable supply chains and distribution and sales networks. But enormous profits are possible with relatively little effort through strategic use of accounting conventions, tax rules, banking laws, stock and commodity exchanges, and exchange rates. When *financial* entrepreneurs look for solutions to America's problems, they come up with remedies to stimulate large-scale capital investment:

accelerated depreciation, tax credits, government subsidies, relaxation of antitrust laws. *Product* entrepreneurs focus on techniques for improving output: instituting better quality controls, improving labor-management relations, helping workers develop additional skills, providing them a share of the profits, and empowering them with more responsibility.

As finance came to dominate the U.S. economy in the 1980s and 1990s, capital was diverted from long-term investment to stock buybacks. Financiers made complicated side bets on whether cash-strapped subprime borrowers would lose their homes. Wall Street traders invested in ways to get a few milliseconds of advantage over other traders, so they could win speculative bets. None of this added value to the economy.

Financial entrepreneurship has become more important than producing and selling real products, even in many traditional manufacturing companies. As Harvard political philosopher Michael Sandel points out, U.S. manufacturing firms got just 18 percent of their profits from their financial investments in 1978, but by 1990, their financial investments were responsible for fully 60 percent of their profits.

The globalization of finance also generated a string of crises around the world. Unrestricted capital flows made countries vulnerable to the whims of global financial markets—to the "electronic herd" of bond traders and investors who moved capital across national borders at the speed of a click on a keyboard. The East Asian financial crisis began in 1997 when Thailand unpegged the Thai baht from the U.S. dollar. To remain competitive, other nations in the region devalued their currencies, which provoked massive flights of capital. Economies that kept more control of foreign capital survived with less damage.

The increasing mobility of capital across borders also allowed U.S. corporations to squeeze their American workers by threatening to move operations overseas—demanding, as conditions for remaining in America, lower wages, fewer benefits, and no unions. As capital grew more mobile, it also became more difficult to tax. Corporate profits and the savings of the superwealthy could move to lower-tax countries at the speed of electronic impulses, hiding behind legal forms and dummy corporations.

I doubt Bob Rubin anticipated these consequences. He simply repeated Wall Street's conventional wisdom in favor of free trade and global capital. The financialization of the American economy was animated by the same market faith as globalization—the assumption that ever more sophisticated financial innovations made the economy more efficient and less risky. Allowing markets to operate freely would direct capital to its most efficient uses and spur economic growth, or so the economic orthodoxy of the era taught.

This was the rationale Bob repeatedly put forward, which led Bill to deregulate the financial industry. The deregulation of finance had started during the Reagan administration when, as I've noted, corporate raiders used borrowed money to buy and dismantle American companies—selling off divisions, squeezing costs, and firing workers—all in the name of maximizing "shareholder value." Financial deregulation continued under George H. W. Bush and under the Clinton administration. Financial houses went from small privately held investment banks to giant corporations whose shares were traded on stock exchanges. Before, when investment bankers made all the profits and suffered all the losses from their bets, they were more cautious. Partners kept their banks small and their transactions relatively simple so they could understand the risks they were taking on. But by the end of Bill's second term, the deregulation of Wall Street had fueled megabanks with employees numbering in the hundreds of thousands and spanning the globe.

There were no longer any constraints on risky bets. Shareholders bore the downside costs while the bankers who made the bets got many of the upside gains in the form of giant bonuses. The entire country would come to bear the downside risks as bankers grabbed the cheapest funding possible to make the riskiest bets with the highest payoffs—which led to the crash of 2008. As the fictitious Gordon Gecko, a corporate raider in the 1987 movie *Wall Street*, proclaimed in a speech to shareholders of an ailing company, "I am not a destroyer of companies. I am a liberator of them! The point is, ladies and gentlemen, that greed—for lack of a better word—is good."

When Brooksley Born, who chaired the Commodity Futures Trading Commission (an agency designed to regulate such things as soybean and pork belly futures), asked Bob—now treasury secretary—for permission to issue rules to monitor risky financial futures contracts, he refused. Bob told Born that the creators of sophisticated financial derivatives on Wall Street knew how to manage them safely on their own. Larry Summers—now deputy treasury secretary—was even more adamant, telling Born that regulating derivatives would "cause the worst financial crisis since the end of World War Two." When Born wouldn't relent, Bob and Fed chief Alan Greenspan went to Congress to get legislation barring her agency from regulating derivatives. It would prove to be a terrible mistake.

The Commodity Futures Modernization Act stopped Born and any other financial regulator from overseeing the burgeoning market in increasingly exotic financial derivatives. In one respect, Bob was correct: Investors soon found a way to manage them safely on their own—or so they thought. They created "credit default swaps," which were supposed to insure them against losses. By 2007, the value of credit default swaps had ballooned to $62 trillion—nearly twice the size of the government securities market, mortgage market, and U.S. stock market combined. Investors were soon to discover, however, that despite its size, the giant credit default swaps market gave them no protection at all. After the calamity of the 2008 financial crisis, Bill conceded that Rubin and Summers had been wrong about derivatives, and that he had been wrong to take their advice.

At Bob's urging, Bill also agreed to repeal the Glass-Steagall Act, a Depression-era law that separated commercial banking from investment banking. It had been enacted to protect ordinary bank depositors from risks created by financial speculators. It also prevented banks from becoming so large as to exert the kind of political influence they wielded before the Great Crash of 1929. But with the repeal of Glass-Steagall in 1999, banks were once again free to become as large as they wished.

And they wished to become very large indeed. Anticipating Glass-Steagall's repeal, Travelers Group, an insurance and brokerage company, announced its intention to merge with Citibank, the biggest New York bank—creating in Citigroup the world's largest financial services company. It was the biggest corporate merger in history. Days after the repeal of Glass-Steagall, Bob accepted a top position at Citigroup.

I feared that all these changes in the rules of the game—linking CEO pay to stock prices, making deficit reduction the major economic goal instead of public investments in the workforce, enacting NAFTA, allowing Chinese accession to the World Trade Organization, and deregulating Wall Street—would widen inequality and further burden American workers. I argued against them. Bob and his allies in the administration, such as Lloyd Bentsen and Larry Summers, argued for them. They responded to my concerns with reassurances that the economy would boom and everyone would benefit.

For a time, the economy did boom—some of it due to the unsustainable dot-com bubble, and some to the normal, temporary upswing in the business cycle. Even the incomes of poor and working-class Americans began to rise. But after the boom petered out, the changes in the rules of the game advocated by Bob Rubin contributed to a permanent rise in the incomes of wealthy Americans while flattening the wages of average working people.

Because I was short enough to fit into the jump seat opposite Bill in the White House limo, I'd try to find out what time he was leaving the Oval Office so I could get in the limo and make my pitches to him in private, arguing against the policies Bob was pushing. Bill listened politely, but I could tell that my constant harping about widening inequality was beginning to make me more of an irritant than a helpful adviser.

I did what I could, which wasn't nearly as much as I wish it had been. I didn't marshal my arguments as effectively as I might have. In meetings, I kept asking whether we could see distribution tables from the Treasury Department, which would give some hint as to winners and losers from various proposals. My questions became increasingly predictable: "What about the impact of this on the working class? What about the poor?" I knew the Treasury had methodologies to answer these questions, but the data never seemed to arrive. I became increasingly cranky. I left several meetings so angry I had to restrain myself from not slamming the giant, heavy wooden doors in the Old Executive Office Building, where many of our meetings took place. Bob Rubin and Larry Summers never raised their voices. They always seemed cool, rational. They knew they had Alan Greenspan on their side, as well as most of corporate America and Wall Street.

I figured that since I couldn't have much effect on the administration's big decisions, I'd retreat to the Labor Department, where I could have a big impact on small decisions that, cumulatively, might provide substantial help to workers. For example, the fate of a batboy in Georgia.

The Batboy in Georgia

Child labor laws bar fourteen-year-olds from working past 7 p.m. on school nights. A hyper-vigilant Labor Department investigator discovered that the Savannah Cardinals, a Class A farm team of the Atlanta Braves, had hired as their batboy fourteen-year-old Tommy McCoy, who often worked late into the night. Next morning, Tommy went to school. The investigator threatened the team with a stiff fine. The team fired little Tommy.

Tommy liked being a batboy. His parents were proud of him. The team was fond of him. The fans loved him. As long as anyone could remember, every kid in Savannah had coveted the job. But now Tommy, who did well in school, was out of the best kid's job in town, and it seemed as if the whole city of Savannah was up in arms. The Cardinals were about to stage a "Save Tommy's Job Night" rally, featuring balloons, buttons, placards, and a petition signed by the fans demanding that Tommy be rehired. ABC News was doing a story on the controversy, which was how I first heard about it, and ABC wanted an on-camera interview with me that same evening, explaining why Tommy had been fired. They couldn't wait to show America the stupidity of the government (and of its new secretary of labor).

I tried to hold ABC off. They said they were running with the story with or without my interview. I called an urgent meeting with the Labor Department's top inspectors. I explained the situation to them, suggesting we let Tommy have his job back. They wouldn't hear of it. "It would look like you're caving in to public opinion," one of the chief inspectors said.

"But," I asked, "isn't it the *public* whom we're here to serve?"

They said the law was clear, that the Savannah team had broken it, and our responsibility was to enforce it.

"But shouldn't we have *priorities*?" I asked. "We have a limited number of inspectors. I can understand going after a building contractor who's hiring kids to lay roofing, but why go after a batboy?"

They said child labor was a serious problem. Children were getting injured working long hours.

"Exactly," I said. "So, let's focus on the *serious* offenses and ignore the less serious."

They warned that if I didn't support the department's investigators, the staff would become demoralized.

"Good! If they become demoralized and stop enforcing the law nonsensically, so much the better," I said.

They said that if I backed down, the Labor Department would lose credibility.

"We'll lose even *more* credibility if we stick with this outrageous decision," I said.

They said there was nothing we could do. The law was the law.

"Nonsense," I said. "We can change the regulation to make an exception for kids at sporting events."

But we'd invite all sorts of abuses, they argued. Vendors would exploit young kids on school nights to sell peanuts and popcorn. Stadiums would hire young children to clean the locker rooms. Parking lots would use children to collect money.

"So, we draw the exception tighter and limit it to batboys and batgirls!"

I was getting nowhere. *World News Tonight* would broadcast the story in minutes.

Then it hit me, like a fastball slamming into my think head: *I was secretary of labor. I could decide this by myself.*

"Thank you," I said, standing. "I've heard enough."

I turned to my assistant and said, "Tell the Savannah team they can keep Tommy. We're changing the regulation to allow batboys and girls. Put out a press release right *now*. Call the producers for *World News Tonight* and tell them I've decided to let Tommy have his batboy job. Tell them our investigator was way off base!"

"But *World News Tonight* is already on the air!" my assistant said.

"Call them *now!*"

I turned on the TV in the corner of my office. ABC's anchor, Peter Jennings, was already reading the news from his monitor. Within moments, he got to the story I was dreading: "The United States Department of Labor has decided that a fourteen-year-old named Tommy McCoy cannot serve as batboy for the Atlanta Braves farm team in Savannah, Georgia. The decision has provoked outrage from the fans. Here's more from . . ."

As Jennings turned it over to ABC's Atlanta correspondent, he appeared to be smirking. Damn. I looked around the table at the inspectors. Did they understand that in seven million living rooms across America people were now saying to each other, "How dumb can government get?" Did they care that the Department of Labor was about to be known as the *Department of Laughable Decisions*?

After two excruciating minutes during which ABC's Atlanta correspondent detailed the story of Tommy and the Labor Department, it was back to Jennings:

"But this tale has a happy ending."

My heart skipped.

"The Labor Department reports that Tommy will get his job back. Secretary of Labor Robert Reich has decided that the Department was—quote—'off base in invoking child labor regulations under these circumstances.'"

Joy! Relief!

The inspectors sitting around my table were dismayed. I tried to explain to them that people in charge of enforcing laws must determine which cases merit attention and resources and which don't. In doing this, they should use common sense. Target employers who are hiring young children for dangerous jobs over, say, a baseball farm team hiring a kid as a batboy.

The inspectors tended to view everyone who broke the law, including the Savannah Cardinals, as equally wrong. They had a view of right and wrong—of the bullies and the bullied—that was far more literal than mine. But not every illegal hire of a child had the same weight. Not everyone who did the hiring was a Mr. Potter. The world was more complicated.

It was about to become even more so.

The Fury in Oklahoma

On October 3, 2024, *The Wall Street Journal* featured a story about corporations maiming and killing workers by not allowing them to lock down machinery when the machinery must be maintained or cleaned. This had been going on for more than three decades.

I vividly recall one morning in 1994 when Joe Dear, who ran OSHA, the Occupational Safety and Health Administration, stormed into my office at the Labor Department. Joe was short and wiry, with the energy of a coiled spring. He had come to OSHA after serving as director of Washington State's Department of Labor and Industries. He was dedicated to worker safety.

Breathlessly, Joe told me that workers at Bridgestone's tire plant in Oklahoma City were getting mangled, even killed, in assembly machines that suddenly restarted when workers were unjamming or cleaning them. The company's other plants had similar horrors. OSHA investigators had repeatedly told Bridgestone executives to install a simple $6 device that would automatically cut off power to the machines whenever a worker locked them down, but the company wouldn't budge. Joe thought it was because the company was afraid its workers would use the device to stop the assembly line in order to gain bargaining leverage in upcoming union negotiations.

"We're hitting them with a $7.5 million fine, the maximum," Joe said.

Joe hadn't sought a fight with the second-largest tire maker in the world. We both knew it would unleash a giant team of lawyers and might drag the case through the courts for years unless we settled for a fraction of the fine. We also knew that final settlement wouldn't be enough to get Bridgestone to mend its ways anyway, if the company figured it was cheaper to pay up and continue risking workers' lives and limbs. Not for the first time had a company made this sort of calculation.

But *something* had to be done. Workers were getting maimed and killed. I was indignant. I felt righteousness coursing through my veins. "We've got to *stop* this, Joe. Maybe they could get away with this shit under the Republicans, but I'll be damned if they do it under our watch."

Joe looked worried. "We can't go any higher with the fine. We might be able to go to court in Oklahoma City and get an emergency order forcing them to comply there. It's dicey."

"Why not use all our ammo?" I felt like I was putting on my holster. "Let's also mobilize public opinion."

"Public opinion?" Joe's worry deepened.

I explained my theory. "Big corporations like Bridgestone spend millions on advertising and marketing to boost their public image. If we get this story on television, we'll embarrass the hell out of them and strike fear in the hearts of every other corporation that's screwing its workers."

Joe hadn't planned on my fury.

"I want to go out there," I said, now simmering. "I'll deliver the legal papers in person. We'll fly out Sunday night and do it Monday morning. Alert the media so they can be on hand. Hold a press conference, maybe with some of the injured workers, including the widow of the worker who was killed."

Press conference? Injured workers? A widow? Joe was warming to the idea. A smile spread across his face. This was no longer a legal matter. It had become an issue of public morality—and public relations.

"Will the employees be with us on this?" I asked.

"No question. You'll be a hero."

"Okay then. We go to Oklahoma City."

It was like I was galloping into town on a large white stallion, a sheriff's badge pinned to my vest. Few feelings in public office are more exhilarating than self-righteous indignation—or as dangerous.

Late Sunday night we met at the Murrah Federal Building in downtown Oklahoma City to plan the final details of our operation. With us were the department's top lawyer, two security agents, and a press aide.

We planned the route that our two vans would follow to the company headquarters, the precise time of our departure, when we'd alert the press so they could set up cameras outside the gate and film us as we entered, the time when we'd alert the company president so he had enough notice to direct company officials to receive us (but not enough to unleash his own lawyers and publicists), what I'd tell the executives inside, and the time and place of the press conference afterward. Several of the injured workers along with the widow of one who had died were ready to appear.

Joe and the rest of the team rode in silence to the Bridgestone plant. A half dozen TV cameras were waiting at the gate to record the spectacle. A guard allowed us through. We parked.

"We've hit the beach, Captain," Joe said.

"Walk slowly and keep your ammo dry."

We walked across the lot to the plant entrance. I imagined the scene on the evening news: barely visible through the mist, the silhouettes of America's runty but courageous secretary of labor leading his small battalion of gallant men to their fates, as they took on Industrial Evil. We were taking on the bullies.

Once we were inside, a nervous receptionist asked us to follow her. We walked down a narrow corridor and into a linoleum-floored room with a Formica table in the center, encircled by several chrome-and-plastic chairs. She said two gentlemen would be with us shortly, then rushed off.

A few minutes later, two grim-faced men entered and asked us to sit. One was a top executive from the company's U.S. headquarters, the other the plant manager. I introduced myself and the others, trying not to let my voice betray my nervousness. "We have come here to present you with court papers alleging that this plant presents an imminent hazard to the safety of its employees," I said gravely. Joe removed an inch-thick pile of legal papers from his briefcase and placed them in the center of the table. The two men stared at the pile, expressionless.

I continued to speak, more forcefully now. "We have urged you to correct these hazards, but they have not been corrected. We have no choice but to seek an emergency order that will require you to equip employees on the assembly line with a simple device to turn off the power when they must clean or unjam the machines. We're also imposing a $7.5 million fine."

I looked intently at the two men. They stared back. They said nothing.

What *now*? At a minimum, I expected them to try to defend themselves, which would have given me the chance to express outrage that they failed to buy a $6 device that could have saved lives and limbs. But there was just silence.

We marched back out of the building and across the parking lot. The camera crews were still lingering outside the gate. I tried to look determined, like someone who has just summoned the full force of the United States government against a common enemy.

A half hour later, the press gathered for the news conference at a downtown hotel to hear of our great battle. The widow, a frail woman in her late fifties, stood beside me. Around us were several of the workers who had been injured or maimed in the plant. In front of me, sitting in two rows of chairs, were other workers from the plant.

I explained why I had come to Oklahoma City, describing the mayhem that the company had caused and what actions the department would take, doing a weak imitation of William Jennings Bryan. "We will *not* allow workers to risk death and dismemberment simply because a company refuses to buy a $6 piece of safety equipment.

American workers are *not* going to be sacrificed on the altar of profits. We are *not* going to allow a competitive race to the bottom when it comes to the lives and limbs of American workers."

The workers applauded. The widow's eyes filled with tears. Reporters asked a few questions. Then, having cleaned up Oklahoma City, we rode off into the sunset on the next commercial flight back to Washington, feeling triumphant.

The triumph was short-lived.

Soon after we left Oklahoma, Bridgestone's vice president for public affairs held a news conference in Oklahoma City to rebut the Labor Department's allegations, claiming the company's procedures for servicing machines were fully adequate and that they didn't need the Labor Department *in Washington* telling them how to run their business.

Then he delivered the bombshell: Bridgestone had decided to close its Oklahoma City tire factory. All 1,100 workers would be out of jobs in weeks. He blamed the federal government, asserting that its safety standards had made the plant uneconomical.

The next morning's *Daily Oklahoman* used my expedition as an illustration of the worst sort of meddling from Washington. In a bitter editorial, it accused me of grandstanding for political purposes. Its front-page story quoted angry tire workers, soon to be unemployed, saying I should never have come to Oklahoma City. One even asserted that safety was never a problem at the plant and that machines must be kept running to be serviced properly.

If it's a choice between a dangerous job and no job, people will choose the dangerous job. I can't blame them. America's safety nets were—still are—in tatters, and we force workers to make this terrible choice repeatedly.

In the end, I asked our legal staff to drop the emergency order if the company would keep its plant open, which they agreed to do.

The bullies won. I was haunted by our failure. All I'd considered was the moral superiority of my position and the thrill of the spectacle. I hadn't imagined Bridgestone would take hostage the livelihoods of more than a thousand people. I hadn't understood that the mounting economic stresses across America would fuel anger at every major institution in society, including a federal government that sought to protect people from some of those stresses.

We must protect workers from corporate greed. That means fines that are high enough to make it truly costly for a corporation to ignore worker safety laws when it's profitable to do so. And safety nets strong enough to enable people to refuse to take on illegally dangerous work.

On February 11, 1992, a twenty-four-year-old army veteran named Timothy McVeigh wrote a letter to the *Lockport Union Sun & Journal* in Lockport, New York:

> The "American Dream" of the middle class has all but disappeared, substituted with people struggling to just buy next week's groceries. . . . At a point when the world has seen communism falter as an imperfect system to manage people, democracy seems heading down the same road. No one is seeing the "big picture." Maybe we have to combine ideologies to achieve the perfect utopian government. Remember, government-sponsored health care was a communist idea. Should only the rich be allowed to live longer? Does that say that because a person is poor he is a lesser human being and doesn't deserve to live as long, because (?) he doesn't wear a tie to work? . . . America is in serious decline. We have no proverbial tea to dump. Should we instead sink a ship of Japanese imports? Is a civil war imminent? Do we have to shed blood to reform the current system? I hope it doesn't come to that, but it might.

On the morning of April 19, 1995, McVeigh parked a rented Ryder truck in front of the Alfred P. Murrah Federal Building in downtown Oklahoma City, the building I had used as a command center. Inside McVeigh's vehicle was a powerful bomb made from a deadly cocktail of agricultural fertilizer, diesel fuel, and other chemicals. McVeigh got out of the truck, locked the door, and headed toward his getaway car. He remotely ignited one timed fuse, then another, and the bomb exploded. In moments, a third of the building was reduced to rubble. One hundred sixty-eight people died, including nineteen children. Several hundred more were injured. It was the worst act of homegrown terrorism in American history. Most of the adults who died or were injured were federal employees, although none were from the Labor Department.

I was devastated. What sort of person would do this? Why target federal workers? What was happening to America?

McVeigh later claimed that his actions were a response to the "abuses and usurpations" by the federal government. He referred to Ruby Ridge in rural Idaho, where a siege by U.S. marshals on the property of Randy Weaver on weapons charges ended in the killing of his wife and son, and to a siege in Waco, Texas, six months later, which ended in the death of seventy-six Branch Davidians.

More than a decade before the bombing, when McVeigh was still in high school, he had read *The Turner Diaries,* a novel about a right-wing rebellion against the federal government. The hero and narrator of the novel, Earl Turner, ignites a second civil war in America by setting off a truck bomb next to the FBI building in Washington. This planted the idea for what McVeigh did in Oklahoma City.

The incendiary political language of the 1990s added further fuel to McVeigh's internal fire. He listened to radio personality Rush Limbaugh, who used his talk show to say such things as "the second violent American revolution is just about—I got my fingers about a quarter of an inch apart—is just about that far away." McVeigh was the personification of evil but he saw himself as a warrior.

In a speech shortly after the bombing, Bill Clinton said, "We hear so many loud and angry voices in America today whose sole goal seems to be to try to keep some people as paranoid as possible and the rest of us all torn up and upset with each other." He went on: "They spread hate. They leave the impression that, by their very words, violence is acceptable. . . . I'm sure you are now seeing the reports of some things that are regularly said over the airwaves in America today. Well, people like that who want to share our freedoms must know that their bitter words can have consequences."

In response to Clinton's speech, Limbaugh denounced "irresponsible attempts to categorize and demonize those who had nothing to do with this. . . . There is absolutely no connection between these nuts and mainstream conservatism in America today." Limbaugh would be proven wrong. The connection between right-wing rhetoric and political violence in America would grow.

Americans were outraged by the bombing and sympathetic to

the families that had lost loved ones. For a moment it seemed as if the nation realized that federal workers weren't faceless bureaucrats but people just like themselves, trying to do their jobs as best they could. But the lull didn't last long. Soon, the anger against government welled up again. I ran into it almost everywhere. Some of it was directed at Bill and Hillary.

Labor Day in Wisconsin

I was perched atop the back seat of a bright-green 1958 Buick open-topped convertible as Imperial Marshal of the Wausau Gala Labor Day Parade. It was a cool, sun-drenched day with a hint of fall in the air. I waved to the few people who sat in lawn chairs along Main Street. Behind the convertible was the Wausau High School Marching Band, and behind them the Wausau Fire Department. Then came several groups holding banners: "Local #311 SEIU" and "Proud to be from Pipefitters Local #44" and "International Union of Electrical Workers Local #353." It seemed like far more people were *in* the parade than watching it.

I was there because Congressman David Obey, chairman of the House Appropriations Committee, had asked me to be. He and his committee doled out money to the Labor Department. His wish was my command.

Obey was perched next to me on the convertible's back seat. Bespectacled and sharp-nosed, he looked like an owl. He waved at anything capable of waving back. I admired him enormously. He was a progressive lawmaker in the tradition of Wisconsin's Robert "Fighting Bob" La Follette. He'd won some important battles for working people over the years. He was also tough and cranky.

"I'm worried," he said to me out of the side of his mouth, then waved to a middle-aged woman in a lawn chair, who smiled and waved back. "How ya' doin', Gladys?" He was talking about the upcoming midterm elections.

"That bad?" I asked.

"*I'll* do okay. But—geez—we're gonna lose a lot of good people." Another wave. He called out, "Hi ya, Gert!"

"Think we could lose the House?"

"Yup." Obey waved to a bald man holding an American flag, and yelled, "Atta-boy, Henry!"

"What's the problem?"

"Lot of things. NAFTA. Health care bill gone to hell. Gays in the military. Guns. This dame Paula Jones. Hillary. Baseball strike."

"They're gonna take it out on the Democrats?"

"Working folk out here don't much like your boss," he said quietly. He turned to wave—"Hi Frankie! Good to see ya!"—then back. "'Specially men. Hey, Arch! How you doin'?"

"What do men have against him?"

Obey didn't say anything for a few minutes. He continued to wave and shout to his constituents, many of them people he'd known for decades.

Then, at a lull in the sidewalk crowd, he turned directly to me. "Factories closing. New jobs pay shit. Guys have to take women's work in fast food, retail, hospitals, hotels. Their wives have to work harder, longer hours. These guys are angry. Humiliated. Furious. They thought Clinton would change all that, but it only got worse. NAFTA and global trade scares the hell out of them. Then he wants to take away their guns! He wants to put gays in the army! He doesn't stand up to a bitch from Arkansas who accuses him of hanky-panky. He puts his bossy law-school graduate wife in charge of healthcare reform, which crashes. Get the picture?" He turned back to the lawn chairs. "Hey, Emma!"

"Not sure I do."

He looked at me as if I was the dumbest kid in the class. "Emasculation! Blue-collar men already lost one testicle before Clinton. Now they're both gone. And they blame *us, Democrats!*" Then another wave. "Beatrice, you look beautiful!"

On the Air in the Midwest

"You're on Talk Radio 95, *The Charles Walton Show,* where you hear the news when it's news! Joining us this evening, the United States secretary of labor! Here to take y-o-o-o-u-u-u-r calls! . . . John from Garden Park. You're on Talk Radio 95!"

"Hello?"

"You're on the air, John! Do you have a question for the secretary?"

"Yes. Mr. Secretary, have you ever held a real job in your entire life?"

"Well, John, I used to teach."

"Just what I thought. You don't know nothing."

"Thank you, John! Diane from Oak Brook, you're on the air!"

"Hi, Charlie."

"Hi, Diane!"

"Love your show, Charlie."

"Thanks, Diane! A question for the labor secretary?"

"Why does the secretary think government has all the answers?"

"I don't think government has all the answers, Diane."

"Yes you do. You and all the other liberals in the Clinton administration. Ever heard of free enterprise? Socialism doesn't work!"

"Thank you, Diane! Next up, Peter from Lakeview! Pete, you're on the air!"

"Great show, Charlie."

"Thanks, Pete! Your question?"

"I don't understand something."

"What is it you don't understand, Pete?"

"I don't understand where these guys get off."

"Your question for the labor secretary, Pete?"

"Mr. Secretary, why do you think you have the right to tax honest hardworking people? It's *our* money."

"Pete, your federal taxes pay for national defense, Medicare, highways, environmental protection, air-traffic control, safe workplaces, all sorts of things you rely on."

"It's *my* money. I should decide what I need. You have no right."

"Thank you, Pete! We're cooking tonight, folks! The board's all lit up! Ted from Orleyville, you're on the air!"

"I really appreciate your show, Charles."

"Thank you, Ted! Your question for the secretary?"

"Yes. Mr. Secretary, you're a fucking—"

"Michelle in Garden View! You're on the air!"

"I'd like to know why we spend billions and billions of dollars on welfare for people who do nothing all day but sit around and watch TV."

"Michelle, all welfare spending is less than 3 percent of the federal budget, and most people on welfare are off it and into jobs within two years."

"You're lying."

"Tony in Lakeview! You're on the air!"

"I just lost my job. My company went to Mexico. I want to ask the labor secretary how anybody can get a good job in America if we have to compete with Mexicans who are paid a nickel an hour?"

"Good question, Tony! Mr. Secretary?"

"Tony, I'm sorry you lost your job. But there are millions of good new jobs out there, some of them exporting to Mexico and other countries. You can get—"

"Good new jobs? Where? The new jobs pay nothing. They pay shit. You're talking out of your asshole."

"Afraid that's all the time we have! Mr. Secretary, thanks so very much for being with us this evening!"

Memo to the President About
the Upcoming Election

TO: POTUS
From: Labor Secretary Robert Reich
RE: Upcoming election
Date: October 2, 1994

We're in danger of losing Congress.

Yes, the economic plan is paying off. More than four million new jobs have been added. But there's a huge amount of frustration and disillusionment in the land. Only a relative few are sharing in the newfound prosperity. The middle class is becoming an *anxious* class.

Only the richest 5 percent of Americans are gaining much ground. In fact, their share of national income in 1993 (48.2 percent) is the highest on record. The gap is the widest since the Census began collecting data almost thirty years ago.

In 1992, Americans voted for "change" because so many were losing ground. Your economic plan spurred the recovery but didn't stop the slide. As a result, these Americans feel betrayed. They're likely to vote for "change" again in 1994.

Polls show that the voters who are most alienated from the administration are *adults without college degrees,* whose incomes have dropped the most. Many are "Reagan Democrats," who were slowest to rally to you in 1992, are still distrustful of government, and are most likely to desert the Democrats this November. Others are the working poor, so disillusioned with politics that they've stopped voting.

The main economic strategies you've embarked on—deficit reduction and free trade—won't reverse the slide.

Deficit reduction has added to national savings and initially reduced long-term interest rates, which has helped middle-class borrowers. But it hasn't benefited the bottom half. Free trade is similarly good for the economy overall, but its benefits aren't shared equally. The higher-skilled and better-educated gain a global market for their services, while those with low skills or no skills have to compete with lower-wage workers around the world.

What's the answer?

Profitable companies must share part of their burgeoning profits with their employees, instead of simply seeking to put a lid on wages. There was once an implicit social contract in this nation which dictated that as companies did better, so should their workers. That compact has come undone. You should propose tax incentives to encourage companies to share profits and upgrade skills, rather than keep a lid on wages or fire workers.

Workers also need stronger unions. You should call for labor law reforms that make it easier to form unions.

They need looser monetary policy from the Fed, so interest rates fall and labor markets tighten. Not much you can do about this but use whatever influence you have.

Signal your clear intention to raise the minimum wage. It will help workers at the bottom (the average minimum-wage worker brings home half the family income), and have a "ripple effect" upward on working-class wages.

Finally, between now and the midterm elections, you (and other Democrats) must at least *acknowledge* the problem. Recognize the frustrations and fears of a large segment of the workforce. Talk about the challenge of widening inequality. Talk about the responsibilities of profitable corporations to share the good times with their employees.

I received no response to this memo.

The Triumph of the Nasties

The growing anger in America had deeper roots, but Bill and Hillary were convenient targets.

Just before the midterm elections, Bob Michel, the House minority leader, a Republican, invited me to his office. His staff said he wanted to talk about what was going on in the Labor Department, but I sensed there was more to it than that. Michel had a kindly face topped by a shock of white hair and spoke in a mellifluous baritone. The overall effect was grandfatherly. He had just announced his decision to retire from the House and not seek another term.

"This place used to be very civil," he said, leaning back in his chair. "Republicans and Democrats often saw things differently, of course, but we respected one another. We could actually get something done. We respected the institution." I heard wistfulness in his voice.

"You see that changing?" I asked, naïvely.

"It's becoming a different world up here. That's a big part of why I'm getting out. There's a new breed. They don't care about getting anything done. All they want to do is tear things down. The right wing is gaining ground. It will be our undoing, eventually."

"You mean [Newt] Gingrich?"

"And his friends." Michel's voice grew softer. "They talk as if they're interested in ideas, in what's good for America. But don't be fooled. They're out to destroy. They'll try to destroy anything that gets in their way, using whatever tactics are available. They don't believe in bipartisanship. I don't really know what they believe in."

I thought Michel's observation true of Washington as a whole, maybe even the nation. The media didn't cause Americans to feel angry; it simply mirrored their feelings. Mean-spirited politicians don't simply appear on the national scene by accident. They're put there by angry voters whose feelings they reflect.

—

After the 1994 midterms, Democrats lost control of both houses of Congress in a wave of anger directed at Bill Clinton, Democratic lawmakers, and, it seemed, government in general. Gingrich took over as House majority leader. The media treated him as the new king of Washington and accorded him the celebrity normally reserved for new presidents at inaugurations. I couldn't help thinking how different it would have been had Bob Michel remained.

Bob Dole took over the Senate. He trumpeted his victory, too. Gingrich and Dole seemed to have taken command of the United States government. In our system, power is found where the public seems to have conferred it, and the two of them were credibly claiming to have most of it. Bill was pained. He came to Washington with a bold agenda, and now all the energy seemed to be on the Republicans' side. Part of the reason they gained the upper hand is they spent much of the previous two years pillorying Bill and Hillary, attacking and ultimately defeating their healthcare plan and raising questions about their ethics.

One day, several of us joined Bill in the ornate Map Room in the basement of the White House. We talked for more than an hour about the situation but didn't come up with anything he found helpful. Finally, he stood up. Worry and frustration showed on his face. "You have to *help* me," he said, slowly, looking around the group. "I don't *want* to use their tactics. I don't want to be *mean*." There was a long pause. Then he said more softly, "This is a cynical age. Doing good and right aren't sufficient anymore. Being mean isn't a disqualification anymore."

Bill's mind seemed to be operating on a different plane than ours. He was considering questions and choices that none of us completely understood. His voice rose. "Gingrich isn't the *only* mean one. Dole went on TV a year ago today, on the very day I was burying my mother, crapping on me about Whitewater. Then he told his troops in the Senate not to do what was right on the crime bill but to vote to defeat me." He looked around the table and pleaded, "I don't want to be like them. But you have to help me."

No one said anything for about a minute. Then Al Gore responded softly. "The people have to see you as optimistic, confident, sure of the direction you're taking the country. If I'd been the object of as much unfair criticism as you and Hillary, I'd be much angrier. But we have the time. There's no reason to panic."

Time? Panic? I couldn't keep one morbid thought out of my mind: If Bill and Gore were to die right then, the law of the land would confer the presidency on Newt Gingrich. Gingrich was a brilliant political operator and an intellectual opportunist. I'd met with him several times in his office, and each time gone away with the distinct impression of a military general in an age where campaign strategy had supplanted military strategy, where explosive ideas had become more important sources of power than bombs. He professed to understand this and spent a great deal of time and energy trying to persuade others that he alone possessed the strategy and the ideas entitling him to be the general of the new Republican right.

Gingrich channeled the growing anger in America. He instructed Republicans to use these words about Democrats: sick, pathetic, lie, anti-flag, traitors, radical, corrupt. In the midterm election he had claimed that "people like me are what stand between us and Auschwitz. I see evil all around me every day." Gingrich liked to think of himself as a revolutionary force, but he behaved more like a naughty boy. He grinned uncontrollably when I congratulated him on a devious legislative ploy; he became defensive when I gently scolded him for misusing certain historical ideas in support of one of his grand theses. His office was adorned with figurines of dinosaurs, as you might find in the bedrooms of little boys who dream one day of being huge and powerful. To characterize Gingrich as "mean" missed this essential quality of naughtiness. His meanness was real, but it was the meanness of a little kid rather than a tyrant. And like all bullies, inside was an insecure little fellow who desperately wanted attention.

Gingrich personified an irony: he gained popularity by supporting views that harmed the people who voted for him and his ilk, such as his vociferous opposition to healthcare reform. Like others who followed him, he channeled the public's anger at the loss of jobs and good wages—and the loss of pride and respect that accompanied them—into distrust of government.

Almost overnight, it seemed, Congress grew nastier. It wasn't just because Republicans were now in charge. Many of the older-guard

Republicans, like Bob Michel, were gone. Some others I had got to know and work with during the previous years had lost their races or had been through unexpectedly tough primaries. The newly elected Republicans seemed surlier, reflecting voters who were surlier. In one congressional hearing soon after the new Congress was installed, my testimony was interrupted by a newly elected congressman who asked, seemingly out of the blue, "Mr. Secretary, are you a socialist?" I said no but was flummoxed. Where did this person come from? Why was he so accusatory?

The former Congress had hardly been all sweetness. The previous year I had walked into an elevator in the Senate office building followed by Senator Strom Thurmond, Republican from South Carolina, and one of his aides. Thurmond was then ninety-two years old.

Thurmond nodded to me. "Nice suit you have on, Mr. Secretary," he said.

"Thank you, Senator."

"Do they make it in an adult size, too?"

Thurmond wasn't smiling. His aide looked decidedly uncomfortable. Did Thurmond intend to be nasty? Was it dementia?

I said nothing. The elevator doors opened. I moved to leave.

"Nice to see you, Mr. Secretary," he said as he waved.

In public, the new congressional Republicans displayed an acrimony I hadn't seen before. They didn't seem to want to build anything; they seemed to want to tear everything down. At my first hearing on the Labor Department's upcoming appropriation, Ernest Istook, newly elected Republican from Oklahoma, whose black-rimmed glasses and bread-dough face made him look like a high school debate nerd, laid into me. "Mr. Sec-re-tar-y," he spit in a low boom-box voice, "I recall April of last year when you made a *personal* visit to Oklahoma City—to my congressional district."

I tried to look calm and confident. Istook glared back. He talked slowly, spitting out small mouthfuls of indignation, savoring every syllable: "You made a huge media event out of announcing you were fining [Bridgestone] $7.5 million. . . . The company saw no way to comply . . . other than to shut down. And *one thousand five hundred people* in my district were worried about whether they would ever be able to go back to work, because *Sec-re-tar-y Reich* had come to town."

I tried to explain but he interrupted. This was political theater, and he didn't want to yield the stage. Indignation in his voice turned to contempt. "This became part of the reason that people in Oklahoma turned against the Clinton administration and its advocates and created a momentum that led to . . . *November.*" He uttered "November" with revolutionary fervor. November! The Gingrich Revolution! The boom box boomed more loudly. "This attitude you displayed when you came into my congressional district created a big-time circus event."

I knew I couldn't win but I tried to explain anyway, "Congressman, I have to do what I think is right. I have to make some hard calls. A worker died. OSHA's conclusion . . ."

"Which was reached *after your personal intervention!*"

"No, Congressman, I decided to intervene only after I got the report from OSHA."

"You *pushed* them toward that decision!"

He was calling me a liar. He was assaulting my integrity. This was war, and I had no idea how to defend myself. "Congressman, the staff at OSHA . . ."

The boom box grew more menacing. "They saluted and went along with what *you wanted*! And now you say you bear no culpability! That you want to blame your *subordinates*! I hope the people in your department are aware of your attitude!"

I was used to disputes over policy when I appeared at congressional hearings, but this was personal. Istook and his ilk didn't want to talk policy. They were intent on character assassination. They were bullies and thugs. They were also reflecting the anger that had grown throughout America, for all the reasons I've cited. Workers were losing faith that they and their children would do better.

Here I was, near the center of official power in America but feeling utterly powerless to do anything about any of this.

Bill was falling ever more under the influence of Bob Rubin, Wall Street, and big money. After losing his bid for universal healthcare, Bill announced that the "era of big government" was over. Meanwhile, the mounting wealth at the top was overflowing into politics in the form of fat-cat donations to candidates on both sides of the aisle.

In August 1996, the Center for Public Integrity, which monitored how money was trying to influence lawmakers, released a ten-page report called "Fat Cat Hotel: How Democratic High-Rollers Are Rewarded with Overnight Stays at the White House." The report examined the connection between such stays in the Lincoln Bedroom during Bill's presidency and financial contributions to the Democratic Party and to Bill's 1996 presidential campaign. A Democratic National Committee memorandum from its finance chair, Terry McAuliffe, had contained the names of potential donors along with Bill's notation: "Ready to start overnights right away—give me the top 10 list back, along with the 100." No charges were ever brought by the Department of Justice in connection with the matter. The bedroom practice was unseemly, but it was not illegal. Yet media stories about it contributed to a growing sense that the system was corrupt, rigged for those at the top.

I began to understand that I was losing the "battle of the Bobs" not just because I lacked convincing policy arguments about trade, unions, the deregulation of Wall Street, or CEO pay. I was also losing because the moneyed interests were gaining power, and they were dead set against my arguments.

Paying Bill Gates $135 for Lunch

No wealthy political donor ever slept in my rental house a mile northwest of the White House, and I didn't dine with billionaires— until one day Bill Gates asked me to lunch. Gates was then CEO of Microsoft and the richest person in America. I was curious and flattered, and accepted his invitation. I had no idea why he asked me to lunch except that I was reputed to have influence with the other Bill, in the Oval Office. Had he known how little influence I had, Gates probably wouldn't have made the effort.

I don't recall much about our lunch except that it was at one of Washington's most expensive restaurants, and that everything Gates said struck me as rather predictable. He was probably as bored with me as I was with him. When I returned to my office, the Labor Department's chief lawyer stopped by to ask if I had enjoyed the lunch and if I had paid for my portion. I was embarrassed to tell him that paying had never occurred to me. I was having lunch with *Bill Gates,* for crying out loud. The chief lawyer patiently explained that federal law barred employees of the executive branch from accepting gifts whose value exceeded $50. "There are exceptions," he said, "but my advice is that you send Gates a check for the value of your lunch."

"Really? A check to *Bill Gates*?" I asked, incredulously. "I don't even know how much it cost!"

He whipped out a piece of paper. "We phoned his office, and you owe him $120."

"But . . ." I stammered.

"Oh, and be sure to make it a personal check," he said. "I can have it delivered to his hotel this afternoon. For safety's sake, add $15 to cover the cost of delivery."

I did what the Labor Department's chief lawyer advised I do. I believe but cannot be sure (this was more than thirty years ago) that Gates cashed my check.

I was reminded of this transaction when it was revealed that ever since he became a Supreme Court justice, Clarence Thomas had been taking lavish vacations and gifts from billionaire Republican donor Harlan Crow. Thomas also sold his relatives' properties to Crow, who had paid tuition for one of Thomas's relatives. Thomas has helped make megadonors like Crow even more powerful.

Over the years, in his Supreme Court opinions, Thomas had repeatedly ruled against requiring politicians to reveal the names of people who donated to them, and against any contribution limits at all. In the Court's notorious 2010 *Citizens United v. Federal Election Commission* decision, which Thomas joined, a bare majority of justices ruled that limits on "independent political spending" by corporations and other outside groups violate the First Amendment right to free speech. The Court thereby overturned election spending restrictions that dated back more than a hundred years. Before *Citizens United,* it was assumed that certain of these restrictions prevented corruption. But in *Citizens United,* the Court's majority held that "independent political spending" presented no substantive threat of corruption, as long as it wasn't coordinated with a candidate's campaign. The ruling dramatically expanded the already outsized political influence of wealthy donors and corporations. Corporations could now spend unlimited funds on campaign advertising. As if this weren't damage enough, the Court's majority also dropped "buying influence" from the definition of "corruption" that it had been using for decades.

Thomas went a step further than the other justices, refusing to sign on to the part of the *Citizens United* opinion upholding donor *disclosure* as a cornerstone of American campaign finance laws. In his partial dissent, Thomas claimed that disclosure rules violate the First Amendment rights of donors by opening them up to criticisms and threats that might "chill" their "speech"—that is, their donations. Thomas ignored the free speech rights of constituents who might wish to hold their elected officials accountable. Thomas subsequently called the trips and gifts from Crow "personal hospitality from a close personal friend" that did not have to be reported.

Is Capitalism Moral?

Republicans sent the White House a bill to eliminate welfare. Polls showed that a majority of the public agreed. With the 1996 election looming, Bill was under pressure to fulfill his campaign promise to "end welfare as we know it." Most of the cabinet were against his signing the Republican bill, but his political advisers urged him to.

"Mr. President, four years ago you promised to end welfare as we know it, and this is as close as you'll get to having a chance to reform the system," said one political adviser.

"The bill isn't perfect, but the welfare system is rotten, so you should sign the bill and pledge to fix the bad parts when you're reelected," said another.

I couldn't think of anything to say at the cabinet meeting that Bill would listen to.

What I wanted to say but didn't was *You're twenty points ahead in the polls, for chrissake. You don't need to hurt people this way. You don't need to settle for this Republican piece of shit. Veto it and explain to the public why you did. Explain that you want to get poor people into jobs, and that to do so requires money. Explain that without adequate job skills or childcare, there's simply no way. And as long as the Fed is intent on raising interest rates (and putting people out of jobs) to control inflation, there won't be enough jobs to go around. So, we'll need public-service jobs. Make all this part of your next campaign. That's the whole point of being reelected, isn't it? Why else do you want to be president?*

He left the meeting and retreated to the Oval Office, where Hillary was waiting. She was his most important political adviser. I felt sure she would advise him to sign the bill. Allowing his cabinet to have our say demonstrated that he respected us enough to hear our objections, but after the meeting I felt sick to my stomach. I wanted to go to sleep and wake up with a knock at the door to find a tall, gangly, sweet-faced twenty-two-year-old holding a bowl of chicken soup in one hand and crackers in the other, saying, "Heard ya weren't feeling too well."

I walked alone all the way down Pennsylvania Avenue back to the Labor Department—past the Department of Justice, in which I had toiled under Robert Bork and Gerald Ford, past the Federal Trade Commission, where I'd worked under Mike Pertschuck and Jimmy Carter. The U.S. Capitol loomed in front of me. I turned left, up the steps of the Labor Department, into the empty great hall, and then into an elevator up to my office. I sat down at my desk and looked out at the Capitol's great gleaming dome. I asked myself if it was worth it. All the time and energy, fourteen hours a day—for what? To stave off the bullies? Hell, I was a member of an administration that was allowing the economic system to bully millions of helpless people.

Just as I was about to hit bottom, my chief of staff, Kitty Higgins, walked in. She saw my face. She had watched me become glummer by the day.

"What's up?" I said, trying to pick my chin off the floor.

"We've got a problem."

The last thing I needed in this world was another problem.

"Tell me. What is it?"

"It's *you!*"

"Me? What do you mean?"

Then she let me have it. "You're the captain. People watch you for subtle cues about whether our team is winning or losing, and whether they're doing what you want them to. Every one of the assistant secretaries and their deputies, along with hundreds of senior staff around here, see that hangdog look in your eyes, the way your shoulders droop . . . What did you think government would be like, anyway? Did you suppose you could snap your fingers . . . and America would change? That's just arrogance, Mr. Secretary. Pure arrogance."

She was right.

Days later, it occurred to me that if we succeeded in raising the minimum wage, we would lift hundreds of thousands of American families out of poverty. Some would no longer need welfare. Bill was willing to go along, but how could we get Congress to raise the minimum wage when Republicans were in control of both houses, and the Chamber of Commerce and the National Restaurant Association were lobbying intensively against it?

I turned to two people who would know how: Ted Kennedy and Minnesota senator Paul Wellstone. They thought it worth a try.

I watched in awe as they managed the minimum wage bill in the Senate, wielding Senate procedural rules like football players executing a complicated play.

I had come to deeply admire both. Kennedy was by then a seasoned warhorse. He had been elected to the Senate in 1964 and reelected seven more times. He walked with a slight limp due to a plane crash years before that had broken his back. Silver-haired and heavyset, still possessing an unmistakable Boston accent and a quick laugh, he was called the "lion of the Senate" even by his Republican colleagues because of his experience, influence, and the raw power of his personality. I saw in him reflections of his brother Robert, at whose funeral at St. Patrick's Cathedral in New York City, in 1968, he had said:

My brother need not be idealized or enlarged in death beyond what he was in life; to be remembered simply as a good and decent man, who saw wrong and tried to right it, saw suffering and tried to heal it, saw war and tried to stop it. Those of us who loved him and who take him to his rest today, pray that what he was to us and what he wished for others will someday come to pass for all the world. As he said many times, in many parts of this nation, to those he touched and who sought to touch him: "Some men see things as they are and say why. I dream things that never were and say why not."

Wellstone was short and wiry, with a wry smile and the energy of a spring coil. He could see the moral issue at the core of every major battle in Congress and was forever optimistic that the public would be with him when he explained his position. Some years later, when Wellstone voted against the Iraq War resolution, I phoned to congratulate him on his courage; polls in Minnesota showed most voters strongly in favor of the resolution. "But please assure me you didn't just give up your Senate seat," I added with a laugh, although I was genuinely worried. Wellstone reassured me. "Don't worry. They elected me because I stay true to my values. When I explain why we shouldn't be in Iraq, they may not agree but they'll vote for me."

What made me so fond of Kennedy and Wellstone was not just their effectiveness in getting bills through the Senate on behalf of working people and the poor—bills that many observers assumed were lost causes, such as the minimum wage in a Republican Congress—but also their spirit. They avoided the cynicism that by then had begun to enshroud much of official Washington—the necessity to placate lobbyists and corporate donors, the ends-justify-means excuses, the partisan mud fights. They were big government liberals, and proud of it. In Massachusetts and in Minnesota they had put together coalitions of working-class men and women, Black people, Latinos, members of organized labor, and the poor that helped them repeatedly win elections. Both sincerely, passionately believed in social justice. They were happy warriors, my comrades in arms.

Before the vote on the minimum wage, I briefed Democratic senators and House members, pointing out that adjusted for inflation the minimum wage was at a forty-year low and that the average minimum-wage worker brought in half the family's income. The reason Democrats and most of their Republican colleagues ultimately voted for the increase had little or nothing to do with my policy arguments. They voted for it because over 80 percent of Americans, in poll after poll, favored raising it. And *they* were in favor because it was the right thing to do. It was a matter of basic fairness. The stock market was soaring. Corporations were enjoying record profits. The people at the top had never had it so good. It was only right that hardworking people at the bottom got a bit of a raise.

The measure passed both chambers. Over 10 million Americans working at the minimum wage would get a raise of ninety cents an hour. That might not sound like much, but it meant an additional $36 a week to many workers and their families who were barely getting by. Soon after the vote, Democratic senators and House members who had shepherded the bill through the Republican Congress gathered to give themselves, and me, and American workers, a round of applause.

Kennedy, Wellstone, and I held a press conference in the Capitol. Standing behind a table of groceries representing what the typical minimum-wage earner could now buy, Kennedy explained it would help Americans "who do some of the most difficult work in our society . . . teachers' aides, janitors, healthcare workers, hardworking men and women who want to be part of the American dream."

Wellstone called it "a matter of simple justice." I noted that most Americans supported the minimum-wage increase even though only a small portion of the public would get any direct benefit from it because it was "a moral issue. . . . Americans said it is fair, it is decent, it is about time."

That afternoon, hundreds of Labor Department employees crowded into the great hall on the first floor of the building and cheered as I entered. I was surprised and touched. There were so few times in those difficult years when I had a clear sense that I was improving people's lives. I and my team had worked hard to get the bill passed. It was a thrilling moment.

"Good work, Mr. Secretary," Kitty said, with a big grin.

I think most Americans dislike welfare because they don't believe in handouts to anyone who's able to work. But they also believe that anyone working full-time should earn enough to be able to keep themselves and their family out of poverty. Most Americans also believe that anyone who wants and needs work should have access to a job, and that if a corporation is doing better, the people who work for it should do better, too. Taken together, these ideas constitute a kind of moral code at the heart of American capitalism. Contrary to economists and right-wing pundits who believe people are motivated entirely by selfishness, this code is broadly supported even though most people aren't affected by it directly or personally. It's supported because it seems *fair*.

It's easy to lose sight of or underestimate the typical American's sense of fairness, but time and again I've seen it and heard it. It's not as theoretical as put forward by philosopher John Rawls, but it's consistent with Rawls's theory. The hate and anger now pervading American politics may have obscured the sentiment for now, but I'm confident our sense of fairness will reemerge. Kennedy and Wellstone never wavered, and they never deployed hate. They worked with their adversaries, coaxing them, reasoning with them, seeking to find common ground. Hate is a dangerous corrosive. It undermines civility, eats away at social trust, and dissolves bonds of community and nation. To me, people who wield hate for personal ambition are among the vilest of human beings. They must be held accountable for the consequences of their hatefulness.

Paul Wellstone died on October 25, 2002, at the age of fifty-eight, in the crash of a charter plane near Eveleth, Minnesota, that also took the lives of his wife, Sheila; his daughter, Marcia; several of his campaign staff; and the plane's two pilots. They were heading to Eveleth to attend the funeral of a steelworker whose son then served in the Minnesota House of Representatives. Wellstone had chosen to attend the funeral rather than a Minneapolis rally and fundraiser with Walter Mondale and Ted Kennedy.

Kennedy died August 25, 2009, of a brain tumor, at his home in Hyannis Port, Massachusetts. He was seventy-seven years old.

I attended the funerals of both men. With each of their passings, I sensed that America had lost parts of its moral bearings.

My Illicit Affair

It began at one of those interminable Washington receptions I had grown to hate. They were always stand-up events where I was expected to engage in small talk with dozens if not hundreds of people I didn't know, moving among groups while trying to balance a drink with a napkin containing cheese puffs or tiny cucumber sandwiches, and shaking hands as if enjoying myself. The hardest part was deciphering what people were saying to me because their voices emanated a foot or more above my ears and the ballrooms were invariably noisy. When encircled by the taller-than-normal men who tended to be senators and members of Congress, I felt as if I'd fallen into a well.

At this particular reception, a senior senator on the Judiciary Committee began telling me something with apparent glee, but he was so very tall and the crowd so noisy that I couldn't hear a word. So I grabbed a nearby chair and stood on it, which put our heads at about the same level.

"I'm Alan Simpson," he said, with great amusement.

"Well, Senator, I'm Robert Reich, and I'm glad to be up here in the stratosphere with you." We shook hands.

"A bit dizzying up here, isn't it?" He laughed.

"Better than down there, where I can't hear a damn thing and get spit on."

"I'd never spit on a cabinet member, not even a Democrat," he said, with mock seriousness.

"Not intentionally, but you'd be surprised how much saliva rains down there. I almost need an umbrella."

By this time several attendees had gathered around us, amused that the extremely tall Republican senator and unusually short Democratic secretary had found common ground—that is, height.

Everything I had learned about Simpson suggested we occupied the opposite extremes of Washington. He was a conservative Republican from Wyoming, a fiscal hawk, close friend of George H. W. Bush, chum of Dick Cheney and George W. Bush, and six-foot-seven. He had served in the Wyoming legislature for thirteen years after being elected in 1964, then been a three-term U.S. senator starting with his election in 1978. Yet within minutes of standing next to him on top of a chair in the middle of that reception, I discovered we had something in common: our senses of humor. He told me that his mother was over a hundred and fit as a fiddle because she walked five miles a day. "The only problem is we have no idea where she is," he deadpanned. I almost fell off my chair.

I asked him if he knew the difference between congressional politics and university politics. "No, tell me!" he asked with a broad grin. "In Congress, it's dog-eat-dog," I explained. "In university politics, it's exactly the opposite." He cracked up.

"You're very funny," he said. "You always seem very serious when I see you on the news."

"CNN doesn't appreciate shtick."

"What's *shtick*?"

"You seriously don't know?"

"No."

"Cow dung on a stick."

He exploded in laughter.

I told him that I took my job very seriously but tried not to take myself too seriously. He said he did the same, but most of his colleagues did the reverse. He then told me about his family, and I told him about mine. We both missed our kids, another point of connection.

We resolved to meet for lunch. When I returned to the Labor Department and asked my assistant to arrange it, she demurred. "You haven't had lunch with most Democratic senators. If you have lunch with Simpson they'll be insulted," she warned. She informed my chief of staff, who was even more determined that I not lunch with Simpson. "You haven't even had lunch with Ted Kennedy!" she said. "Besides, it would be wrong. Republicans hate us. What would people think?" Simpson's staff was against our lunch, too (he later told me). They said it was inappropriate for a senior Republican senator from one of the most conservative states in the nation to have lunch with the most liberal member of Clinton's cabinet. "Your constituents in Wyoming will have a fit," they told him.

We snuck out for lunch. Neither of our staffs knew where we'd gone. Alan suggested a bistro at some distance from the Capitol and the Labor Department where we wouldn't be found. We spent hours sharing personal stories, laughing, talking about our families. It was the start of a beautiful friendship. When I think of the poisoned politics of our time, when Republicans and Democrats often loathe one another, I'm grateful for Alan.

In subsequent months and years we saw quite a lot of each other. It was an illicit relationship by the emerging norms of Washington, but we didn't care. After I left the administration and Alan retired from the Senate and accepted a temporary position at the Kennedy School's Institute of Politics, we grew even closer. We did a public television show together on Boston's WGBH where we discussed the issues of the week for thirty minutes, mixing humor and politics. We called it *The Long and the Short of It*. We began each episode by walking toward each other from opposite sides of the stage set, in silhouette—Alan's long, lanky frame almost entirely filling one side of it and my stubby one filling barely two-thirds—and shaking hands before sitting down, when the stage lights would go on and we'd go at it. We often disagreed on the issues but did it with so much warmth and evident enjoyment of each other's company that many people wrote in to say they loved watching us because we were such a relief from the usual political fare. The show lasted only one season, but we had a wonderful time doing it.

We also appeared in various forums, such as the institute run by Leon and Sylvia Panetta in Monterey, California. On these occasions, Alan and I often shared regrets about what was happening to American politics. "They hate each other," he said, of the crop of Democrats and Gingrich Republicans who followed us into Washington.

When Trump first ran for president in 2016, I asked Alan why he thought more Republicans weren't speaking out against Trump. "They're scared," he said.

"Scared of Trump?"

"No," he said, lowering his voice. "They're scared of the kind of people Trump is attracting and what he's bringing out in them."

"You mean, they're scared of being physically harmed?"

"Friend, it only takes one nutcase."

Alan had become a controversial figure among Trump Republicans for his liberal views on women's rights and gay rights. He had long been controversial among liberals and Democrats for other positions he took. He served on the Senate Judiciary Committee that skewered Anita Hill and confirmed Clarence Thomas. As the Republican co-chair of Obama's commission on the federal deficit, he called Social Security recipients "greedy geezers." When California's Alliance for Retired Americans protested one of his appearances in the state, he called their view "a nefarious bunch of crap." In an email to an official of the Older Women's League who complained that he wanted to cut Social Security, he compared the program to "a milk cow with 310 million tits," and ended with "call when you get honest work."

He made some errors, but I admired his sincerity and passion for democracy. Alan wasn't in anyone's pocket, and he bemoaned the role of big money in politics. "If this crap continues," he told me one day when we were doing *The Long and the Short of It,* "in a few years, some wealthy bozo is gonna buy the whole damn presidency. It's ludicrous."

The last time we spoke was when I phoned to congratulate him on being awarded the Presidential Medal of Freedom by President Biden.

"I saw it was you calling," he said. "I wouldn't have answered if it was anyone else."

"Congratulations, Alan," I said. "You could be the last Republican in the United States with any sense of civic responsibility."

"No," he said. "Just up the road from where we live is a Republican cow. Very responsible. Doesn't shit anywhere outside her pasture."

Alan Simpson died March 14, 2025, at the age of ninety-three.

My Family Leave Act

After the 1996 election, I put on a positive face in public, even though I privately felt like a total failure. Being secretary of labor was the best job I'd ever have in my life, and I was proud of what the Labor Department had achieved—raising the minimum wage; implementing the Family and Medical Leave Act, which gave workers the right to take twelve weeks off from their jobs for medical emergencies or the births of their children; keeping workers safe and attacking sweatshops inside America. But I had lost many fights in the White House and had begun wondering if the job was worth everything I was sacrificing, especially my family.

One of the central dilemmas in my life has been trying to find a better balance between work and family. I've usually failed miserably. I used to assume that a better balance meant more of what you really wanted and less of what you didn't. For me, though, and perhaps many of you, that metaphor doesn't help.

Working families don't have it easy in America, and the work-family challenges are particularly daunting for women—especially women of color. The pandemic made it even harder. But for many people it's at least *possible* to live cheaper, scale back, give up the rat race. I've even met a few people who've done the reverse—more work and less family, because they love their job and find the world of spouse and kids harder to manage. So they've hired a babysitter, gratefully sent the kids off to college, or got a divorce. Now they are happily focused on work.

I know someone who found balance by cutting back on both. She had had it with a boss who kept piling it on and a family that relied on her to do everything for them. She simply needed more time for herself.

If you're like me, though, and, I suspect, some others, you love your job and you love your family, and you desperately want more of both. I was doubly blessed, in a way, yet the downside is that I had no way of getting work and family into better balance. I was inevitably shortchanging one or the other, never able to do enough of what I truly valued because I wanted more of both.

I used to think it was just a matter of improving my "time-management" skills. But a family doesn't need you only when you block out time for them, and work doesn't present new opportunities or crises on a predictable schedule. In the end, I had no room for better "balance." I had to make a choice.

One night toward the end of my four years as secretary, after Clinton had won reelection, my workload seemed under control for the first time. I planned to be home to say good night to my boys, who were then young teenagers. I hadn't been home in almost a week. Instead, another work crisis intervened. When I phoned home to tell them I might not make it back in time for bed, my younger son, Sam, said that was okay. "But will you wake me up when you come in, Dad?" he asked.

I said it might be early in the morning, and he needed his sleep.

"I'd like it if you'd wake me," Sam responded. "I just want to know you're here with us."

That did it. My job meant a great deal to me, but my two teenage boys meant more, especially because I knew they would be gone from the nest and on their own in a precious few years.

Finding a better balance? I'd been kidding myself into thinking there was one.

The next day I told Bill I'd be leaving and explained why. He said he understood. He had the same dilemma but couldn't leave for another four years.

I tried not to feel I was letting him down or turning my back on America. I told myself I had done everything I possibly could.

Home Again

I went home. Sam was on the cusp of thirteen, Adam was sixteen. With time to spare for the first time in years, I was eager to do all sorts of things with them. But they had other things on their minds. "Sorry, Dad. I'd really like to go to the game with you, but . . . well, you see, David and Jim and I are gonna hang out in the Square." "That's a cool movie, Dad, but . . . well, to tell the truth, I'd rather see it with Diane."

I suggested we make a plan, mark our calendars. But when the time came, there was always someone or something else.

Teenage boys can't be scheduled. They're like clamshells. They open just for a moment, to take in a little nourishment or expel some dirt. But then they clam up tight again. If you're around when they open, you have a chance to see something truly beautiful inside and you have a quick chance to connect. "Quality time?" Teenage boys mostly have better things to do.

A few weeks after I had left my job, around 10 p.m., when I was relishing going to bed at a decent hour, Adam wandered into the kitchen. "Can you listen to me practice my debate, Dad? The competition is tomorrow. I need your advice."

He wanted my advice! I tried to hide my glee. "Sure," I said calmly. I feared that if I conveyed my tidal wave of enthusiasm the clam would shut tight against the surge. I listened to him for the full five minutes. It was terrific, and I told him so. He smiled bashfully.

"Any criticisms?" he asked. "Must be something I can improve on."

"Well, I suppose you could speak more slowly at the start," I said, oblivious to the dangerous currents, "and try to give your main argument a little bit more emphasis, like this . . ."

I plunged in. I repeated part of his argument, but with dramatic flair. I added a few points he hadn't thought of. I entertained the imaginary audience with witty asides, silenced them with bold logic, charmed them with clever examples.

Out of the corner of my eye I saw the shell closing. All he had wanted was a little advice, a helpful hint. He didn't want his dad to take control. He merely wanted his dad on his side in this competition. He didn't want to feel in competition with his father.

"Thanks, Dad," he said in a tight voice. He left the room. I felt like a fool.

After that, I contented myself with driving the boys to their friends' houses, and to tennis matches and debates and drum lessons. Those moments in the car were quiet, private, unscheduled. Sometimes the clamshells opened. When they did, I listened, trying not to be judgmental or to take control or to say too much. We joked about all sorts of things.

Usually, I dropped them off a few blocks from where they were heading. It wouldn't be cool to be seen being driven by your dad. Teenagers pretend to one another that they don't exist within families.

Adam and Sam are now grown men with their own families. When they can't make time for their old dad, he understands. When they do make the time, he couldn't be happier.

Looking back on my years as secretary of labor, I'm proud of what was accomplished. Yet I was part of an administration that failed to slow the larger trends that eventually would threaten American democracy—widening inequality, the siphoning of the nation's wealth to the top, and the corruption of politics by big money. Reversing them would have been difficult, but I was haunted by the sense that we hastened them.

I watched the storm clouds gather, worrying about the eventual tempest.

PART V

The Gathering Storm

My Unfortunate Prescience

After the disastrous—for Democrats—midterm election of 1994, I gave a speech at the Democratic Leadership Council. I wanted to try to explain why, in my view, the Democrats had lost both the House and the Senate. I attributed the losses to what I had heard and seen when I went on the road: the anger and frustration, the sense of falling behind, the loss of status and pride. Voters took it out on Democrats because they'd been running Congress for many years and were now occupying the presidency as well.

I also felt it necessary to sound an alarm about the future, because I worried about the consequences of widening inequality.

> My friends, we are on the way to becoming a two-tiered society composed of a few winners and a larger group of Americans left behind, whose anger and disillusionment are easily manipulated. Once unbottled, mass resentment can poison the very fabric of society, the moral integrity of society, replacing ambition with envy, replacing tolerance with hate. Today the targets of that rage are immigrants and welfare mothers and government officials and gays, and an ill-defined counterculture. But as the middle class continues to erode, who will be the targets tomorrow?

The audience seemed startled at my warning. My colleagues in the White House were furious. Speeches by cabinet members were supposed to be approved in advance by the White House, but I doubted Clinton's political advisers would approve this one because it was so foreboding. So I had sent an anodyne and boring speech to the White House instead. I thought I could get away with it because I doubted the media would pay much attention to what I had to say. I was wrong. It made headlines. I was ordered to the White House, where Leon Panetta, Bob Rubin, George Stephanopoulos, and other top advisers told me in no uncertain terms that I had violated White House rules. They accused me of not being a team player and barred me from making any further speeches.

I told them I didn't work for them. I had been nominated by the president and confirmed by the Senate, and they had no power over me. I'd be silent only if Bill Clinton directed me to be, and I knew he wouldn't tell me to stop speaking my mind.

His top advisers did have a point. Cabinet officers must be team players, otherwise the executive branch can't function. I was wrong to have decided on my own what to say to the public. Yet I never regretted giving that speech.

Of course, I wish I had been less prescient. The tinder was there. Global trade, the deregulation of Wall Street, the raiders and the corporate obsession with share values, the corporate assault on unions, the Powell memo, the Supreme Court's opening of big money into politics, the lack of help for people stranded in the old economy to adapt to the new. It was a combustible mixture. All it took was a match. The match was Fox News.

When Roger Ailes Didn't
Offer Me a Job

When Fox News premiered in 1996, it tried to appeal to liberals as well as traditional conservatives. I was often invited to appear on Sean Hannity's show, then co-hosted by liberal Alan Colmes. The chip on Hannity's shoulder had not yet grown into a tree stump. I even guest-hosted Bill O'Reilly's show several times when he was on vacation.

But soon, Roger Ailes—whom Rupert Murdoch hired to be the

station's CEO—discovered that angry venom brought more viewers, especially from an American working class that seemed to be growing more enraged by the day, and concocted the miasma that became today's Fox News. Stephen Metcalf, writing in *The New Yorker,* posited that "Ailes did more to degrade the tone of public life in America than anyone since Joseph McCarthy."

Ailes was born in Warren, Ohio, in 1940, with hemophilia, a condition that didn't stop his father from beating him with an electrical cord, according to various biographical accounts, but caused his mother to keep her distance for fear of bruising the child. I'm no psychoanalyst, but I'd guess that the combination of a fearsome disease, a cruel father, and a distant mother might produce someone who wanted to inflict fear and pain on others.

Ailes thought of Warren as the real America, which had been hollowed out by Wall Street and demeaned by New York and Washington power mongers. He majored in television and radio at Ohio University. His parents divorced while he was in college, his mother saying in court that her husband had threatened to kill her. (The court found him guilty of "extreme cruelty" to his wife.)

After graduation, Ailes took a job at KYW-TV, in Cleveland, where he met Richard Nixon, then running for president. According to Joe McGinniss's *The Selling of the President 1968,* Nixon remarked to Ailes, "It's a shame a man has to use gimmicks like this [television] to get elected," to which Ailes replied, "Television is not a gimmick."

Ailes became Nixon's television producer and, according to McGinniss, "sold" Nixon to America. He helped repair Nixon's image after his disastrous first debate with John F. Kennedy, even changing the way Nixon's face was lit when he appeared on television. Years later, at NBC's *America's Talking,* the channel Ailes ran before Fox News, he continued to manipulate optics—encouraging female anchors to wear short skirts and sit at translucent desks where their legs were backlit.

In the 1980s, Ailes's politics grew more conservative, along with those of the Republican Party. Between 1980 and 1986, Ailes helped thirteen Republican senators and eight members of Congress get elected, including Dan Quayle and Mitch McConnell. He also played key roles in the presidential campaigns of Ronald Reagan and George H. W. Bush, helping the latter turn likable Michael Dukakis into an advocate of furloughing dangerous Black convicts.

Ailes famously advised Reagan to disarm Walter Mondale in a 1984 presidential debate by saying "I am not going to exploit, for political purposes, my opponent's youth and inexperience." Ailes is also credited with what he called the "Orchestra Pit Theory" of political coverage: "If you have two guys on a stage and one guy says, 'I have a solution to the Middle East problem' and the other guy falls in the orchestra pit, who do you think is going to be on the evening news?"

Ailes met Rush Limbaugh in the late 1980s at the Twenty-One restaurant in Manhattan. The way Limbaugh described it, Ailes approached him and introduced himself by saying, "My wife loves you." Years later, Limbaugh said that discovering Ailes was "like finding a soul mate." From then onward, they were comrades in arms.

On Limbaugh's radio show, which first aired in 1984, he talked nonstop for hours, picking fights with listeners and staking out a far-right political position. His mixture of ridicule and indignation toward liberals caught on with listeners. Ten years later, Limbaugh had an audience of 20 million, tuning in on some 650 stations. His show wouldn't have been possible before Ronald Reagan's Federal Communications Commission relaxed the so-called fairness doctrine. That doctrine held that radio and TV stations were "public trustees" and should air competing views on important issues. Broadcasters should not take sides. But by the mid-1980s, the commission was no longer enforcing the fairness doctrine. The Reagan commissioners believed that the rise of cable TV made lots of viewpoints available to the public that did not exist when print and over-the-air broadcasting were the only conduits.

"What Rush realizes, and what a lot of listeners don't," an Atlanta station manager explained, "is that talk-radio programming is entertainment, it is not journalism." Yes, it was entertainment—but entertainment with an edge that channeled the growing anger of America's working class toward liberals and so-called coastal elites who seemed to look down on regular people. By 1995, self-described conservatives accounted for roughly 70 percent of all talk-radio listeners.

Limbaugh's politically incorrect in-your-face offensiveness drove liberals nuts, which made it even more popular. It was bullying, to be sure, but bullying in *response* to the bullying that millions of working-class Americans felt they were enduring at the hands of people holding the reins of power in Washington, New York, Hollywood, and wherever else big decisions were being made.

Ailes loved Limbaugh's cruel use of humor. During a brief foray into national television, at Ailes's urging, Limbaugh showed clips of me making speeches as labor secretary with just the top of my head visible at the bottom of the screen. The studio audience (and presumably viewers at home) ate it up. Would Limbaugh have been as effective had he chosen to be a class warrior rather than a culture warrior—if he had ridiculed the super-wealthy and the captains of industry? Possibly, but government was an easier target and, as I've said, class warfare was still frowned upon in America.

Ailes's own bullying got him fired from NBC after a meeting at which he called his associate David Zaslav "a little fucking Jew prick." An investigation by NBC concluded that Ailes had a "history of abusive, offensive, and intimidating statements/threats and personal attacks made to and upon a number of other people." Although Ailes signed an agreement not to "engage in conduct that a reasonable employee would perceive as intimidating or abusive," his days with NBC were numbered.

When NBC released Ailes from his non-compete agreement, Rupert Murdoch tapped him to run his fledgling Fox News in 1996. Limbaugh's anti-liberal mockery on talk radio had demonstrated to Ailes that there was a large audience for what Fox News could dish out. So he built Fox News the same way Rush built right-wing talk radio—with his middle finger firmly directed at the liberal establishment. Fox viewers were eager to say "f*ck you" to city slickers who thought they were culturally superior. It was the same elite that George W. Bush mocked when he ran for president against John Kerry in 2004—the "Chardonnay-and-brie set" who found a "new nuance" each day on Iraq. Bush drew out the word "nuance" to emphasize Kerry's French cultural elitism. "In Texas, we don't do *nuance*," Bush said to laughter and applause.

Ailes found that a mixture of lies, nastiness, derisive humor, and paranoid conspiracy theories would grab millions of viewers while, not incidentally, making him very rich. Ailes also knew that with the end of Soviet communism, the political right needed an overarching

236 · COMING UP SHORT

demonic force. He found it in America's cultural left. Ailes instructed his producers to focus on progressives, left-wing professors, and liberal intellectuals with positions on gays, lesbians, trans people, immigrants, Black people, and crime that mainstream conservative viewers would find offensive. In time, the middle-finger mockery gained a deadly serious undertone. In 2016, those who wanted to f*ck the liberal establishment supported for president a neofascist who would also give the finger to the Constitution and the rule of law.

In 1998, Ailes asked me to drop by his office in New York City. The Monica Lewinsky scandal was exploding, and Fox News's prime-time ratings were soaring because of it. I had said publicly, in defense of the president's insistence that he "didn't have sex with that woman," that I believed him because the Bill Clinton I knew wouldn't jeopardize his presidency for sex with a White House intern. (But, as I said earlier, I also knew about the allegations of extramarital affairs. During Clinton's 1992 campaign, one of his trusted staffers was put in charge of what were crudely called "bimbo eruptions"—women claiming to have had sex with him when he was governor of Arkansas.)

When I arrived, Ailes's secretary asked me to take a seat in her outer office. After almost an hour, she told me he was ready to see me. His corner office, behind a door made of steel with a wooden veneer, was at the end of a long row of offices with nameplates engraved in gold. There were lots of security guards. His office was tastefully decorated and had large windows looking out over midtown Manhattan. He had small eyes and large jowls hanging from fat cheeks, giving the overall impression of a giant bulldog. He didn't sit in his chair so much as ride it, like someone on a big horse or a Harley motorcycle— lunging forward, somewhat menacingly.

Ailes didn't smile or engage in small talk. He began our meeting oddly, saying he was solidly working class and he hated CNN. When I asked him why the hate, he mumbled something about "fucking Ted Turner" and then whipped a few papers off his desk and began reading them. I sat across from him in silence for several minutes. Was this some sort of humiliation ritual?

He looked up and said he liked my "on-air presence" and wondered if I'd be interested in some "further engagement" with Fox

News. Without waiting for an answer, he asked how well I knew Bill Clinton. I said I knew him well but wasn't going to criticize him publicly about Monica Lewinsky. Ailes said he'd get back to me with a proposal. I never heard from him again.

By 2004, Ailes had turned Fox News into a major political force. It was a key part of the Republican effort to "swift boat" Democratic presidential candidate John Kerry by lying about his military service and denigrating the circumstances related to his combat medals. Although George W. Bush had avoided military service altogether, Fox News's continuous attacks on Kerry again confirmed Ailes's "Orchestra Pit" strategy. Viewers were captivated by Kerry's fall. Glenn Beck's show, a crude jumble of sensationalist lies and pseudo-historic lectures, debuted the day before Obama's inauguration and fueled the Tea Party movement.

In October 2012, Murdoch renewed Ailes's contract for another four years. If completed, Ailes would have served as head of Fox News Channel for twenty years. He was earning well over $20 million a year. But on July 6, 2016, former Fox News anchor Gretchen Carlson filed a sexual harassment lawsuit against him, alleging that he fired her for rebuffing his advances. Her allegations emboldened more than a dozen other female employees at Fox to step forward and reveal their own terrifying experiences with Ailes. He had sexually harassed and attacked a slew of women in the very office where I had visited him. What those women endured there was stomach-wrenching. Ailes was the worst kind of bully—cruel, manipulative, exploitative, even sadistic. After Fox's popular anchor Megyn Kelly told investigators that Ailes made unwanted sexual advances toward her at the start of her career, Murdoch told Ailes he had the choice of resigning or being fired. He chose resignation, plus a $40 million exit package.

Ailes may have left Fox, but his legacy of cruel bullying lived on. By then, Fox had become 2016 presidential candidate Donald Trump's main media enabler. The same evening Ailes walked away from Fox—July 21, 2016—Trump accepted the Republican Party's presidential nomination, delivering his dark "American carnage" speech to many of the same people Ailes had cultivated over two decades—

mostly lacking college degrees, overwhelmingly white, older, largely rural, and bitter over being economically bullied and left behind by an establishment that barely knew they existed.

The bully Roger Ailes bequeathed to the bully Donald Trump a bullied American working class.

Gored

I admired many things about Al Gore, especially his leadership on climate change. But during the Clinton administration, he was so worried about being viewed as a "tree hugger" that he distanced himself from every major environmental issue we dealt with. He was also a fiscal hawk. Even though the country was running a budget surplus by the 2000 election, Gore would not propose that the surplus be used for better schools or more affordable healthcare or even to slow climate change. He wanted to use it to pay down the national debt. This struck me as absurd. It was a once-in-a-lifetime opportunity for the government to take an active role without worrying about the deficit. To me Gore's timidity was inexcusable.

Moreover, the so-called new ideas George W. Bush was peddling were terrible, not because they were "too risky," as Gore claimed, but because they would further split the nation into the have-mores and have-lesses. The huge tax break Bush was contemplating would mainly benefit people who became much richer in the 1990s. The school vouchers Bush touted would skim off good students with ambitious parents and leave needier students behind in poorer schools. Bush's idea to privatize Social Security accounts would likely increase the savings of the wealthier and younger while risking the more meager savings of lower-income workers. His privatized medical savings accounts would attract healthier Americans while leaving the less healthy in higher-risk groups. Why didn't Gore slam Bush on these grounds?

The 2000 election was a travesty. It was effectively decided by two of the most powerful forces in American politics: cable news and the Supreme Court.

On Election Night, the networks initially announced Gore had won Florida. Later that evening, Fox News called it for Bush. (Roger Ailes had hired Bush's first cousin, John Ellis, to run Fox News's "decision desk." I and much of the rest of America suspected a conflict of interest when Fox News decided Bush had won.) CNN then followed Fox News, naming Bush the winner. Gore initially conceded and phoned Bush to congratulate him. Then Gore reversed himself and *un*-conceded. When Bush indignantly told Gore that his "little brother"—the governor of Florida, Jeb Bush—said that he had won, Gore replied: "Let me explain something. Your little brother is not the ultimate authority on this." The ensuing brouhaha revealed that our electoral system had no clear method for deciding on or declaring a winner in a very tight race. This would cause far more confusion and mischief two decades later.

No one disputed that Gore had won the popular vote. The election turned on a relative handful of votes necessary to capture Florida's electoral college votes. The Florida Supreme Court supported Gore's demand that a manual recount be held in four counties. The next thirty-six days were agonizing nail-biters for the country. Then, on December 12, the Supreme Court did something I never expected it to do in a presidential election: In a bitterly divided five-to-four decision, it overruled the Florida Supreme Court and ordered that the recount be stopped because different standards of counting votes in different counties would violate the equal protection clause of the Constitution. It looked like a partisan coup. The five justices in the majority had all been nominated by Ronald Reagan or George H. W. Bush. Justice John Paul Stevens, who had been nominated by Gerald Ford, wrote in an angry dissent: "Although we may never know with complete certainty the identity of the winner of this year's Presidential election, the identity of the loser is perfectly clear. It is the Nation's confidence in the judge as an impartial guardian of the rule of law."

To me, *Bush v. Gore* signified a loss of innocence in America. The Supreme Court had determined the winner of a presidential election in an overtly partisan way. Never in living memory had the Court so blatantly extended its reach beyond what were considered the boundaries of its legitimacy. I assumed *Bush v. Gore* would mark the nadir of the Supreme Court in the eyes of the American public. I would be proven wrong.

Falling for Barack

The first term of the Bush presidency was a disaster and not just because George W. was incompetent. The attack on the World Trade Center on September 11, 2001, triggered a "war against terrorism" that turned the United States into a blatant torturer and war-crazed marauder across broad swaths of the Middle East. It unleashed a vicious wave of Islamophobia in America and gave rise to bizarre conspiracy theories. Alex Jones, a radio host, told his hundreds of thousands of listeners, "All the terrorism that we've looked at from the World Trade Center and Oklahoma City to Waco has been government actions. They need this as a pretext to bring you and your family martial law. They're either using provocateur Arabs and allowing them to do it or this is full complicity with the federal government." All the while, inequalities of income, wealth, and political power were soaring in America, but the fear of terrorism seemed to wipe everything else from the public's mind.

I had been scheduled to fly that morning from Boston to San Francisco. I heard news of the attack on my way to the airport. I tried to get through to my family to tell them I was safe, but it was impossible. When I returned home, no one was there. I watched the chilling footage, the twin towers collapsing, nearly three thousand Americans killed. No one knew how many planes were involved. For Bush's own safety, he had been whisked away from a school he was visiting. My stomach was in a knot. The nation would need strong and careful leadership. I doubted Bush was up to the job.

In moments of national emergency there exists a window of time in which people can be reminded of our common good and the duties we owe one another as members of the same society. The first responders to the disasters that day were not only heroes; they also exemplified the nation we could be. What did Bush ask us to do in the wake of the attack? To shop.

The 2004 Democratic convention was held in Boston. I was living just a few miles from it but mostly stayed away. By then, political conventions were colossal bores. After the chaos of the Democratic convention in Chicago in 1968, the parties made sure that their conventions would no longer be contests between contending factions and rival camps. Winning candidates would be determined by voters in primary elections and caucuses. Conventions had become long-winded television infomercials to showcase the candidates and advance possible future candidates. Halfway interesting things, however, did occur behind the scenes in gossipy corridors where media celebrities mingled with political celebrities or in hotel bars where ambitious young people made connections. Sometimes, although rarely, they heralded the arrival of a new political voice.

I stopped by Boston's Fleet Center on Tuesday, July 27, to hear a young Black state senator from Chicago's Hyde Park, Barack Obama, who was running to become a U.S. senator from Illinois. People had told me good things about him.

I've never been a great believer in the power of a single speech to change the trajectory of politics or even the career of an aspiring politician. Franklin D. Roosevelt enhanced his career with his rousing speeches nominating Alfred E. Smith in 1924 and 1928. At the Democratic convention of 1948, Hubert Humphrey, then the thirty-seven-year-old mayor of Minneapolis, stepped into the national spotlight with an impassioned platform speech on civil rights. But New York governor Mario Cuomo's presidential aspirations went nowhere despite his widely praised 1984 stem-winder, "A Tale of Two Cities." Jesse Jackson's moving speech to the 1988 Democratic convention in Atlanta (which had me in tears) did not put him on a fast track toward the presidency.

Even a convention speech that bombs doesn't do lasting damage. At the 1988 Democratic convention in Atlanta, Bill Clinton made an introduction of Michael Dukakis that I thought would end Bill's political career. When he showed the speech beforehand to me and to Strobe Talbott, our old friend from Oxford days, we urged him to pare it back. He already had a reputation for being long-winded, and the text seemed to go on forever. But this was to be Bill's moment in the sun, and he was determined to bask in it. The speech lasted thirty-two minutes. The loudest applause came when he uttered "in conclusion."

Yet the words Obama uttered over seventeen minutes in 2004 changed his career overnight and would ultimately change America. After the speech, observers from across the political world hailed it as an instant classic, and Obama was drawing comparisons (deservedly or not) to Martin Luther King, Jr., and John F. Kennedy.

No one had expected it. Obama's speech wasn't even given in prime time. Talking to reporters on the first morning of the convention, New Mexico's Governor Bill Richardson, the convention's chairman, ticked off the names of those scheduled for the first night, including Al Gore, Jimmy Carter, and Bill Clinton. "You'll see exciting speeches the second day," he continued. Then, drawing a blank, he hollered to a nearby aide, "Who are they?" One speaker was Obama, who was little known outside Illinois before the convention. As the *Philadelphia Daily News* headlined on the morning of his keynote address: "Who the Heck Is This Guy?"

As soon as Obama began, I was transfixed.

There's not a liberal America and a conservative America— there's the United States of America. There's not a black America and white America and Latino America and Asian America; there's the United States of America. . . . We all share the hope that we can tuck in our children at night and know they are fed and clothed and safe from harm. That we can say what we think, write what we think, without hearing a sudden knock on the door. That we can have an idea and start our own business without paying a bribe or hiring somebody's son. . . . People don't expect government to solve all their problems. But they sense, deep in their bones, that with just a change in priorities, we can make sure that every child in America has a decent shot at life, and that the doors of opportunity remain open to all. They know we can do better. . . . In the end, that's what this election is about. Do we participate in a politics of cynicism or a politics of hope?

The words were pitch perfect, as was his delivery. He knew how to use his powerful voice—speeding up for dramatic emphasis and slowing down for focus, sounding thoughtful in some places and passionate in others. I remembered Bill's announcement of his presidential run in Little Rock, twelve years before. Obama's talk had the same qualities—intelligence, vigor, youth. After four years of George W. Bush, the nation was desperate for a voice of intelligence and hope.

By the time I visited Obama in his Senate office a year later, he was already a rock star. I had no doubt he'd make a run for it in 2008. Obama had asked me to come by. I figured it was an audition for becoming an adviser for his presidential campaign. We talked about the people who were being left behind in the economy, not just the poor but the working class. He got it. But I pushed too hard. I wanted him to come out clearly in favor of raising taxes on the wealthy so there'd be enough money to give every child in America good preschool and every family adequate childcare and eldercare, along with affordable healthcare. I talked too fast and pressed too aggressively. I should have sat back and let him ask me questions. At the end of a half hour, he politely ushered me out—around the young people camping out in the reception area who squealed when he appeared.

I didn't fail my audition entirely: He asked me to be one of his economic advisers, among many others. We met several times in the year leading up to the election, but I always had the feeling he was on guard against my unsubtle advocacy. In one such meeting, I sat directly across from him at a large conference table. Bob Rubin was two seats to his left; Larry Summers, to his right. Obama said he was aware of the "battle of the Bobs" in the Clinton administration. Then, looking first at me and then at the other Bob, he said he'd have been more open to my argument in 1993 than Bill Clinton had been. "I probably wouldn't have been as obsessed with deficit reduction." Yet I still sensed a certain caution, even in this off-the-record meeting. All smart politicians are careful. None wants to get too far ahead of where the public is. But Obama seemed particularly anxious not to come off as too liberal. I wondered where the caution was coming from.

After a campaign that rallied Americans to his call for "change we can believe in," Obama was elected president. The morning after the election, he invited me to a meeting at the Chicago Hilton. About twenty advisers and campaign aides gathered around a large table in a nondescript hotel conference room before he arrived. We were proud and excited. I thought about what to say to him. *Congratulations, Mr. President, on making history* seemed too much about his being the first Black man to become president. *And now the real work begins!* felt trite. *Good luck, Mr. President* was a snooze. Then he swept through the door and began shaking everyone's hands. When he got to me, I couldn't speak. My throat swelled. My eyes filled with tears. My mind flashed to Mickey Schwerner, Martin Luther King, Jr., Bobby Kennedy. America had just elected a young Black man to be our next president.

Obama shook my hand, gave me a big grin, and moved on. He didn't have much time. He had to deal with the implosion of Wall Street.

The Perfect Storm

Remember the scene in *It's a Wonderful Life* where the Jimmy Stewart character tries to quell a run on his bank by explaining to depositors that their money was needed for loans to others in the same community, and if they'd just be patient, they'd get their deposits back? Bank runs were common in the early 1930s. But Franklin D. Roosevelt's administration enacted laws and regulations requiring banks to have more money on hand, barring them from investing their depositors' money for profit (in the Glass-Steagall Act), insuring deposits, and tightly overseeing the banks. Banking became far more secure.

As I've noted, this lasted until the 1980s, when Wall Street financiers, seeing the potential for big money, got the Reagan administration to start dismantling these laws and regulations, culminating in 1999 when congressional Republicans and Bill Clinton (at the urging of Bob Rubin) repealed what remained of Glass-Steagall.

Clinton left office during a strong upturn in the business cycle. The economy had grown considerably, the stock market had soared, and the budget showed a surplus. But the *structure* of the economy—the rules that determined who got what—had become more rigged in favor of those at the top and against the bottom half. Cheap goods were rushing in from China and manufacturing jobs were disappearing from America. Technologies run by software, such as computer-controlled machine tools, were taking over many of the remaining assembly jobs. Most manufacturing workers couldn't easily upgrade their skills.

At the same time, CEO pay and the wealth of private equity and hedge fund managers were skyrocketing. The deregulation of Wall Street was widening inequality even as it pushed corporations to suppress wages and bust unions. As wealth began concentrating at the top, the wages of the bottom half continued to languish, and the middle class began shrinking. The frustrations I had seen in the heartland when I was labor secretary continued to grow.

Some middle-class families coped with stagnant or declining wages by having wives and mothers move into paid work. The huge increase in women workers during these years wasn't the result of new opportunities open to women as much as it was the need to prop up family incomes. Before the late 1970s, most middle-class women were "homemakers," meaning they worked at cleaning their homes and raising their children but didn't get paid for it. Now, as male wages flattened or declined, women had to get jobs to keep family incomes on the upward trajectory they were expected to be on—while continuing to clean their homes and raise their children.

When this first coping mechanism was exhausted, everyone worked longer hours. But two-income families could work only so many hours; they also needed to take care of their kids. This limited how far this second coping mechanism could go to restoring the middle class.

The third coping mechanism was for middle-class families to cash in on the rising value of their homes. Low interest rates, fueled by China's investment of its massive export earnings in the U.S. capital market, allowed many Americans to qualify for home mortgages. This sent house prices soaring. As a result, existing homeowners could refinance their mortgages or take out home equity loans, borrowing against the value of their homes to support levels of consumption their incomes alone couldn't support. In 2003 alone, American homeowners extracted more than $850 billion by refinancing or taking out home equity loans.

Wall Street was more than happy to finance the speculative frenzy and package it in the sort of derivatives that Brooksley Born had warned about in the 1990s. Savings banks flipped mortgages to investment banks, which then bundled them into mortgage-backed securities with varied levels of risk. They then sold these securities to investors, who bet on whether borrowers would default on their mortgages. To insure against default, Wall Street created "credit default swaps"—insurance-like contracts that were supposed to pay out in case of default. These exotic financial derivatives—like most of Wall Street's bets on bets—were largely exempt from regulation, courtesy of the Clinton administration and Congress.

Eight years after Bill agreed to repeal Glass-Steagall, hell broke loose. The highly leveraged derivatives that insured mortgage-backed securities detonated, the debt bubble burst, and the financial system—along with the world economy—was brought to the brink of economic Armageddon. Millions of Americans lost their savings, jobs, and homes. Wall Street's frenzy proved to be a house of cards, a gigantic Ponzi scheme. Who would be left holding the bag and bearing the losses?

The 2008 financial crisis, the worst collapse since 1929, which led to the worst recession in decades, was the direct result of financial deregulation. Alan Greenspan, who had retired as chairman of the Fed in 2006, called it "a once-in-a-century credit tsunami." Pressed by critics, Greenspan acknowledged that the crisis had forced him to rethink his free market ideology. "I have found a flaw," he told a congressional committee. "I made a mistake in presuming that the self-interests of organizations, specifically banks and others, were such that they were best capable of protecting their own shareholders and their equity in the firms. . . . I was shocked."

Shocked that the "free market" would succumb to greed, self-dealing, betting, and fraud? Shocked that decades of deregulation of Wall Street would have plunged the nation and the world into crisis? Until then I had no idea you were so gullible, Alan.

The crisis shattered the prevailing assumption that ever more sophisticated financial innovations made the economy more efficient and less risky. When the bubble burst, the Bush administration moved to protect investment banks. Treasury Secretary Henry "Hank" Paulson, former CEO of Goldman Sachs, and Timothy Geithner, president of the New York Fed, arranged a rescue of the investment firm Bear Stearns but allowed Lehman Brothers to go under. Paulson and Geithner argued that Lehman was in such bad shape from its risky real estate investments that the Fed didn't have legal authority to rescue it. The stock market crashed. AIG, an insurance giant that had underwritten hundreds of billions of dollars' worth of credit on "the Street," faced collapse. So did Citigroup, which Bob Rubin had joined. The bank had bet heavily on risky mortgage-related assets.

Paulson asked Congress for $700 billion to bail out the financial industry, restoring investor confidence in the biggest banks by enabling them to pay their debts. He and Fed chair Ben Bernanke insisted that a taxpayer bailout of Wall Street was the only way to avoid another Great Depression.

I testified before a House committee that was trying to decide how large the bailout should be, one of many "experts" trying to advise Congress. Neither I nor anyone else could answer the question with confidence—nothing like this had happened before, at least not since the Great Crash of 1929 that had ushered in the Great Depression. The economy had changed so much since then that there was no way to estimate how much would be necessary to save it this time.

I huddled with congressional staffers. Why not force the banks to reorganize their debts under the bankruptcy, so there would be an orderly sale of bank assets to their major creditors? I asked. The aides told me that, according to the Wall Street bankers they consulted with, bankruptcy would be too slow and would "destabilize" financial markets. I said those markets had grown to be too large a part of the economy; it was time they shrank. No, I was told, the biggest banks were so large that their implosion would take much of the world economy—and ours—with them. But why save just the financial system? I repeatedly asked. What about homeowners whose houses were now worth less than what they owed on them? What about workers who lost their jobs? What about those who lost their savings? Didn't they deserve as much help as the bankers? I never got good answers to these questions.

I ran into Bob Rubin at the 2008 Democratic convention that nominated Barack Obama for president. It was the first time I'd seen Bob since I left Washington. Even in a busy corridor filled with politicians and reporters, and even with Wall Street imploding, Bob seemed his usual serene self. I asked him why he thought the financial crisis had occurred. He said it was a "perfect storm."

When Obama took over as president, he endorsed the Bush administration's Wall Street bailout—the so-called Troubled Assets Relief Program, or TARP. TARP seemed to me an appropriate acronym for a program shielding the big banks from financial losses while keeping the rest of the nation permanently in the dark about the deals that went on under the tent.

Obama appointed a team of Clinton-era economic advisers led by Geithner, who became Obama's treasury secretary, and Larry Summers, who became director of the National Economic Council. These were the same people who, working under Bob Rubin in the 1990s, had prepared the way for the financial crisis by deregulating Wall Street. Summers had supported repealing the Glass-Steagall Act and opposed regulating derivatives. Geithner, as chair of the New York Fed, had been responsible for overseeing Wall Street in the years leading up to the crisis. Geithner worked with Hank Paulson to create TARP. Obama's other economic appointments were a hit parade of individuals who had served in Rubin's Treasury Department. They were intelligent people. I had no reason to doubt their integrity. But, as with Larry, I doubted their judgment.

During the Clinton years, these economists had promoted finance-driven globalization. They had deregulated the financial industry. Their policies had hurt much of working America, cost millions of good jobs, and led to the 2008 financial crisis. Yet Obama followed their advice to restore the profitability of Wall Street banks rather than reduce the power of finance or help the millions of Americans who lost their jobs, homes, and savings.

Soon after he was installed in the White House, Obama branded Wall Street bankers "shameful" for giving themselves nearly $20 billion in bonuses as the economy was deteriorating and the government was spending billions to bail out their banks. In a private meeting, the CEOs of the biggest banks reportedly sought to explain to him why they and their top executives deserved the bonuses. "These are complicated companies," one CEO offered. Another said: "We're competing for talent on an international market." Obama stopped the conversation short. "Be careful how you make those statements, gentlemen. The public isn't buying that. My administration is the only thing between you and the pitchforks."

Ultimately, some ten million homeowners lost their homes to foreclosure. This was not an inevitable result of the financial crisis. It was a policy choice. When I saw Summers at an event in Washington, I asked him why the administration wasn't doing more to help homeowners.

"It's very complicated," he said, waving his arms.

"What's complicated about it? Why not just require banks to write down the value of people's mortgages, with the government subsidizing part of the loss?"

"Can't be done without inviting a lot of fraud," he answered, definitively. That seemed to be the end of the conversation. But hadn't the banks committed the biggest fraud by concealing their risky bets from investors and bank regulators?

Obama put in place a program to "modify" home loans that did little to stem the foreclosures. Asked why the program wasn't working, Geithner replied that its purpose was not to keep people in their homes but to "foam the runway" for the banks, spreading out the pace of foreclosures so that the banks could better handle them. The Federal Reserve also provided large subsidies to the big banks in the form of free loans. Estimates of the true cost of the bailout varied from half a trillion dollars to several trillion.

The wealth of American homeowners fell by $16 trillion. In effect, Obama had shifted the costs of the banks' speculative binge onto ordinary Americans. This deepened mistrust of a political system increasingly seen as rigged in favor of the rich and powerful. In the end, no top banker was ever held accountable, let alone indicted or jailed.

In late 2010, the Financial Crisis Inquiry Commission, the panel responsible for determining who and what caused the financial meltdown, voted to refer Robert Rubin to the Department of Justice for investigation, stating it believed Rubin "may have violated the laws of the United States in relation to the financial crisis" by misleading Citigroup's investors and the market by hiding the extent of the bank's subprime exposure, stating at one point that it was 76 percent lower than what it actually was. I doubted Bob had intentionally misled investors. I knew him as a man of honor and rectitude. But had he unwittingly allowed some of his subordinates to mislead investors?

Nothing came of the referral.

A package of regulations was put in place, called Dodd-Frank, after the two legislators who pushed it through Congress—Connecticut senator Chris Dodd, who chaired the Senate Banking Committee, and Massachusetts representative Barney Frank, who chaired the House Financial Services Committee. The law and its regulations were not nearly as strict as those of the 1930s. Dodd-Frank required only that the banks submit to stress tests by the Fed and hold a certain minimum amount of cash on their balance sheets to protect against financial shocks. The new law didn't prohibit banks from gambling with their investors' money or reinstitute the Glass-Steagall Act that separated investment banking from commercial banking. Wall Street lobbyists, backed with generous campaign donations from the Street, wouldn't abide any tougher medicine.

That, sadly, was the real lesson of the bailout of Wall Street—how power was wielded to cushion the top executives and shareholders of big banks and other financial institutions from the downsides of risks they took on and from accountability for their errors, while allowing them to take all the upside gains. It was, in effect, a form of socialism for the rich. That lesson was not lost on America. It spawned two related, although temporary and seemingly opposite, political movements.

Tea Partiers, Occupiers, and Other Angry People

The financial crisis of 2008 ended Americans' ability to turn their homes into piggy banks and use the rising values of their homes to procure second mortgages or as collateral to borrow against. This— along with the bailout of the bankers who had created the crisis— brought a rude shock to millions of American families. They could no longer hope, or pretend, that they were still living the American dream of upward mobility in a system that rewarded hard work and didn't play favorites. It was as if a veil suddenly dropped from their eyes to reveal an ugly landscape they had avoided seeing for years.

One political consequence was the Tea Party, comprising angry conservative Republicans. Emerging in 2009 and gaining momentum through nationwide rallies and widespread media coverage, their candidates appeared on ballots across America in the fall of 2010. TARP and the bailout of Wall Street was the trigger. At the Utah Republican convention that ousted incumbent senator Robert Bennett in 2010, the Tea Party mob repeatedly shouted "TARP! TARP! TARP!" In those midterm elections, these activists were instrumental in shifting power in the House of Representatives back to Republicans and shifting the national debate back to curbing government spending and lowering the U.S. debt. It felt like a repeat of 1993, when after twelve years of Ronald Reagan's and George H. W. Bush's wild spending and massive tax cuts (mostly for the rich), Bill Clinton was saddled with cleaning up the mess; as we have seen, he did, at the expense of much of what he campaigned on. Now, after George W. Bush cut taxes and racked up near-record spending, much of it helping the big Wall Street banks, Republicans suddenly became deficit hawks again, and the Tea Partiers in their ranks took aim at Obama.

A parallel response emerged on the political left. On September 17, 2011, a small group of people set up tents in downtown Manhattan's Zuccotti Park, renamed it Liberty Park, and announced their intention to "Occupy Wall Street." This marked the start of a short-lived movement that focused on the widening inequities of American life. Almost overnight, central squares and public parks across major cities became centers of a struggle against American capitalism's grotesque distribution of wealth and power.

When asked at a news conference about the Occupy Wall Street movement, Obama responded: "These days, a lot of folks who are doing the right thing aren't rewarded and a lot of folks who aren't doing the right thing *are* rewarded." He predicted that the frustrations fueling the Occupiers would "express itself politically in 2012 and beyond until people feel like once again, we're getting back to some old-fashioned American values."

Although the Tea Party and Occupy movements took aim at different parts of the American political economy—Tea Partiers were incensed at government, Occupiers felt Wall Street and big corporations were to blame—both condemned "corporate welfare" and "crony capitalism," worried about excessive coziness between big business and big government. Both took aim at America's elites.

Occupy is credited with spurring policy initiatives such as Obama's "Buffett Rule," a proposed minimum 30 percent tax on top incomes. It never became law because those at the top, who'd have to pay more in taxes, told their political patrons (both Republican and Democratic) to nix it. But a "Millionaires Tax" did go into effect in California, raising the state's tax rate on incomes in excess of $1 million, from 13.3 percent to 14.4 percent, the highest in the nation.

In truth, Occupy was a fractured, disorganized mess. Its camps soon reeked of spoiled food and inadequate port-o-johns. Its decision-making system required total consensus before any action was taken, which meant almost no action was ever taken. Occupy organizers held such deep antipathy toward politics and hierarchies that they were unable to translate the movement into any politics at all, which spelled inevitable irrelevance.

At one point, Oakland's Occupy encampment invited me to speak. When I arrived, I was told I wouldn't be allowed to.

"Why not?" I asked.

"Because you were in the Clinton administration," one of them said, "and we're anarchists."

"But I was invited here to speak."

"You won't be speaking."

"If you're anarchists, you can't stop me." Some of the people who had invited me to speak moved menacingly toward the anarchists. Two anarchists picked up clubs. I thanked them all and promptly left.

On November 9, a crowd of over a thousand students set up tents on Berkeley's Sproul Plaza and declared "Occupy Cal." In a near replay of what had occurred almost fifty years before at the start of the Free Speech Movement, Berkeley's chancellor summoned riot police from Oakland and Alameda County to break up the encampment. The police attacked students and faculty. They tore down the tents and made thirty-nine arrests. I joined in the protest but stayed clear of the police.

For days thereafter, Sproul Plaza teemed with art, music, dance performances, rallies, and marches. It culminated with the annual Mario Savio Memorial Lecture, which I delivered from the steps of the same administration building students had occupied in 1964. As evening approached, some three thousand students and faculty filled the plaza. I was unprepared for such a crowd. I didn't have a speech or notes. I didn't want to sound like an aging boomer nostalgic for Berkeley of the 1960s, yet I couldn't ignore the parallels between the 1964 Free Speech Movement and the Occupy movement. I lacked the eloquence of Mario Savio, but there I was, near the exact place where he'd spoken, surrounded by thousands of students expecting rousing words.

I spoke about the near record levels of inequality, how wealth at the top was corrupting our politics, about the ideals of social justice and the common good that had animated the Free Speech and civil rights movements. I said that the sentiments Savio expressed in 1964 were relevant to 2011 and praised Occupy Cal protesters for their moral courage. I told them that democracy depends upon the ability of people to come together and make their voices heard. I warned that if America continued in the direction it was going, the bullies would be in charge, and I congratulated those in the crowd for trying to stop them, protect the powerless, give voice to those without one, and fight for democracy. "The days of apathy are over. Once this has begun, it cannot be stopped, and it will not be stopped," I shouted into the mic, and urged students to continue fighting for equal opportunity and equal political rights, just as an earlier generation of protesters had. "You are already making a huge difference," I told them, hoping to hell I was right.

The biggest difference between the 1964 Free Speech Movement and the 2011 Occupy movement was how much worse inequality had become. That included the soaring cost of public higher education. When Savio addressed Berkeley students, tuition and fees at the university were almost negligible. Now it was difficult for a young person from a middle-class family to afford the tab. Most had to go into debt. Yet the typical middle-class family was earning only slightly more (adjusted for inflation) than it had earned in the mid-1960s. Had America made any real progress since then?

As my speech ended, the crowd chanted "Whose university? *Our* university!" It was the same phrase I had heard almost fifty years before. American populism had never died. It had just morphed into two different sets of grievances—one cultural, one economic. The cultural ones were, in many respects, products of the economic grievances, although Republicans tried to hide that ineluctable fact.

The Two Faces of Populism

Both the Tea Party and the Occupy movement reflected a deepening suspicion of those at the top. The former's cultural populism— seeded by Newt Gingrich, Rush Limbaugh, Roger Ailes, and Fox News—felt like a political movement but it was more like a boisterous and angry club that the discontented could join, one with its own signs and symbols, its own conspiracy theories and villains. Occupy's economic populism, on the other hand, was a mix of ideas and political strands stretching from left-of-center Democrats to labor unions to democratic socialists all the way to anarchists. It was more of an attitude than a political movement. You couldn't belong to it. You could only perform within it—demonstrate, march, petition, write your members of Congress.

Both faces of populism had long histories. In the early twentieth century, economic populism predominated. Americans reclaimed the economy and democracy from the robber barons of the first Gilded Age. The Progressive Era, as it was called, emerged because millions of Americans saw that wealth and power concentrated at the top was undermining American democracy and stacking the economic deck. Wisconsin's "Fighting Bob" La Follette instituted the nation's first minimum-wage law. Presidential candidate William Jennings Bryan attacked the big railroads, giant banks, and insurance companies. Ohio's Senator John Sherman led the way to America's first antitrust legislation. President Theodore Roosevelt used that legislation to bust up the giant trusts. Suffragists like Susan B. Anthony helped secure women the right to vote. Reformers like Jane Addams successfully pushed for laws protecting children and the public's health. Organizers like Mary Harris "Mother" Jones spearheaded labor unions.

In 1910, Roosevelt warned that "a small class of enormously wealthy and economically powerful men, whose chief object is to hold and increase their power" could destroy American democracy. Roosevelt's answer was to tax wealth. The estate tax was enacted in 1916 and the capital gains tax in 1922.

In the 1912 presidential campaign, Woodrow Wilson promised "a crusade against powers that have governed us . . . that have limited our development . . . that have determined our lives . . . that have set us in a straitjacket to do as they please." The struggle to break up the trusts would be, in Wilson's words, a "second struggle for emancipation." Wilson signed into law the Clayton Antitrust Act, which strengthened antitrust laws and protected unions. He also established the Federal Trade Commission to root out "unfair acts and practices in commerce," and he successfully pushed for the first permanent national income tax.

Teddy Roosevelt's fifth cousin, Franklin D. Roosevelt, saw the 1929 crash as an opportunity to renegotiate the relationship between capitalism and democracy. He attacked corporate and financial power by giving workers the right to unionize, the forty-hour workweek, unemployment insurance, and Social Security. FDR instituted a high marginal income tax on the wealthy—those making more than $5 million a year were taxed up to 75 percent—and regulated finance.

Accepting nomination for reelection as president in 1936, FDR spoke of the need to redeem American democracy from the despotism of concentrated economic power. He reviewed what had led to the Great Crash:

> Through new uses of corporations, banks and securities, [an] industrial dictatorship [now] reached out for control over Government itself . . . [T]he political equality we once had won was meaningless in the face of economic inequality. A small group had concentrated into their own hands an almost complete control over other people's property, other people's money, other people's labor—other people's lives. . . . Against economic tyranny such as this, the American citizen could appeal only

to the organized power of Government. The collapse of 1929 showed up the despotism for what it was. The election of 1932 was the people's mandate to end it.

Roosevelt warned the nation against the "economic royalists" who had pressed the whole of society into service. "The hours men and women worked, the wages they received, the conditions of their labor . . . these had passed beyond the control of the people, and were imposed by this new industrial dictatorship," he thundered. What was at stake, he said, was nothing less than the "survival of democracy."

On the eve of his 1936 reelection, FDR told the American people that big business and finance were determined to unseat him. He said that during his first term of office:

We had to struggle with the old enemies of peace—business and financial monopoly, speculation, reckless banking, class antagonism, sectionalism, war profiteering.

They had begun to consider the Government of the United States as a mere appendage to their own affairs. We know now that Government by organized money is just as dangerous as Government by organized mob.

Never before in all our history have these forces been so united against one candidate as they stand today. They are unanimous in their hate for me—and I welcome their hatred.

Yet by the 1950s, the Democratic Party had given up on economic populism. Gone from their presidential campaigns were tales of greedy businessmen and unscrupulous financiers. Postwar prosperity had created the largest middle class in the history of the world and reduced the gap between rich and poor. By the mid-1950s, a third of all private-sector employees were unionized, and blue-collar workers received generous wage and benefit increases regularly. Keynesianism had become a widely accepted antidote to economic downturns—substituting the management of aggregate demand for class antagonism. Even Richard Nixon purportedly claimed, "We're all Keynesians now." Who needed economic populism when fiscal and monetary policy could even out the business cycle, and when the rewards of growth were so widely shared? As I've noted, postwar fears of Soviet communism also put a damper on the older Democratic class politics. And then the civil rights and anti–Vietnam War movements spawned an anti-establishment, anti-authoritarian New Left that distrusted government as much if not more than it distrusted Wall Street and big business.

The split—dramatically revealed on television during the protests at the 1968 Democratic National Convention in Chicago and animating the hardhat riot of 1970—eventually gave rise to Bernie Sanders's candidacy in the 2016 primaries, and the struggle within the Democratic Party between his populists and Hillary Clinton's mainstream Democrats.

The Republican Party, meanwhile, embraced cultural populism. As I've shown, Richard Nixon and his protégé Pat Buchanan saw in it the means of destroying the New Deal coalition and attracting the white working class to the Republican Party. Ronald Reagan deployed cultural populism to argue that Washington insiders and arrogant bureaucrats had stifled the economy and hobbled individual achievement. The rot at the top of America was a cultural elite out of touch with average working Americans, and who coddled the poor—including "welfare queens," Reagan's racist dog-whistle.

In the 2004 presidential election, Republicans described Democrats as an effete group of "latte-drinking, sushi-eating, Volvo-driving, *New York Times*–reading, body-piercing [and] Hollywood-loving" people out of touch with the real America. George W. Bush attacked John Kerry as a "Massachusetts liberal" and made his joke about no "nuance" in Texas. House Republican leader Tom DeLay opened his campaign speeches by saying "Good morning or, as John Kerry would say, *Bonjour.*"

The Democrats' failure to embrace economic populism as they did under FDR enabled Republican cultural populism to fill the void, offering Americans who were losing ground an explanation for what had gone wrong and a set of villains to blame. As Democratic pollster Stanley Greenberg concluded after the 2016 election, "Democrats don't have a '*white* working-class' problem. They have a '*working-class problem*' which progressives have been reluctant to address honestly or boldly. The fact is that Democrats have lost support with *all* working-class voters across the electorate."

Before Trump's election in 2016, Democrats had occupied the White House for sixteen out of twenty-four years. During the first two years of both the Clinton and the Obama administrations, Democrats controlled Congress. They scored some important victories for working families, including the Affordable Care Act, an expanded Earned Income Tax Credit, and the Family and Medical Leave Act. I'm proud of having been part of a Democratic administration during that time. But I was also terribly frustrated during those years by the "battle of the Bobs" inside the Clinton White House, the so-called New Democrat political operatives who focused on suburban swing voters and ignored the old Democratic working class, and the corporate Democrats in Congress who refused to do more for average workers and failed to see that if the middle class continued to shrink, authoritarianism would only grow. As I've noted, Clinton used his political capital to pass free trade agreements without providing millions of blue-collar workers who consequently lost their jobs with the means of getting new ones that paid at least as well. His North American Free Trade Agreement and acquiescence to China joining the World Trade Organization undermined the wages and economic security of manufacturing workers across the nation, hollowing out the Rust Belt.

Both Clinton and Obama stood by as corporations busted trade unions, the backbone of the working class. Neither Clinton nor Obama spent any political capital to reform labor laws by allowing workers to form unions with a simple up-or-down majority vote, or even to impose meaningful penalties on companies that fired workers for trying to form unions. During the 2008 campaign, Obama was instructed to not even use the words "labor union," since most workers were not members and unions were thought to be unpopular. Under Clinton and Obama, corporate power continued to rise and union membership to fall as a portion of the workforce. Antitrust enforcement continued to ossify.

Both Clinton and Obama depended on big money from corporations and the wealthy. Both turned their backs on campaign finance reform. In 2008, Obama was the first presidential nominee since Richard Nixon to reject public financing in his primary and general election campaigns, yet he never followed up on his reelection promise to pursue a constitutional amendment to overturn the *Citizens*

United v. FEC decision. Throughout these years, Democrats drank from the same campaign funding trough as the Republicans—from big corporations, Wall Street, and the very wealthy.

In the decades immediately after World War II, Republican legislators were significantly more likely than Democratic legislators to hail from Ivy League universities. It's the reverse today. In the 1940s, educated Americans voted Republican. Today, they vote Democrat. Between the 1980s and 2020s, the Democratic Party went from being the party of American workers to the party of college-educated professionals.

Meanwhile, big money poured into the American political system. By the 2016 election, the richest 100th of 1 percent of Americans— 24,949 extraordinarily wealthy people—accounted for a record-breaking 40 percent of all campaign contributions flowing to both parties. That same year, corporations flooded the presidential, Senate, and House elections with $3.4 billion in donations, an amount far beyond the wildest fantasies of Lewis Powell when he wrote his 1971 memo to the corporate chiefs of America. Labor unions no longer provided any countervailing power, contributing only $213 million.

The most powerful force in American politics has come to be anti-establishment fury at a "rigged system." There is no longer a big-government left or a small-government right, or a moderate "center." Because Democrats have not embraced economic populism, the only populist version available to voters without college degrees has been the Republican cultural one.

By the 2020s, Republicans saw the culture wars as the central struggle of American public life. Donald Trump blamed America's problems on immigrants, Democrats, socialists, the mainstream media, the "Deep State" (including the FBI, Justice Department, prosecutors, and unfriendly judges), "coastal elites," and, wherever possible (and usually indirectly), women and people of color. JD Vance, Trump's choice for vice president, called women who chose not to have children "childless cat ladies" and lied that Haitian immigrants were eating people's pets in Springfield, Ohio.

Republican cultural populism is entirely bogus. The biggest change over the previous four decades, the change lurking behind the insecurities and resentments of the working class, has had nothing to do with identity politics, "woke"ism, critical race theory, transgender kids, immigration, "cat ladies," or any other Republican cultural bogeymen. It has been a giant upward shift in the distribution of income and wealth; in the power that has accompanied that shift; and the injuries to the pride, status, and self-esteem of those who have been left behind.

Anti-Establishment Rage

In the fall of 2015, I visited Michigan, Wisconsin, Ohio, Pennsylvania, Kentucky, Missouri, and North Carolina. I was doing research on the changing nature of work in America. I spoke with many of the people I had first met when I was secretary of labor. Several brought their friends and grown children to my informal meetings, which became a kind of free-floating focus group spread across states that had once been economic powerhouses but were now economic basket cases. Two decades before, many of these people had expressed frustration that they weren't doing better. I remembered the Labor Day parade in Wisconsin when David Obey told me how upset his constituents were, and my painful appearances on Midwest radio stations when callers gave me hell. But in 2015, I sensed something new: The frustration I heard two decades before had morphed into raw anger.

The people I met were furious with their employers, the federal government, and Wall Street. They were irate that they hadn't been able to save for their retirements, indignant that their children weren't doing any better than they did at their children's age, and enraged at those at the top—especially the bankers. Several people I talked with had lost jobs, savings, or homes in the financial crisis or the Great Recession that followed it. Now, most were back in jobs— which paid no more than they had two decades before in terms of purchasing power. I heard the term "rigged system" so often that I began asking people what they meant by it. They spoke about the bailout of Wall Street, political payoffs, insider deals, CEO pay, and "crony capitalism."

These complaints came from people who identified themselves as Republicans, Democrats, and independents. A few had joined the Tea Party; some had briefly been involved in the Occupy movement. Yet most of them didn't consider themselves political. They were white, Black, and Latino, from union households and non-union. The only characteristic they had in common was their position on the income ladder: middle class or below. All were struggling.

Many of the conservative Republicans and Tea Partiers I met condemned big corporations getting sweetheart deals from the government because of lobbying and campaign contributions. A group of farmers in Missouri were livid about the emergence of "factory farms"—owned and run by big corporations—that abused land and cattle, damaged the environment, and ultimately harmed consumers. They claimed that giant food processors were using their monopoly power to squeeze the farmers dry, and the government was doing squat about it because of Big Agriculture's money and influence.

In Cincinnati I met with Republican small-business owners who were still hurting from the bursting of the housing bubble and the bailout of Wall Street. "Why didn't underwater homeowners get any help?" one of them asked rhetorically. She answered her own question: "Because Wall Street has all the power." Others nodded in agreement. Whenever I suggested in a public appearance that big Wall Street banks be busted up—"any bank that's too big to fail is too big, period"—I got loud applause. In Kansas City I met with Tea Partiers who were angry that hedge fund and private equity managers had wangled their own special "carried interest" tax deal. "No reason for it," said one. "They're not investing a dime of their own money. But they've paid off the politicians." In Raleigh, I heard from local bankers who thought Bill Clinton should never have repealed the Glass-Steagall Act. "Clinton was in the pockets of Wall Street just like George W. Bush was," said one.

Most of the people I met in America's heartland wanted big money out of politics and thought the Supreme Court's *Citizens United* decision was shameful. Most were also opposed to trade agreements, including NAFTA, that they believed had made it easier for corporations to outsource American jobs and destroy their communities. Most, regardless of political party, thought the economic system was biased in favor of the rich.

The more conversations I had, the more I understood the connection between people's view of "crony capitalism" and their dislike of government. They didn't oppose government per se. In fact, most favored additional spending on Social Security, Medicare, education, and infrastructure. Rather, they saw government as the vehicle for big corporations and Wall Street to exert their power in ways that hurt the little guy. They called themselves Republicans, but many of the inhabitants of America's heartland were economic populists. Heartland Republicans and progressive Democrats remained wide apart on cultural issues, such as immigration or abortion or LGBTQ rights. But wherever I went, the economic populist upsurge was real.

With the 2016 political primaries looming, I asked my "focus groups" which candidates they found most attractive. At that time, Hillary Clinton and Jeb Bush were assumed to be the Democratic and Republican candidates, respectively. Yet almost no one I spoke with mentioned either Clinton or Bush. They talked about Bernie Sanders and Donald Trump, oftentimes *both* as candidates they'd support for president. When I asked why, they said Sanders or Trump would "shake things up," or "make the system work again," or "stop the corruption," or "end the rigging."

The following year, Sanders—a seventy-four-year-old Jew from Vermont who described himself as a democratic socialist and wasn't even a Democrat until the 2016 presidential primaries—came within a whisker of beating Hillary in the Iowa caucus, routed her in the New Hampshire primary, garnered over 47 percent of the caucus-goers in Nevada, and ended up with 46 percent of the pledged delegates to the Democratic National Convention from primaries and caucuses. Had the Democratic National Committee not tipped the scales against him by deriding his campaign and rigging campaign financing in favor of Hillary Clinton, I believe Sanders would have been the party's nominee in 2016.

Trump, a sixty-nine-year-old egomaniacal billionaire reality TV star who had never held elected office or had anything to do with the Republican Party and who lied compulsively about almost everything, of course won the Republican primaries and went on to beat Clinton, one of the most experienced and well-connected politicians in modern America. Granted, he didn't win the popular vote, and had some help from Vladimir Putin, but he won.

Something very big was happening: a rebellion against the establishment. Hillary and Jeb Bush had deep bases of funders, well-established networks of political insiders, experienced political advisers, all the name recognition you could want, but neither of them could convince voters they weren't part of the system, and therefore part of the problem.

When I did my interviews, the overall economy was doing well in terms of the standard measures of employment and growth. But those indicators didn't reflect the economic insecurity most Americans felt and continue to feel, nor did they show the seeming unfairness most people experienced. The indicators didn't reveal the linkages many Americans saw, and still see, between wealth and power, crony capitalism and stagnant real wages, soaring CEO pay and their own loss of status, the emergence of a billionaire class and the undermining of democracy, and between globalization and the loss of their communities. The standard measures didn't show the frustration of American workers without college degrees who for decades have had to work harder with very little to show for it, and whose lifespans have shrunk.

Much of the political establishment denies what has occurred. They prefer to attribute the rise of Trump and, more broadly, what might be called Trumpism—political paranoia, xenophobia, white Christian nationalism, and cultural populism—solely to racism. Racism did play a part, but to understand why it has had such a strong impact, especially on the voting of white people without college degrees, it's important to see what drove the racism. After all, racism in America dates back to long before the founding of the Republic, and even modern American politicians have had few compunctions about using racism to boost their standing. Richard Nixon's "law and order" campaign on behalf of "the silent majority" was an appeal to it, as was Ronald Reagan's condemnation of "welfare queens" and George H. W. Bush's use of Willie Horton against Michael Dukakis. Racial dog-whistles could even be heard behind Bill Clinton's promises to "end welfare as we know it" and "crack down on crime."

What gave Trump's racism—as well as his hateful xenophobia, misogyny, and jingoism—particular virulence was his capacity to direct the intensifying anger of the working class into these channels. It was not the first time in history that a demagogue has used scapegoats to deflect public attention from the real causes of their distress, and it won't be the last.

In 2016 Trump galvanized millions of blue-collar voters living in communities that never recovered from the tidal wave of factory closings. He understood what resonated with these voters: He promised to bring back jobs, revive manufacturing, and get tough on trade and immigration. "We can't continue to allow China to rape our country, and that's what they're doing," he said at one rally. "In five, ten years from now, you're going to have a workers' party. A party of people that haven't had a real wage increase in eighteen years, that are angry." Speaking at a factory in Pennsylvania in June 2016, Trump decried politicians and financiers who had betrayed Americans by "taking away from the people their means of making a living and supporting their families."

Trump failed to bring back manufacturing jobs. Although promising at a rally in Youngstown, Ohio (which had lost about 50,000 well-paying unionized steelworker jobs during the previous forty years), that all the empty factories would be "coming back," they did not. By 2019, the last large plant in the area, a GM factory that had employed almost 5,000 workers, closed its doors. During Trump's first term, the trade deficit grew to its highest level since 2008. Because Trump's 2017 tax cuts lowered the tax rates on foreign profits, corporations offshored even more jobs. More than 300,000 jobs were lost to offshoring and trade during his first term.

Worries about free trade used to be confined to the political left. But by 2016, according to the Pew Research Center, people who said free-trade deals were "bad for America" were more likely to be Republican. The problem wasn't trade itself. It was a political-economic system that had failed to cushion working people against trade's downsides or to share trade's upsides—in other words, a system that was rigged against them. Big money—campaign donations from wealthy individuals and big corporations—was at the root of the rigging. This was the premise of Sanders's 2016 campaign. It was also central to Trump's appeal ("I'm so rich I can't be bought off"), although once elected he delivered everything big money wanted. And, of course, his promises were empty ones.

In the 2016 primaries, Bernie Sanders did far better than Clinton with blue-collar voters. He did this by attacking trade agreements, Wall Street greed, income inequality, and big money in politics. Sanders sought to remedy the disease of the Democratic Party—its abandonment of economic populism and of the American dream.

The End of the American Dream

In his 1931 book *The Epic of America,* historian James Truslow Adams wrote that the American dream is "of a land in which life should be better and richer and fuller for everyone, with opportunity for each according to ability or achievement," and "regardless of the fortuitous circumstances of birth or position." Adams wrote this at the height of the Great Depression. His dream became reality in the first decades after World War II as America's middle class burgeoned. Almost everyone's income rose, and their children did even better than they did. The formula for a better life was simple: Play by the rules and work hard.

But starting in the late 1970s, the dream began to fade. The standard explanation for the decline of the American dream posits that globalization and technological change made most Americans less "competitive," thereby justifying their flat or declining wages and decreasing job security. Germany, Japan, and other nations whose economies had been pummeled during World War II recovered, with the help of the victors, to become powerful economic competitors.

The standard explanation, however, disregards another and more fundamental cause: the increasing concentration of political power in America's corporate and financial elite. The typical inhabitant of Germany, Japan, and of other advanced economies has continued to enjoy rising living standards, now often higher than that of the typical American, even though these other economies have faced the same challenges of globalization and technological change as has America. The difference is that their corporate and financial elites have not had as much power as America's. This imbalance has allowed the American economic elite—America's oligarchy—to reorganize the market for its own benefit through changes in laws and regulations. Those changes have enhanced their wealth but not that of typical Americans.

Most Americans don't pay a great deal of attention to national indicators showing how fast the economy is growing, how many new jobs are being created, and the rate of inflation. Instead, they look at their own efforts to create a better life for themselves and their children. And, as I've explained in these pages, those efforts no longer seem to pay off. Most Americans have been catching on. An October 19–24, 2023, *Wall Street Journal*/NORC poll found that only 36 percent of voters said the American dream—"that if you work hard you'll get ahead"—still holds true. This was down from 53 percent in 2012, and 48 percent in 2016. An NBC News poll conducted November 10–14, 2023, found that a record-low 19 percent of voters said they felt confident that life for their children's generation will be better than for their own generation, while 75 percent were not confident their children will be better off. As the American dream faded, and as inequalities of income and wealth soared, many Americans felt increasingly infuriated.

When most people stop believing that they and their children have a fair chance at the American dream, public trust in the major institutions of society declines, as has happened in America, especially since the financial crisis and bank bailouts. In a 2024 survey by Pew, more than 80 percent of respondents believed that most political figures "don't care" about people like you and me. (In Sweden, by comparison, just 43 percent of people believe this.) In that same survey, more than a quarter of Americans thought that an autocracy, in which a leader can bypass Congress and the courts, would be a "somewhat" or "very good" form of government. I doubt this is because they support autocracy; they more likely want a different system that's presumably better. It is not surprising that many Americans became vulnerable to the rants of a demagogue who promised radical change by taking a wrecking ball to democracy, and even reelected him.

By 2016, when Trump was first elected president, the richest 1 percent of Americans owned more wealth than the bottom 90 percent put together. Between 1972 and Trump's first election, the pay of the typical American worker dropped 2 percent when adjusted for inflation, although the American economy had more than doubled in size. If you were a young man with only a high school degree, your pay dropped much further.

The underlying story is not simply one of economic frustration and anxiety. Economics cannot be separated from politics, power, and social status. Nor can it be separated from expectations of doing better if one adheres to the implicit social contract of hard work and diligence. Americans born in the early 1940s had a 92 percent chance of obtaining a higher household income than their parents, once they became adults. In this way, they would live out the American dream. But Americans born in the 1980s had only a fifty-fifty chance of doing better than their parents.

Arguably, losing a job or income did not make a person any more likely to support Trump in 2016, 2020, or 2024. The people most likely to support him felt they had lost ground compared to where they thought they *should* and *would* be if the game weren't rigged. Most Americans without college degrees—over 60 percent of adult Americans—were working longer hours than people like them had worked in the 1970s and 1980s, with fewer sick days or vacations and less job security. Nearly one out of every five was in a part-time job. Two-thirds were living paycheck to paycheck. Employment benefits such as pensions were shrinking.

In 1980, the U.S. had a typical life expectancy for a rich country. But by 2024 it ranked lower than its peers, lower even than many poor countries. In addition, the gap in life expectancy between America's most affluent and everyone else was widening. Working-class men without college degrees were succumbing to opioids, suicide, chronic liver cirrhosis, and poisoning, including drug overdoses.

In her thoughtful book *Stolen Pride,* sociologist Arlie Hochschild notes that many Americans who were blocked from access to the American dream initially blamed themselves and felt ashamed. One reaction to that was to draw on a fund of pride based on race, ethnicity, religion, region, or nationality. Her in-depth interviews in Trump country—in Louisiana and western Kentucky—revealed that Trump stepped into the breach created by the absence of a Democratic narrative that spoke to the anguish of many Americans left behind. Trump focused instead on their victimhood, on what had been "stolen" from them: their jobs, their communities, their land, and their pride.

Trump's baseless assertion that the 2020 election was "stolen" from him fit into that narrative. He paired his lie with the truth of their lost pride. He bonded with his followers by telling them in essence that everyone who shamed him also shamed them, everyone who tried to oppress him also oppressed them, the powers that tried to keep him down were the same that kept them down. Having established this bond, it was easy for him to shift from shame to blame. Younger working-class men who had been marginalized in an economy that no longer respected or rewarded their work found in Trump a tough guy who lashed out at the forces trying to hold them down, a seeming macho man who blamed his (and their) problems on cultural elites.

When I read Hochschild's analysis, I thought back to David Obey's warning to me in 1994: "Factories closing. New jobs pay shit. Guys have to take women's work in fast food, retail, hospitals, hotels. Their wives have to work harder, longer hours. These guys are angry. Humiliated. Furious. They thought Clinton would change all that, but it only got worse. NAFTA and global trade scares the hell out of them. Then he wants to take away their guns! He wants to put gays in the army! He doesn't stand up to a bitch from Arkansas who accuses him of hanky-panky. He puts his bossy law-school graduate wife in charge of health-care reform, which crashes. Get the picture?"

In a telling survey, *New York Times* investigative reporters Michael H. Keller and David D. Kirkpatrick compared two kinds of Republican voter in 2020: those living in the congressional districts of the 139 Republican House members who voted not to certify the results of the 2020 election, and those living in the Republican districts of the sixty-four Republican House members who voted to certify the results. The first group were on average poorer, with annual incomes 10 percent lower than those in the second group. The first group had fewer college and high school diplomas per capita; suffered higher death rates from suicide, drug overdoses, and alcohol-related liver failure; were more likely to reside in areas in which they were a decreasing racial majority; and were more likely to watch Fox News.

In his third run for the presidency in 2024, Trump cast himself as a martyr on behalf of his followers, fusing his identity with theirs. When he announced his candidacy, he told supporters, "In 2016, I declared: I am your voice. Today, I add I am your warrior. I am your justice. And for those who have been wronged and betrayed, I am your retribution." After being charged with retaining government secrets, he told a Republican gathering in Michigan: "I'm being indicted for you." On August 3, 2023, the day of his indictment for seeking to overturn the 2020 election, he posted, in all caps, "I AM BEING ARRESTED FOR YOU." A week later, at a campaign event in New Hampshire, he said, "They want to take away my freedom because I will never let them take away your freedom. They want to silence me because I will never let them silence you."

When Trump was found guilty, he asserted that the system had been rigged against him—*and* against them, his followers. Trump's claim was baseless, yet the rigging of the American system against working people was real. That distinction was lost on many working Americans who saw in Trump a larger version of themselves. Trump wasn't wrong. He was *wronged.*

The Rigging of the Market

During the 1950s and 1960s, my father owned a shop in which he sold women's clothing to the wives of factory workers. This was an era when the income of a factory worker or schoolteacher or baker or salesman or mechanic was enough to buy a home, have two cars, and raise a family. During those years, the earnings of the typical

American worker doubled, just as the size of the American economy doubled.

Over the next four decades, the size of the American economy more than doubled again, but the earnings of the typical American (adjusted for inflation) barely budged. As I've explained, forty years of stagnant wages, increasingly insecure jobs, and the erosion of the middle class were not the consequences of the so-called free market. They were the results of a massive shift in power. Wealth is not a zero-sum game in which some can gain it only at the expense of others. But *power* is zero-sum. Some can gain power only if others lose it. And what has happened to much of America is a consequence of a massive shift in power—to the top.

Since 1971, when Lewis Powell urged the leaders of American corporations to devote a portion of their profits to politics, America has witnessed the largest and most entrenched system of legalized bribery in its history. This money—from Wall Street moguls, hedge fund and private equity mavens, corporate CEOs and the top executives just below them, and venture capitalists—along with that of the superwealthy, has altered the rules of the "free market" for the benefit of large corporations and the rich, further enlarging their wealth and power. By 2024, the wealthiest 1 percent of Americans brought home more than 40 percent of the country's total income, up from 10 percent in the 1950s and 1960s, and they had over 30 percent of the nation's wealth. Families in the bottom half of the distribution had only 2 percent of total wealth. Families in the bottom quarter were in debt.

Hidden behind the supposedly neutral supply-and-demand curves of textbook economics is the question of whether the system is improving the lives of most people or is mainly making the rich even richer. The issue is not more or less government. It is whom the system is working for. As I said, most Americans don't oppose government per se. Most want additional spending on Social Security, Medicare, education, and infrastructure, but view government as the vehicle for big corporations and Wall Street to exert power in ways that hurt them. If democracy were working as it should, the people making the rules would be acting on behalf of the vast majority, the common good. But since Powell summoned the moneyed interests into politics, that has hardly been the case.

I watched the stream of money into politics in the late 1970s turn into a tsunami by the 2020s. Starting in 1974, when I went to work in the Justice Department under Gerald Ford and Robert Bork, through my time at the Federal Trade Commission under Jimmy Carter, when I was briefly the "Democrats' new guru" in the 1980s, through my years as secretary of labor under Bill Clinton, then advising Barack Obama, and then as a professor studying the structure of the American economy, I watched this gusher fuel an ever more vicious cycle: Big money bought changes in laws and regulations that ratcheted wealth and power upward, making it easier for the wealthy and powerful to gain *further* legal changes that ratcheted even more wealth and power upward.

All of this has taken a profound toll on public trust. When the game is widely seen as rigged in favor of those at the top, society shifts from a system of mutual obligations to a system of private deals. Rather than be founded on the common good, political relationships increasingly are viewed as contracts whose participants seek to do as well as possible for themselves, often at the expense of others not at the table. When it's all about making deals, one "gets ahead" by getting ahead of others. Duty is replaced by self-aggrandizement and self-promotion. Calls for sacrifice or self-denial are replaced by personal demands for better deals.

Laws that limit campaign donations have been weakened or repealed by the Supreme Court, allowing wealthy individuals and corporations more leeway to bribe politicians—yes, *bribe* them. I've already mentioned the court's decisions in *Buckley v. Valeo* (1976) and *Citizens United v. Federal Election Commission* (2010). On June 26, 2024, the Court dealt its latest blow to federal anti-corruption law in *Snyder v. United States,* which held that "gratuities"—gifts and payments provided *after* a public official does what the briber wants—are not technically "bribes" and therefore are not illegal. Bribes, said the Court in this bizarre 6–3 decision, are only issued *before* the desired official act.

The central question is not capitalism versus some different system. It is what *form* of capitalism. What are the rules to be, and who is to make them? It was once thought acceptable to own and trade human beings, to take the land of Indigenous people by force, to put debtors in prison, and to exercise vast monopoly power. It must now be asked: Is it morally acceptable that the typical worker's wage has stagnated for the last forty years while most of the economy's gains have gone to the top? Do we believe that people who are fabulously rich are succeeding because of their own inherent worthiness or because the game is rigged in their favor? Have people who are poor failed, or has the system failed them? Is it morally acceptable that the pay of American CEOs of big companies has gone from an average of 20 times that of the typical worker forty years ago to over 350 times today? Are the denizens of Wall Street—who in the 1950s and 1960s earned modest sums but are now paid tens or hundreds of millions annually—really "worth" that much more now than they were then?

The people who now hold a record share of the nation's wealth justify their wealth by utilizing three myths.

The first is "trickle-down" economics. They claim that their wealth benefits everyone else as they invest it and create jobs. Yet for over forty years, as wealth at the top has soared, very little has trickled down. In his first term, Trump provided a giant tax cut to the wealthiest Americans, promising it would generate $4,000 more income for everyone else. It never materialized. The superwealthy rarely create jobs or increase wages. Most jobs are created when average working people have enough money to buy the goods and services produced by the private sector, thereby pushing companies to hire more people and pay higher wages.

The second myth is the "free market." The ultra-rich claim they're being rewarded by the impersonal market for creating and doing what people are willing to pay them for. The wages of other Americans have stagnated, they say, because most Americans are worth less in the market now that new technologies and globalization have made their jobs redundant. But there's no reason why the "free market" would reward the rich vast multiples of what they were rewarded decades ago. The market can induce great feats of invention and entrepreneurialism with lures of hundreds of thousands or even millions of dollars—not necessarily billions. The ultra-wealthy have *rigged* the so-called free market in America for their own benefit, campaign contributions from big corporations and the wealthy smoothing the way.

The third myth is that they are superior human beings, rugged individuals who "did it on their own" and therefore deserve their billions. Yet 60 percent of America's billionaires are heirs to fortunes passed on to them by wealthy ancestors. Others had the advantages that come with wealthy parents.

There is simply no moral justification for today's extraordinary concentration of wealth at the very top. So much wealth in so few hands is easily turned into political power—distorting our politics, rigging our markets, and granting unprecedented influence to a handful of people. Even before Trump 1 and Trump 2, it was destroying our democracy.

The (Republican) Party's Over

The death of the Republican Party is tragic to me personally. As I told you, I got my first job in government in Republican Gerald Ford's administration. I argued Supreme Court cases in Ford's Department of Justice. Years later, as secretary of labor under Bill Clinton, I worked closely with Republicans in the House and Senate to enact the Family and Medical Leave Act, raise the minimum wage, and protect workers' pensions. My father was a Republican who voted for Dwight Eisenhower for president in 1952 and 1956. His father, my grandfather Alexander Reich, was a Republican who voted for Alf Landon for president in 1936 and Wendell Willkie in 1940.

The Republican Party once stood for limited government, active opposition to Soviet aggression, and a balanced budget. Now it stands only for Trump and his authoritarian neofascism, demanding total loyalty to him. It has turned his big lie about the 2020 election being stolen into a litmus test of that loyalty. It has no principled core, no sense of right and wrong.

Gerald Ford is as far from the current Republican Party as was or is any Democratic president. Sad to say, in 2024, the board of the Gerald R. Ford Presidential Foundation declined to present the Gerald R. Ford Medal for Distinguished Public Service to former Wyoming representative Liz Cheney out of fear that Trump would be reelected and retaliate against the organization by taking away its tax-exempt status.

In response, Pulitzer Prize–winning photographer David Hume Kennerly resigned from the board. In his resignation letter he wrote that "Gerald Ford became president, in part, because Richard Nixon had ordered the development of an enemies list and demanded his underlings use the IRS against those listed. That's exactly what the executive committee fears will happen if there's a second coming of Donald Trump." Kennerly added:

Did [Lieutenant] Gerald Ford meet the enemy head-on [in World War II] because he thought he wouldn't get killed? No. He did it despite that possibility. This executive committee, on the other hand, bolted before any shots were fired. You aren't alone. Many foundations, organizations, corporations, and other entities are caught up in this tidal wave of timidity and fear that's sweeping this country. I mistakenly thought we were better than that. This is the kind of acquiescent behavior that leads to authoritarianism. President Ford most likely would have come out even tougher and said that it leads directly to fascism.

Nixon infected the modern Republican Party with a sickness that would ultimately kill it. Trump applied the coup de grâce.

"Two years ago, I won this primary with 73 percent of the vote," Liz Cheney said in 2022. "I could easily have done the same again. The path was clear. But it would've required that I go along with President Trump's lie about the 2020 election. It would've required that I enable his ongoing efforts to unravel our democratic system and attack the foundations of our republic. That was a path I could not and would not take."

Cheney lost the 2022 Republican primary to Trump-endorsed Harriet Hageman, who received 65.8 percent of the vote to Cheney's 29.5 percent.

I disagreed with Cheney on almost all the substantive issues she voted on while in Congress, but on the transcendent issue of democracy—the foundation on which all other issues depend—I salute her leadership, her dedication, and her commitment. And I grieve for the Republican Party that has lost her and what was left of its moral authority. The Republican Party purged their honest lawmakers who refused to go along with Trump's Big Lie, the most dangerous one in American history in terms of its consequences for Americans' confidence in democracy.

On April 14, 2024, on ABC's *This Week,* host George Stephanopoulos asked New Hampshire's Republican governor Chris Sununu about his switch from supporting former South Carolina governor Nikki Haley for the Republican presidential nomination to supporting Trump: "Your words were very, very clear on January 11, 2021," Stephanopoulos reminded Sununu. "You said that President Trump's rhetoric and actions contributed to the insurrection. No other president in history has contributed to an insurrection. So, please explain."

Sununu responded, "For me, it's not about him as much as it is having a Republican administration."

Near the end of the interview, Stephanopoulos said: "Just to sum up, you would support him for president even if he is convicted in classified documents. You would support him for president even though you believe he contributed to an insurrection. You would support him for president even though you believe he's lying about the last election. You would support him for president even if he's convicted in the Manhattan case. I just want to say, the answer to that is yes, correct?"

Sununu replied, "Yeah, me and 51 percent of America."

Stephanopoulos: "I'm asking you about right and wrong. You're comfortable with the idea of supporting someone who's convicted of a federal crime as president?"

Sununu: "No, I don't think any American is comfortable with any of this. They don't like any of this, of course, but I mean, when it comes to actually looking at each of these trials as they kind of take place whether it's this year or next year or as they kind of line up. Right now this is about an election. This is about politics."

I could hardly believe what I was hearing. Politics is *not* about right and wrong? It has no moral content? Is it *only* about winning?

Governor Sununu's willingness to destroy American democracy so his party could stay in power—a rejection of our system of government and an abrogation of the self-government that generations of Americans have fought and died for—is shared by most Republican officeholders today.

The Republican Party's end is tragic because America needs two parties capable of governing; two parties with a sense of the common good, even if their interpretations of it differ; two parties dedicated to democracy, even if politics is sometimes dirty and often frustrating. The death of the party is a testament to how fragile our democracy has become. It illustrates what happens when presidents are not held accountable. It is evidence of what occurs when a large portion of the public feels it's been cheated. It shows that many Americans have lost sight of our history and ideals or have become so cynical and hopeless that they are willing to chuck it all in favor of an atrocious human being who claims to be on their side.

The Republican Party has turned from a governing institution into a crazed cult, intent on turning America into an authoritarian nation. It represents a clear and present danger to the future of the United States and the world. A large, angry, anxious working class craves a strongman who will shake up the system. But such strongmen are utterly inconsistent with democracy. As I write this, politicians who call themselves Republicans have taken over both chambers of Congress and Donald Trump has been reelected president. We will see if these people are capable of governing America.

In the spring of 2024, Elon Musk and entrepreneur and investor David Sacks reportedly held a secret billionaire dinner party in Hollywood. Its purpose was to defeat Joe Biden, who was still in the running, and reinstall Donald Trump in the White House. The guest list included billionaire tech financier Peter Thiel, Rupert Murdoch, financier Michael Milken, billionaire co-founder of Uber, Travis Kalanick, and Steven Mnuchin, Trump's treasury secretary.

At the same time, Musk turned up the volume and frequency of his anti-Biden harangues on his X platform. Starting in January 2024, Musk repeatedly attacked Biden, on everything from his age to his policies on immigration and healthcare. Biden "obviously barely knows what's going on," Musk posted. "He is just a tragic front for a far-left political machine." Musk also repeatedly praised Trump, arguing that he was a victim of media and prosecutorial bias in the criminal cases he faced. When Kamala Harris became the Democratic nominee, Musk turned the heat up even higher, in favor of Trump and against Harris.

By the end of the 2024 campaign, Musk had more than 200 million followers on X, and because he owned the platform, he was able to manipulate the algorithm to maximize the number of people who saw his posts. No other leader of a social media firm had been as willing to tip the political scales toward authoritarian leaders around the world—not just toward Trump, but also Javier Milei, the president of Argentina; Jair Bolsonaro, former president of Brazil; and Narendra Modi, prime minister of India. Some of this helped Musk's business interests. In India, he secured lower import tariffs for Tesla vehicles. In Argentina, he solidified access to lithium, the mineral most crucial to Tesla's batteries. By contrast, Musk slammed Biden for his decisions on electric vehicle promotion and subsidies, most of which have favored unionized U.S. auto manufacturers. Musk and his Tesla company are viciously anti-union.

But something deeper was going on. Musk, Thiel, Murdoch, and their cronies were leading a movement against democracy. Thiel, the billionaire tech financier, wrote, "I no longer believe that freedom and democracy are compatible." But if freedom is not compatible with democracy, what is it compatible with? Thiel donated $15 million to the successful Republican Ohio senatorial campaign of JD Vance in 2022. Vance alleged that the 2020 election was stolen and that Biden's immigration policy meant "more Democrat voters pouring into this country." Later, Thiel helped persuade Trump to choose Vance as his vice president.

Billionaire money gushed into the 2024 election. Musk alone donated more than a quarter of a billion dollars in support of Trump. Just fifty families injected more than $600 million into the 2024 election cycle, according to a report from Americans for Tax Fairness. Most of this went to the Trump Republican Party. Trump also solicited a group of top oil executives to raise $1 billion for his campaign, promising that if elected he would "immediately" reverse dozens of environmental rules and green energy policies adopted by President Biden. Trump said this would be a "deal" for them because of the taxation and regulation they would avoid thanks to him.

Speaking from the World Economic Forum's confab in Davos, Switzerland, in January 2024, Jamie Dimon—chair and CEO of JPMorgan Chase, the largest and most profitable bank in the United States, and one of the most influential CEOs in the world—heaped praise on Trump's policies while president. "Take a step back, be honest," Dimon said. Trump "grew the economy quite well. Tax reform worked."

What planet had Dimon been on? Under the first Trump administration, the economy lost 2.9 million jobs. Even before the pandemic, job growth under Trump 1 was slower than it was under Biden. Most of the benefits of Trump's tax cut went to big corporations like JPMorgan Chase and wealthy individuals like Dimon, while the costs grew the budget deficit. If not for those Trump tax cuts, along with the Bush tax cuts and their extensions, the ratio of the federal debt to the national economy would now be declining.

But the increasing flow of billionaire money to Trump and his Republican Party was not motivated solely by the lure of tax cuts and regulatory rollbacks. The goal of these American oligarchs has been to roll back *democracy*. When asked if he was becoming more political, Musk admitted (in a podcast in November 2023), "If you consider fighting the woke mind virus, which I consider to be a civilizational threat, to be political, then yes. Woke mind virus is communism rebranded." Communism rebranded? What nonsense.

A former generation of wealthy American conservatives backed candidates like Barry Goldwater because they wanted to *conserve* American institutions. Musk, Thiel, Murdoch, and their fellow billionaires in the anti-democracy movement don't want to conserve anything that occurred after the 1920s, including Social Security, civil rights, and even women's right to vote. As Thiel wrote: "The 1920s were the last decade in American history during which one could be genuinely optimistic about politics. Since 1920, the vast increase in welfare beneficiaries and the extension of the franchise to women— two constituencies that are notoriously tough for libertarians—have rendered the notion of 'capitalist democracy' into an oxymoron." If it is becoming an oxymoron, it's because billionaire capitalists like Musk and Thiel were intent on killing democracy by supporting Trump and the neofascists surrounding him.

Thiel defines freedom as the capacity to amass extraordinary wealth without paying taxes on it, but most of us define it as living under the rule of law with rights against arbitrary authority and a voice in what's decided. If we want to guard what's left of our freedom, the anti-democracy movement must be met with a bold *pro*-democracy movement that protects the institutions of self-government both from authoritarian, neofascist strongmen like Trump and his wannabes, *and* from big money like Thiel's, Musk's, and Murdoch's.

The 1920s marked the last gasp of the Gilded Age, when America's robber barons ripped off so much of the nation's wealth that the rest of America had to go deep into debt both to maintain their standard of living and to maintain overall demand for the goods and services the nation produced. When that debt bubble burst in 1929, we got the Great Depression, and then Benito Mussolini and Adolf Hitler emerged to create the worst threat to freedom and democracy the modern world had ever witnessed.

If America learned anything from that Gilded Age and the fascism that grew like a cancer in the 1930s, it should have been that gross inequalities of income and wealth fuel gross inequalities of political power—as Musk, Thiel, and other billionaires have been putting on full display—which in turn generate strongmen who destroy both democracy and freedom. Ironically, under fascist strongmen, no one is safe, not even oligarchs.

The Final Battle?

Just before the 2024 election, I spoke with a young conservative who admitted that Trump was an "odious thug," but argued that America and the world had become such a mess that we need such a person as president.

"Think of Putin, Xi, Kim, Ali Khamenei, Netanyahu—they're all odious thugs," he said. "We need our *own* odious thug to stand up to them."

I said that direct confrontation could lead to more bloodshed, even nuclear war.

He continued: "We need an odious thug to shake up Washington, stir up all the ossified bureaucracies now destroying America, do all the things no one has had the balls to do." I winced. He charged: "We need someone to take control!"

As soon as he uttered those last words, he and I both knew the conversation was over. He had spilled the beans. He was impatient with the messiness and slowness of democracy. He wanted a dictator.

I was born in 1946. At that time, the world had just experienced what can occur when a loathsome person who exudes "strength" takes over a major nation and threatens the world. Some of my relatives died fighting Nazis or perished in Nazi concentration camps. I can't help but wonder if the young conservative I spoke with would feel differently were he my age.

The first rally of Trump's 2024 election campaign on March 25 in Waco, Texas—exactly thirty years after a deadly siege between law enforcement and the Branch Davidians resulted in the deaths of more than eighty members of that religious cult and four federal agents—opened with a choir of men imprisoned for their role in the January 6 insurrection singing "Justice for All," intercut with the national anthem and with Trump reciting the Pledge of Allegiance with his hand on his heart. Behind, on big screens, was footage from the Capitol riot.

Trump then repeated his bogus claim that the 2020 presidential election was "rigged." He praised the rioters of January 6. He raged against the prosecutors overseeing multiple investigations into his conduct as "absolute human scum." He told the crowd that "the thugs and criminals who are corrupting our justice system will be defeated, discredited, and totally disgraced." He then declared:

> Our enemies are desperate to stop us and our opponents have done everything they can to crush our spirit and to break our will. But they failed. They've only made us stronger. And 2024 is the final battle, it's going to be the big one. You put me back in the White House, their reign will be over and America will be a free nation once again.

As indictments piled up against him and his poll numbers among Republicans rose, Trump's "final battle" came into ever sharper focus. It was a battle against the rule of law and democracy and against all those who opposed him. Unfortunately for the nation, the Republican Party united behind Trump. If not defending the January 6 rioters outright, GOP lawmakers attacked special counsel Jack Smith, the Justice Department, the Manhattan district attorney, and other current and prospective prosecutors seeking to hold Trump accountable.

Americans hold different views about many things, but most of us oppose authoritarianism and reject fascism. We value the Constitution and the Bill of Rights. We are committed to democracy, even with its many flaws. We want a system that seems fair, where inequalities of income and wealth appear reasonably connected to the common good and where people have an equal chance to get ahead regardless of their race or religion. We support the rule of law and want to live in a nation where no one is above it. We want to be able to sleep at night without worrying that a president might unleash armed lackeys to drag us out of our homes because he considers us to be his enemy.

"Authoritarianism" isn't adequate to describe what Trump wants for America. "Fascism" would be more appropriate. Fascism stands for a coherent set of ideas different from, and more dangerous than, authoritarianism. To fight them, it's necessary to know what they are and how they fit together. Borrowing from cultural theorist Umberto Eco, historians Emilio Gentile and Ian Kershaw, political scientist Roger Griffin, and former U.S. secretary of state Madeleine Albright, let me offer five elements that distinguish fascism from authoritarianism.

- The rejection of democracy, the rule of law, and equal rights under the law in favor of a strongman who interprets the popular will.

"The election was stolen." (Trump, 2020)
"I am your justice. . . . I am your retribution." (2023)
Authoritarians believe society needs strong leaders to maintain stability. They vest in a dictator the power to maintain social order through the use of force (armies, police, militia) and bureaucracy.

By contrast, fascists view strong leaders as the *means of discovering* what society needs. They regard the leader as the embodiment of society, the voice of the people.

- The galvanizing of popular rage against cultural elites.

"Your enemies" are "media elites" . . . "the elites who led us from one financial and foreign policy disaster to another." (2015, 2016)
Authoritarians do not stir people up against establishment elites. They use or co-opt those elites in order to gain and maintain power.

By contrast, fascists galvanize public rage at presumed (or imaginary) cultural elites and use *mass rage* to gain and maintain power. They stir up grievances against those elites for supposedly displacing average people, and seek revenge. In so doing, they create mass parties. They often encourage violence.

- Nationalism based on a dominant "superior" race and historic bloodlines.

"Tremendous infectious disease is pouring across the border. . . . The United States has become a dumping ground for Mexico and, in fact, for many other parts of the world." (2015)

"I think any Jewish people that vote for a Democrat, I think it shows either a total lack of knowledge or great disloyalty." (2019)

"Getting critical race theory out of our schools is not just a matter of values, it's also a matter of national survival. . . . If we allow the Marxists and Communists and Socialists to teach our children to hate America, there will be no one left to defend our flag or to protect our great country or its freedom." (2022)

Authoritarians see nationalism as a means of asserting the power of the state, glorifying the state. They want it to dominate other nations. They worry about foreign enemies encroaching on its territory.

By contrast, fascists see a nation as embodying what they consider a "superior" group—based on race, religion, and historic bloodlines. Nationalism is a *means* of asserting that superiority. They worry about disloyalty and sabotage from "others" within the nation, who are scapegoated, excluded, or expelled, sometimes even killed. Fascists believe schools and universities must teach values that extol the dominant race, religion, and bloodline. Schools should not teach inconvenient truths (such as America's history of genocide and racism).

- Extolling brute strength and heroic warriors.

"You'll never take back our country with weakness, you have to show strength and you have to be strong." (January 6, 2021)

"I am your warrior." (2023)

The goal of authoritarianism is to gain and maintain state power. For authoritarians, "strength" comes in the form of large armies and munitions.

By contrast, the ostensible goal of fascism is to strengthen society. Fascism's method of accomplishing this is to reward those who win economically and physically and to denigrate or exterminate those who lose. Fascism depends on organized bullying. For the fascist, war and violence are means of strengthening society by culling the weak and extolling heroic warriors.

- Disdaining women and non-standard forms of gender identity and sexual orientation.

"When you're a star, they let you do it. You can do anything. Grab 'em by the pussy. You can do anything." (2005)

"You have to treat 'em like shit." (1992)

I will *"promote positive education about the nuclear family, the roles of mothers and fathers and celebrating, rather than erasing, the things that make men and women different." (2023)*

Authoritarianism imposes hierarchies and seeks order.

By contrast, fascism is organized around the particular hierarchy of *male dominance*. The fascist heroic warrior is male. Women are relegated to subservient roles. In fascism, anything that challenges the traditional heroic male roles of protector, provider, and controller of the family is considered a threat to the social order. Fascism seeks to eliminate homosexual, transgender, and queer people because they are thought to challenge or weaken the heroic male warrior.

These five elements of fascism reinforce each other. Rejection of democracy in favor of a strongman depends on galvanizing popular rage. Popular rage draws on a nationalism based on a supposed superior race or ethnicity. That superior race or ethnicity is justified by a social Darwinist idea of strength and violence, as exemplified by heroic warriors. Strength, violence, and the heroic warrior are centered on male power. These five elements also find expression in the white Christian nationalist movement Trump is encouraging. It is also the direction most of the Republican Party is now heading in. These are not simply elements of authoritarianism but the essential elements of fascism.

Trump won the 2024 election. He also won a plurality of the popular vote. He chose JD Vance as his vice president and named Elon Musk a key adviser. There are many theories for why Trump triumphed once again, notwithstanding his attempt to overturn the results of the 2020 election and his many other faults and failings. High on the list must be the deep and growing antipathy Americans feel toward a system that increasingly seems to be rigged against them—an antipathy that began when inequalities of income and wealth started widening more than four decades ago and soared as big money engulfed American politics. Rush Limbaugh and Roger Ailes harnessed that antipathy to build media empires. The Wall Street financial crisis brought the antipathy to a boiling point. Trump then exploited it with bigoted cultural populism when he ran in 2016, 2020, and 2024. But Democratic politicians (with the stark exception of Bernie Sanders) refused to respond to the antipathy with an economic populism that connected it to the increasing political power of big corporations and the wealthy. Yet the reality is this: Americans can preserve our democracy and share our prosperity only by attacking and countering concentrated wealth and the political corruption that accompanies it.

PART VI

The Long Game

My Mother's Advice

When I was young and frustrated about one thing or another, my mother reassured me that "everything works out in the end." The saying drove me nuts. "When is the *end*?" I'd ask her. "Next week? Next year? After we die? In a century? What are we supposed to do in the meantime? Just *wait*?"

I worried, first, that much could go wrong while we waited. The famed British economist John Maynard Keynes once wrote, "In the long run, we're all dead." His point was that most people don't care that the economy *eventually* will correct itself; people often can't afford to wait. For us, there is the climate crisis, widening inequality, attacks on democracy, big money polluting our politics, mass shootings, police violence and institutional racism, nuclear proliferation, and uncontrolled and unregulated artificial intelligence, among other challenges. Responding intelligently and fairly to all requires a fully functioning democracy. "The arc of the moral universe is long, but it bends toward justice," the Rev. Martin Luther King, Jr., once assured us. But how much more injustice must be endured until the universe finishes bending?

I also worried that my mother's type of optimism could lead to passivity. I learned from Mickey Schwerner and others in the civil rights movement, from Mario Savio and others in the Free Speech Movement, and from friends in the anti–Vietnam War movement, that nothing important works out in the end unless we work hard for it *now*. We must all be activists.

Over time, I've come to understand that the choice isn't between gaining immediate wins or falling into passivity. Being an activist for social justice means working hard but not expecting the goals to be achieved anytime soon. It requires accepting that they may not be achieved in our lifetime but that seeking them is essential for our lives to matter. It means taking on some challenges you're likely to fail at, but which may inspire others along the way. It means regarding some failures as noble experiments. It means seeking to achieve big, important things that will change people's lives for the better, even if you come up short.

Let me introduce you to three good friends who have played the long game with patience and accomplishment. The first is Fred Wertheimer. Ever since I met him in the 1970s when he worked as legal counsel for Common Cause, the nonpartisan citizens' lobby, Fred has been trying to make American democracy work better. Heavyset, with tufts of hair exploding around an otherwise bald head, and a large, wrinkled face, Fred is no one's idea of Jimmy Stewart going to Washington. Yet step-by-step, Fred has achieved some remarkable things. He led the successful campaign to pass the Federal Election Campaign Act of 1972, still the major U.S. law regulating political campaign fundraising and spending. In the 1980s, when he was Common Cause's legislative director, Fred helped create the current system of public financing of presidential campaigns. By the 1990s, when he was president of Common Cause, Fred had become such an effective advocate for campaign finance reform that when Newt Gingrich became Speaker of the House in 1995, he threatened to eliminate Common Cause's nonprofit tax exemption, calling the organization a "left-wing, socialist" group. Fred stood up to Gingrich's bullying. As Fred told PBS's *Frontline* in 1995:

> Gingrich [has used] issues of ethics and corruption [as] partisan weapons, not moral concepts . . . he built a financial empire based on special interest and private influence money. He did everything he could to block . . . serious reforms of the system that were undertaken. And now of course he's the king of this corrupt system. The money is flowing his way. And . . . he's continuing a pattern of trying to make sure the corrupt system stays in place. . . . [It's] the ultimate test for Newt Gingrich's revolutionaries, because you can't be a revolutionary if you're doing it floating on an ocean of huge campaign contributions from corporate America and wealthy individuals. . . . He is going to do what he's done throughout his history, which is . . . make sure that this corrupt system in Washington stays in place. . . . When you look at the way business is done in Washington and in

terms of lobbyists, huge campaign contributions, people buying and selling access and influence over government policy, Newt Gingrich is a career Washington inside politician . . . perhaps the leading practitioner of the Washington influence money game, the opposite of revolutionary. He is the chief protector, preserver, and defender of this corrupt system. . . . a front for the establishment class that has exercised disproportionate, improper influence over government policy in recent decades through the use of money.

As I write this, Fred is still at it, lobbying Congress to expand voting rights while trying to curtail the ability of big corporations and the ultra-wealthy to bribe legislators. It's a Sisyphean task, especially with the current Republican-appointed majority on the Supreme Court. Not long ago, I asked Fred if he ever gets discouraged. He chuckled. "Discouraged?" he said, almost surprised I asked. "This is my life. This is what I *do*."

Another friend, Annie Leonard, has been fighting climate change almost all her adult life. She is a wellspring of positive energy. When I first met her, I was awed by her combination of childlike cheerfulness and deadly serious commitment. Annie has a deep laugh and a razor-sharp mind. In the late 1980s, she began working with Greenpeace on a campaign to ban rich nations from dumping their waste into poor ones. Annie traveled around the world to track garbage and hazardous waste. "I was sneaking into the factories where it was being disposed, interviewing the workers, taking hair samples and soil samples to prove the environmental health harm," she later explained. Annie helped make the public aware of the problem, including public appearances and congressional testimony that contributed to the 1992 Basel Convention, an international treaty to protect less developed countries from the dumping of hazardous waste by transnational corporations based in developed countries. In 2007, Annie created and narrated a hugely popular animated documentary about the life cycle of material goods called *The Story of Stuff,* and wrote a book version of it. A whirlwind of energy, she also co-created and coordinated the Global Alliance for Incinerator Alternatives; served on the boards of the International Forum on Globalization and the Environmental Health Fund; and in 2014 became the executive director for Greenpeace USA. In March 2022, she co-founded the Jane Fonda Climate PAC, with the well-known actress and climate activist. She is on the board of directors of Inequality Media Civic Action, the nonprofit I co-founded.

Annie has had setbacks, as we all have, but she has never relented. She is playing the long game for the same reason Fred plays it—it's her life; it's what she does.

The third friend I want to tell you about is Christopher Edley Jr., who played the long game in pursuit of racial justice and better schools for poor kids. I worked with Chris on and off for forty-three years—on the Harvard faculty, on several presidential campaigns (Mondale and Dukakis), in the Clinton administration (he served as an associate director of the Office of Management and Budget), and at Berkeley, where we both taught. I first met him when he joined the faculty of Harvard Law School in 1981. Among his many students in subsequent years was Barack Obama.

I remember one evening in Cambridge in the 1980s when Chris and I walked past a fence on the way to dinner. Scaling it would have saved us twenty minutes. He patiently explained to me why it was possible for me to scale it, even at my height, but not for him, a young Black man. For him, scaling a fence could be a death sentence if police were summoned.

Yet Chris had the courage to speak truth to power and did so without fear or rancor. When affirmative action was coming under assault, Bill Clinton asked him to oversee a review of affirmative action under the slogan "mend it, don't end it." Chris was eager to oblige. He produced an impeccable report that made the case that affirmative action needed almost no mending. When Clinton's political advisers pushed Chris to go public with his defense of affirmative action and take on the critics, he told them there was no reason to dignify the critics' arguments. A few years later, he wrote that the "real goal" of critics of affirmative action was "to protect the current distribution of privilege and opportunity that has produced white-male elites in virtually every sector."

Chris never flagged and never grew bitter or cynical. He used facts, arguments, and logic to pulverize people who tried to block him. Chris's testimony before the Senate Judiciary Committee against the nomination of Clarence Thomas to the Supreme Court was a model of careful reasoning. He meticulously showed that Thomas, then a federal appeals court judge, was too politically partisan to be entrusted with a job on the highest court. Chris even had the courage to tell Obama, the day after he won the presidency, that he was making a dreadful mistake in his choice of chief of staff. Chris thought Rahm Emanuel too shrill and intemperate to do the job well. Giving Obama his candid opinion about Emanuel was an act of kindness to the newly elected president, even though it likely cost Chris a job in his administration.

Like Annie, Chris had a wonderful sense of humor, which I've come to believe is also essential for playing the long game. He saw humor in everything from the hypocrisies of left-wing politicians to the absurdities of academic politics. ("Why do professors fight so bitterly? Because the stakes are so low." "Washington is the kind of place where your friends stab you in the front.")

He became dean of the Berkeley Law School, transforming it from a first-rate institution into a hugely innovative first-rate institution. He then agreed to be the interim dean of Berkeley's School of Education (but did so reluctantly, he said, because he was tired, which should have been a warning sign to those of us who knew and loved him). Education, especially of poor kids who are disproportionately children of color, was his passion. He founded the Opportunity Institute, which funded innovative educational projects across the country, focusing primarily on disadvantaged kids. He co-founded the Civil Rights Project at Berkeley Law, which generated influential books, papers, and conferences. It became a model for research programs within law schools. Like Annie, he served on the board of directors of the little nonprofit I co-founded.

I was in the middle of writing this memoir when I got word that Chris had died. As I write about him now, what comes to mind are not his extraordinary achievements but our friendship. When an old friend passes, you can't replace them with another old friend. You have only a limited number of people who have shared your history, moved through life with you, talked and laughed and pondered their lives with you. It's these cumulative understandings, the sweetness and depth of long familiarity, that give meaning to old friendships. Chris died while still playing the long game, a part of which is to inspire people along the way. He will continue to inspire me.

My Failure at the Short Game

In 2002, I decided to run for governor of Massachusetts. I lost, but I'm glad I tried because hundreds of my students helped me, learning politics from the inside. Many have continued to be political activists since then. I lost the short game but they're part of the long one.

Before I ran, I thought I knew everything there was to know about getting elected—which made me think I could get elected, too. I'd been involved in dozens of campaigns. I'd advised candidates running for governor, senator, and president. I'd worked for three presidents. I was wrong. It takes several particular personality traits to successfully run for a major public office (none of which I have).

First, *you need to be sufficiently narcissistic to be able to sell yourself to voters (and anyone you need to help bankroll your campaign)*. In 2002, so many Massachusetts residents urged me to run that I thought voters (and donors) would flock to me once I announced. But the moment I said I was *running,* the burden of proof instantly shifted onto me. Even my most ardent supporters wanted to know: What made me think *I* would be a good governor? Many of the people who I assumed would be generous with their dollars in support of my campaign became skinflints overnight.

I could promote policy *ideas*—I'd done that all my life—but I was terrible at promoting *myself.* Putting myself out there was embarrassing. Telling complete strangers why they should be enthusiastic about *me* made me want to crawl into a hole and disappear. Standing every morning at exits to the MBTA, Boston's subway system, trying to introduce myself and shake as many hands as possible was excruciating. Dialing for dollars, hour after hour, when most people who answered my phone calls promptly hung up on me, was more humiliating than anything I'd experienced since being ridiculed by the bullies of Lewisboro Elementary School.

Donald Trump is a masterful self-promoter because he's a pathological narcissist. He boasts about himself nonstop and has probably done so since he was an infant. No matter that his bragging requires that he tell wild lies, engage in vile smears, and display a grandiosity that should cause people to cringe; he does it all without moral constraint. It's *all* he does. He's the extreme. But you've got to be big on self-promotion to get anywhere in electoral politics.

You need to be wildly extroverted. You have to get *more* energy out of every encounter with a total stranger—every handshake, pat on the back, morsel of conversation—than the energy you *lose* in such an encounter. Bill Clinton lived off this contact energy. He'd see people standing along the side of a road and order his driver to stop so he could get out and shake their hands. When I rode anywhere with him, we were always late because he needed contact highs along the way. By the end of a day of such encounters, Bill had more energy than he had when the day began. Al Gore was the opposite; he seemed to lose a bit of energy with each encounter, so that by the end of a day of campaigning, he was depleted. I was drained after a few hours.

Trump is not a typical extrovert. He gets energized when he dominates and causes others to be submissive.

You need to be a method actor. You must be able to *will* yourself into feeling whatever the situation demands, so you come off as authentic even if it's a pure ruse. Ronald Reagan was a master of this, presumably because acting had been his career before politics. Clinton was almost as good. Obama and Biden, far less so. Nixon and George W. Bush were lousy method actors—even when they told the truth, they seemed to be lying. I long ago gave up trying to fathom where Trump's acting came from.

I was awful at method acting. On St. Patrick's Day 1992, I was supposed to give humorous remarks in several of Boston's Irish enclaves, but our family pet had just died, and I came off as strangely somber. On another occasion, I wanted to show indignation about the war in Iraq, but my best friend was clowning around on the fringe of the crowd, and I burst out laughing.

You need a thick skin. Your political opponents and the media inevitably will find your vulnerabilities and attack them. Biden had one of the thickest; Trump, the thinnest. I thought I was impervious. After all, I'd been a cabinet official at a time Republican lawmakers had turned into attack dogs. But when one of my opponents in the governor's race accused me of lying about getting Bill Clinton's endorsement, I was livid. When another said I became a professor because I couldn't make it in the real world, I was furious. When I was attacked for endorsing gay marriage, I lost several nights' sleep.

You mustn't cede control of your campaign to political consultants. Once you declare your candidacy or even your possible interest in becoming a candidate, you'll be descended upon by people who make their money by advising candidates on how to run and finance their campaigns and by buying advertisements for them. Most of these people have no idea who you are, have no interest in what your values are, and don't even care very much about whether you're elected. They want to pocket the money you raise, by getting a cut of the cost of advertising and marketing you. I discovered this too late in the campaign, after the "consultants" had already spent all the money I raised and antagonized the volunteers and unpaid organizers I really needed.

You must be respectful of the media and not become incensed by their "gotcha" reporting. I considered myself media savvy before I ran for office, but the moment I declared I was running, I was in the snake pit. As I said earlier, it seemed like the only thing the media wanted to report about me was my height.

Needless to say, I didn't become governor of Massachusetts. The experience taught me I was terrible at being a politician (and, contrary to my mother's advice, everything does not work out in the end). I never again ran for office, but I've continued to fight the bullies—on social media, in my books and articles, in my advice to candidates, and in the mainstream media. Running for office made me even more keenly aware of the role and responsibility of that media in a democracy in danger of coming apart. Part of playing the long game is understanding how and why the media is failing us and what it must do to help the public fully understand the nature of the crisis we're in.

Rejecting "Both-sides-ism"

The media coverage of Trump's anti-democracy movement has been he said/she said, as if they were covering normal American politics instead of a contest between democracy and neofascism. After Joe Biden asserted early in his presidency that democracy was threatened, *The New York Times* quoted Republican House minority leader Kevin McCarthy claiming Democrats are the ones "dismantling Americans' democracy," without pointing out that McCarthy himself was one of 139 House Republicans who voted to overturn the results of the 2020 presidential election even after the attack on the Capitol.

During the 2024 presidential campaign, Trump made the preposterous claim during an event in Wisconsin that children were getting sex-change operations at school, saying "Can you imagine you're a parent, and your son leaves the house and you say, 'Jimmy, I love you so much. Go have a good day in school' and your son comes back with a brutal operation. Can you even imagine this?" It was a transphobic lie; the rest of his speech was full of similar hate-filled rants that would have dominated coverage about any other politician. Yet Reuters covered the event under the headline: "Trump Revs Up

Small-Town Base in Wisconsin." During the September 2024 presidential debate between Trump and Kamala Harris, Trump issued a whirlwind of conspiracy theories about stolen elections, crowd sizes, and Haitian immigrants eating pet cats and dogs. How did the *Times* headline describe the debate? "Harris and Trump Bet on Their Own Sharply Contrasting Views of America."

Believing that "balanced journalism" must give equal weight both to liars and to truth-tellers is dangerous to those seeking to protect democracy. Playing the long game requires calling the media on this outrage. As CNN's then White House reporter John Harwood correctly pointed out:

> The core point [President Biden] made in that political speech about a threat to democracy is true. Now, that's something that's not easy for us, as journalists, to say. We're brought up to believe there's two different political parties with different points of view and we don't take sides in honest disagreements between them. But that's not what we're talking about. These are not honest disagreements. The Republican Party right now is led by a dishonest demagogue. Many, many Republicans are rallying behind his lies about the 2020 election and other things as well. And a significant portion—or a sufficient portion—of the constituency that they're leading attacked the Capitol on January 6. Violently. By offering pardons or suggesting pardons for those people who violently attacked the Capitol . . . Donald Trump made Joe Biden's point for him.

Shortly after Harwood said this on the air, a source told Dan Froomkin of *Press Watch* that Harwood was being let go despite his long-term contract with the network, and that Harwood used his last broadcast to "send a message."

More of our ablest journalists must be willing and able to tell America the truth and their bosses must allow them to do so. It is not "partisan" to explain what Trump and his anti-democracy movement are seeking. It is not "taking sides" to point out that the Trump Republicans are trying to establish an authoritarian government in America. It is not "violating journalistic standards" to tell the unvarnished truth about the crisis we are facing today. A failure to call out the Trump Republicans for what they are—liars, enablers, and accessories to crimes against the Constitution—itself violates the most basic canons of journalistic ethics.

I hope I have successfully demonstrated that America is facing a dangerous moment. The Republican Party in thrall to Trump is veering toward fascism. Yet too much of the media covered the 2024 election through the prism of the horse race and other outdated norms of politics-as-usual.

Chris Licht, soon after he became CNN's chairman and CEO, canceled Brian Stelter's Sunday morning media analysis program *Reliable Sources,* explaining that its ratings weren't sufficient. But that seemed a cover for why Stelter's show was really canceled: Stelter had become a cogent critic of the media's coverage of Trump. On his last show, Stelter said: "It's not partisan to stand up for decency and democracy and dialogue. It's not partisan to stand up to demagogues. It's required. It's patriotic. We must make sure we don't give platforms to those who are lying to our faces." Licht told the staff at CNN that he wanted less criticism of Trump and the Republican right, saying they should stop referring to Trump's "Big Lie" because the phrase sounded like a Democratic talking point. Licht also said he wanted more conservative guests.

Licht and CNN's new corporate overseer was Warner Bros. Discovery, whose CEO, David Zaslav, wanted Licht to reposition CNN to have more "straight news reporting" and fewer "opinionated" views from hosts. He said he wanted CNN to be for "everybody . . . Republicans, Democrats." But as Republicans have moved into the netherworld of authoritarianism, CNN's news coverage would never satisfy them—Fox News had that sewn up—nor should CNN even try. If we learned anything from Trump and his lapdogs at Fox News, it was that facts, data, and logic were no longer relevant to the Republican base. Even "straight news reporting" depends on what stories are featured, which facts are highlighted, and the context surrounding the news. How could it be possible to report on Trump or any number of Republican leaders without mentioning the Big Lie, or say they'd broken norms if not laws? The anti-democracy movement in America (as elsewhere) is among the biggest challenges facing the world today. Wouldn't *failing* to report on it in a way that sounded alarms be a gross dereliction of duty?

It's impossible to know for sure what motivated Zaslav, but keeping shareholders happy may be a part of it. The leading shareholder in Warner Bros. Discovery at that time was John Malone, a multibillionaire cable magnate. (Malone had been a chief architect in the merger of Discovery and CNN.) Malone described himself as a "libertarian," although he traveled in right-wing Republican circles. In 2005, he held 32 percent of the shares of Rupert Murdoch's News Corporation. He was on the board of directors of the right-wing Cato Institute. In 2017, he donated $250,000 to Trump's inauguration. Malone said he wanted CNN to be more like Fox News because, in his view, Fox News had "actual journalism." Malone wanted the "news" portion of CNN to be "more centrist."

When you follow the money behind important irresponsible decisions at the power centers of America today, the road often leads to right-wing billionaires.

Before CNN fired Brian Stelter, he wrote in his newsletter that Malone's comments "stoked fears that Discovery might stifle CNN journalists and steer them away from calling out indecency and injustice." (A source told *Deadline*'s Dominic Patten and Ted Johnson that even if Malone didn't order Stelter's ouster, "it sure represents his thinking.") Sadly, there are still many in America—and not just billionaires like Malone—who believe that holding Trump accountable for what he has done (and continues to do) to this country is a form of partisanship that has no place in so-called balanced journalism. This view is itself dangerous.

Equally dangerous is the eagerness of the media to hire former White House aides, even those who have tried to wreck our democracy, which is why I found it troubling that CBS News hired as an on-air contributor Mick Mulvaney, who served as acting chief of staff under Trump and led his Office of Management and Budget. Mulvaney was also an active enabler of Trump's deceit and attempted coup. On a major network, a "guest" appears from time to time when a program's producer invites them; guests are unpaid. I've been a frequent guest on several networks. "On-air contributors" appear regularly as paid contractors, which gives them the cachet and authority of being part of a network's news division.

Mulvaney's first appearance for CBS News occurred on a *Money-Watch* segment in which he was asked to explain Biden's plan for taxing the super-rich. The anchor, Anne-Marie Green, introduced Mulvaney as "a former OMB director" and "the guy to ask about this." But she said nothing about *whose* OMB he directed, suggesting that he was simply a budget expert offering an expert analysis rather than a fierce Trump partisan. Then she asked him whether a "regular working-class American" should care about Biden's tax proposal. Mulvaney's answer: "It's easy to look at it and say, 'Don't worry, you're not going to pay this,'" but regular working Americans would have to "*prove* that they don't have to pay it," and such a burden "could be troublesome: every single year proving that you're not worth a hundred million dollars."

This was just about as misleading as it gets in broadcast media (except for Fox News). Nothing in Biden's proposal to tax the super-rich required that people prove they were *not* super-rich. Mulvaney's claim was pure demagoguery. But that's what should have been expected from him. Mulvaney was complicit in Trump's attempted extortion of Ukraine's President Volodymyr Zelensky in 2019, threatening to withhold U.S. aid to fight Russian aggression unless Zelensky came up with dirt on Hunter Biden. (This was the call in which Zelensky's request "we need more Javelins," anti-tank missiles which proved crucial in Ukraine's defense against Russian invasion, was met with Trump's "I would like you to do us a favor though.") When the quid pro quo came to light, Mulvaney brushed it off: "I have news for everybody: Get over it. There's going to be political influence in foreign policy." After Trump withheld the aid, Mulvaney asked White House budget officials for legal justification to withhold it until Zelensky announced an investigation of Hunter Biden.

And there was the time Mulvaney called COVID a "media hoax" designed to bring down Trump. And the time he predicted that if Trump lost in 2020, he would "concede gracefully." When CBS made him an on-air contributor, Mulvaney was already a high-powered lobbyist for corporate interests, another fact that CBS somehow failed to mention in its announcement of his position and when it introduced him on air.

When I was growing up, CBS News was the home of news legends like Edward R. Murrow and Walter Cronkite, pioneers who set the standards for broadcast news. Now that same division was reaching into the cesspool of Trump conspirators and enablers because Neeraj

Khemlani, its co-head, explained to the staff that when it came to contributor hires, "getting access to both sides of the aisle is a priority because we know the Republicans are going to take over, most likely, in the midterms."

Access to *what*? To the Big Lie about the 2020 election? To lies about COVID? To bonkers economics? To insights about how to pull off a coup that nearly destroyed American democracy and continues to threaten it? Since when does CBS News's decisions about who to hire depend on predictions about which party will prevail in the midterm elections, anyway? What if the party that's predicted to win is so contemptuous of democracy that it continues to claim, without basis in fact or law, that the last presidential election was stolen? Would the CBS News of the 1950s hire as an on-air contributor Senator Joseph McCarthy because the news division wanted access to "both sides"? (In fact, Edward R. Murrow exposed McCarthy as a liar and demagogue.)

If there were ever any doubts that "both sides" of the political aisle are about the same, January 6, 2021, should have laid them to rest. One of America's two national political parties has embraced (and been embraced by) an anti-democratic extremist fringe. CBS News, like every news outlet and platform, has a cardinal responsibility to protect American democracy from this growing menace. To fulfill this responsibility, it must report accurately what is occurring. It should not pander to the menace by hiring a person who had a hand in it and will further obscure the truth.

Nor should the producers of daytime talk shows chase ratings and ad dollars by pandering to this growing menace, distorting the public's understanding of what's important or the core choices lying ahead. I'm certainly not going to play this game, even if the number-one-rated daytime TV talk show wants me to.

Refusing Dr. Phil

I received an email from an associate producer at the *Dr. Phil* show. She had come across my film *Inequality for All* and wanted to know "if I'd be interested in joining Dr. Phil as an expert guest for an upcoming episode."

Hey, why not? *Dr. Phil* was the highest rated daytime TV talk show in America with over two million viewers. I had lots to say to those viewers about the perils of widening inequality. Then I read the rest of the email: "For this conversation we will be asking questions like do college admissions enroll minorities over prospective Caucasian students? Are Caucasian teachers and professors being laid off to 'make up for past discriminations' against minority educators, as seen in Minneapolis?" These were the only questions included in the email. In other words, it would be a show about favoritism to Black people over white people.

What was going on? *Dr. Phil* is carried by CBS, not Fox News. Phil McGraw himself isn't a rabid right-winger, at least not that I know of. (He did appear on Fox News soon after the start of the pandemic to argue against temporarily closing the economy, claiming that the likelihood of dying from COVID was no greater than that of dying in a car accident or drowning in a swimming pool. By that time 3,000 people had died of the infection. Two years later, it had taken the lives of 1 million.) But my beef wasn't with Dr. Phil. It was with the people who produce popular TV talk shows.

Producers and celebrity hosts like Dr. Phil decide two hugely important things: the topics to be discussed, and how those topics are framed. These decisions determine what issues the public focuses on (out of an almost infinite number bubbling up each day) and what's debatable about them (out of an almost infinite number of possibilities). These two determinations in turn fuel public emotions, ranging from anger, indignation, and outrage, to hope, pride, and confidence. They affect our daily conversations, shape our politics, divide or connect Americans, and help set the national agenda.

Take the contract agreement between the Minneapolis teachers union and the Minneapolis school district, the issue Dr. Phil's associate producer wanted me to talk about. That contract stipulated that if school budgets must be cut, white teachers would be laid off before those from "underrepresented" populations, regardless of seniority. If school budgets then expanded, "underrepresented" teachers would be reinstated before white teachers, regardless of seniority.

MAGA outlets, blogs, and social media sites went nuts over this. Racial preferences for Black people have become an infuriating, hot-button issue, especially among struggling working-class whites. Viewed this way, this issue has lent itself to the right-wing trope that "coastal elites" have rigged the economic game against white working people in favor of "less-deserving" people of color.

Presumably, this is the debate Dr. Phil's producer had in mind. But it was the wrong issue and the wrong debate. Go a bit deeper and you'll see that the goal of the Minneapolis school board was to remedy continuing effects of past discrimination, by supporting *"the recruitment and retention of teachers from underrepresented groups"* (emphasis added). This has been a particularly important goal in Minnesota's schools, where 5.6 percent of licensed teachers identify as a teacher of color or Native American, compared to 30 percent of students.

Research shows that having teachers of color in the classroom has a positive impact on students of color, including improved test scores and graduation rates, presumably because teachers of color are more likely to know what students of color are up against, having once been in that position themselves. They also give such students role models that they emulate. But in a *last-in, first-out* seniority system, teachers of color are more likely to be laid off when budgets are cut because they entered the school system more recently. In the Minneapolis public schools, fewer teachers of color are tenured than white teachers because state law requires that teachers be on probation until they complete three consecutive years of work. So the new Minneapolis contract served an important public purpose in a system where seniority and tenure otherwise discriminated *against* people of color. The contract helped level the playing field and ensure more teachers of color were in classrooms.

There wasn't a chance I'd be able to explain all this on the *Dr. Phil* show. I'd be lucky if I got out two sentences before another guest, representing the "other side" of the issue, jumped down my throat, charging "reverse racism!" Millions of daytime TV viewers were likely to learn from this discussion only that government was favoring Black teachers over white teachers, and that lots of people were mad about it.

I sent my regrets.

That the national conversation is in the hands of producers and celebrity hosts chasing ratings and advertising dollars, with no regard for how they're distorting the public's understanding of what's important or the core choices lying ahead, is disgraceful.

The media is the national classroom through which millions of Americans gain an understanding of what our democracy is, or should be, struggling with. I have tried on occasion to teach the country within that classroom. And for many years I've also used social media to post videos about what I've considered to be important issues.

Around 2010, my younger son, Sam, who then worked for a popular online comedy brand called CollegeHumor (later, Dropout TV), told me I should spend less time and energy writing books and more making films and videos. We were in the kitchen of our house in Berkeley, drinking coffee, when Sam decided it was time for a heart-to-heart.

"Dad, how many books have you written?" he asked, with the hint of a grin.

"I'm not sure."

"Maybe fifteen?"

"In that neighborhood," I responded. "Why do you ask?" I recognized the grin. For thirty years Sam had enjoyed provoking me.

"You've spent a lot of time writing books."

"Yes. So, what's your point?"

"You might want to reconsider how you're spending your time."

"So, you think I've wasted my time?"

"Not exactly wasted," Sam said. "I mean, some people have bought them."

Sam was coming in for the kill. He'd been thinking about this conversation.

The night before, over dinner, I related that I'd recently been at a fundraising event at someone's house in Oakland where I found a copy of one of my first books on a shelf and told the host how excited I was to see it. The host, looking embarrassed, suggested I pull the book out from its place on the shelf. When I did and opened it, I saw that the entire inside had been hollowed out to create a safekeeping place for jewelry. My book made such an excellent safe because no one would ever think to pull it off the shelf. Sam laughed, but the story emboldened him to begin our conversation the next morning.

Sam continued: "I mean, the reason you write is to reach people."

"Of course."

"And as an educator you especially want to reach young people, right?"

"Sure, because young people are still open to lots of ideas, and if you get into their heads, you might influence them for life."

Sam's eyes lit up. "Okay, then. Have you thought about social media?"

He might as well have asked "Have you thought about a zebra?" I had no idea what he was getting at.

"You mean, the Internet?"

"I guarantee you, Dad, that if you put as much time and energy into making videos for the Internet as you put into writing books, you'd reach five times as many young people."

I was skeptical. I had watched some of Sam's comedy videos, but I didn't make the connection, at least not at first. But Sam was patient with me, explaining how it was done, encouraging me to try. And I did try. I teamed up with a young filmmaker named Jake Kornbluth and we made a bunch of three-minute videos about politics and the economy. A few went viral. Then we made the feature film *Inequality for All*, which won an award at the Sundance Film Festival, went into hundreds of movie theaters, and has since found its way into thousands of high school classrooms. After that, I was fortunate to find several other hugely talented young people who have helped me make more films and videos.

Sam was wrong about one thing, though. The videos and films didn't reach five times as many young people as my books. A more accurate ratio would be fifty times as many; maybe five hundred times as many.

Turning to videos to communicate made sense because, as I learned, the brains of many young people are wired differently from the brains of old boomers like me. I already sensed this in classrooms where I taught undergraduates. My students were more sensitive to visual cues than verbal cues. They learned more when I jumped into the aisles of the lecture hall and role-played various characters, engaging them in verbal jousting, than when I delivered a lecture. They reacted more to live performances than to words. They were wired for action, sound, speed, movement.

So if I wanted to explain to them some of the ideas I've written about here, I needed ways to convey those ideas that weren't just words on a page, but which jumped out at them, challenging several of their senses simultaneously. Film and video—accompanied by music, animated graphics, and the stories of real people—could reach those young brains. That's basically what I've been doing since Sam persuaded me to take the leap. Even on TikTok (I believe, but have no way of proving, that I'm the oldest person to fast-dance on TikTok). I still write, of course, because I love writing, and I believe in the power of written words. Hence, this book. Although I've retired from teaching, I still appear in the classroom from time to time, trying to work my magic. The challenge is how to communicate with Gen Z across a half century divide.

That, too, is part of the long game.

Talking with Gen Z

Most of the people I deal with daily—the people I talk with, meet with, collaborate with, teach, Zoom with, make videos with, and have lunch and coffee with—are fifty years younger than I am, in their mid- to late twenties. I don't dwell on the half-century gulf between us, but it occasionally slams me in the face—as when I catch our reflection in the window of a coffee shop and wonder for an instant about the identity of that little old man in our midst, or when I make a casual reference to Humphrey Bogart or Archibald Cox and they stare back blankly, when I refer to "the Rosemary Woods stretch," or being "Borked" or "swift-boated," and they don't have the slightest idea what I'm talking about.

Recently some of us got into a conversation about clothing, and I mentioned that I'd stored my tony jacket in my valise above the chest of drawers in the den. I might as well have been talking ancient Greek.

I miss lots of what *they* say, too. Recently, one of them opined that "inflation is high-key, skyrocketing right now." I got the skyrocketing part. But high-key? Another told me, reassuringly, that the "vibe" of something I'd written was "immaculate." I was not reassured. When one asked another if she'd seen me "clap back at Elon Musk," I didn't know whether to feel complimented or upset.

One of my graduate students, referring to another who had driven a Mustang to someone's weekend baby shower, exclaimed, "What a flex!"

"A flex?" I asked.

"A flex! A flex," she said more loudly, as if she were talking to someone hard of hearing.

I *am* becoming hard of hearing, damn it. But that wasn't the problem.

Face it: A half century is a chasm in the landscape of living memory. A person who tries to speak across it can seem to warp the time-space continuum. When I was a boy, I remember my father telling me that when *he* was a boy he watched veterans of the Civil War march in New York City. I was astonished. How could he be that old? How could the Civil War have occurred that recently?

Most of my *undergraduate* students were born after 9/11. They don't remember a time when the United States was united over anything. They have a hard time believing I've lived most of my life before the Internet. When I tell them I was born before television, they look at me as if I'm a fossil. I suppose I am.

When I tell my undergraduates that I once advised Barack Obama, they're somewhat impressed. Labor secretary to Bill Clinton? Their eyes begin to glaze over. Worked for Jimmy Carter? Not particularly interested. Interned for Bobby Kennedy? Campaigned for Eugene McCarthy? They look puzzled, as if I've entered the misty expanses of ancient history. Sometimes I follow this by telling them I started my career as an assistant to Abraham Lincoln. This used to elicit a laugh. I'm beginning to fear it won't much longer. But every day I consider myself blessed for having the great good fortune to spend most of my time with these young people. They inspire me. They push me. They make me laugh. They help me play the long game. They're going to inherit the mess my generation has bequeathed them. Instead of being bitter or angry, they have all sorts of ideas for how to clean it up, fix it, make the world better. They have the energy and determination to succeed. They keep me optimistic and sane. They make me hopeful that the common good can be resurrected.

Now, please don't get me wrong—it's not all about chronological age. I know some young people who act as rigid and compulsive as the stiffest of my boomer peers, and have come across elderly people with the youngest hearts I've ever known. But overall, I draw huge amounts of strength and happiness from the young people I deal with every day. I also derive it from several older people I deal with every once in a while. One such person is Bernie Sanders.

Loving Bernie

Bernie phoned.

"Bob?"

The Brooklyn patois was unmistakable. "Bernie!"

"Listen, I want you to know that I recommended you to be the next secretary of labor." Bernie is not one for small talk.

Biden's first labor secretary, Marty Walsh, was leaving and apparently Bernie was pushing me as his replacement.

"But I've been there. Done that. Don't want to do it again."

"Just wanted to give you a heads-up. You'll be getting some calls from the media."

Did Bernie even hear what I said?

"Thanks, Bernie."

"Bye."

"Bye, and . . ." He was already off the phone.

Let me just come right out and say it: I love Bernie Sanders. For years now, he has been leading us into the future.

I love his authenticity. Some people have liked Donald Trump because he says whatever he wants, but he's an asshole. Bernie's authenticity comes from saying what he wants and speaking the truth. Although Bernie is blunt, when he growls that "this *grotesque* level of income and wealth inequality is *immoral,*" he means it. And he's right.

I love his chutzpah. Bernie once announced that Starbucks' anti-labor CEO Howard Schultz had agreed to testify before the Senate Committee on Health, Education, Labor and Pensions, which Bernie chaired, because he had threatened him with a subpoena if he didn't. The National Labor Relations Board had filed more than eighty complaints against Starbucks for refusing to negotiate in good faith with its workers in more than 280 of their stores that voted to unionize. "I look forward to hearing from Mr. Schultz as to when he intends to end his illegal anti-union activities and begin signing fair first contracts with the unions," Bernie said.

I love him because he sounds like a vintage record (even his voice has the crackle of worn vinyl).

I love him because he's never been afraid to call himself a democratic socialist. Soon after he began running for the 2016 Democratic presidential nomination, his campaign manager warned me he was about to make a speech to "introduce" the public to democratic socialism. I was impressed that he had the guts to do this but worried about his timing. "Does he have to do it *now*?" I asked. The campaign manager told me Bernie was committed to doing it and couldn't be persuaded otherwise. It was pure Bernie.

Since the nineteenth century, the word "socialism" has been used to scare people away from doing anything big that we need done. But America is changing. As early as 2011, the Pew Research Center found that almost half of all voters under the age of thirty held a positive view of socialism while only 46 percent held a positive view of capitalism. In the 2016 Democratic primaries and then again in 2020, young people all over America wore buttons reading "Feel the Bern."

I love Bernie because he has endless patience for important things and no patience for unimportant conversation. In 2010, he delivered an eight-and-a-half-hour speech on the Senate floor to protest the extension of tax cuts instituted during George W. Bush's presidency. I was in the Capitol at the time and dropped by his office to congratulate him on his marathon. He quickly thanked me, then waved me off to take a phone call.

Just before the California Democratic primary in 2020, he gave a stem-winder of a speech in Oakland. We had a late dinner at a small dive on Shattuck Avenue that was empty except for the two of us—until a supporter spied us through the window and came bounding in with a Bernie poster.

"Senator, would you sign my . . . ?"

"Not now! We're eating!" Bernie barked.

In all my years in and around politics I'd never come across a candidate willing to do this.

I love Bernie because he's a true *populist,* a word that has got a terrible rap since Trump arrived on the scene but should be redeemed. It means for the people and against the powerful. Trump pretends to be a populist, but he's always wanted to be one of the powerful since he entered politics and has been in their pockets.

I love Bernie because he has almost single-handedly changed the national conversation, turning proposals that had once been on the

Democratic fringe into respectable and, in some cases, mainstream Democratic positions: creating jobs by rebuilding infrastructure; providing free tuition at public universities; breaking up the big banks; guaranteeing workers paid medical and family leave.

I love Bernie because even in his eighties his indignation hasn't faded, nor has his energy.

When he entered Congress in 1991 as an independent, he wasn't particularly well liked. That may have had something to do with his telling the press that Congress "is not working. It is failing. Change is not going to take place until many hundreds of these people are thrown out of their offices," and charging that "Congress does not have the courage to stand up to the powerful interests. I have the freedom to speak my mind." Congressman Barney Frank shot back: "Bernie alienates his natural allies. His holier-than-thou attitude— saying, in a very loud voice, he is smarter than everyone else and purer than everyone else—really undercuts his effectiveness." Joe Moakley, another Massachusetts Democrat, then chairman of the powerful House Rules Committee, complained that Bernie "screams and hollers, but he is all alone."

Bernie's lack of popularity on Capitol Hill didn't hold him back. He was reelected to the House seven times and was one of the founding members and the first chair of the Congressional Progressive Caucus, which has grown steadily from six members in 1991 to seventy-one, as of this writing. His ascent to the Senate in 2006 was astonishing: he beat the Republican candidate, Richard Tarrant, one of the wealthiest men in Vermont, by 33 percentage points.

I backed Bernie in 2016 when he ran for the Democratic nomination for president against Hillary Clinton and backed him again in 2020. I took some crap for doing this from Clinton people, but I'm glad I did it. The system needed shaking up. It needed Bernie's candidacy even if he wasn't going to get the nomination. Bernie exemplifies the long game.

I love Bernie because he has more guts than any politician I know. Hell, he has more guts than just about anyone I know.

Restoring Democratic Capitalism

Here's something else that makes me optimistic and fortifies me for the long game. It took one of the oldest presidents in American history, who had been in politics for over half a century, to return the nation to an economic paradigm that dominated public life between 1933 and 1980 and is far superior to the one that has dominated it since. Call it democratic capitalism.

The Great Crash of 1929 followed by the Great Depression taught the nation a crucial lesson that we forgot after Ronald Reagan's presidency: that markets are human creations. The economy that collapsed in 1929 was the consequence of allowing nearly unlimited borrowing, encouraging people to gamble on Wall Street, and permitting the Street to take huge risks with other people's money. Franklin D. Roosevelt and his administration reversed this. During World War II, they controlled prices and put almost every American to work. Subsequent Democratic and Republican administrations enlarged and extended democratic capitalism. Wall Street was regulated, as were television networks, airlines, railroads, and other common carriers. CEO pay was modest. Taxes on the highest earners financed public investments in infrastructure (such as the national highway system) and higher education.

America's postwar industrial policy spurred innovation. The Department of Defense and its Defense Advanced Research Projects Administration developed satellite communications, container ships, and the Internet. The National Institutes of Health did trailblazing basic research in biochemistry, DNA, and infectious diseases. Public spending rose during economic downturns to encourage hiring. Meanwhile, antitrust enforcers broke up AT&T and other monopolies. Small businesses were protected from giant chain stores. Labor unions thrived. By the 1960s, a third of all private-sector workers were unionized. Large corporations sought to be responsive to all their stakeholders.

But then, as I've noted, America took a giant U-turn. Corporate campaign donations overwhelmed American politics, altering the rules of the economic game in favor of big corporations and the ultra-wealthy. The goal of economic policy shifted from the common good to economic growth, even though Americans who were already well-off gained most from that growth. And the means shifted from public oversight of the market to deregulation, free trade, privatization, "trickle-down" tax cuts, and deficit reduction—all of which helped the moneyed interests make even more money. In sum, after Reagan's presidency, democratic capitalism, organized to serve public purposes, all but disappeared, replaced by corporate capitalism organized to serve the moneyed interests.

Joe Biden almost revived democratic capitalism. He learned from the Obama administration's mistake of spending too little to pull the economy out of the Great Recession that the pandemic required substantially greater spending, which would also give working families a cushion against adversity. So he pushed for and got the giant $1.9 trillion American Rescue Plan. This was followed by a $550 billion initiative to rebuild the nation's bridges, roads, and public transit, as well as broadband, water, and energy systems. The year 2022 saw the biggest investment in clean energy sources in American history—expanding wind and solar power, electric vehicles, carbon capture and sequestration, and hydrogen and small nuclear reactors. Then came the largest public investment ever made in semiconductors, the building blocks of the next economy.

Notably, these initiatives helped companies that employ American workers. He also embarked on altering the balance of power between capital and labor, as had FDR. Biden put trustbusters at the head of the Federal Trade Commission and the Antitrust Division of the Justice Department. And he remade the National Labor Relations Board into a strong advocate for labor unions.

Unlike his Democratic predecessors, Biden did not reduce all trade barriers. He focused them on industries that were crucial to America's future—semiconductors, electric batteries, electric vehicles. Unlike Trump, Biden did not give a huge tax cut to corporations and the wealthy. It's also worth noting that, in contrast with every president since Reagan, Biden did not fill his White House with former Wall Street executives. Not one of his economic advisers, not even his treasury secretary, was from the Street.

Biden's larger achievement was to change the economic paradigm that had reigned since Reagan. His democratic capitalism was neither socialism nor "big government." It was, rather, a return to an era when government organized the market for the common good.

Biden also did something that Donald Trump could never do: He put his country over ego, ambition, and pride. He bowed out with grace and dignity.

Presidents don't want to bow out. Both Richard Nixon and Lyndon Johnson had to be shoved out of office. Biden was hardly perfect; in my view, his legacy will forever be tainted by his failure to stop Benjamin Netanyahu from creating a bloodbath in Gaza. His main problem was he was old and losing some of the capacities that dwindle with old age. Even among people who are not president, old age inevitably triggers denial. How many elderly people do you know who accept that they can't do the things they used to do or think they should be able to do? How many willingly give up the keys to their car? It's not surprising Biden resisted. Yet he cared about this country and was aware of the damage a second Trump administration could do to America. Some complain that Biden should have bowed out earlier, giving his vice president, Kamala Harris, more time to campaign. Maybe so. But having watched several presidents close up, I give him huge credit for bowing out at all. Why did he do it? He cared for the country. He feared he couldn't get reelected, and he knew that Donald Trump was deeply dangerous. In other words, Joe Biden demonstrated that a critical part of the long game is reclaiming patriotism.

Reclaiming Patriotism

My father loved America. He served proudly in World War II. He always paid his taxes in full and on time. "It's an honor," I remember him saying about paying taxes. "It's for America." He called Joe McCarthy a "son of a *bitch*" because, he said, "McCarthy hates America. He's just out for himself."

My father would have despised Donald Trump.

Trump conducted the second formal rally of his 2024 presidential campaign in Pickens, South Carolina, where an estimated fifty thousand turned up under the scorching sun to hear him. There, he advanced his version of patriotism based on white Christian nationalism.

He began by celebrating the town's namesake, Francis Pickens, who was governor of South Carolina when it was the first to secede from the Union on the eve of the Civil War. Trump assured the crowd he wouldn't let "them" change the town's name. He commended the Supreme Court for rejecting affirmative action "so someone who has not worked as hard will not take your place." He saluted the court's decision to overrule *Roe v. Wade* so "radical left Democrats will not kill babies." He promised to stop "men competing in women's sports" and prevent classroom teachers from teaching the "wrong" lessons about sexuality or history. He condemned foreign governments that "send" over the border "people in jails and insane asylums" and promised to deny entry to "all communists and Marxists." And he declared America's most dangerous opponents not to be Russia, China, or North Korea but "enemies within" America.

The true meaning of patriotism is the opposite of Trump's exclusionary white male Christian nationalism. It's closer to the love of America my father expressed. Over the last three-quarters of a century, I've seen America's ideal of inclusion become more of a reality. In my lifetime, America has made incremental progress toward equal rights for women, Black people, immigrants, Native Americans, Latinos, LGBTQ+, Muslims, Jews, atheists, and agnostics. Much work needs to be done, of course, but the nation is far better for the progress it has made.

White male Christian nationalism has nothing to do with patriotism. True patriots don't fuel racist, religious, or ethnic divisions. Patriots aren't homophobic or sexist, nor are they blind to social injustices, whether ongoing or embedded in American history. They don't ban books or prevent teaching about the sins of the nation's past. They don't censor truths that may make people uncomfortable, facts that are inconvenient, realities that people would rather not face.

True patriots are not uncritically devoted to America. They are devoted instead to the *ideals* of America—the rule of law, equal justice, voting rights and civil rights, freedom of speech and assembly, freedom from fear, and democracy. True patriots don't have to express patriotism in symbolic displays of loyalty like standing for the national anthem and waving the American flag. They express patriotism in taking a fair share of the burdens of keeping the nation going, sacrificing for the common good. This means paying their fair share of taxes rather than lobbying for lower taxes or seeking tax loopholes or squirreling away money abroad. It means refraining from making large political contributions that corrupt American democracy. It means blowing the whistle on abuses of power even at the risk of losing one's job. It means volunteering time and energy to improving one's community and country.

Patriotism is not found in baseless claims that millions of people vote fraudulently, or in pushing for laws based on the Big Lie that the 2020 election was stolen, which make it harder for people to vote. Patriotism lies instead in strengthening democracy, defending the right to vote, and ensuring that *more* Americans are heard. Patriots understand that when they serve the public, their responsibility is to maintain and build public trust in the institutions of democracy. They don't put loyalty to their political party above their love of America. They don't support an attempted coup. They don't try to hold on to power after voters have chosen not to reelect them. They don't make money off their offices. When serving on the Supreme

Court, they recuse themselves from cases where they may appear to have a conflict of interest. They don't disregard precedent to impose their own ideology.

America's problem is *not* as described by Trump and his white male Christian nationalists, that the nation is losing its whiteness or its dominant religion, or that too many foreigners are crossing its borders. It is not that men are competing in women's sports or children are using school bathrooms inconsistent with their sex at birth, or that teachers are not celebrating the nation's history.

America's problem is that too many Americans, including its lawmakers, are failing to understand what patriotism requires. The "we" that should be at the center of patriotism—the duties that should bind us to one another—are also essential to our economy, our communities, our workplaces.

Creating "We" Workplaces

Recently I went into a Starbucks and asked the barista behind the counter a simple question: "How is it to work here?"

He was understandably cautious in answering. After all, I could have been a corporate stooge. (Starbucks was then doing whatever it could to bust unions, including firing workers who might have been trying to organize a union.)

Then he said, reluctantly, "They treat us okay."

"*They*." That was the key word.

Let me give you a simple way to test for a good workplace. I came up with it years ago when as secretary of labor I visited them all over America. I call it the "we-they" test: Ask a frontline worker a general question like "How is it to work here?" or "How's your job?" or "How would you describe this workplace?" Then listen for the pronoun. If workers describe the company as "they" or "them," it's a tip-off that workers regard the company and its executives as being on a different team. If workers describe the company as "we" or "us," the company instills a sense of pride and ownership in its workers. Even a statement like "they aim for high quality here" suggests a workplace where employees regard the company and its top executives as being on the other side of the divide.

Over the years, I've discovered that "we" companies achieve higher levels of quality, productivity, and service than "they" companies. I could give you many examples, but let me offer the L-S Electro-Galvanizing Co. in Cleveland, in the heart of the Rust Belt, which passed the "we" test with ease when I visited it.

L-S Electro-Galvanizing won awards for quality. Its customers were loyal, and its profits were mounting. The company's equipment for putting zinc coatings on cold-rolled steel was available to all competitors (including those abroad with cheaper labor), but its workers were constantly discovering better ways to use their equipment and serve their customers. The galvanized steel emerging from the factory was consistently high quality, tailored exactly to customer specifications and sold at a competitive price.

L-S's workplace was organized from the bottom up. When I visited, I couldn't tell managers from employees. All wore the same uniforms, parked in the same parking lots, ate in the same cafeteria. Worker committees did the hiring, decided on pay scales linked to levels of skill, and set production targets. They rotated jobs, so that every worker gained knowledge of the entire system. More than 10 percent of payroll was spent on training. And jobs were secure. Even during the recession, when its customers were scaling back, the company kept everyone on board.

All prospered together when the company did well. Workers received gain-sharing bonuses based on plant productivity and profit-sharing bonuses based on company performance. Almost no one ever quit.

L-S was unionized. As odd as it may seem, unionized workers are more likely to use the "we" pronoun than non-unionized. That's probably because unionized workers have a voice and more security, and are better paid. They're not continuously at war with management. For everyone to do better, workers and managers must get along.

By contrast, Starbucks consistently failed my "we" test. Apart from its small number of unionized workers, its workers had no sense of ownership or control. Top executives regarded them as replaceable parts. All decisions came from the top. The company's militant anti-unionism was both a source and a consequence of this culture.

All workplaces aren't "we" workplaces because top executives don't want to give up control. They don't want to entrust frontline workers with day-to-day decisions. Meanwhile, America's frontline workers feel bruised and beaten by years of promises unkept, real wages and benefits cut, and jobs eliminated. Many of them were dubbed "essential" during the pandemic, but they continue to be treated like cow dung.

Playing the long game requires empowering workers. Worker empowerment should be good for everyone. It should include sharing the profits.

Sharing the Profits

One idea to spread the benefits of economic growth was tried with great success in the early twentieth century. It emerged in 1916 from the tumultuous period when America shifted from farm to factory, when Sears, Roebuck and Co., then one of America's largest corporations with over 30,000 employees, announced that it was embarking on a major experiment—profit-sharing. The firm gave workers shares of stock, making them part owners.

Shortly thereafter, the Bureau of Labor Statistics issued a report suggesting that it was a means of reducing the "frequent and often violent disputes" between employers and workers. Profit-sharing gave workers an incentive to be more productive since the financial success of the company would be shared. It also reduced the need for layoffs during recessions because payroll costs dropped as profits did.

It all proved a huge success. Other companies that joined the profit-sharing movement in the first half of the twentieth century included Procter & Gamble, Pillsbury, Kodak, and U.S. Steel.

By the 1950s, Sears workers had accumulated enough stock that they owned a quarter of the company. And by 1968, the typical Sears salesperson could retire with a nest egg worth well over a million dollars (in today's dollars). The downside was that when profits went down, workers' paychecks would shrink. And if a company went bankrupt, workers would lose all their investment in it. The best profit-sharing plans have been in the form of cash bonuses that employees can invest however they wish, on top of predictable wages. At Lincoln Electric, for instance, which has had profit-sharing since 1934, employees receive a cash bonus worth, on average, 40 percent of their annual base earnings.

Profit-sharing with employees has all but disappeared in large corporations, which since the start of the 1980s and the advent of private equity managers have focused on maximizing shareholder returns. Sears phased out its profit-sharing plan in the 1970s (and filed for bankruptcy protection in 2018). At the same time, profit-sharing with top executives has soared as big Wall Street banks, hedge funds, private equity funds, and high-tech companies have doled out huge amounts of stock and stock options. As a result, share prices have gone into the stratosphere while wages have barely risen. Researchers have found that increases in share prices before the late 1980s were related to overall economic growth. Since then, a large portion of the dramatic increases in those prices have come out of what used to go into wages.

As of this writing, Jeff Bezos, who now owns around 10 percent of Amazon's shares of stock, is worth $210 billion overall. Other top Amazon executives hold hundreds of millions of dollars of Amazon shares. But most of Amazon's employees, such as warehouse workers, haven't shared in the bounty. Amazon used to give out stock to hundreds of thousands of its employees. But in 2018 it stopped doing so and instead raised its minimum hourly wage to $15. The wage raise got headlines and was good PR, but Amazon's decision to end stock awards was more significant. If Amazon's 1.2 million employees together owned the same proportion of its stock as Sears workers did in the 1950s—a quarter of the company—each employee by 2024 would own shares worth an average of over $350,000.

America's trend toward higher profits, higher share prices, and mounting executive pay, but near stagnant wages, is unsustainable economically and politically. Profit-sharing should be encouraged by lowering taxes on corporations that share profits with all their workers, and raising taxes on those that don't. Sharing profits with workers is a logical and necessary step to making the system work for the many, not just the few. Another is supporting businesses that lie at the hearts of our communities. Both are critical parts of the long game.

Making Community Count

I've got a special place near my heart for Dan & Whit's general store in Norwich, Vermont. It was there for me during my undergraduate years in college in nearby Hanover, New Hampshire, often on snowy evenings when I couldn't get supplies elsewhere. Years later when my parents retired to Vermont, Dan & Whit's was there for them, too.

Like many places around the country, Vermont has been struggling to find enough workers to fill jobs. But unlike most urban centers, where the obvious answer is to pay workers more, rural towns can't always count on higher wages to elicit more job applicants because populations are thin and often declining. Unlike profitable national retail chains, mom-and-pop businesses can't always absorb higher labor costs anyway. They can't simply pass them on to customers in higher prices either, because small-town customers might not have the ability to pay.

So in late 2021 when Dan & Whit's owner Dan Fraser put up a "Help Wanted" sign, the inhabitants of Norwich knew it was bad news. (I never met the younger Dan but I'm sure I met his grandfather, who passed the store on to his father, who passed it on to Dan.) Dan would have to close the place down if he didn't get help.

It turned out that Dan didn't need to do anything. Dan's customers began applying for the jobs. Rick Ferrell, a local doctor, took on a shift at the register. A retired finance director applied for the deli counter. A nurse, a teacher, a psychology professor, a therapist, a school principal—nearly two dozen customers have stepped up to stock shelves, do the inventory, and clean up the place, so that Dan & Whit's can remain open. (Virtually all of these new hires are donating their hourly wages to some of Dan's favorite charities.)

I've spent a lot of time over the years examining what happens to communities when important businesses close, often because some bean counters in headquarters hundreds or thousands of miles away decide it's not worth the cost of keeping the businesses going where they are. Economists often praise capitalism's wondrous "efficiencies" at moving assets to their "highest and best uses." There's something to that. But what's left out of the equation are the social costs of these moves, which can be high.

When asked why the people of Norwich stepped in to help Dan keep going, employee Dianne Miller said it was "because Dan & Whit's is the heartbeat of this community." Others described it as the "heart of the town." That's the best quick summary of the social benefits of a place like Dan & Whit's I've ever heard.

Communities *do* have hearts. When such businesses disappear, the community loses not only an economic asset but a place that allows it to be a community, a place where people meet up, congregate, exchange gossip and information, barter, learn about common problems, sometimes decide to act. I remember Dan & Whit's as such a place. I can't imagine Norwich without it. Luckily, it won't have to be. But this isn't just a "feel good" story about one country town coming together to save an iconic general store. It seems to me there's an important lesson here for all of us, wherever we live.

American capitalism is the harshest form of capitalism in all the world's advanced economies. It takes almost no account of social costs and benefits. Businesses swoop in and swoop out wherever and however profits can be maximized and losses minimized. But communities are different. They aren't nearly as footloose as financial capital. They're built on *social* capital, which often takes years to accumulate and can't be cashed in.

I think people owe something to businesses that are the hearts of our communities. Maybe we shouldn't allow big chains or Walmarts to drain our main streets of the commerce they need to survive. Even if Walmart's items are cheaper, the social costs of losing the small businesses that undergird our community are often way higher.

Maybe we should donate some of our own time and labor to account for the importance of these core businesses. Maybe those of us who can afford it should buy shares in them, to give them an added financial cushion. At the very least, we owe them our patronage—rather than, say, the Waltons or Jeff Bezos.

Meanwhile, we need to create a recycled economy.

Recirculating Stuff

Every holiday, birthday, special occasion, and just plain recreational shopping ends up filling shelves and closets with more *stuff*. I for one don't want anything more, thank you. My shelves are already overflowing with books. My attic is full of old chairs and tables, chafing dishes, pictures, games, children's toys, ski equipment, stereos, a broken easel. My closet can't accommodate any more clothes, most of which I haven't worn in years.

Once a year (usually around the holidays), I drop off as much old stuff as I can at Goodwill Industries or the Salvation Army. I have to admit I also prowl around thrift stores on the off chance I'll find some quirky thing I've been looking for (or maybe a friend or relative would love to have)—a vinyl recording of Leonard Cohen from the late 1960s, a funny tie, memorabilia from one of FDR's presidential campaigns.

A few months ago, a few of my neighbors systematically began putting stuff they no longer want on the sidewalk at the end of the street, hoping others will pick it up. They organized it so well that I've started putting stuff there, and even picked up a few things, like some exercise weights I'd been looking for. In all these ways, I've become a small part of a *recycled* economy. Maybe you have, too.

At different times of our life, we want different things. When kids are small, they have certain needs; as they grow up, different needs and wants. When they leave home and we downsize, lots of stuff goes into the attic. Tastes change over the years, too. Technologies alter or advance. There are the gifts that don't suit, the clothes that no longer fit, the purchases that are later regretted. All create a need for recycling.

This got me wondering: *What if we were all more intentional about recycling stuff? What if there were a systematic way of donating things we no longer need and of finding stuff we'd like to have?* I'm not talking about recycling our garbage or waste; I'm imagining an entire *system* based on continuously recycling stuff, without any of it being bought or sold.

Something like this is already up and running in the form of "Buy Nothing" groups. Started in 2013 as a local network in Bainbridge Island, Washington, these groups now have 4.3 million members in forty-four countries. Members can offer or request any item or service, as long as it's legal. (Buying, selling, and bartering are prohibited.) A Buy Nothing app was downloaded more than 125,000 times in a month.

A recycling system in which all the stuff people no longer want is continuously recirculated to people who want it could be increasingly important as we face a worsening clash between infinite wants on a planet with finite resources. Imagine how much less *waste* there'd be if the stuff *already* out there were continuously recirculated. The United States now produces more plastic waste than any other country, according to the National Academy of Sciences. The average American generates about 287 pounds each year. And think of the greenhouse gas emissions we'd avoid in a recycled economy. A 2020 paper published in *Nature* attributes overconsumption and the relentless pursuit of economic growth to the explosive rise in such emissions now threatening our planet.

But wait, you might say, consumer spending is about 70 percent of gross domestic product. Our economy depends on *consumption*. Remember George W. Bush telling Americans that the most patriotic thing we could do after 9/11 was to *buy*? If consumer spending were substantially reduced because we recycled lots more stuff, the Gross Domestic Product would take a dive. Tens of thousands of retailers and wholesalers might close. Millions could lose their jobs and live-lihoods. Hell, we just lived through a pandemic-induced recession that showed how bad things can get.

Yet that's *not* the inevitable tradeoff, because life in a recycled economy would be a lot cheaper. We wouldn't need to buy nearly as much, so we wouldn't need to earn nearly as much, which means working less and spending more time with our families or on lei-sure pursuits. Most of us already have too many possessions we don't need or want any longer, or we have the wrong stuff for this particu-lar time in our lives. We just need a better system for reallocating what is already produced that's not wanted or not being used by the people who have it, and getting it to the people who want it. Not only would this generate less waste and a cleaner environment, it might also make a dent in poverty by more systematically getting items to people who need them.

I offer these ideas—creating "we" businesses, sharing the prof-its, supporting businesses that lie at the hearts of our communities, and moving to a recycling economy—because they're all within our grasp. They're commonsense ways of softening an otherwise harsh economy. They can help make our society healthier. That's critical to the long game.

So is changing our idea of leadership.

Leading America

People vested with formal authority to run major businesses, gov-ernment, universities, the media, charities, and faith-based institu-tions carry around in their heads a presumed definition of what it means to be a successful "leader." These days, it's usually focused on accumulating for themselves and their organizations more power or wealth, or both, and doing whatever it takes to get it. I've found that definition to be profoundly inadequate. The long game requires a new and different conception of leadership, one in which leaders see part of their responsibility as building public trust in the institutions they oversee.

As I've said, CEOs half a century ago understood that corporations were not just for shareholders but also for employees, communities, customers, and the public. Banks existed not to make wild bets with other people's money but to protect depositors' and investors' savings and to prudently lend them. Health insurers existed to provide insurance to everyone who needed it, not to make big money by cherry-picking the healthiest. Most of the news media existed to report the news—it might be tilted left or right—but not to enrich their top executives, top talent, and major investors. Political parties existed to organize and inform voters, not to corrupt our democracy with giant campaign contributions and negative ads.

Over time, these institutions and their leaders seem to have forgotten that their legitimacy depends on advancing the common good and that leadership is a public trust. The ethos of doing whatever it takes to win has eroded that trust.

In the long game, political victories that undermine trust in politics shouldn't be considered wins because they're net losses for society. Record-breaking corporate profits achieved by eroding the public's trust in business are derelictions of duty, not successes. Lobbying and campaign donations that result in laws and regulations favoring the lobbyists and donors are failures of leadership. A nonprofit that pulls in piles of funding isn't a success if the money comes with strings attached that compromise its integrity.

The standard justification for today's whatever-it-takes-to-win leadership is that not acting in that manner potentially puts them out of a job, allowing their political or economic competitors to prevail. That assumes that the people who put such people into positions of power—voters, investors, members of various organizations—want them to do whatever it takes to win. Many of these backers, however, understand their own obligations to the common good, and don't support strategies that harm everyone over the longer term.

One example: On the eve of the Senate's final vote on repealing the Affordable Care Act in July 2017, Senator John McCain returned to Washington from his home in Arizona where he was being treated for brain cancer to cast the deciding vote against repeal. He also took to the Senate floor to condemn the whatever-it-takes politics that had overtaken Washington, beginning by saluting a former generation of senators for whom the common good was more important than winning particular legislative battles. "I've known and admired men and women in the Senate who played much more than a small role in our history, true statesmen, giants of American politics," he said.

> They came from both parties, and from various backgrounds. Their ambitions were frequently in conflict. They held different views on the issues of the day. And they often had very serious disagreements about how best to serve the national interest. But they knew that however sharp and heartfelt their disputes, however keen their ambitions, they had an obligation to work collaboratively to ensure the Senate discharged its constitutional responsibilities effectively.... That principled mindset, and the service of our predecessors who possessed it, come to mind when I hear the Senate referred to as the world's greatest deliberative body.

McCain then admonished his current colleagues for eroding the common good, in words aimed as much at voters as at his fellow senators. "Our deliberations today ... are more partisan, more tribal, more of the time than any other time I remember," he said. He reminded them that winning was not as important as upholding and strengthening the institutions of governing.

> Our system doesn't depend on our nobility. It accounts for our imperfections, and gives an order to our individual strivings that has helped make ours the most powerful and prosperous society on earth. It is our responsibility to preserve that, even when it requires us to do something less satisfying than "winning." Even when we must give a little to get a little. Even when our efforts manage just three yards and a cloud of dust, while critics on both sides denounce us for timidity, for our failure to "triumph."

This wasn't the first time McCain refused to pander to the worst in contemporary American politics, even though that might have been an easier path to victory. One of my fondest memories of McCain occurred in the 2008 presidential campaign when he was running against Barack Obama. It occurred at a town hall event in Minnesota when McCain responded to a supporter who said he was "scared" at the prospect of an Obama presidency. "I have to tell you," McCain said, "Senator Obama is a decent person and a person you don't have to be scared of as president of the United States." At this, the Republican crowd booed. "Come on, John!" one audience member yelled out. Others shouted that Obama was a "liar" and a "terrorist." A woman holding a microphone said, "I can't trust Obama. I have read about him and he's not, he's not uh—he's an Arab. He's not . . ." At this, McCain snapped the microphone from her and replied: "No, ma'am. He's a decent family man [and] a citizen that I just happen to have disagreements with on fundamental issues and that's what this campaign's all about."

Our best chance of reversing whatever-it-takes politics over the long term is through political leaders like McCain who demand that politicians attend to the common good rather than win by under-mining it, and who help educate the public about the importance of doing this. That is the essence of political leadership.

An American president is not just the chief executive of the United States, and the office he (or, one day, hopefully, she) holds is not just a bully pulpit to advance certain policy ideas. Nor is it a position from which to reward supporters and punish political opponents. A president is also a moral leader, pledged to pursue the common good. It is hardly the case that every president has been an exemplar, but a president inevitably helps set the moral tone of the nation. The values a president enunciates and demonstrates ricochet through society, strengthening or undermining its citizens. Cicero observed more than two thousand years ago that "the administration of the government, like the office of a trustee, must be conducted for the benefit of those entrusted to one's care, not of those to whom it is entrusted."

As one of George Washington's biographers, Douglas Southall Freeman, explained, Washington believed he had been entrusted with something of immense intrinsic worth and that his duty was to uphold it for its own sake and over the long term. By June 1775, when Congress appointed him to command the nation's army, Washington had already "become . . . the embodiment of the purpose, the patience, and the determination necessary for the triumph of the revolutionary cause. He had retained the support of Congress and won that of New England in like manner and measure, by directness, by deference, and by manifest dedication to duty."

Two hundred forty years later, in the 2016 presidential campaign, candidate Donald Trump was accused of failing to pay his income taxes. His response was, "That makes me smart." His comment conveyed a message to millions of Americans that paying taxes in full is not an obligation of citizenship. Trump also boasted about giving money to politicians so they would do whatever he wanted. "When they call, I give. And you know what, when I need something from them two years later, three years later, I call them. They are there for me." In other words, it's perfectly okay for business leaders to pay off politicians, regardless of the effect on our democracy.

After Trump launched an attack on NFL players who kneeled during the national anthem to protest structural racism and police violence, Steve Kerr, coach of the Golden State Warriors, responded by explaining what the players were seeking in terms of core American values. "Just think about what those players are protesting," said Kerr.

> They're protesting excessive police violence and racial inequality. Those are really good things to fight against. And they're doing it in a nonviolent way. Which is everything that Martin Luther King preached, right? A lot of American military members will tell you that the right to free speech is exactly what they fight for. And it's just really, really upsetting that the leader of our country is calling for these players to be "fired."

Kerr went on to talk about our duty to make America more tolerant.

> The fact is we live in an amazing country, but it's a flawed one. I consider myself unbelievably lucky to live here, so please spare me the "If you don't like it you can get out" argument. I love living here. I love my country. I just think it's important to recognize that we as a nation are far from perfect, and it's our responsibility to try to make it better. And one of the ways to

do that is to promote awareness and understanding and acceptance. Not just acceptance but embracing our diversity, which when you get down to it is not only who we are but truly what makes us great.

Before Trump, the peaceful transfer of power was assumed to be a central feature of American democracy. Think of Al Gore's gracious concession speech to George W. Bush in 2000, after five weeks of a bitterly contested election and just one day after the Supreme Court ruled in favor of Bush: "I say to President-elect Bush that what remains of partisan rancor must now be put aside, and may God bless his stewardship of this country."

Bush's response was no less civil: "This evening I received a gracious call from the vice president. We agreed to meet early next week in Washington and we agreed to do our best to heal our country after this hard-fought contest."

Many voters continued to doubt the legitimacy of Bush's victory, but there was no civil war. Think of what might have occurred if Gore had bitterly accused Bush of winning fraudulently and blamed the five Republican appointees on the Supreme Court for siding with Bush for partisan reasons. Think what might have happened if, during his campaign, Bush had promised to put Gore in jail for various improprieties, and then, after he won, accused Gore (or Bill Clinton) of spying on him during the campaign and trying to use the FBI and CIA to bring his downfall. These statements, close to ones Trump actually made after losing the 2020 election, might have imperiled the political stability of the nation. They would have sacrificed the common good to an extreme form of whatever-it-takes-to-win politics. Instead, Gore and Bush made the same moral choice their predecessors had made at the end of every previous American presidential election, and for the same reason: They understood that the peaceful transition of power confirmed the nation's commitment to the Constitution, which was far more important than their own losses or wins. It was a matter of public morality. Trump had no such concern.

This is the essence of Trump's failure of leadership—not that he chose one set of policies over another, not only that he divided rather than united Americans, or even that he behaved in childish and vindictive ways unbecoming a president, but that he sacrificed the processes and institutions of American democracy to achieve his personal goals. By saying and doing whatever it took to win, he abused the trust we place in a president to preserve and protect the nation's capacity for self-government.

CEOs and directors of major corporations are also entrusted with the common good. It is no excuse for them to argue they have no choice but to do whatever it takes to maximize share prices. No law requires them to do this. As I've said, the idea that the sole purpose of a corporation is to maximize share prices is relatively new, dating back to the 1980s.

In the summer of 2014, the managers, employees, and customers of a New England chain of supermarkets called Market Basket joined together to oppose the board of directors' decision earlier that year to oust the chain's popular chief executive, Arthur T. Demoulas. Their demonstrations and boycotts emptied most of the chain's seventy stores. Arthur T., as he was known, had kept prices lower than his competitors, paid his employees more (along with profit-sharing), and gave them and his managers more authority to make decisions. Just before he was ousted, he offered customers an additional 4 percent discount, arguing they could make better use of the money than the shareholders could. Arthur T. viewed Market Basket as a joint enterprise from which everyone should benefit, not just its shareholders—which was why the board fired him. Yet eventually consumers and employees won. The boycott was so costly that the board sold the company to Arthur T.

What happened next? Management experts—business school professors, management consultants, and economists—were skeptical that Market Basket could ever make it in the dog-eat-dog world of American capitalism. Yes, it was a heartwarming story, they noted condescendingly, but Arthur T. would not emerge as a modern-day George Bailey because the George Baileys of America were extinct if they ever lived at all. The naysayers pointed to Market Basket's pile of debt along with its higher-than-normal pay and lower-than-normal prices. It was in a doom loop.

Yet a decade later, the naysayers were proven wrong. By 2024, Market Basket was thriving. Demoulas Super Markets, as the business was now formally known, stretched across four New England states, with revenue projected of $7.6 billion that year, roughly double its revenues in 2014. It had twenty more stores than a decade before, ninety in all, and about 40 percent more workers. Dunnhumby, a marketing firm that specializes in the retail sector, ranked Market Basket among the five best-run supermarket chains in the United States. The money Arthur T. borrowed to buy the business was paid back in full. And the chain has never abandoned its core strategy of low prices, nor its end-of-the-year bonus system or its profit-sharing retirement plan.

CEOs of big corporations might say the example of Market Basket doesn't apply to them because it's not a publicly held company whose shares are traded on major stock exchanges. Market Basket doesn't have to worry about failing to maximize share prices, and thereby succumb to corporate raiders or activist investors. True, but Arthur T.'s business model could be applied even where many shareholders are involved. For example, Patagonia, a large apparel manufacturer based in Ventura, California, has organized itself as a "benefit corporation," a for-profit company whose articles of incorporation require that it consider the interests of workers, the community, and the environment, as well as shareholders. Benefit corporations are certified and their performance is regularly reviewed by nonprofit third-party entities, such as B Lab. By 2024, forty-one states and the District of Columbia had enacted laws allowing companies to incorporate in this way, thereby giving CEOs and directors explicit legal authority to consider the interest of all stakeholders.

CEOs might still argue that if they want to raise money in public capital markets they must attend solely to the interests of shareholders, or competitive forces will wipe them out. That argument assumes that CEOs are powerless to change this. But since markets are based on rules, and the heads of large companies have outsized political influence over what those rules are to be, they could show admirable leadership by pushing for laws that require CEOs to consider all their stakeholders.

Enlightened CEOs could make the economy work for everyone rather than for a privileged few. Rather than reflexively seek tax cuts, they could push to *raise* taxes on corporations as well as on people like themselves and other wealthy Americans and dedicate the funds to better schools for all American kids. They could seek a higher minimum wage, bigger wage subsidies (in the form of the Earned Income Tax Credit), more portable pensions, universal healthcare, and other measures that would raise wages and make American workers and their families more secure. They could fight for laws that make unionizing easier.

If this sounds far-fetched, it's only because of how far we've come from the era when the heads of American business viewed themselves as "corporate statesmen," trustees of the common good. In the 1940s and 1950s, CEOs of major corporations lobbied for measures to expand jobs. They argued that unions "serve the common good." In the 1960s, many of these CEOs lobbied for stronger environmental protections and for passage of the Environmental Protection Act.

Nothing is stopping CEOs and top executives on Wall Street from putting an end to the rigged system. They could reduce the needs of candidates to raise vast sums of campaign money by supporting public financing of campaigns. They could back stricter limits on the "revolving door" between industry and government personnel, and laws requiring full disclosure of the sources of all campaign funding. Why shouldn't CEOs and top Wall Street executives be among the vanguard seeking a constitutional amendment allowing lawmakers to *limit* lobbying and campaign spending? For too long CEOs have abdicated their duty to their country. We are now living with the consequences.

As taught in professional schools and required for obtaining many professional licenses, ethics is straightforward and superficial. It involves fulfilling legal responsibilities, avoiding obvious conflicts of interest, and behaving in an aboveboard manner—that is, avoiding legal troubles or public relations disasters.

But responsible leadership extends far beyond the ethics taught in professional schools. Playing the long game requires an understanding that the purpose of leadership is not simply to win. It is to serve.

Making Society Healthy

In 2023, a panel of medical experts—the U.S. Preventive Services Task Force—recommended for the first time that doctors screen all adult patients under sixty-five for anxiety disorders. The advisory group said the guidance was intended to help prevent mental health disorders from going undetected and untreated. It made a similar recommendation for children and teenagers.

This advice highlights the extraordinary stress levels that have plagued the United States in recent years. Some say we need more psychiatrists, psychologists, and therapists, that America is short on mental health resources on all levels. Lori Pbert, a clinical psychologist and professor at the University of Massachusetts Chan Medical School, who serves on the task force, calls mental health disorders "a crisis in this country."

But wait. Maybe what people feel are valid descriptions of personal experience rather than symptoms of mental illness. Maybe we need to stop thinking about anxiety and depression as "disorders" and start regarding them as rational responses to a *society* that's become ever more disordered. So many Americans are concerned by the soaring costs of living and the growing insecurity of jobs and incomes. So many are terrified by Trump's and his followers' attacks on democracy. Who doesn't worry about mass shootings at their children's or grandchildren's schools? Who isn't affected by the climate crisis? Who hasn't been unnerved by ongoing war and the threat of terrorism?

For many Americans there is additional anxiety about increasingly brutal racism; attacks on Asian Americans, Hispanic Americans, and Jews; mounting misogyny and anti-abortion laws; homophobia and transphobia; and the growing coarseness and ugliness of what we see and read in social media. It would be weird if these people *weren't* stressed.

Studies show that women have nearly double the risk of depression as men. From 2014 to 2019, the suicide rate among Black Americans increased by 30 percent. Are women and Black people suffering from a "disorder," or are they responding to reality, or both?

White men without college degrees are particularly vulnerable to "deaths of despair" from suicide, overdoses, and alcoholic liver diseases, with contributions from the cardiovascular effects of rising obesity, according to the American Council on Science and Health. Are they suffering from a "disorder," or are they responding to a fundamental change in American society, or both? As I've noted, economists Anne Case and Angus Deaton argue that deaths of despair among whites would not have happened, or been so severe, had the white working class not been left behind.

Even if we had far more mental-health professionals, what would they do against these formidable foes? Prescribe more pills? If anything, Americans are already overmedicated. Even when mental-health care is covered by insurance, it usually limits the length of treatment—which does indeed encourage the use of drugs. I believe we need better access to mental-health care and increased staffing, but we must also try to make our society healthier as part of the long game. Americans need more job security, stronger safety nets, higher wages. Americans need to reject Trumpism and the reckless power of big money. We must take a leading role in ending the climate crisis, and do everything possible to overcome racism, homophobia, and misogyny. That, too, will make us healthier.

These goals are difficult to achieve, of course. But without *seeking* to achieve them, without making their achievement central to what we try to do as a people, we will not get healthier no matter how many resources are thrown at the problem. Brutality is our common enemy. A civil society is, or should be, our common goal.

For those of you who may be skeptical that we can win this long game, there's reason to believe we can. What keeps me optimistic is our young people.

Watching the Moneyed
Class Get Run Over

More than a third of Harvard's graduating seniors are heading into finance and management consulting, two professions notable for how quickly their practitioners make *bags* (slang for sacks of money), reports *The New York Times*. Similar percentages show up in other prestigious universities. Frankly, I'm not surprised that a third of graduating seniors at the nation's most prestigious private universities are heading into finance and consulting. In this era of raging income inequality and billionaire robber barons, the potential bags in finance and consulting are gigantic. At Goldman Sachs salaries start at $105,000 to $164,000 and are soon in the stratosphere. At McKinsey, they begin at $100,000 to $140,000 and also rise steeply.

Think of the lure: Make a bag and then do whatever you want to do without ever again worrying about money. Make a bag and support whatever good causes you believe in without having to work at social change. Make a bag and you'll never have to grovel to those with wealth and power.

When I graduated Dartmouth College in 1968, almost no one I knew went into finance or consulting. In those days, inequalities were minuscule compared to now. The bags at that time could have fit into a glove compartment. One of the least discussed but most profound consequences of America's surging inequality is the number of talented young people now devoting themselves to making bags. Remarkably, though, *most* talented young people are not yet in the bag.

For most of the last forty-two years, I've taught at several of America's most prestigious universities. The biggest change I've seen over the years is not how starry-eyed students have become about finance and consulting but how passionate they've become about making the world better. Graduates who are out to make a bag are still there, of course. But many graduates are joining nonprofits, entering politics, or becoming community organizers, public defenders, teachers, healthcare workers, diplomats, staffers on congressional committees, union organizers, scientists, or environmental activists.

Conservative columnist David Brooks bemoans this progressive trend. In a June 2024 column entitled "The Sins of the Educated Class," he laments that at elite universities "the share of progressive students and professors has steadily risen, and the share of conservatives has approached zero." He cites a May 2023 survey of Harvard's graduating class showing 65 percent identifying as progressive or very progressive. Brooks believes that the Gen Z cohort at prestigious universities is so tormented by the cognitive dissonance between their positions of privilege and their commitments to social justice that they must "prove to themselves and others" that they're "on the side of the oppressed."

I don't see it like that. At least since the start of Donald Trump's first presidency in January 2017, the larger meaning of "progressive" has shifted to someone who wants to preserve and protect democracy. To be a progressive is no longer to be on the political left as the left used to be defined—seeking a larger government—but to be on the side of the Constitution, the rule of law, and a modicum of decency. I believe this is why so many more undergraduates now deem themselves progressive.

I agree with Brooks that elite universities should dismantle arrangements that let the privileged members of society pass down their educational privileges to their children while locking out most everyone else—for example, by ending affirmative action for legacies and calling on the private sector to remove college prerequisites for decent-paying jobs. But Brooks and other conservatives are dead wrong about *which* elite is holding back the rest of America. It's not the educated class. It's the moneyed class. They overlap but they are not the same.

Trump and much of his Republican Party are criticizing the educated class in order to pose as populists on the side of average working people. Consider Representative Elise Stefanik, chair of the House Republican Conference (and Harvard class of '06), who doesn't miss an opportunity to attack elite universities and their presidents, or Senator Josh Hawley (Stanford '02 and Yale Law '06), who calls the student demonstrations against the slaughter in Gaza signs of "moral rot."

JD Vance (Yale Law '13) has called university professors "the enemy," proposed legislation to restrict the consideration of race in admissions, and sought to crack down on the encampments that emerged on college campuses during student protests. According to Vance, America's colleges and universities are controlled by left-wing politics, and he has approved of authoritarian Hungarian prime minister Viktor Orbán's approach to state universities:

> The closest that conservatives have ever gotten to successfully dealing with left-wing domination of universities is Viktor Orbán's approach in Hungary. I think his way has to be the model for us: not to eliminate universities, but to give them a choice between survival or taking a much less biased approach to teaching. [The government should be] aggressively reforming institutions, such as Harvard, in a way to where they're much more open to conservative ideas.

Republicans promised the moneyed class that in return for their support in the 2024 election, they'd receive an extension of Trump's 2017 tax cuts—which disproportionately boosted the wealth of big corporations and the rich—as well as additional tax cuts and regulatory rollbacks. It's estimated that this will expand the national debt by $4.5 trillion over the next decade, rendering it impossible for the government to invest in things average Americans desperately need, such as childcare, eldercare, affordable housing, and, yes, affordable higher education.

Brooks warns that if present trends continue, we could face a populist uprising, "a multiracial, multiprong, right/left alliance against the educated class." That class must "seriously reform the system or be prepared to be run over," says Brooks.

I think it's the moneyed class who should be prepared to be run over. The educated class, on the other hand, is growing in part because of the extraordinary success and impact of great public universities, such as the University of California, Berkeley, where I've spent the last twenty years.

My Last Class

When I arrived at Berkeley in 2004, I had no idea I'd be spending the next two decades there. And I didn't appreciate the university's power as one of the most successful engines of upward mobility in America.

Before Berkeley, I'd taught at two prestigious private universities, Harvard and Brandeis. My own college education had occurred at Dartmouth, Oxford, and Yale. I had visited Berkeley briefly in the late 1960s, as a research and teaching assistant to Sim Van der Ryn, a professor of architecture who was in the forefront of the "green architecture" movement, and in more recent years I had given occasional lectures at Berkeley as I did at other public universities, but I didn't really understand public universities.

During my first week on the Berkeley faculty, I was contacted by several professors from the department of computer science, asking if I'd drop by to talk with them about widening inequality in America.

"Um, sure," I stammered, wondering why computer scientists would want to hear from me. "Maybe you can give me some guidance on what you'd like me to talk about?"

"The whole problem," one of them said. "We need to understand it better."

I was about to ask why they thought they needed to understand inequality better when another of them broke in. "You see, we teach a lot of students who come from poor families. First-generation Americans, or the first in their families to attend a university. It would help us to know a bit more about their experience of poverty."

"We don't teach just about software and gadgets," said another. "We want our students to apply what they learn here in ways that improve people's lives. So it would be helpful to understand what's happening to America."

"We teach ethics," said another. "We don't *call* it ethics, but that's what it is. We want our students to do good in the world." I stared at him for a moment in wonderment. In all my years of teaching up until that point, I had never heard a scientist say anything remotely like this. For a moment he seemed embarrassed, maybe interpreting my momentary shock as criticism. "You see," he said slowly, "we're a *public* university. We have a duty . . ."

He didn't have to say another word. Suddenly I realized I was at a different kind of institution than the prestigious universities I had attended or taught in until then. The word "duty" summed it up: Public universities exist for the *public*. They have a responsibility to the public.

In most universities, the boundaries between disciplines are like moats. Rarely do professors from, say, computer science, show much curiosity about what's taught in, say, public policy and economics. But at a place like Berkeley, disciplinary boundaries are so porous that I kept meeting professors who taught courses that bridged disciplines, and research teams comprised of professors from many different backgrounds. That fluidity, too, seemed connected to the publicness—the duty—of a great public university. Instead of looking inward, the faculty was continuously looking outward. Rather than becoming narrower, they were broadening their fields of study.

The other thing that has struck me about great public universities like Berkeley is that they take seriously their obligation to teach a wide cross section of students. Diversity is real. As my colleague David Kirp has pointed out, in the wake of the Supreme Court's 2023 ruling that gutted affirmative action, enrollment of Black and Latino students declined in most colleges and universities. Fewer Black students were enrolled at most of the fifty top-ranked schools than before the Court's ruling. But Berkeley managed to maintain its diversity.

How did Berkeley do it? About one-third of Berkeley's undergraduates start at a community college. (By contrast, fewer than 1 percent of Harvard University students transfer from any institution.) What's more, 90 percent of Berkeley's transfer students graduate—the same rate as their classmates. David asks: How can elite universities maintain a diverse student body in a post–affirmative action world? His answer: Recruit community college graduates. Community colleges enroll more than 40 percent of America's undergraduate students.

More than a million students graduate from these schools every year. Admitting more of them to top-notch four-year universities would lead to greater racial, ethnic, and economic diversity on those campuses. David notes that in New York City, more than half the community college students are Black or Hispanic—twice the percentage of white students—while in Texas, 94 percent of the students in two-year institutions are minorities. Community college students are often older, more likely to be single parents, veterans, or the first in their family to attend college. In short, top-tier universities can boost diversity without relying on quotas by recruiting community college graduates.

After they graduate, some of these students pay it forward by supporting the next generation. David says that one of his former students, who enrolled in community college after a stint in prison, graduated from Berkeley with honors. He's pursuing a graduate degree in public policy and plans to be a strong voice for prison reform. While enrolling community college graduates won't compensate for the damage done by the Supreme Court's decision to gut affirmative action, it can be an important part of the answer.

I've been a teacher for most of the last forty-two years. I've done lots of other things, but I've always come back to teaching. That's been my home. My calling. I couldn't imagine not teaching.

I knew I wanted to be a teacher from the first day I walked into my first class to teach public policy to graduate students at Harvard in September 1981. By then I knew a lot about how public policies were made. I had interned for a senator (Bobby Kennedy), clerked for a federal judge (Frank Coffin), advised the commissioners at the Federal Trade Commission, worked at the Justice Department, argued before the Supreme Court, and eventually served in a president's cabinet and run a department of the federal government. I knew the dance of legislation, the ways laws are turned into regulations, how regulations are enforced, how legislators and judges keep their eyes on the people who interpret and enforce the law. I knew how little actual policy making has to do with economic analysis but also the importance of sound and careful thinking along the way about what the public needs. I saw relationships among politics, law, economics, and the histories and the norms of particular institutions: I understood all of it as a system moving through time, adapting itself to different pressures and forces as it moved. I also saw how large a part big money was coming to play—money flowing from large corporations to lobbying and law firms and to public relations firms, money flowing from corporations and wealthy individuals into political campaigns, money flowing into so-called think tanks and nonprofits whose analyses were utilized by corporations to make their cases before legislators and judges.

I felt I had a lot to teach but also a lot to learn, and I learned a great deal from my students—from their questions, their insights, their excitement, their intense interest in every aspect of law, politics, economics, and history, and from their idealism that remained intact even as I revealed the sobering underbelly of our system of self-government.

The moment I began teaching, I felt as if I was eating a wonderful meal for the first time. I instantly fell in love with teaching. I loved the *liveness* of it—the energy in the classroom, the electricity that would spark when I said something that students hadn't thought about or provided a framework that made sense of what they previously had considered random phenomena. Sometimes I lectured. More often, I played roles and assigned roles to them: a legislator, a judge, a corporate CEO, a Wall Street investment banker, a labor leader, an environmental advocate, an investor, a consumer, a citizen. I'd create dramatic situations based on real events, and we'd take off. Almost every time, the students were enthralled. Almost every time, I learned something new.

Teaching is about getting students to reexamine the assumptions they entered the classroom with, getting them to see all the moving parts of our political-economic system and understand it in a dynamic way—viewing it as a system that's changing and adapting through time, having them question why they believe something is true about the system, pushing them to think critically, and to understand how and why the system has evolved as it has. During the pandemic, I had to teach remotely via my computer and the Internet. What a bore! I tried as hard as I could to make the virtual classrooms alive, but remote teaching drained the lifeblood out of the classrooms because the interactions were so limited.

Teaching is not about conveying facts or thoughts or even theories. It's about conveying energy and excitement. If my students wanted to know what I think about something, they could read my books. What I could give them in the classroom was my enthusiasm, curiosity, and enjoyment about the subject we were learning about. Rather than use our classroom time together to lecture, I wanted to grab their interest, stir their own excitement. I had to figuratively grab them by the shoulders and shake them, laugh with them, run up and down the aisles of the classroom, asking them questions, keeping them surprised and engaged.

If I couldn't touch their emotions, I couldn't get them to think hard. Touching their emotions meant connecting with them. Telling stories that illustrated the points I wanted them to understand. Having them tell their own stories. Using humor—not telling jokes but punctuating our lessons with self-deprecating stories drawn from my life (some of which I've shared with you in these pages) and with gentle digs at conventional wisdom. When they laughed, they opened themselves up to being receptive to the more serious things we talked about. Laughter made even the largest classes intimate. We were all sharing in the joy of being together. Every class was different. Each had its own personality. Every semester was like meeting a new person, gradually getting to know them, coming to understand what made them tick, how they thought, what they considered interesting or alarming or amazing or funny.

My biggest class at Berkeley contained about eight hundred students every spring semester. I called it "Wealth and Poverty." It was comprised mostly of juniors and seniors, many of whom, as I've said, had begun as transfer students from community colleges. Many were the first in their families to attend a university. When we talked about poverty, many offered personal stories. Some of their stories were harrowing.

How was it possible to teach eight hundred students and talk about their personal stories? By walking up and down the aisle, asking them questions, and then repeating their answers to the entire classroom. And using those answers to launch into a discussion of whatever it was they experienced, knowing that their stories would be shared by others and knowing that some of the more privileged in the class would learn something new and powerful and possibly painful.

I also used silence. Silence punctuated our role-playing. Silence encased my questions and their answers after I repeated them. It followed my stories and their stories. Silence allowed the class to think about what they saw and heard. Silence focused their attention. Many young people today have very little silence in their lives. Maybe that's why they have difficulty focusing. The silences I brought to teaching were a critical part of connecting with my students.

Often these days, when I'm in an airport or on the main street of a large city, someone comes up to me. Some are middle aged. "Professor Reich!" they say. I usually have to explain that I've had so many students over the years that I can't remember them. They're forgiving. "Where did I teach you and when?" I ask. They tell me they were in the class of 2004 at Berkeley or the class of 1997 at Brandeis or the class of 1984 at Harvard, or wherever and whenever. And they are kind enough to tell me that they still remember our class together, how much it meant to them, still means to them even today. I don't know whether they're just being polite, but I'm pleased they remember. I ask them what they're doing now. A large number are working in nonprofits or in the public sector or are helping community groups—in housing, public health, education, labor organizing. Some are serving in government. I like to think I've played a small part in motivating them to do what they're doing.

The psychologist Erik Erickson wrote about the stages of a person's life. The last stage he called the "generative" stage, when people focus on contributing to the next generation, on leaving a positive legacy. I never thought much about this until I came to the last semester of teaching. I hated the thought of not teaching. Teaching was the most generative thing I've done in my life, apart from being a father. But I told myself that I should leave when I could still do it well, when I could still be generative. I owed it to my students.

My last class was especially bittersweet. I tried not to reveal how much I was hurting inside. Because so many of them were seniors, I always used my last class to talk about them and their futures. And then I made myself available after class to shake their hands, sign their books, pose for selfies with them. This last time, I felt a particular connection with them. They were graduating. So was I.

I won't lie. Retiring from teaching—from the calling I love—has been painful. Most people who "retire" stop what they call "working" and begin what they call "playing." But what if your work is also your play? What if it's your calling? What if it's deeply meaningful to you? For the most part, people don't especially enjoy what they do on the job. My father spent most of his working life anxious about earning enough for his family to live on. The moment he turned sixty-five he stopped working and began collecting Social Security, and he spent the next thirty years playing golf.

I had my yearly doctor's appointment recently. My doctor is a young woman, not much older than many of my graduate students. Everything checked out fine. When she asked me what was new in my life, I told her I had retired from teaching. She congratulated me. I burst into tears. I'd been hiding from myself just how much I miss it.

Retirement is often confused with aging, but I think the relationship is the reverse. Meaningful work—work that's more play than work—can lead to a longer life. As Oliver Wendell Holmes, Sr.—poet, writer, educator, and physician—once said, people "do not quit playing because they grow old; they grow old because they quit playing."

I am no longer teaching courses, but I haven't quit playing. My long game isn't nearly over.

But I can't deny it: I am growing old.

Growing Old

Joe Biden and Donald Trump were the oldest Democratic and Republican candidates for president, respectively, in history. I don't think concerns about Biden's age reflected an "ageist" prejudice so much as an understanding that people in their eighties do wither—and he looked and acted withered. I speak with a certain authority. As I write this, I'm seventy-eight years old. I feel fit, I swing dance and salsa, and can do twenty pushups in a row. Yet I confess to a certain loss of, shall we say, *fizz.*

It's now thought a bit disappointing if a person dies before eighty-five. (My mother passed at eighty-six; my father, two weeks before his one hundred and second birthday, so I'm hoping for the best, genetically speaking.) Three score and ten is the number of years of life set out in the Bible. Modern technology and Big Pharma should add at least a decade and a half. Beyond this is an extra helping. "After eighty, it's gravy," my father used to say. His helping of gravy lasted almost twenty-two years.

People treat you differently when you get old. When I was younger, I recall telling an elderly friend, *You look great.* He responded glumly that there were four ages to life: youth, middle age, old age, and You look great.

As the Grateful Dead said, "No one gets out of this alive." This reality occurs to me with increasing frequency. I find myself reading the obituary pages with ever greater curiosity about how long people lasted and what brought them down. I remember a *New Yorker* cartoon in which an older reader of the obituaries sees headlines that read only "Older Than Me" or "Younger Than Me."

"Bodily decrepitude," said Yeats, "is wisdom." I have accumulated somewhat more of the former than the latter. I still have my teeth—unlike my grandfather, whom I vividly recall storing his choppers in a glass next to his bed—and have so far steered clear of a heart attack or stroke (I pray I'm not tempting fate by stating this fact). But I've had both hips replaced. Even with hearing aids, I have a hard time understanding someone talking to me in a noisy restaurant. (You'd think that the sheer market power of 60 million boomers losing their hearing would be enough to generate at least one set of quiet restaurants. But no—restaurants seem to be getting louder, in fact.)

When I get together with old friends, our first ritual is an "organ recital"—how's your back? knee? heart? hip? shoulder? eyesight? hearing? prostate? hemorrhoids? digestion? The recital can run (and ruin) an entire lunch. The question my friends and I jokingly (and brutishly) asked one other in college—"Getting much?"—now refers not to sex but to sleep. I don't know anyone over seventy-five who sleeps through the night. When he was president, Bill Clinton prided himself on getting only about four hours. But he was in his forties then. (I also recall cabinet meetings where he dozed off.)

My memory for names is horrible and getting worse. (I once asked Ted Kennedy how he recalled names, and he advised that if a man is over fifty, just ask "How's the back?" and he'll think you know him.) I often can't remember where I put my wallet and keys or why I've entered a room. Certain proper nouns have disappeared altogether; even when rediscovered, they have a diabolical way of disappearing again.

I have lost much of my enthusiasm for travel and feel, as did Philip Larkin, that I would like to visit China, but only on the condition that I could return home that night.

I'm told that after the age of sixty, one loses half an inch of height every five years. This presents a challenge for me considering that at my zenith I didn't quite make it to five feet. If I live as long as my father did, I may vanish.

I'm also noticing I have less patience, perhaps because of an unconscious "use by" timer that's now clicking away. Increasingly I wonder why I'm wasting time with this or that buffoon. I'm less tolerant of long waiting lines, automated phone menus, and Republicans.

Cicero thought "older people who are reasonable, good-tempered, and gracious bear aging well. Those who are mean-spirited and irritable will be unhappy at every stage of their lives." Easy for Cicero to say. He was forced into exile and murdered at the age of sixty-three, his decapitated head and right hand hung up in the Forum by order of the mean-spirited and irritable Marcus Antonius.

The style sections of the papers tell us that the seventies are the new fifties. Septuagenarians are supposed to be fit and alert, exercise like mad, have rip-roaring sex, and party until dawn. Not so. Inevitably, things begin falling apart. My aunt, who lived far into her nineties, often quoted the old adage "Getting old isn't for sissies." Toward the end she repeated it every five minutes.

I'm feeling more and more out of it. I'm doing videos on TikTok and Snapchat, yet when my students talk about Ariana Grande or Selena Gomez or Jared Leto I don't have a clue who they're talking about (and frankly don't care).

Philosopher George Santayana claimed to prefer old age to all others. "Old age is, or may be as in my case, far happier than youth," he wrote. "I was never more entertained or less troubled than I am now." True for me too, in a way. Despite Trump, the Republican Party, climate change, near-record inequality, potential nuclear war, and another strain of COVID making the rounds, I remain upbeat—largely because I still spend most days with people in their twenties who buoy my spirits.

Santayana also said that the reason old people have foreboding about the future is they cannot imagine a world that's good without themselves in it. I don't share that view. To the contrary, I think I and my generation—including Bill Clinton, Hillary Clinton, George W. Bush, Donald Trump, Al Gore, Newt Gingrich, and Clarence Thomas—did not make a better world. We failed to stop the bullies. Some of us contributed to the brutality. Others I've known and worked with and have mentioned in these pages have played the long game admirably, but compared to what needed to be done, compared to what could and should have been done, they have also failed.

It is far too easy to attribute failure to a generation, way too simplistic to blame those with the power to change society for the better who did not exercise such power. Most of the people I have worked with did the best they could under circumstances over which they felt little control. But the stark reality—as I have traced it in these pages and lived it over the past seventy-eight years—is that the richest and most powerful nation in modern history, the America that emerged victorious from World War II and whose democracy was a beacon for much of the rest of the world, is now coming up short. Trump and Trumpism are consequences, not causes. As I hope I've made clear, the causes have been growing for more than forty years. We could have addressed them. We did not.

The responsibility to remedy this—to restore genuine opportunity, strengthen democracy, and contain the bullies—now falls to those who come after us. They include my wonderful, brilliant students.

Acknowledgments

This book benefited from the insights of Jaz Brisack, John Isaacson, Michael Lahanas-Calderón, Heather Lofthouse, Vishal Narayanaswamy, Adam Reich, and Sam Reich. I am also grateful to many people I've had the privilege to know and work with over the years, among them Olena Berg, Bill Clinton, Maria Echeveste, Sophia Efthimiatou, Tom Glynn, Kitty Higgins, Anita Hill, Arlie Russell Hochschild, Annie Leonard, Jacob Kornbluth, Barack Obama, Bernie Sanders, Gail Shearer, Tom Sugrue, Strobe Talbott, Martha Tierney, Laura Tyson, Elizabeth Warren, Fred Wertheimer, and Tracy Weston.

I also want to express thanks to several people whose lives were enormously influential on mine but are no longer with us. They include Robert Bork, Frank M. Coffin, Joe Deer, Bob Edgar, Christopher Edley, Jacques Feuillon, Karen Hobart Flynn, John Kenneth Galbraith, Ted Kennedy, Richard Neustadt, Michael Pertschuk, Alan Simpson, Paul Wellstone, and Tom Williamson. I am grateful to my colleagues at the University of California at Berkeley, for fostering the intellectual community that continues to be my home, and to more than four decades of hardworking and eager students at Berkeley, Brandeis, and Harvard, who taught me more than I ever taught them. Thanks are especially due to Michael Nacht, Henry Brady, and Dean David C. Wilson of the Goldman School of Public Policy at Berkeley; to my able assistant there, Aarin Walker; and to Steve Silberstein and Doug Goldman for valued support.

My talented colleagues over the past few years at Inequality Media have been a source of ideas and insights, for which I continue to be enormously grateful. They include Zoe Beck, Alessandra Bosco, Naomi Bradford, Emily Denny, Daniel Davis, Anna Ely, Court Fuller, Michael Lahanas-Calderón, Heather Lofthouse, Katie Milne, Vishal Narayanaswamy, Kyle Parker, and Andrew Santana. This book would not have been written but for the help and prodding of my literary agent and friend, Rafe Sagalyn, and my gifted editor and friend, Jonathan Segal, both of whom have been at my side from the start of my book-writing days, as well as the thoughtful editing of Emily Cunningham, assisted by Isabel Ribeiro and Ellen Feldman. Finally, and in countless ways, I am indebted to my partner and wife, Perian Flaherty, whose love and myriad insights continue to inspire and sustain me.

Notes

Part I: The Bullies

Starters

11 Fred Trump, Donald's father: Biographical details on Donald Trump from Benjamin C. Waterhouse, *Donald J. Trump: Life Before the White House,* Miller Center of Public Affairs, University of Virginia, 2023; on George W. Bush, from the George W. Bush White House Archives, 2020; on Bill Clinton, from the William J. Clinton Presidential Library and Museum, 2016.

11 3.4 million of us: U.S. Census Bureau, American Community Survey, various tables.

12 The war and the Depression decade: See Thomas Piketty, *Capital in the Twenty-First Century* (Cambridge, MA: Harvard University Press, 2014).

It's a Wonderful Life

13 If you don't already know it: Details about the movie *It's a Wonderful Life* from Jeanine Basinger, *The It's a Wonderful Life Book* (New York: Alfred A. Knopf, 1986).

15 When *It's a Wonderful Life* was released: Travis Andrews, "It's a Wonderful Life Is a Holiday Classic. The FBI Thought It Was Communist Propaganda," *Washington Post,* December 21, 2017.

My Father and the SOBs

16 On Labor Day, just after we moved in: The dialogue between the old men of the town and my parents was related to me by my parents several years later. Like most of the dialogue in this book, I have reproduced it based on my memory, as best I can.

16 "Legally, you have a right": In 1946, New York State passed a law prohibiting racial or religious discrimination through restrictive covenants in real property deeds. In *Shelley v. Kraemer* (1948) the Supreme Court held that restrictive covenants in real property deeds that prohibited the sale of property to persons "not of the Caucasian race" unconstitutionally violate the equal protection provision of the Fourteenth Amendment.

17 McCarthy ridiculed the "pitiful squealing": See John Nichols, *The Fight for the Soul of the Democratic Party* (New York: Verso, 2020).

18   Representative John Elliott Rankin: See Richard Seymour, *Cold-War Anticommunism and the Defense of White Supremacy in the Southern United States,* PhD thesis, London School of Economics, 2006.

18   In December 1946: See John Nichols, *The Fight for the Soul of the Democratic Party* (New York: Verso, 2020).

20   Cohn proved himself useful: On the relationship between Roy Cohn and Donald Trump, see Marie Brenner, *Ruthless: How Roy Cohn's and Donald Trump's Dark Symbiosis Changed America* (New York: Simon & Schuster, 2018).

21   During Ronald Reagan's 1980 presidential campaign: On Roy Cohn, Donald Trump, and Roger Stone, see George Packer, "The Mafia Style in American Politics," *The Atlantic,* October 23, 2019.

My Expulsion

24   On average, according to a 2024 survey: See "This Is How Much Childcare Cost in 2024," *Care,* January 17, 2024.

Sitting on the Vice President's Lap

25   "the most damaging indictment": Alex Ross, "Uncommon Man," *The New Yorker,* October 7, 2013.

25   "The dangerous American fascist": "The Danger of American Fascism," *New York Times Sunday Magazine,* April 9, 1944.

26   "Those who fan the fires": Cited in John Nichols, *The Fight for the Soul of the Democratic Party* (New York: Verso, 2020). For an excellent biography of Wallace, see John Culver, *American Dreamer: A Life of Henry A. Wallace* (New York: W. W. Norton, 2000).

27   "We must remember": Cited in Nichols, *Fight for the Soul.*

The Dangers Lurking in Lewisboro School

30   Soon afterward, the U.S. Supreme Court: In *Ingel v. Vitale* (1962), the court ruled that state officials cannot create an official school prayer or encourage its recitation in public schools because it violates the First Amendment.

30   But seventy years later: In *Bremerton v. Kennedy* (2023), the court ruled that the school district violated football coach Joe Kennedy's First Amendment rights by restricting his private prayers, which the court said amounted to speech, even though his prayers occurred on the football field in front of his players and arguably induced his players to join him in prayer.

31   As I write this, the MAGA governor: Rick Rojas, "Louisiana Requires All Public Classrooms to Display Ten Commandments," *New York Times,* June 19, 2024.

How Alice Camp Saved Me

32   Why should investment bankers: Although pay is hardly the main reason people teach, it's also true that paying teachers more might produce better teachers. Eric A. Hanushek of Stanford University has found that an excellent teacher (who's

just one standard deviation better than average, or better than 84 percent of teachers) raises each student's lifetime earnings by $20,000. So, if twenty students are in the class, an extra $400,000 is generated compared with a teacher who is merely average. See Eric A. Hanushek, "The Economic Value of Higher Teacher Quality," NBER Working Paper Series, Working Paper 16606, National Bureau of Economic Research, Cambridge, MA, 2010.

My Father's Recitations

34 In the summer of 1954: Hurricane Carol remains one of the worst hurricanes to hit Connecticut and Rhode Island, causing almost a half-billion dollars of damage. See Hugh Cobb, "The Siege of New England," *Weatherwise* 42, no. 5 (1989): 5.

What Happened to My Protector, Mickey

40 "Freedom Summer" of 1964: See Bruce Watson, *Freedom Summer: The Savage Season of 1964 That Made Mississippi Burn and Made America a Democracy* (New York: Penguin Books, 2011). See also Seth Cagin and Philip Dray, *We Are Not Afraid: The Story of Goodman, Schwerner, and Chaney and the Civil Rights Campaign for Mississippi* (Macmillan, 1988).

41 Johnson was proud: See Johnson's Address on the Civil Rights Bill, July 3, 1964, Library of Congress.

41 Goldwater told Republican delegates: Senator Barry Goldwater, Address Accepting the Nomination at the Republican National Convention in San Francisco, July 16, 1964, Library of Congress.

43 That fall, some University of California, Berkeley, students: See Samuel Farber, "The Berkeley Free Speech Movement, 56 Years Later," *Jacobin*, September 3, 2020. See also Reginald Zelnik and Robert Cohen, eds., *The Free Speech Movement: Reflections on Berkeley in the 1960s* (Berkeley: University of California Press, 2002).

43 "There is a time": See Mario Savio's speech before the FSM sit-in, December 3, 1964, Free Speech Movement Archives.

44 As Savio later told *The Washington Post*: Karlyn Barker, "Rebel with Cause," *The Washington Post*, November 8, 1996. See also Robert Cohen, *Freedom's Orator: Mario Savio and the Radical Legacy of the 1960s* (New York: Oxford University Press, 2009).

44 FBI director J. Edgar Hoover: See Seth Rosenfeld, "How the Man Who Challenged 'the Machine' Got Caught Up in the Wheels and Gears of J. Edgar Hoover's Bureau," *San Francisco Chronicle*, October 10, 2004.

45 In the twenty years following: See Kareem Crayton, "The Voting Rights Act Explained," Brennan Center for Justice, July 17, 2023.

46 The decision opened the floodgates: Kevin Morris and Coryn Grange, "Growing Racial Disparities in Voter Turnout, 2008–2022," Brennan Center for Justice, March 2, 2024.

Stopping Bullies

46   "nasty, brutish, and short": See Thomas Hobbes, *Leviathan: Or the Matter, Form, and Power of a Commonwealth, Ecclesiastical and Civil* (Cambridge University Press, 1904).

Why I'm So Short

49   I had inherited a mutation: According to Johns Hopkins Medicine, multiple epiphyseal dysplasia is a condition that affects the ends of the long bones, otherwise known as epiphyses (singular: epiphysis). The condition results from a problem in the cartilage oligomeric matrix protein, which accumulates in the cartilage and causes premature destruction, and can lead to early arthritis.

50   "twenty years ago": See Jane Brody, "Weighing the Use of Growth Hormones for Children," *New York Times*, March 29, 2021.

51   David Sandberg: See "Height and Social Adjustment: Are Extremes a Cause for Concern and Action?" *University of Michigan Research, Pediatrics*, September 2004, pp. 744–50.

51   Yet when psychologists: See Leslie Martel and Henry Biller, *Stature and Stigma: The Biopsychosocial Development of Short Males* (Lexington, MA: Lexington Books, 2019).

51   In another study: See Burkhard Bilger, "The Height Gap," *The New Yorker*, April 5, 2005, p. 34.

51   A paper published in 2013: See Gert Stulp, Abraham Buunk, Simon Verhulst, and Thomas Pollet, "Tall Claims? Sense and Nonsense About the Importance of Height of U.S. Presidents," *Leadership Quarterly* 24, no. 1 (February 2013): 159–71.

52   A survey of the heights: See Vivek Kaul, "The Necktie Syndrome: Why CEOs Tend to Be Significantly Taller than the Average Male," *Economic Times*, September 30, 2011.

Part II: Coming Up

The Old Left, the New Left, and the Left Out

55   My introduction to the New Left: See *The Port Huron Statement*, Students for a Democratic Society, 1962. See also Richard Flacks and Nelson Lichtenstein, eds., *The Port Huron Statement: Sources and Legacies of the New Left's Founding Manifesto* (Philadelphia: University of Pennsylvania Press, 2015); Todd Gitlin, *The Sixties: Years of Hope, Days of Rage* (New York: Bantam Books, 1987). See also Louis Menand, "The Making of the New Left," *The New Yorker*, March 22, 2021.

58   The trail-blazing progressive authors: See John Kenneth Galbraith, *The Affluent Society* (Boston: Houghton-Mifflin, 1958); Rachel Carson, *Silent Spring* (Boston: Houghton-Mifflin, 1962); Michael Harrington, *The Other America* (New York: Simon & Schuster, 1962); Betty Friedan, *The Feminine Mystique* (New York: W. W. Norton, 1963); Ralph Nader, *Unsafe at Any Speed* (New York: Grossman Publishers, 1965).

The Absurdity of Ayn Rand

60 Rand's philosophy: There is a large literature on Rand and her intellectual legacy. Among the books I have found most valuable are Anne C. Heller, *Ayn Rand and the World She Made* (New York: Doubleday, 2009); Chris Matthew Sciabarra, *Ayn Rand: The Russian Radical* (University Park: Penn State University Press, 2013); Jennifer Burns, *Goddess of the Market: Ayn Rand and the American Right* (New York: Oxford University Press, 2009).

61 Years later, Donald Trump: On the relationship between Rand and Donald Trump, see Jonathan Freedland, "The New Age of Ayn Rand: How She Won Over Donald Trump and Silicon Valley," *The Guardian*, April 11, 2017.

My Unforgivable Hypocrisy

67 The College Handbook: Before the mid-1960s, American undergraduates were subject to several restrictions on their sexual lives that would be considered absurd today. Women had curfews, typically 10 or 11 p.m. (I vividly recall a sign in one Wellesley College dormitory, "Gentlemen Will Withdraw by 10 p.m."). Another typical rule required that if a young man and woman were together in a dormitory room, at least three of their four legs had to be touching the floor, leading to some complex acrobatics and oddly timed interventions from "dorm mothers" or "dorm fathers."

My Date with Hillary

70 Fifty years later: See Kate Phillips and Elizabeth Bumiller, "Taking the Mystery Out of a Date," *New York Times*, August 6, 2007. Here's the *Times* report in its entirety: "So who was the mystery 'boy from Dartmouth' with whom Hillary Rodham spent a Saturday night when she was an undergraduate at Wellesley? Ms. Rodham—that would be Senator Hillary Rodham Clinton, Democrat of New York and presidential candidate—wrote about the date in one series of letters to a childhood friend. Based on the evidence, however, this probably was not an affair of the heart. The boy appears to have been Robert B. Reich, a politically active student at Dartmouth College who went on to become friends with Bill Clinton when they were Rhodes scholars at Oxford, and then served as President Clinton's first secretary of labor. In a video blog posting and in an interview, Mr. Reich recalled that because both he and Ms. Rodham were student class presidents, he proposed a 'presidential summit' date. They went to see Michelangelo Antonioni's film 'Blowup.' 'She wanted a lot of butter on her popcorn,' Mr. Reich said. . . . A lot of butter. Significant? You be the judge."

Getting Chewed Out by Bobby Kennedy

73 "Look," he said: Johnson was clearly worried that Kennedy might challenge him for the Democratic presidential nomination in 1968, mainly due to Johnson's pursuit of the Vietnam War. But Kennedy resisted entreaties from the anti–Vietnam War left of the Democratic Party to take Johnson on—at least until Minnesota

senator Eugene McCarthy demonstrated Johnson's vulnerability and Johnson withdrew from the race.

For followers of Robert F. Kennedy, Johnson was a boorish bully with no class or breeding—a "politician" in the worst sense of the word. For loyalists to Johnson, Kennedy and his clan comprised effete bluenoses and cool, dispassionate Harvard intellectuals who sneered at their man because of his Texas Hill Country beginnings. The Kennedy camp's disdain for Johnson had nothing to do with his mostly liberal policies (excluding Vietnam), but seemed to have been based on his aggressive, homespun manner. See Jeff Shesol, *Mutual Contempt: Lyndon Johnson, Robert Kennedy, and the Feud That Defined a Decade* (New York: W. W. Norton, 1997).

Getting Clean for Gene

74 He claimed that America: See Tim Pugmire, "McCarthy Takes a Risk," *MPR News,* St. Paul, Minnesota, November 20, 2006.

74 McCarthy had encouraged Bobby Kennedy: See Dominick Sandbrook, *Eugene McCarthy: The Rise and Fall of Postwar American Liberalism* (New York: Knopf, 2004). See also "Remembering Gene McCarthy," *Online NewsHour,* New York, *PBS,* December 12, 2005.

76 Sarah and I reached New Hampshire: See "Crusade of the Ballot Children," *Time* magazine, March 22, 1968, pp. 28–29.

76 JOHNSON SAYS HE WON'T RUN: *New York Times,* April 1, 1968.

76 It is hard to convey: See George Christian, "The Night Lyndon Quit," *Texas Monthly,* April 1988, pp. 21–29.

77 Almost immediately, Kennedy soared: Among the best books on Robert F. Kennedy's 1968 campaign are Thurston Clarke, *The Last Campaign: Robert F. Kennedy and 82 Days That Inspired America* (New York: Henry Holt, 2008); and David Halberstam, *The Unfinished Odyssey of Robert Kennedy* (New York: Random House, 1969).

78 On Thursday, April 4: Murray Schumach, "Martin Luther King Jr.: Leader of Millions in Nonviolent Drive for Racial Justice," *New York Times,* April 5, 1968.

78 Without skipping a beat: See Rick Perlstein, *Nixonland: The Rise of a President and the Fracturing of America* (New York: Charles Scribner, 2009), p. 257.

80 Humphrey's loss to Nixon: See Benjamin Brown, "1968: The Year That Broke the Democratic Party," *Texas Orator,* July 11, 2024. See also Perlstein, *Nixonland.*

When Bill Clinton and I Didn't Inhale Together

81 Women were not allowed: It wasn't until 1976 that women became eligible to apply for Rhodes Scholarships. The first women were admitted in 1977. The Rhodes Trust applied for the change after Parliament passed a law in 1975 prohibiting sexual discrimination. In 1976, Britain's minister of education, Shirley Williams, removed the word "manly" from the will of Cecil Rhodes, the last barrier preventing women from participating in the scholarship.

82 My other recollection: By the late 1950s, Lyndon Johnson, then the Senate majority leader, and Bobby Baker, the secretary of the Senate, had formed such a close and symbiotic relationship that Baker was dubbed "Little Lyndon." Baker referred to himself as the "101st senator." In 1967, Baker was convicted of tax evasion, conspir-

acy to defraud the government, and theft. After appeals, he went to prison in 1971 and served fifteen months. "Russia wouldn't have treated me the way this country has," Baker said at the start of his sentence. "But I have no great resentment. No, this is a great country. It's done a lot for me. I like to think I have done a lot for it." See Neil Genzlinger, "Bobby Baker, String-Puller Ensnared in Senate Scandal, Dies," *New York Times,* November 17, 2017.

The Biggest Moral Quandary of Our Young Lives

83   It was a time: An abundance of research and commentary has focused on how many young men in the wealthiest or most educated cohort served in Vietnam. The consensus is that they served in significantly lower percentages than young men who were poorer or less well-educated. See Thomas Wilson et al., "Vietnam Military Service: A Test of the Class Bias Thesis," *Armed Forces and Society* 21, no. 3 (Spring 1995); Arnold Barnett, Timothy Stanley, and Michael Short, "America's Vietnam Casualties: Victims of a Class War?" *Operations Research* 40 (1966): 856–66. For other views, see James Fallows, "What Did You Do in the Class War, Daddy?" *Washington Monthly,* October 1, 1975, pp. 5–20; James Fallows, "Vietnam: Low-Class Conclusions," *The Atlantic,* April 1993, pp. 38–44; Roger Rosenblatt, "Those Who Go and Those Who Stay," *Life* magazine, October 1990, p. 21; Christian D. Appy, *Working-Class War* (Chapel Hill: University of North Carolina Press, 1993).

83   Our small band: For more on this tumult and what happened to the band, see Alessandra Stanley, "Most Likely to Succeed," *New York Times,* November 22, 1992.

84   Bill got his extended deferment: Just before the 1992 presidential election, Colonel Holmes, to whom Bill Clinton wrote his letter, issued a scathing statement, asserting that Clinton had deceived him. See William C. Rempel, "Ex-ROTC Leader Says Clinton Deceived Him, Cheated Military," *Los Angeles Times,* September 17, 1992.

My T-Group in Big Sur

88   T-groups were big: See Leland P. Bradford, Jack Gibb, and Kenneth Benne, eds., *T-Group Theory and Laboratory Methods* (Hoboken, NJ: John Wiley & Sons, 1964). In 1946, the civic leaders of Bridgeport, Connecticut, asked psychologist Kurt Lewin to convene a series of conversations with community members to help ease racial tension in the city. Lewin assembled a team of psychologists and educators to run the conversations, in which members and facilitators interacted directly and learned from each other in real time. This was essentially the first T-group. In 1947, Lewin created the National Training Laboratories Institute for Applied Behavioral Science to advance the methodology. By the mid-1960s, T-groups were embraced by corporate America, major universities, and the U.S. military. Various forms of "encounter groups" and "consciousness seminars" emerged, often under the umbrella label of the "human potential movement."

The Riot That Started the Culture Wars

93   It was also the day: On the hardhat riot, see David Paul Kuhn, *The Hardhat Riot: Nixon, New York City, and the Dawn of the White Working Class Revolution* (New York: Oxford University Press, 2020).

94   Nixon then exploited: The paraphrase of Colson and quotes from Haldeman, Buchanan, and Brennan are from Kuhn, *The Hardhat Riot.*

95   As the journalist Pete Hamill: Pete Hamill, "The Revolt of the White Lower Middle Class," *New York* magazine, April 14, 1969, p. 21.

95   Pat Buchanan, writing in 1988: See Nicole Hemmer, "The Man Who Won the Republican Party Before Trump Did," *New York Times,* September 8, 2022. See also Nicole Hemmer, *Partisans: The Conservative Revolutionaries Who Remade American Politics in the 1990s* (New York: Basic Books, 2022).

95   Three years later: Hemmer, "The Man Who Won."

At Yale Law with Bill, Hillary, and Clarence

97   My introduction obviously didn't take: See Hillary Clinton, *Living History* (New York: Simon & Schuster, 2003); Bill Clinton, *My Life* (New York: Alfred A. Knopf, 2004).

97   All of us were there: For a useful assessment of *Roe v. Wade,* see Mary Ziegler, *Roe: The History of a National Obsession* (New Haven, CT: Yale University Press, 2023).

98   Neither he nor they: See *Dobbs, State Health Officer of the Mississippi Department of Health et al. v. Jackson Women's Health Organization et al.,* decided June 24, 2022. Justice Samuel Alito wrote the opinion for the Court, in which the court reversed *Roe v. Wade.* Justice Clarence Thomas wrote a concurring opinion. On the failure of Alito or Thomas to give a coherent argument, see Laurence Tribe, "Deconstructing Dobbs," *New York Review of Books,* September 22, 2022, pp. 3–8.

98   In October 1991: See Anita Hill, *Speaking Truth to Power* (New York: Random House, 1997). See also Katelyn Fossett, "30 Years After Her Hearing, Anita Hill Still Wants Something from Joe Biden," *Politico,* October 1, 2021, pp. 15–23.

To Be Borked

101   A few years after: See Robert Bork, *The Antitrust Paradox: A Policy at War with Itself* (New York: Free Press, 1978).

101   I enjoyed sparring: After his nomination was rejected by the Senate, Bork's writings became darker and angrier. See *The Tempting of America: The Political Seduction of the Law* (New York: Free Press, 1990); *Slouching Toward Gomorrah: Modern Liberalism and American Decline* (New York: Regan Books, 1996); *A Country I Do Not Recognize: The Legal Assault on American Values* (Palo Alto, CA: Hoover Institution, 2005).

101   Bork was known as a conservative: See Jeffrey Segal, "Amicus Curiae Briefs by the Solicitor General During the Warren and Burger Courts: A Research Note," *Western Political Quarterly* 41, no. 1 (1988).

101   In 1970, Nixon authorized: For histories of Richard Nixon and the Watergate scandal, see Bob Woodward and Carl Bernstein, *All the President's Men* (New York:

Simon & Schuster, 1974); Leon Friedman and William F. Levantrosser, eds., *Watergate and Afterward: The Legacy of Richard M. Nixon* (Palo Alto, CA: Stanford University Press, 1992).

107 In 2005, I testified: See *Hearings Before the Committee on the Judiciary, United States Senate, on the Nomination of John G. Roberts to Be Chief Justice of the Supreme Court of the United States—Panel VI* (Washington, DC: U.S. Government Printing Office, 2005).

109 Bork's nomination was controversial: See *Hearings Before the Committee on the Judiciary, United States Senate, One Hundredth Congress First Session, on the Nomination of Robert H. Bork to Be Associate Justice of the Supreme Court of the United States—Part 1 of 5* (Washington, DC: U.S. Government Printing Office, 1989). See also Stephen L. Carter, *The Confirmation Mess* (New York: Basic Books, 1994).

Part III: The Giant U-Turn

The Worst Memo in American History

115 In 1971, unbeknownst to me at the time: For background on the Powell memo, see Jacob Hacker and Paul Pierson, *Winner-Take-All Politics: How Washington Made the Rich Richer and Turned Its Back on the Middle Class* (New York: Simon & Schuster, 2011). See also Richard Roberts, "How the Powell Memorandum Changed Capitalism—and What We Can Learn from It Today," *Medium*, August 23, 2021.

115 Powell's memo, distributed widely: The full text of the Powell memorandum can be found at Lewis F. Powell, Jr., "The Memorandum: Attack on the American Free Enterprise System," August 23, 1971, available at the Powell Papers, Lexington, VA, Washington and Lee University School of Law.

119 Ironically, Powell wrote his memo: See John Rawls, *A Theory of Justice* (Cambridge, MA: Harvard University Press, 1971).

The Truth About Jimmy Carter

121 My boss at the FTC: Michael Pertschuk spent his career, first as a staff member in the Senate, then as chairman of the Federal Trade Commission, as a staunch consumer advocate. See Michael Pertschuk, *When the Senate Worked for Us: The Invisible Role of Staffers in Countering Corporate Lobbies* (Nashville, TN: Vanderbilt University Press, 2017). For a short biography of Pertschuk, see Sam Roberts, "Michael Pertschuk, Antismoking and Auto Safety Crusader, Dies at 89," *New York Times*, November 29, 2022.

122 "Thirty to forty years from now": Quoted in Haynes Johnson, "A Carter Issue Turns on Him," *Washington Post*, February 11, 1978.

My Six-Foot, Eight-Inch Mentor and Friend

123 Ken had run: The best biography of Ken Galbraith is Richard Parker, *John Kenneth Galbraith: His Life, His Politics, His Economics* (Chicago: University of Chicago Press, 2006).

124 Ken didn't regard economics: See Parker, *John Kenneth Galbraith*.

126 When he wrote *The Affluent Society:* For a discussion of Galbraith and his views about inequality, see my "Trouble We're In," *American Prospect,* November 20, 1998.

When I Became a Feminist

132 Surely, such bullying: See Jennifer Kingsten, "Harvard Tenure Battle Puts 'Critical Legal Studies' on Trial," *New York Times,* August 30, 1987. See also Carol Kleiman, "Evidence Tenuous for Denied Tenure," *Chicago Tribune,* October 14, 1993.

133 But sexism: See Erin Fuchs, "Harvard Law Is Finally Dealing with Its Huge Sexism Problem," *Business Insider,* December 10, 2013.

The Raiders of the Lost Economy

135 Before then it was assumed: For a good review of the history of corporate social responsibility, see M. Agudelo, L. Johannsdottir, and B. Davidsdottir, "A Literature Review of the History and Evolution of Corporate Social Responsibility," *International Journal of Corporate Social Responsibility* 4, no. 1 (2009).

136 In 1985, after winning: See Glenn Collins, "Icahn Ends RJR Nabisco Proxy Fight," *New York Times,* February 28, 1997.

137 Not surprisingly, Icahn was: See Patrick Radden Keefe, "Carl Icahn's Failed Raid on Washington," *The New Yorker,* August 21, 2017.

139 Within Dunlap's first two years: On Al Dunlap, see John A. Bryne, *Chainsaw: The Notorious Career of Al Dunlap in the Era of Profit-at-Any-Price* (New York: Harper Business, 1999).

139 I duked it out: Quotes from Dunlap and me can be found in the transcript "Corporate Layoffs and the Fate of American Workers," *ABC Nightline,* February 14, 1996, https://drive.google.com/file/d/1V7CMh2zsJNirg6nW3mUzzPY6vr5AZOkb /view.

142 Dunlap's undoing: See *Securities and Exchange Commission v. Albert Dunlap et al.,* May 15, 2001, https://www.sec.gov/enforcement-litigation/litigation-releases /lr-17710.

142 the sixth-worst CEO: Cited in Paul Tuscano, "Portfolio's Worst American CEOs of All Time," CNBC, April 30, 2009.

143 The free-market theorist: See Milton Friedman, "A Friedman Doctrine—The Social Responsibility of Business Is to Increase Its Profits," *New York Times Sunday Magazine,* September 13, 1970.

144 Jared Kushner's real estate company: See Morgan G. Stater, "Maryland State Lawmaker Files 'Jared Kushner Act' to Prevent Tenant Arrests," *The Hill,* January 1, 2018, p. 12.

145 To remedy this: Closing the loophole has allegedly been a top priority of Democrats, including Democratic presidents Clinton, Obama, and Biden. But it never gets closed. To get the Inflation Reduction Act passed in the Senate, Democrats dropped their most recent attempt to close the carried interest loophole. See Eric Reed, "The Carried Interest Loophole and the Inflation Reduction Act Concession," *SmartAsset,* November 8, 2022.

Part IV: Failure

The New Democrats

152 He was part of a cohort: See Jon F. Hale, "The Making of the New Democrats," *Political Science Quarterly* 110, no. 2 (June 1995): 207–32; Jeff Faux, "The Myth of the New Democrats," *American Prospect*, October 1, 1993, pp. 11–23.

152 "will do it for the Democrats!": Mondale quoted in Tom Wraight, "Rethinking the American Industrial Policy Debate," *Journal of Policy History* 36, no. 2, published online by Cambridge University Press, March 14, 2024.

153 The irony wasn't lost on me: See Jeff Faux, "Industrial Policy: The Road Not Taken," *The American Prospect*, December 21, 2009, pp. 18–25; Sydney Blumenthal, "Drafting a Democratic Industrial Plan," *New York Times*, August 28, 1983; Richard McGahey, "Industrial Policy's Problem," *New York Times*, July 6, 1984.

153 As governor, he had presided: See David Lampe, ed., *The Massachusetts Miracle: High Technology and Economic Revitalization* (Cambridge, MA: MIT Press, 1988).

154 "two key economic advisers": Hobart Rowen, "A Battle for Dukakis' Economic Mind," *Washington Post*, July 20, 1988.

155 the infamous Willie Horton ad: The ad can be seen at https://edition.cnn.com /2018/11/01/politics/willie-horton-ad-1988-explainer-trnd/index.html.

155 Lee Atwater, who bragged: See Peter Baker, "Horton Ad Set Tone on Race in Politics That Still Stings for African Americans," *New York Times*, December 3, 2018.

Watch Bill Run!

159 Fifty million Americans tuned in: See Michael Kruse, "The TV Interview That Haunts Hillary Clinton," *Politico*, September 23, 2016.

160 The overall theme: I had written about this in several articles and in my book *The Work of Nations* (New York: Alfred A. Knopf, 1992). I gave Bill a copy of the book, and he told me it had influenced his thinking about the economy and what he needed to do if elected. Many of its themes found their way into Bill's campaign book, co-authored with vice presidential candidate Al Gore, *Putting People First: How We Can All Change America* (New York: Three Rivers Press, 1992).

161 Bill's economic team was divided: The strongest proponents of NAFTA were Bob Rubin, Lloyd Bentsen, Larry Summers, and Leon Panetta. Laura Tyson said she had reservations. I expressed concern about what would happen to American workers. Bentsen said anyone who lost a job because of NAFTA would be eligible for Trade Adjustment Assistance. The social consequences of NAFTA continue to be debated. I think it safe to say that the nation's failure to create any system for getting new jobs to workers who lost their old jobs due to trade, technological change, or for any other reason—new jobs that paid at least as well as the old ones with at least as much job security—magnified the social costs of economic change.

The Deficit Obsession

163 the federal budget deficit: See Michael Linden, "The Real Heroes of the 1998 Budget Surplus: Clinton and His Economy," *Center for American Progress*, March 7, 2011.

163 Interest on the national debt: The great switch by the super-rich—from paying the government taxes to lending the government money—has gone almost unnoticed. Yet it was a critical piece of the puzzle. Tax rates on the super-rich plummeted under Ronald Reagan, George W. Bush, and Donald Trump, and loopholes grew wider. Meanwhile, more and more of the nation's income and wealth have gone to the top. Treasury bills—essentially, loans to the U.S. government—have proven good and safe investments. Had the super-rich financed the U.S. government the way they did before 1981—by paying taxes rather than lending the government money—the budget deficit would have been far lower, and the government would have had more leeway with which to finance services most Americans depend on.

164 Reagan and David Stockman: Stockman later had a change of heart. In 2011, he contended that the party of Reagan had spent three decades compounding the errors that he had a hand in engineering in the early 1980s—and a reckoning loomed. The cost of Reagan's tax cut ballooned from $500 billion over five years to $1 trillion after lobbyists added special-interest tax breaks for various industries. And on the spending side, the Reagan administration went hog-wild throwing money at the Pentagon. As a result, he said, the deficit ballooned. "I was horrified," Stockman recalled. See David Corn, "Reagan: Morning After in America," *Mother Jones*, February 4, 2011, pp. 12–21.

164 Al Gore was upset: The memo in question was dated December 12, 1991, see "World Bank Analyst Suggests Transferring Pollution to the Poor," *Jornal do Brasil* 2 (February 1992), quoted in "Nomination of Lawrence H. Summers," *Hearing Before the Committee on Finance, Senate,* 103rd Congress (1993). In a 1998 *New Yorker* profile, John Cassidy reported that "the memo was composed by a young economist who worked for Summers and that Summers, after a cursory review of it, co-signed to stimulate internal debate."

Becoming Secretary

166 "Our purpose is to discover": Here again I have reconstructed the dialogue as best I can recall. Some is drawn from my diary, which I began to maintain in some detail at this time.

166 "We're on your side": This political vetting was accompanied by a vetting by the FBI, which included providing a list of every employer I'd had, every country I'd ever visited, and other details of my private life. The purpose of a political vetting is to avoid any surprises that may compromise a potential cabinet secretary. The purpose of the FBI vetting is to ensure that a potential cabinet secretary is not a security risk to the United States.

167 Some days later, Bill and I: I also mentioned to Bill that Ron Brown, whom Bill had been eyeing for secretary of commerce, would make an excellent partner for me if I were to become secretary of labor, because Ron and I could then experiment with various ways to improve labor-management relations. Brown and I subsequently traveled to Paris in the spring of 1993 to attend a summit involving economic ministers. On April 3, Brown left Paris to attend a trade mission when a U.S. Air Force CT-43 carrying him and thirty-four other people crashed into a mountainside on approach to Croatia's Dubrovnik Airport. There were no survivors.

168 My coaches helped me cram: I have reconstructed the dialogue as best as I can recall, with the help of my diary.

171   After introductions: This is drawn from "Secretary of Labor Confirmation Hearings," *Federal News Service Transcript*, January 7, 1993.

172   Then an unexpected question: From "Secretary of Labor Confirmation Hearings," *Federal News Service Transcript*, January 7, 1993.

174   I was confirmed: That was typical of the time. Barring controversy, presidential nominees to the cabinet were confirmed unanimously.

Breakfast with Greenspan

175   Our breakfast was pleasant: I did not know it at the time, but Greenspan had been communicating with Bob Rubin, who was the vehicle through which Greenspan signaled to Clinton what Greenspan demanded in terms of deficit reduction as a condition for not hiking interest rates too much.

The Real Reason CEO Pay Exploded

177   But now CEOs' pay was exploding: The following dialogue is drawn from my contemporaneous notes.

The Battle of the Bobs

180   "For 15 years, Democratic Party": See David Leonhardt, "The Bottom Line on Obamanomics," *New York Times*, August 22, 2008.

180   "Government or the market": I have developed this argument in *Saving Capitalism: For the Many, Not the Few* (New York: Alfred A. Knopf, 2015).

181   I disagreed: The argument that public investments would do more to boost business investment than private investments fueled by lower interest rates is by no means settled. Indeed, the debate continues to rage. As I write this, the Biden administration has bet on significant public investments, yet the Federal Reserve Board has raised interest rates to slow the economy in order to ward off inflation.

182   Often, Bill went along with Rubin: Rubin and Clinton might have been exactly right if the goal was getting the economy growing, at least through the next few years—and getting Clinton reelected in 1996. In retrospect, though, I think history has shown they were wrong. By failing to invest as much as necessary in the American workforce, education, and infrastructure; opening the U.S. economy far wider to imports from Mexico and China; deregulating Wall Street; failing to make it easier for workers to join unions; failing to constrain CEO pay; and failing to aggressively attack monopolies, Clinton accepted the neoliberal shibboleths of the era, which resulted in widening inequality and greater corruption of our political system—thereby setting the stage for a right-wing populist reaction, including Donald Trump.

182   This prompted James Carville: Louis Uchitelle, "Ideas and Trends: The Bondholders are Winning; Why America Won't Boom," *New York Times*, June 12, 1994.

182   "It is the economic equivalent": See William J. Clinton, "Remarks at Vietnam National University in Hanoi, Vietnam, November 17, 2000," The American Presidency Project.

183   I wasn't allowed to speak out: I agreed with the academic theory that free trade helps everyone, but I also knew that the real world didn't conform to academic

theory. Labor unions were strongly opposed to NAFTA because they saw foreign trade undermining their bargaining power, and they were proven correct. Yet I had to argue to the unions that NAFTA would create more jobs in the United States. There was some evidence for this, but more jobs didn't mean higher wages, and more jobs didn't mean additional jobs in the places where jobs would be lost. Yet I was representing the president, and he was committed to getting NAFTA enacted.

183 The Clinton administration lobbied: Rubin; Leon Panetta, Clinton's first budget director; and Lloyd Bentsen, secretary of the treasury, all argued that passing NAFTA should be the administration's highest priority. I recall Bentsen banging his finger on the table in the Roosevelt Room, saying, "We must get NAFTA done right away." My job was to get organized labor on board or at least minimize the political damage. It was a difficult and thankless task.

184 A 2021 study documented: See J. Choi, I. Kuziemko, E. Washington, and G. Wright, "Local Economic and Political Effects of Trade Deals: Evidence from NAFTA," National Bureau of Economic Research Working Paper 29525, November 2021.

184 Economists have estimated: See David Autor, David Dorn, Gordon Hanson, and Kevah Majlesi, "A Note on the Effect of Rising Trade Exposure on the 2016 Presidential Election," Appendix to Autor, Dorn, Hanson, and Majlesi, "Importing Political Polarization? The Electoral Consequences of Rising Trade Exposure," National Bureau of Economic Research Working Paper 22637, December 2017. See also Autor, Dorn, and Hanson, "The China Shock: Learning from Labor-Market Adjustment to Large Changes in Trade," *Annual Review of Economics* 8 (2016): 205–40.

185 By the time Bob and I: There are various ways of measuring the financial sector's profits as a share of total U.S. corporate profits, but there's no doubt they have exploded over the last thirty years. See R. Greenwood and D. Scharfstein, "The Growth of Finance," *Journal of Economic Perspectives* 27, no. 2 (Spring 2013): 3–28. See also Jordan Weissmann, "How Wall Street Devoured Corporate America," *The Atlantic*, March 5, 2013, p. 22.

185 In early 1980, I wrote an essay: See Reich, "The Paper Entrepreneurs Are Winning Over the Product Entrepreneurs," *New York Times*, May 23, 1980.

186 As finance came to dominate: After the stock market crash of 1929 and the Great Depression, the U.S. government passed the Securities Act of 1933 and the Securities and Exchange Act of 1934 to prevent a crash from recurring. The 1934 legislation did not bar stock buybacks per se, but it barred companies from manipulating their stock prices. Corporations understood that if they undertook a stock buyback, they could be accused by the SEC of trying to manipulate their stock price. It was not until Ronald Reagan appointed John Shad to head the SEC that the agency adopted rule 10b-18, which provides a "safe harbor" for companies to do stock buybacks, as long as they do not buy more than 25 percent of the stock's average daily trading volume in a single day. See William Lazonick, "Profits Without Prosperity," *Harvard Business Review*, September 2014.

186 As Harvard political philosopher: See Michael J. Sandel, *Democracy's Discontent: A New Edition for Our Perilous Times* (Cambridge, MA: Harvard University Press, 2022), p. 297.

188 Larry Summers—now deputy treasury secretary: See Mike Konczal, "Can Larry

Summers Play Nice with Other Financial Regulators?" *Washington Post,* August 4, 2013. See also Robert Kuttner, "Falling Upward: The Surprising Survival of Larry Summers," *American Prospect,* July 12, 2020, pp. 1–5.

188   By 2007, the value: See Inaki Aldasoro and Torsten Ehlers, "The Credit Default Swap Market: What a Difference a Decade Makes," *BIS Quarterly Review,* June 2018, pp. 27–37.

188   At Bob's urging: See Joseph Kahn, "Former Treasury Secretary Joins Leadership Triangle at Citigroup," *New York Times,* October 27, 1999.

189   But after the boom petered out: See Greenwald, Lettau, and Ludvigson, "How the Wealth Was Won: Factors Shares as Market Fundamentals," National Bureau of Economic Research Working Paper 25769, revised October 2023.

The Batboy in Georgia

191   But now Tommy: See "Batboy Is Called Out by Labor Officials, Who Vow a Review," *New York Times,* May 28, 1993. See also, "More Batty Thinking from the Feds," *Orlando Sentinel,* May 28, 1993; "Stossel Takes On Outdated Child Labor Laws," ABC News, August 6, 2002.

The Fury in Oklahoma

193   On October 3, 2024: See John Keilman, "Factory Workers Are Dying Because Machines Aren't Being Turned Off," *Wall Street Journal,* October 3, 2024.

196   A half hour later: See Steve Lackmeyer and Charles T. Jones, "Court Order Shuts Down Dayton Tire US. Fines Plant $7.5 Million," *The Oklahoman,* April 19, 1994.

197   Soon after we left: See Sam Howe Verhovek, "Tire Factory Shuts Doors in Dispute Over Safety," *New York Times,* April 20, 1994.

198   Timothy McVeigh wrote a letter: See James Barron, "Terror in Oklahoma: The Suspect," *New York Times,* April 27, 1995.

199   He listened to radio personality: Limbaugh's comments about a "violent American revolution" came on February 22, 1995, two months before the Oklahoma City bombing.

Labor Day in Wisconsin

200   I admired him enormously: You can get some sense of why from his memoir, *Raising Hell for Justice: The Washington Battles of a Heartland Progressive* (Madison: University of Wisconsin Press, 2007).

On the Air in the Midwest

202   "You're on Talk Radio 95": I changed the name of this radio host to "Charles Walton" because it's not the most flattering portrait, but the callers and what they said are accurate.

Memo to the President About the Upcoming Election

204 TO: POTUS: I sent this memo to Bill Clinton on October 3, 1994.

The Triumph of the Nasties

206 Just before the midterm elections: Michel epitomized the congressional Old School, especially among Republicans. He prized collegiality, collaboration, civility, and courtesy as essential political virtues. He had a reverence for institutional norms and customs in what he fondly terms "the people's House." He got what he wanted from the GOP rank and file because he was a patient listener, a flexible goal-setter, and gentle persuader. See David Hawkings, "Bob Michel, Last Leader of the 'Old School' House GOP, Dies at 93," *Roll Call*, February 17, 2017.

207 Gingrich and Dole seemed: See McKay Coppins, "The Man Who Broke Politics," *The Atlantic*, November 2018, pp. 18–26.

208 Gingrich channeled the growing anger: See generally Julian Zelizer, *Burning Down the House: Newt Gingrich, the Fall of a Speaker, and the Rise of the New Republican Party* (New York: Penguin Press, 2020).

Paying Bill Gates $135 for Lunch

212 The chief lawyer patiently explained: See 5 U.S. Code Section 7353, "Gifts to Federal Employees."

212 The Court thereby overturned: See *Citizens United v. Federal Election Commission*, 558 U.S. 310, decided January 21, 2010. See also Michael Waldman, "The Case That Could Wipe Out 100 Years of Campaign Finance Laws," Brennan Center for Justice, October 7, 2009.

213 Corporations could now spend: Mimi Murray and Digby Marziani, "Money in Politics After *Citizens United*," Brennan Center for Justice, April 19, 2012.

Is Capitalism Moral?

213 "The bill isn't perfect": The old welfare program was perhaps better than nothing but it had many faults. Perhaps its worst was that it discouraged work. Under Reagan, the phase-out rate was 100 percent—meaning that every additional dollar earned caused benefits to be cut by one dollar. For a useful history of welfare in the United States, see Jason DeParle, *American Dream: Three Women, Ten Kids, and a Nation's Drive to End Welfare* (New York: Penguin Books, 2005). Many reformers have preferred a guaranteed job program to welfare.

214 I felt sure: Indeed, he would. See John Harris and John Yang, "Clinton to Sign Bill Overhauling Welfare," *Washington Post*, August 1, 1996.

215 I watched in awe: For an excellent background on Kennedy during this time, see Nick Littlefield and David Nexon, *Lion of the Senate* (New York: Simon & Schuster, 2016); on Wellstone, see Bill Lofty, *Paul Wellstone: The Life of a Passionate Progressive* (Ann Arbor: University of Michigan Press, 2005).

216 "My brother need not be": See "Tribute to Robert F. Kennedy," St. Patrick's Cathedral, New York City, June 8, 1968, version released to the press, available at the John F. Kennedy Presidential Library and Museum, Columbia Point, Boston.

My Illicit Affair

220 Everything I had learned: The best reference on Simpson's life is the Wikipedia entry for Alan K. Simpson.

222 As the Republican co-chair: See Michael Hiltzik, "Why Is This Foul-Mouthed Enemy of Social Security Receiving a Presidential Honor?" *Los Angeles Times,* July 5, 2022.

Part V: The Gathering Storm

My Unfortunate Prescience

231 I gave a speech: For the entire speech, see Robert Reich, "A New Middle Class," Democratic Leadership Council, C-SPAN, November 22, 1994.

When Roger Ailes Didn't Offer Me a Job

233 "Ailes did more to degrade": See Stephen Metcalf, "How Roger Ailes Degraded the Tone of Public Life in America," *The New Yorker,* May 19, 2017. For an excellent biography of Ailes, see Gabriel Sherman, *The Loudest Voice in the Room: How the Brilliant, Bombastic Roger Ailes Built Fox News—and Divided a Country* (New York: Random House, 2014).

233 "It's a shame a man has to use": See Joe McGinniss, *The Selling of the President 1968* (New York: Trident Press, 1969), p. 245.

234 "I am not going to exploit": See Stephen D. Wrage, "Fox News's Roger Ailes; The Man Who Single-Handedly Rogered America," *The Globalist,* August 2, 2016.

234 "What Rush realizes": Cited in Bob Baker, "What's the Rush?" *Los Angeles Times,* January 20, 1991.

237 It was a key part: See Albert Eisle, "Swift Boat Ads Were Too Hot for Fox News," *The Hill,* December 8, 2004, pp. 2–3.

Gored

239 When Bush indignantly told Gore: See "In Interview, Bush Admits He Was 'Abrupt' When Gore Called Back," *Washington Post,* December 6, 2000.

239 Then, on December 12: See *Bush v. Gore,* 531 U.S. 98 (2000). See also Anthony Lewis, "A Supreme Difference," *New York Review of Books,* June 10, 2010, p. 2; Jack M. Balkin, "*Bush v. Gore* and the Boundary Between Law and Politics," *Yale Law Journal* 110 (May 2, 2001): 1407.

239 To me, *Bush v. Gore:* As I write this, the court's legitimacy has plummeted to a new low. Only 43 percent of Americans say they approve of the way the Supreme Court is handling its job, down from 62 percent when the court decided *Bush v. Gore.* See Megan Brenan, "Views of Supreme Court Remain Near Record Lows," *Gallup News,* September 29, 2023, revised July 1, 2024.

Falling for Barack

241 What did Bush ask: In an address to the nation on the evening of the 9/11 attacks, Bush reassured the public that the American economy was still "open for business." He went on to tell the public to "get down to Disney World in Florida" to help shore up the nation's hurting airlines. "Take your families and enjoy life the way we want it to be enjoyed," he said.

242 No one had expected it: See David Bernstein, "The Speech," *Chicago* magazine, May 29, 2007, pp. 1–7.

The Perfect Storm

247 The 2008 financial crisis: Much has been written about the relationship between deregulation of financial markets and the 2008 financial crisis. Among the most thoughtful are Kimberly Amadeo, "Causes of the 2008 Financial Crisis," *The Balance,* updated June 6, 2024; Martin Baily, Robert Litan, and Matthew Johnson, "The Origins of the Financial Crisis," Brookings Institution, November 2008; Colin McArthur and Sarah Edelman, "The 2008 Housing Crisis," Center for American Progress, April 13, 2017.

249 In a private meeting: See Eamon Javers, "Inside Obama's Bank CEO's Meeting," *Politico,* April 3, 2009.

250 The wealth of American homeowners: See Laurie Goodman and Christopher Mayer, "Homeownership and the American Dream," *Journal of Economic Perspectives* 32, no. 1 (Winter 2018): 31–58. See also William Rohe and Mark Lindblad, "Reexamining the Social Benefits of Homeownership After the Housing Crisis," Joint Center for Housing Studies, Harvard University, August 2013.

Tea Partiers, Occupiers, and Other Angry People

252 One political consequence: For a good summary of the Tea Party Movement, see Nella Van Dyke and David S. Meyer, eds., *Understanding the Tea Party Movement* (New York: Routledge, 2014). See also Jeremy Peters, "The Tea Party Didn't Get What It Wanted, but It Did Unleash the Politics of Anger," *New York Times,* August 28, 2019.

252 A parallel response: For a good summary of the Occupy Movement, see Alasdair Roberts, "Why the Occupy Movement Failed," *Public Administration Review* 72, no. 5 (September–October 2012): 754–62.

253 On November 9: See "'Occupy' Protesters Rebuild UC Berkeley Camp," CBS News, November 16, 2011; Jennifer Gollan, "Berkeley Crackdown Raises Fear of Move Backward," *New York Times,* November 18, 2011.

The Two Faces of Populism

255 Both faces of populism: In my view, the best overall history of American populism and progressivism between 1890 and 1940 is still Richard Hofstadter, *The Age of Reform* (New York: Random House, 1955).

257 Yet by the 1950s: See Robert Kuttner, *The Life of the Party: Democratic Prospects in 1988 and Beyond* (New York: Viking, 1987).

258 The Republican Party, meanwhile: For a thoughtful examination of Pat Buchanan, see Ari Berman, "The Conservative Who Turned White Anxiety into a Movement," *The Atlantic,* April 22, 2024, pp. 1–13. For an analysis that puts Richard Nixon at the center, see Harold Meyerson, "The Roots of Today's Republicans," *American Prospect,* October 23, 2023.

258 As Democratic pollster: See Stanley B. Greenberg, "The Democrats' 'Working-Class Problem,'" *American Prospect,* June 1, 2017.

260 By the 2016 election: See Eugene Mazo and Timothy Kuhner, *Democracy by the Wealthy: Campaign Finance Reform as the Issue of Our Time* (Cambridge: Cambridge University Press, 2018).

260 That same year: See Karl Evers-Hillstrom, "More Money, Less Transparency: A Decade Under Citizens United," *OpenSecrets Report,* January 14, 2020.

260 Labor unions no longer: Ibid.

Anti-Establishment Rage

261 I was doing research: Part of that research resulted in the documentary *Saving Capitalism,* directed by Jake Kornbluth and Sari Gilman, produced by Eden Wurmfeld, released November 21, 2017.

264 Much of the political establishment: See, for example, Victor Davis Hanson, "Why Trump Won," Hoover Institution, November 11, 2016; German Lopez, "The Past Year of Research Has Made It Very Clear: Trump Won Because of Racial Resentment," *Vox,* December 15, 2017.

265 Worries about free trade: See Shanay Gracia, "Majority of Americans Take a Dim View of Increased Trade with Other Countries," Pew Research Center, July 29, 2024. See also Bruce Stokes, "Republicans, Especially Trump Supporters, See Free Trade Deals as Bad for U.S.," Pew Research Center, March 31, 2016.

The End of the American Dream

266 In his 1931 book: See James Truslow Adams, *The Epic of America* (Little, Brown, 1931; Routledge edition, 2017).

267 Most Americans have been: See Aaron Zitner, "Voters See American Dream Slipping Out of Reach," *Wall Street Journal,* November 24, 2023.

267 An NBC News poll: See NBC News Survey, Hart Research Associates/Public Opinion Strategies, November 2023.

268 The people most likely: See U.S. Bureau of Economic Analysis, "Real Median Household Income by State, Annual," Federal Reserve Economic Data (FRED), Federal Reserve Bank of St. Louis; Raj Chetty, David Grusky, Maximilian Hell, Nathaniel Hendren, Robert Manduca, and Jimmy Narang, "The Fading American Dream: Trends in Absolute Income Mobility Since 1940," *Science* 356, no. 6336 (April 24, 2017): 398–406.

268 But by 2024 it ranked lower: See Shameek Rakshit, Matthew McGough, and Krutika Amin, "How Does U.S. Life Expectancy Compare with Other Countries," Peterson–KFF Health System Tracker, January 30, 2024. See also "Life Expectancy at Birth," *World Factbook,* U.S. Central Intelligence Agency, 2023.

268 In her thoughtful book: See Arlie Hochschild, *Stolen Pride* (New York: The New Press, 2024).

269 In a telling survey: See Michael H. Keller and David D. Kirkpatrick, "Their America Is Vanishing. Like Trump, They Insist They Were Cheated," *New York Times,* October 23, 2022.

The Rigging of the Market

271 Hidden behind: See "Distribution of Household Wealth Since 1989," DFA: Distributional Financial Accounts, Federal Reserve, updated to June 14, 2024.

272 On June 26, 2024, the Court dealt: See *Snyder v. United States,* 2024.

The (Republican) Party's Over

275 In his resignation letter: See Neil Vigdor, "Board Member Says Group Declined to Honor Liz Cheney for Fear of Trump," *New York Times,* April 10, 2024.

275 "Two years ago, I won": See Max Greenwood, "Liz Cheney Defeated in Wyoming Primary," *The Hill,* August 16, 2022.

277 In the spring of 2024: See Theodore Schliefer, "Guess Who's Coming to Dinner," *Puck,* April 30, 2024.

277 At the same time, Musk turned up: See Kate Conger and Ryan Mac, "Elon Musk Ramps Up Anti-Biden Posts on X," *New York Times,* May 24, 2024.

278 No other leader: See Ryan Mac, Jack Nicas, and Alex Travelli, "Elon Musk's Diplomacy: Woo Right-Wing World Leaders. Then Benefit," *New York Times,* May 13, 2024.

278 "I no longer believe": See Peter Thiel, "The Education of a Libertarian," *From Scratch,* Cato Institute, April 13, 2009.

278 Vance alleged: See Amy Sherman, "JD Vance's Ad About 'Open Border' and Immigrant Voters Is Wrong," *PolitiFact,* April 8, 2022.

278 Just fifty families injected: See Zachary Tashman and William Rice, "Just Fifty Families," Americans for Tax Fairness, May 13, 2024.

279 "Take a step back": See Kevin Breuninger, "Jamie Dimon Praises Trump, Warns MAGA Criticism Could Hurt Biden," CNBC, January 17, 2024.

279 "If you consider fighting": See Lex Fridman, "Transcript for Elon Musk: War, Aliens, Politics, Physics, Video Games, and Humanity," Podcast #400, November 18, 2023.

279 "The 1920s were the last decade": Thiel, "Education of a Libertarian."

The Final Battle?

283 Borrowing from cultural theorist: See Umberto Eco, "Ur-Fascism," *New York Review of Books,* June 22, 1995; Emilio Gentile, "Fascism as Political Religion," *Journal of Contemporary History* 25, no. 2/3 (May–June 1990): 229–51; Roger Griffin, ed., *Fascism: An Introduction to Comparative Fascist Studies* (Cambridge, UK: Polity, 2018); Madeleine Albright, *Fascism: A Warning* (New York: Harper, 2018).

Part VI: The Long Game

My Mother's Advice

289 The famed British economist: Keynes's famous quote is found in his *A Tract on Monetary Reform* (London: Macmillan, 1923).

290 "Gingrich [has used] issues of ethics": Fred Wertheimer's comments about Newt Gingrich can be found at "The Long March of Newt Gingrich," *PBS Frontline*, January 1996.

291 "I was sneaking into": See Joe Wilensky, "After 25 Years, 'Story of Stuff' Creator Finishes Her Degree," *Cornell Chronicle*, May 25, 2013.

292 When affirmative action: See the interview with Christopher Edley, Jr., in "Affirmative Action and the Culture of Intolerance," Penn National Commission on Society, Culture, and Community, University of Pennsylvania, June 11, 1997.

292 "to protect the current distribution": See Christopher Edley, Jr., Opening Remarks, "Roundtable on Race in America," *The Atlantic*, November 13, 1997, pp. 2–3.

292 Chris's testimony: See *Hearings Before the Committee on the Judiciary, United States Senate, One Hundred Second Congress, on The Nomination of Clarence Thomas to Be Associate Justice of the Supreme Court of the United States*, September 17 and 19, 1991, Part 2 (Washington, DC: U.S. Government Printing Office, 1993), p. 2.

Rejecting "Both-sides-ism"

297 *The New York Times* quoted: See Carl Huise, "Behind Kevin McCarthy's Extraordinary Downfall as Reflects an Ungovernable G.O.P.," *New York Times*, October 23, 2023.

298 "The core point [President Biden]": See Jeremy Barr, "'Is There a Purge?': Cohn Harwood's CNN Exit Viewed as Strategy Shift," *Washington Post*, September 2, 2022.

298 a source told Dan Froomkin: See Dan Froomkin, "Was Biden Right? Or Was Biden Wrong? The National Press Won't Say," *Press Watch*, September 2, 2022.

299 Chris Licht, soon after: See Claire Atkinson, "CNN Cancels 'Reliable Sources,' Axing Brian Stelter and Show Staff, with More Familiar Faces Expected to Exit as Network CEO Chris Licht Sets Strategy," *Business Insider*, August 18, 2022. Two years later, after Licht was fired from CNN, Stelter was rehired as chief media analyst and author of its "Reliable Sources" newsletter.

300 A source told *Deadline*'s: See Dominic Patten and Ted Johnson, "CNN Boss Chris Licht Warns Anxious Staffers Over 'More Changes' After Axing of 'Reliable Sources' and Exit of Brian Stelter," *Deadline*, August 19, 2022.

300 Mulvaney's first appearance: See Jon Allsop, "On Mick Mulvaney, Ketanji Brown Jackson, Cynicism, and Idealism," "The Media Today" newsletter, *Columbia Journalism Review*, April 6, 2022.

302 "getting access to both sides": See Tom Porter, "A CBS News Exec Said the Network Is Hiring More Republicans Because 'We Know' They'll Take Over After the Midterms," *Business Insider*, March 31, 2022. Khemlani was removed as co-head of CBS News in 2023.

Refusing Dr. Phil

304 Research shows that having: See Jill Rosen, "Black Students Who Have One Black Teacher Are More Likely to Go to College," *Hub,* Johns Hopkins University, November 12, 2018.

305 Around 2010, my younger son: As I write this, Sam is CEO of Dropout TV.

307 Turning to videos to communicate: My belief that the brains of young people are wired differently than those of old geezers like me comes mainly from my observations of students during my forty years of teaching, and my experiences with social media. I don't mean to imply that human brains have suddenly changed, but that the experiences of young people—mostly through their mobile phones and the Internet—have been radically different from the experiences of my generation, resulting in far different capacities. The scientific research on this suggests this, but is not determinative. See, for example, Carlin Flora, "Are Smartphones Really Destroying the Lives of Teenagers?" *Scientific American,* February 1, 2018, pp. 22–28.

Restoring Democratic Capitalism

313 America's postwar industrial policy: See Robert Reich, "Why the U.S. Needs an Industrial Policy," *Harvard Business Review,* January 1982.

314 Joe Biden almost revived: See Joseph Stiglitz, "Time Is Up for Neoliberals," *Washington Post,* May 13, 2004.

Creating "We" Workplaces

319 I could give you many examples: See Cash Powell, Jr., "L-S Electro-Galvanizing: Factory Without Walls: Successful Start-up with Participative Management," *Manufacturing Excellence,* Association for Manufacturing Excellence, July/August 1994, pp. 45–50; Bert Painter, "Variable Pay in High Performance Work System," moderntimesworkplace.com, 1995, pp. 1– 20.

Sharing the Profits

320 It emerged in 1916: See Sam Pizzigati, "When Sears Shared," Inequality.org, July 8, 2017.

320 Shortly thereafter, the Bureau of Labor Statistics: See Boris Emmet, "Profit Sharing in the United States," U.S. Department of Labor, Bureau of Labor Statistics (Washington, DC: Government Printing Office, 1917).

321 America's trend toward higher profits: "The Productivity-Pay Gap," Economic Policy Institute, updated October 2022, analysis of data from Bureau of Labor Statistics Labor Productivity and Costs program, wage data from the BLS Current Employment Statistics, BLS Employment Cost Trends, BLS Consumer Price Index, and Bureau of Economic Analysis National Income and Product Accounts.

Making Community Count

322 It turned out that Dan: See Steve Hartman, "A Beloved General Store Was on the Verge of Closing amid a Worker Shortage—Until Customers Stepped In to Help," *CBS Evening News,* updated December 3, 2021.

Recirculating Stuff

325 Something like this is already: See Laura Fenton, "What Is a Buy Nothing Group? Here's Everything You Should Know," *Real Simple,* updated April 15, 2024.

325 The United States now produces: See Tik Root, "U.S. Top Contributor to Plastic Waste, Report Shows," *Washington Post,* December 1, 2021. See also "Reckoning With the U.S. Role in Global Ocean Plastic Waste," Committee on the United States Contributions to Global Ocean Plastic Waste, National Academies of Science, Engineering, and Medicine (Washington, DC: National Academies Press, 2022).

325 But wait, you might say: Thomas Wiedmann, Manfred Lenzen, Lorenz KeyBer, and Julia Steinberger, "Scientists' Warning on Affluence," *Nature Communications* 11 (June 19, 2020).

Leading America

327 On the eve of the Senate's final vote: See "McCain's Speech on the Senate Floor," full text and video, CNN, July 25, 2017.

328 This wasn't the first time: See Jonathan Martin and Amie Parnes, "McCain: Obama Not an Arab: Crowd Boos," *Politico,* October 10, 2008.

329 "the administration of the government": See M. Tullius Cicero, "Voluntas Populi," *De Officiis,* Book I: *Moral Goodness,* published online by Cambridge University Press, November 24, 2022.

329 As one of George Washington's biographers: See Douglas Southall Freeman, *George Washington: A Biography* (Clifton, NJ: Augustus M. Kelley Publishers, 1948), p. 29.

330 "That makes me smart": See Russ Buettner, Susanne Craig, and Mike McIntire, "Long-Concealed Records Show Trump's Chronic Losses and Years of Tax Avoidance," *New York Times,* September 27, 2020.

330 "When they call, I give": See Andrew Prokop, "Donald Trump Made One Shockingly Insightful Comment During the First GOP Debate," *Vox,* August 6, 2015.

330 "Just think about": See Steve Kerr (as told to Chris Ballard), "Mr. President: You Represent All of Us. Don't Divide Us. Bring Us Together," *Sports Illustrated,* September 24, 2017, pp. 23–26.

332 Yet a decade later: See John Chesto, "Market Basket Protests: 10 Years Later, Grocer's Business Is Better Than Ever," *Boston Globe,* August 27, 2024.

Making Society Healthy

335 In 2023, a panel of medical experts: Dennis Thompson, "Screen All Adults Under Age 65 for Anxiety Disorders, Expert Panel Says," *Medical Press,* June 20, 2023.

335 "a crisis in this country": See Emily Baumgaertner, "Health Panel Recommends Anxiety Screening for All Adults Under 65," *New York Times,* September 20, 2022.

336 Studies show that women: See Debra Brody, Laura Pratt, and Jeffrey Hughes, "Prevalence of Depression Among Adults Aged 20 and Over: United States, 2013–2016," NCHS Data Brief No. 202, National Center for Health Statistics, February 2018.

336 From 2014 to 2019: See Baumgaertner, "Health Panel Recommends Anxiety Screening."

336 White men without college degrees: See Anne Case and Angus Deaton, "Life Expectancy in Adulthood Is Falling for Those Without a BA Degree, but as Educational Gaps Have Widened, Racial Gaps Have Narrowed," *Proceedings of the National Academy of Science* 118, no. 11 (March 16, 2021).

Watching the Moneyed Class Get Run Over

338 In a June 2024 column: See David Brooks, "The Sins of the Educated Class," *New York Times,* June 7, 2024.

339 "The closest that conservatives": See Katherine Knott, "J.D. Vance Called Universities 'The Enemy,' Now He's Trump's VP Pick," *Inside Higher Education,* July 16, 2024, pp. 1–4. See also Rod Dreher, "'I Would Like to See European Elites Actually Listen to Their People for a Change': An Interview with J.D. Vance," *The European Conservative,* February 22, 2024, pp. 12–15.

Growing Old

347 "Bodily decrepitude":

> *Speech after long silence; it is right,*
> *All other lovers being estranged or dead,*
> *Unfriendly lamplight hid under its shade,*
> *The curtains drawn upon unfriendly night,*
> *That we descant and yet again descant*
> *Upon the supreme theme of Art and Song:*
> *Bodily decrepitude is wisdom; young*
> *We loved each other and were ignorant.*

William Butler Yeats, "After Long Silence," in *Words for Music Perhaps and Other Poems,* 1932.

348 "older people who are reasonable": See Marcus Tullius Cicero, *How to Grow Old: Wisdom for the Second Half of Life,* translated and with an introduction by Philip Freeman (Princeton, NJ: Princeton University Press, 2016). Originally entitled *On Old Age* and written in 44 BC.

Index

ILLUSTRATION CREDITS

A NOTE ABOUT THE AUTHOR

Robert B. Reich is professor emeritus at the University of California, Berkeley. He has served in three presidential administrations, Republican and Democrat, including as secretary of labor under Bill Clinton, for which *Time* magazine named him one of the ten most effective cabinet secretaries of the twentieth century. He has written eighteen books, including *The Work of Nations* (translated into twenty-two languages) and the bestsellers *The System, The Common Good, Saving Capitalism,* and *Locked in the Cabinet.* His articles have appeared in *The New Yorker, The Atlantic, The New York Times, The Washington Post,* and *The Wall Street Journal.* Reich is a columnist for *The Guardian* and writes a daily newsletter at https://robertreich .substack.com/. With Jacob Kornbluth, Reich co-created the award-winning film *Inequality for All* and the Netflix original *Saving Capitalism.* He co-founded Inequality Media and is a cofounder of The American Prospect and the Economic Policy Institute. Reich is a fellow of the American Academy of Arts and Sciences. He lives in Berkeley.

A NOTE ON THE TYPE

This book was set in Minion, a typeface produced by the Adobe Corporation specifically for the Macintosh personal computer and released in 1990. Designed by Robert Slimbach, Minion combines the classic characteristics of old-style faces with the full complement of weights required for modern typesetting.

Composed by North Market Street Graphics,
Lancaster, Pennsylvania

Designed by Michael Collica